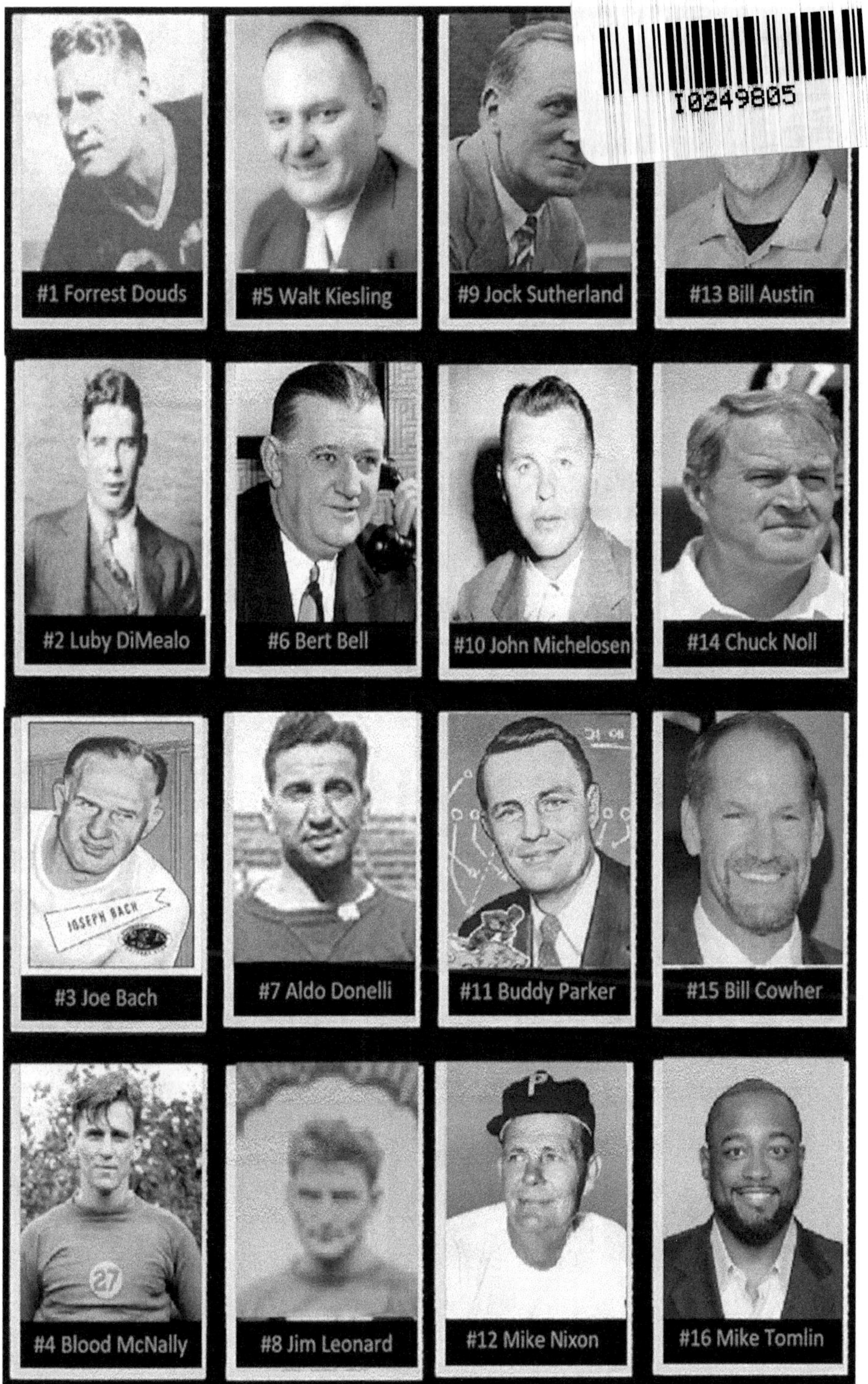

#1 Forrest Douds #5 Walt Kiesling #9 Jock Sutherland #13 Bill Austin

#2 Luby DiMealo #6 Bert Bell #10 John Michelosen #14 Chuck Noll

#3 Joe Bach #7 Aldo Donelli #11 Buddy Parker #15 Bill Cowher

#4 Blood McNally #8 Jim Leonard #12 Mike Nixon #16 Mike Tomlin

Great Moments in Pittsburgh Steelers Football

This book begins at the beginning of Football and goes right to the Mike Tomlin era.

This book is written for those of us who love Pittsburgh Steelers Football. Those who are not the top fans of the Steelers will also want possession of this book, so they can get a leg up on the facts missing from bookshelves of those Steelers fans who do not have this book.

The book first tells the story about the precursor teams to the Pirates and then the founding of the Pittsburgh Pirates as a new National Football League (NFL) team from Pittsburgh in 1933. But it reaches back even further in history than 1933 to find the precursor professional football teams from the turn of the century when Pro Football was just beginning. This book actually takes the Steelers fan on a journey from when there was no football at all, to where American football was only a dream, and then to where American football was played only by colleges with a mixture of soccer and rugby rules.

After explaining how primitive man played football, this book quickly moves on to describe the beginning of football in the US and it recounts the first "American Football Game" in 1869. From there, the progression includes college football teams that loved the new sport and their football graduates looking for a place to play football after college. Eventually all of this builds up to the NFL, and of course the Pittsburgh Pirates, who became The Pittsburgh Steelers, then the Steagles, Card-Pitt, and then a return to the Steelers name.

It moves on to the team's first football game in 1933, and the first Steelers coach, an unknown named Forrest Douds. Then of course it moves to the new era Pirates/Steelers after thirty years of tough going until the team hired the phenomenal immortal—Chuck Noll and then the "to-be" immortals, Bill Cowher and Mike Tomlin, who between all of them chalked up six Super Bowl wins, tops in the entire NFL After thirty years, management eventually hired great coaches. The current coach, Mike Tomlin became the youngest head coach to win the grand prize of football, when the Steelers defeated Arizona in Super Bowl XLIII.

It seems like yesterday but for those pros trying to create a league out of nothing, there would have been nothing without their hard work. And of course, this great book about the Steelers eventually gets a deep look at the great and soon-to-be-immortal-Patriots' coaches including Chuck Noll, Bill Cower, Mike Tomlin, Jock Sutherland, and Buddy Parker. Mike Tomlin, the current coach, of course has his own Super Bowl belt with a big notch in it for the win over Arizona.

The book you are reading now captures the great moments in Steelers Football even before the Steelers were the Pittsburgh Steelers. This Steelers-first book takes the reader through stories about the Steelers 16 coaches, most of whom in early times had losing records and it progresses to great stories about the 85 seasons worth of great games (1571 games) with 655 great wins. The book often stops in time and talks about a particular great player such as John Stallworth, Jack Ham , Jack Lambert, Jerome Bettis, Hines Ward, Franco Harris, Rod Woodson, , Mel Blount, Le'Veon Bell, Antonio Brown, Ben Roethlisberger, and of course the inimitable Terry Bradshaw, a great QB with four Super Bowl Rings-- the greatest Steeler of all time. He matches his talent with an outstanding personality. Though other teams are looking to pass them, the view from the back is not as good as the Steelers' view.

I dare you to pick up this book. If you are an avid Steelers fan, you will never put it down again. You cannot ever get enough of Steelers' greatness, but we do provide as many stories together in one spot as we can in this can't miss book.

Brian Kelly

Great Moments in Pittsburgh Steelers Football

Author: Brian W. Kelly
Copyright © 2018 Brian W. Kelly
Publisher/ Editor, Brian P. Kelly

All rights reserved: No part of this book may be reproduced or transmitted in any form, or by any means, electronic or mechanical, including photocopying, recording, scanning, faxing, or by any information storage and retrieval system, without permission from the publisher, LETS GO PUBLISH, in writing.

Disclaimer: Though judicious care was taken throughout the writing and the publication of this work that the information contained herein is accurate, there is no expressed or implied warranty that all information in this book is 100% correct. Therefore, neither LETS GO PUBLISH, nor the author accepts liability for any use of this work.

Trademarks: A number of products and names referenced in this book are trade names and trademarks of their respective companies.

Referenced Material: *The information in this book has been obtained through personal and third-party observations, interviews, and copious research. Where unique information has been provided or extracted from other sources, those sources are acknowledged within the text of the book itself or at the end of the chapter in the Sources Section. Thus, there are no formal footnotes nor is there a bibliography section. Any picture that does not have a source was taken from various sites on the Internet with no credit attached. If resource owners would like credit in the next printing, please email publisher.*

Published by: LETS GO PUBLISH!
Publisher & Editor: Brian P. Kelly
Mail Location: P.O. Box 621, Wilkes-Barre, PA
Email: info@letsgopublish.com
Web site www.letsgopublish.com

Library of Congress Copyright Information Pending
Book Cover Design by Michele Thomas, Editing by Brian P. Kelly

ISBN Information: The International Standard Book Number (ISBN) is a unique machine-readable identification number, which marks any book unmistakably. The ISBN is the clear standard in the book industry. 159 countries and territories are officially ISBN members. The Official ISBN For this book is on the outside cover:

978-1-947402-38-6

The price for this work is : USD $19.95

10   9   8   7   6   5   4   3   2   1

Release Date: July 2018

LETS GO
PUBLISH!

Pittsburgh Steelers Season Records from 1933 to September 2018

Total 619-552-21 PCT .521 All-time regular season record (1933–2017)
Playoff: 36-25 All-time postseason record (1933–2017)
Overall: 655-577-21 Regular & postseason record (1933–2017)

Total Games   1571
Total Wins   655
Total Losses   577
Total Ties   21   * Prior to Overtime Rules
Stats from   1933   * Through June 2018

Pittsburgh Pirates

Year	Coach	League/Conf/Div	Pl	Record	Pct.
1933	#1 Forrest Douds	NFLEast	5th	3 6 2	.364
1934	#2 Luby DiMeolo	NFLEast	5th	2 10 0	.167
1935	#3 Joe Bach	NFLEast	3rd	4 8 0	.333
1936	#3 Joe Bach	NFLEast	2nd	6 6 0	.500
1937	#4 John Blood McNally	NFLEast	3rd	4 7 0	.364
1938	#4 John Blood McNally	NFLEast	5th	2 9 0	.182
1939	#4 John Blood McNally	NFLEast	4th-T	1 9 1	.136

- McNally's record was 0-3 before he resigned

1939 #5 Walt Kiesling → 1–6–1 record in final 8 games of 1939 season

Pittsburgh Steelers

Year	Coach	League	Pl	Record	Pct.
1940	#5 Walt Kiesling	NFLEast	4th	2 7 2	.273
1941	#6 All coaches 1941	NFLEast	5th	1 9 1	.136

- Shared with coaches #5,7 (0-2)
- Art Rooney convinced Bell to resign- 0-2 record
- Aldo Donelli took over 5 games record 0-5
- Walt Kiesling came back finished year at 1-2-1

1941	#6 Bert Bell	NFLEast	5th	0-2-0	.136
1941	#7 Aldo Donelli	NFLEast	5th	0-5-0	.136

- Shared with coaches #5,6 (0-5)

1941	#5 Walt Kiesling	NFLEast	5th	1 9 1	.136

- Shared with coaches #6,7 (2-0-2)

1942	#5 Walt Kiesling	NFLEast	2nd	7 4 0	.636

Pittsburgh & Philadelphia = Steagles

1943	#5 Walt Kiesling	NFLEast	3rd	5 4 1	.550

Chicago Cardinals & Pittsburgh = Card-Pitt

1944	#5 Walt Kiesling	NFLEast	5th	0 10 0	.000

Pittsburgh Steelers 1945 until today

Year	Coach	League/Conf/Div	Pl	Record	Pct.
1945	#8 Jim Leonard	NFLEast	5th	2 8 0	.200
1946	#9 Jock Sutherland	NFLEast	3rd-T	5 5 1	.500

- Bill Dudley – Joe F. Carr Trophy (MVP)

Year	Coach	League/Conf/Div	Pl	Record	Pct.
1947	#9 Jock Sutherland	NFLEast	2nd	8 4 0	.667

- Lost Eastern Divisional Playoff (Eagles) 21–0

Year	Coach	League/Conf/Div	Pl	Record	Pct.
1948	#10 John Michelosen	NFLEast	3rd-T	4 8 0	.333
1949	#10 John Michelosen	NFLEast	2nd	6 5 1	.542
1950	#10 John Michelosen	NFLAmerican	3rd-T	6 6 0	.500
1951	#10 John Michelosen	NFLAmerican	4th	4 7 1	.375
1952	#3 Joe Bach	NFLAmerican	4th	5 7 0	.417
1953	#3 Joe Bach	NFLEastern	4th	6 6 0	.500
1954	#5 Walt Kiesling	NFLEastern	4th	5 7 0	.417
1955	#5 Walt Kiesling	NFLEastern	6th	4 8 0	.346
1956	#5 Walt Kiesling	NFLEastern	4th-T	5 7 0	.500
1957	#11 Buddy Parker	NFLEastern	3rd	6 6 0	.500
1958	#11 Buddy Parker	NFLEastern	3rd	7 4 1	.625
1959	#11 Buddy Parker	NFLEastern	4th	6 5 1	.542
1960	#11 Buddy Parker	NFLEastern	5th	5 6 1	.458
1961	#11 Buddy Parker	NFLEastern	5th	6 8 0	.429
1962	#11 Buddy Parker	NFLEastern	2nd	9 5 0	.643

- Lost Playoff Bowl(Lions) 17–10 exhibition game

Year	Coach	League/Conf/Div	Pl	Record	Pct.
1963	#11 Buddy Parker	NFLEastern	4th	7 4 3	.607
1964	#11 Buddy Parker	NFLEastern	6th	5 9 0	.357
1965	#12 Mike Nixon	NFLEastern	7th	2 12 0	.143
1966	#13 Bill Austin	NFLEastern	6th	5 8 1	.393
1967	#13 Bill Austin	NFLEasternCent	4th	4 9 1	.321
1968	#13 Bill Austin	NFLEasternCent	4th	2 11 1	.179
1969	#14 Chuck Noll	NFLEasternCent	4th	1 13 0	.071

- Joe Greene – Defensive Rookie of the Year

Year	Coach	League/Conf/Div	Pl	Record	Pct.
1970	#14 Chuck Noll	NFLAFCCentral	3rd	5 9 0	.357
1971	#14 Chuck Noll	NFLAFCCentral	2nd	6 8 0	.429
1972	#14 Chuck Noll	NFLAFCCentral	1st	11 3 0	.786

- Won Divisional Playoffs(Raiders) 13–7
- Lost Conference Championship(Dolphins) 21–17
- Chuck Noll – AFC Coach of the Year
- Franco HarrisOffensive Rookie of the Year
- Joe Greene – Defensive Player of the Year
- Franco Harris– AFC Offensive Rookie of the Year

Year	Coach	League/Conf/Div	Pl	Record	Pct.
1973	#14 Chuck Noll	NFLAFCCentral	2nd	10 4 0	.714

- Lost Divisional Playoffs(Raiders) 33–14

Year	Coach	League/Conf/Div	Pl	Record	Pct.
1974	#14 Chuck Noll	NFLAFCCentral	1st	10 3 1	.750

- Won Divisional Playoffs(Bills) 32–14
- Won Conference Championship(Raiders) 24–13
- Won Super Bowl IX (1)(Vikings) 16–6
- Jack Lambert– Defensive Rookie of the Year
- Joe Greene – Defensive Player of the Year
- Franco Harris– Super Bowl MVP

1975 #14 Chuck Noll   NFLAFCCentral   1st   12 2 0   .857
- Won Divisional Playoffs(Colts) 28–10
- Won Conference Championship(Raiders) 16–10
- Won Super Bowl X (2) (Cowboys) 21–17
- Mel Blount – Defensive Player of the Year
- Lynn Swann – Super Bowl MVP

1976 #14 Chuck Noll   NFLAFCCentral   1st   10 4 0   .714
- Won Divisional Playoffs(Colts) 40–14
- Lost Conference Championship(Raiders) 24–7
- Jack Lambert– Defensive Player of the Year
- Jack Lambert– AFC Defensive Player of the Year

1977 #14 Chuck Noll   NFLAFCCentral 1st   9 5 0   .643
- Lost Divisional Playoffs(Broncos) 34–21

1978 #14 Chuck Noll   NFLAFCCentral   1st   14 2 0   .875
- Won Divisional Playoffs(Broncos) 33–10
- Won Conference Championship (Oilers) 34–5
- Won Super Bowl XIII(3) (Cowboys) 35–31
- Terry Bradshaw – Super Bowl MVP
- Terry Bradshaw – Bert Bell MVP

1979 #14 Chuck Noll   NFLAFCCentral   1st   12 4 0   .750
- Won Divisional Playoffs(Dolphins) 34–14
- Won Conference Championship (Oilers) 27–13
- Won Super Bowl XIV(4) (Rams) 31–19
- Jack Lambert– AFC Defensive Player of the Year
- Terry Bradshaw – Super Bowl MVP

1980 #14 Chuck Noll   NFLAFCCentral   3rd   9 7 0   .563
1981 #14 Chuck Noll   NFLAFCCentral   2nd   8 8 0   .500
1982 #14 Chuck Noll   NFLAFCCentral   4th-T   6 3 0   .667
- Lost First Round(Chargers) 31–28

1983 #14 Chuck Noll   NFLAFCCentral   1st   10 6 0   .625
- Lost Divisional Playoffs(Raiders) 38–10

1984 #14 Chuck Noll   NFLAFCCentral   1st   9 7 0   .563
- Won Divisional Playoffs(Broncos) 24–17
- Lost Conference Championship(Dolphins) 45–28
- Louis Lipps – Offensive Rookie of the Year
- John Stallworth – Comeback Player of the Year

1985 #14 Chuck Noll   NFLAFCCentral   3rd   7 9 0   .438
1986 #14 Chuck Noll   NFLAFCCentral   3rd   6 10 0   .375
1987 #14 Chuck Noll   NFLAFCCentral   3rd   8 7 0   .533
1988 #14 Chuck Noll   NFLAFCCentral   4th   5 11 0   .313
1989 #14 Chuck Noll   NFLAFCCentral   2nd   9 7 0   .563
- Won Wild Card Playoffs(Oilers) 26–23
- Lost Divisional playoff(Broncos) 24–23
- Chuck Noll – Maxwell Football Club Coach of the Year

1990 #14 Chuck Noll   NFLAFCCentral   3rd   9 7 0   .563
1991 #14 Chuck Noll   NFLAFCCentral   2nd   7 9 0   .438
1992 #15 Bill Cowher   NFLAFCCentral   1st   11 5 0   .688
- Lost Divisional Playoffs(Bills) 24–3
- Bill Cowher – NFL Coach of the Year
- Barry Foster – AFC Offensive Player of the Year

Year	Coach	League/Conf/Div	Pl	Record	Pct.
1993	#15 Bill Cowher	NFLAFCCentral	2nd	9 7 0	.563

- Lost Wild Card Playoffs(Chiefs) 27–24 (OT)
- Rod Woodson– Defensive Player of the Year

1994	#15 Bill Cowher	NFLAFCCentral	1st	12 4 0	.750

- Won Divisional Playoffs(Browns) 29–9
- Lost Conference Championship(Chargers) 17–13
- Greg Lloyd – AFC Defensive Player of the Year

1995	#15 Bill Cowher	NFLAFCCentral	1st	11 5 0	.688

- Won Divisional Playoffs(Bills) 40–21
- Won Conference Championship (Colts) 20–16
- Lost Super Bowl XXX(Cowboys) 27–17

1996	#15 Bill Cowher	NFLAFCCentral	1st	10 6 0	.625

- Won Wild Card Playoffs(Colts) 42–14
- Lost Divisional Playoffs(Patriots) 28–3
- Jerome Bettis– Comeback Player of the Year

1997	#15 Bill Cowher	NFLAFCCentral	1st	11 5 0	.688

- Won Divisional Playoffs(Patriots) 7–6
- Lost Conference Championship(Broncos) 24–21

1998	#15 Bill Cowher	NFLAFCCentral	3rd	7 9 0	.438
1999	#15 Bill Cowher	NFLAFCCentral	4th	6 10 0	.375
2000	#15 Bill Cowher	NFLAFCCentral	3rd	9 7 0	.563
2001	#15 Bill Cowher	NFLAFCCentral	1st	13 3 0	.813

- Won Divisional Playoffs(Ravens) 27–10
- Lost Conference Championship (Patriots) 24–17
- Kendrell Bell – Defensive Rookie of the Year

Year	Coach	League/Conf/Div	Pl	Record	Pct.
2002	#15 Bill Cowher	NFLAFCNorth	1st	10 5 1	.656

- Won Wild Card Playoffs(Browns) 36–33
- Lost Divisional Playoffs(Titans) 34–31
- Tommy Maddox – Comeback Player of the Year

2003	#15 Bill Cowher	NFLAFCNorth	3rd	6 10 0	.375
2004	#15 Bill Cowher	NFLAFCNorth	1st	15 1 0	.938

- Won Divisional Playoffs(Jets) 20–17
- Lost Conference Championship (Patriots) 41–27
- Bill Cowher – Sporting News Coach of the Year
- Ben Roethlisberger– Offensive Rookie of the Year

2005	#15 Bill Cowher	NFLAFCNorth	2nd	11 5 0	.688

- Won Wild Card Playoffs(Bengals) 31–17
- Won Divisional Playoffs(Colts) 21–18
- Won Conference Championship(Broncos) 34–17
- Won Super Bowl XL(5) (Seahawks) 21–10
- Hines Ward – Super Bowl MVP

2006	#15 Bill Cowher	NFLAFCNorth	3rd	8 8 0	.500
2007	#16 Mike Tomlin	NFLAFCNorth	1st	10 6 0	.625

- Lost Wild Card Playoffs(Jaguars) 31–29

2008	#16 Mike Tomlin	NFLAFCNorth	1st	12 4 0	.750

- Won Divisional Playoffs(Chargers) 35–24
- Won Conference Championship (Ravens) 23–14

- Won Super Bowl XLIII(6) (Cardinals) 27–23
- James Harrison – Defensive Player of the Year
- Santonio Holmes – Super Bowl MVP
- Mike Tomlin – Motorola NFL Coach of the Year

Year	#	Coach	League	Conf	Finish	W	L	T	Pct
2009	#16	Mike Tomlin	NFL	AFC North	3rd	9	7	0	.563
2010	#16	Mike Tomlin	NFL	AFC North	1st	12	4	0	.750

- Won Divisional Playoffs(Ravens) 31–24
- Won Conference Championship (Jets) 24–19
- Lost Super Bowl XLV(Packers) 31–25
- Troy Polamalu– Defensive Player of the Year

Year	#	Coach	League	Conf	Finish	W	L	T	Pct
2011	#16	Mike Tomlin	NFL	AFC North	2nd	12	4	0	.750

- Lost Wild Card Playoffs(Broncos) 29–23 (OT)

Year	#	Coach	League	Conf	Finish	W	L	T	Pct
2012	#16	Mike Tomlin	NFL	AFC North	3rd	8	8	0	.500
2013	#16	Mike Tomlin	NFL	AFC North	2nd	8	8	0	.500
2014	#16	Mike Tomlin	NFL	AFC North	1st	11	5	0	.688

- Lost Wild Card Playoffs(Ravens) 30–17

Year	#	Coach	League	Conf	Finish	W	L	T	Pct
2015	#16	Mike Tomlin	NFL	AFC North	2nd	10	6	0	.625

- Won Wild Card Playoffs(Bengals) 18–16
- Lost Divisional Playoffs(Broncos) 23–16

Year	#	Coach	League	Conf	Finish	W	L	T	Pct
2016	#16	Mike Tomlin	NFL	AFC North	1st	11	5	0	.688

- Won Wild Card Playoffs(Dolphins) 30–12
- Won Divisional Playoffs(Chiefs) 18–16
- Lost Conference Championship (Patriots) 36–17

Year	#	Coach	League	Conf	Finish	W	L	T	Pct
2017	#16	Mike Tomlin	NFL	AFC North	1st	13	3	0	.813

Lost Divisional Playoffs(Jaguars) 42–45

Dedication

I dedicate this book

To my wife & children and my wonderful brothers and sisters.

Wife—Patricia A. Kelly
Sons & Daughters—Brian P. Kelly, Michael P. Kelly, Katie P. Kelly

Angel Edward J. Kelly, Jr.

Carol & Amelia Kelly

Nancy "Ann" Flannery & Angel Jim Flannery

Mary A. Daniels & Bill Daniels

Joseph A. Kelly & Diane Kelly

I surely am a lucky person to have

Such a great family

Mom & Dad—Angels Edward J Kelly Sr. and Irene McKeown Kelly

Acknowledgments:

I appreciate all the help that I have received in putting this book together as well as all of the other 154 books from the past.

My acknowledgments were so large at one time that readers complained that they had to go through too many pages to get to page one.

And, so I put my acknowledgment list online, and it continues to grow. Believe it or not, it would cost about a dollar more to print my books with full acknowledgments.

Thank you and God bless you all for your help. Please check out www.letsgopublish.com to read the latest version of my heartfelt acknowledgments updated for this book.

In this book, I received some extra special help from many fine American patriots including Dennis Grimes, Gerry Rodski, Wily Ky Eyely, Angel Irene McKeown Kelly, Angel Edward Joseph Kelly Sr., Angel Edward Joseph Kelly Jr., Ann Flannery, Angel James Flannery Sr., Mary Daniels, Bill Daniels, Angel Robert Garry Daniels, Angel Sarah Janice Daniels, Angel Punkie Daniels, Joe Kelly, Diane Kelly, Angel Harry Ashford, Angel Josephine Ashford. Brian P. Kelly, Mike P. Kelly, Katie P. Kelly, Angel Ben Kelly, and Budmund (Buddy) Arthur Kelly.

Thank you all!

Table of Contents

Table of Contents... xvii
Chapter 1 Introduction to the Book........................... 1
Chapter 2 Art Rooney & the Pirates.......................... 13
Chapter 3 History of Pirates / Steelers Football Stadiums 23
Chapter 4 Pirates Launch First Football Team 53
Chapter 5 The Evolution of Modern Football............. 69
Chapter 6 The First American College Football Game........ 73
Chapter 7 Moving Closer Towards American Football 85
Chapter 8 Origin of the Oval-Shaped Sports-Ball 99
Chapter 9 The Birth of Play with Pay........................ 107
Chapter 10 When Pro Football Was Unorganized 113
Chapter 11 NFL's Fast Start from 1920 The Steelers............ 121
Chapter 12 After the Pirates, Steelers History 131
Chapter 13 The 1940's & 1950' Same Old Steelers............... 147
Chapter 14 Three Great Coaches – Noll, Cowher, & Tomlin 153
Chapter 15 The Pittsburgh Steelers Seasons 1 to 3; 1940-'42. 185
Chapter 16 1943 Steagles; 1944 Card-Pitt 193
Chapter 17 Five Coaches from 1945 through 1956............... 207
Chapter 18 Coach Buddy Parker, 1957 to 1964.................... 221
Chapter 19 Coaches Nixon & Austin 1965 to 1968 233
Chapter 20 Coach Chuck Noll I, 1969 to 1982..................... 241
Chapter 21 Coach Chuck Noll II, 1969 to 1982 313
Chapter 22 Coach Bill Cowher 1992 to 2006 343
Chapter 23 Coach Mike Tomlin 2007 to 2017+ 409
Other books by Brian Kelly: (amazon.com, & Kindle).......... 452

References

I learned how to write creatively in Grade School at St. Boniface. I even enjoyed reading some of my own stuff.

At Meyers High School (HS Diploma) and King's College (BS Data Processing), and Wilkes-University, (MBA Accounting & Finance) I learned how to research, write bibliographies and footnote every non-original thought included in my writings. I learned to hate ibid, and op. cit., and I hated assuring that I had all citations were written down in the proper sequence. Having to pay attention to details took my desire to write creatively and diminished it with busy work.

I know it is necessary for the world to stop plagiarism, so authors and publishers can get paid properly, but for an honest writer, it sure is annoying. I wrote many proposals while with IBM and whenever I needed to cite something, I cited it in place, because my readers, IT Managers, and company management, could care less about tracing the vagaries of citations. I always hated to use stilted footnotes, or produce a lengthy, perfectly formatted bibliography. I bet most bibliographies are flawed because even the experts on such drivel do not like the tedium.

I wrote 154 other books before this book and several hundred articles published by many magazines and newspapers and I only cite when an idea is not mine or when I am quoting, and again, I choose to cite in place, and the reader does not have to trace strange numbers through strange footnotes and back to bibliography elements that may not be readily accessible or available.

Yet, I would be kidding you, if in a book about the great moments in Pittsburgh Football, I tried to bluff my way, so you would think that I knew everything before I began to research and write anything in this book. I spent as much time researching as writing. I might even call myself an expert of sorts now for all the facts that I have uncovered.

Without any pain on your part, you can read this book from cover to cover to enjoy the stories about the many great moments in both the Pittsburgh Pirates of the NFL and their successor, The Pittsburgh Steelers. Both generations of Pittsburgh Teams made their mark on the football world.

This book is not intended for historians per se, but it does teach a lot of football history. It is for regular people of all levels of intelligence. It is for people who want to have a fun read, who like smiling when Steelers Football is the topic. It is fun reading about each of Pittsburgh's 655 wins. This book is for people who love Pittsburgh Pennsylvania Football and perhaps it is also for some Steeler detractors who want to have command of the facts before they defend a point of view.

There are lots and lots of facts in this book. This book is not for sticklers about the mundane aspects of writing that often cause creative writers to lay bricks or paint houses instead of writing. It is for everyday people, like you and I, who enjoy the Steelers because they are the Steelers and who enjoy football because it is football. It is that simple.

When the Steelers play a team and they win or lose, that is a historical fact, but to discover such facts, it does not require fundamental or basic research. The NFL itself as well as the Steelers, copyright their original material but not publicly available facts. They copyright so they can say "no" if somebody else's creativity affects the league or the franchise negatively. Even the NFL does not own publicly well-known facts that are readily available about legacies such as Chuck Noll, Bill Cowher, Mike Tomlin, or even future immortals and all of the many Pittsburgh top seasons.

The championships and the coaches and the great players are well known and well defined, though some may think the facts belong to the NFL. Facts are facts, period. So, what? As the author of this book, I care but it is a sports book. I use a judicious approach to assure that I am not throwing the bull when I intend to be presenting the facts.

Nonetheless, this is not a book about heavy math algorithms, or potential advances to the internal combustion engine, or space travel, or the eight elements necessary to find a cure for cancer. So, I refuse to treat this book 100% seriously. It is a sports book. If you find a fault, I will fix it. This is a book about sports and sports legends and stories about sporting events that have been recorded seven million times already someplace else. Pennsylvanians should be pleased. Though I tried for sure to get it all right and I used the work of others to assure so, I bet I made a mistake or two. Tell me about them. Don't sue me!

What is my remedy for the *harmed* if I have made a mistake? I did not write this book to harm anybody. If I did not write this book, would the *harmed individuals* from the book be unharmed? So, at the very least, I can *unpublish* those parts of the book. If any reader is harmed, let me know, and I will do whatever must be done for all to be OK

Preface:

These three great quotes from Mike Tomlin, Steelers Head Coach help demonstrate why he is a Super Bowl caliber coach.

1. "We don't live in our fears. We live in our hopes."

2. "It's not about what you're capable of. It's about what you're willing to do."

3. "The good teams, the dominant teams, aren't necessarily dominant in stadiums, but they are dominant largely in moments, when they do what's required to get out of stadiums with victories."

When the 2017 season began, everybody thought the Steelers were going to do well and most thought that Mike Tomlin's mastery of the game would have set the Pittsburgh Steelers up well for another Super Bowl. It would have been their seventh Super Bowl win but unfortunately, after coming in first in their division NFL's AFC North, The Steelers were knocked out in the Divisional Championship at the hands of the Jacksonville Jaguars L (42-45) in a major offensive battle. Ben Roethlisberger again was at peak, but the D had a tough time with the Jags.

To recap, like so many great teams in Steeler history. This team won the AFC North championship. They did not have to compete in a Wild-Card game. Instead, they got a first-round bye headed into the postseason and just missed taking the conference's top seed after Week 17. This would give them home-field advantage throughout the playoffs. The loss to the Jags was disheartening to say the least but the Steelers are up on their feet and looking forward to a solid 2018 season and a seventh Super Bowl this coming season.

The oddsmakers do like the Steelers, and they like the Patriots and the Eagles also, but Big Ben and the Steelers are right there at the top. Two PA teams out of three are the non-New England contenders. Pittsburgh was among a few consistent favorites in 2018 championship odds released by prominent Las Vegas sports books in the hours after the Philadelphia Eagles defeated the New England Patriots in the 2017 championship game played in February 2018, in Minneapolis.

The Westgate Superbook has already clocked in the odds with the the Steelers at 8/1 behind only the Patriots (5/1) and Eagles (6/1). Mike Tomlin and Ben Roethlisberger and a host of inspired Steelers are ready to get back those three points they lost to the Jaguars in the 2017 Playoffs. 42-45 is too many points when the Steelers get the 42.

And, so, like most teams that expect to win the Super Bowl every year, there is talk about firing Mike Tomlin. There are many good arguments, however, that say Mike Tomlin will probably not — and should not be fired from Pittsburgh. He had a fine year.

Tomlin orchestrated a 13-3 regular season and made a three point error in the playoffs (13-4) Don't forget he also won 48 games in four seasons, and the Steelers have built their success over the past half-century on stability. Coaches last a while at Pittsburgh and they all seem to win Super Bowls—at least once, and sometimes as many as four.

Pittsburgh has had three coaches in the past 49 seasons, with Chuck Noll lasting 23 years. Tomlin is seen as cold and calculating when he and the organization feel it is necessary. He has never had a losing season during the 11 years he has coached for the Steelers. Even Sports Illustrated says, "Keep Tomlin," by agreeing that there is no one good enough to replace him. Who ya gonna call? But all that said and done, the Steelers do need to make some structural changes to their coaching staff. Let's hope Mike Tomlin gets it right and that the 8-1 odds become 4-1 before opening day.

After writing about Notre Dame, Penn State, Clemson, Alabama, Florida, Syracuse, and Army, Brian Kelly, your author was moved by the Steeler's great seasons, especially from Chuck Noll to the present and the work of Ben Roethlisberger and Mike Tomlin in modern times to take a shot at writing a book about one of his favorite Pennsylvania pro-teams. Kelly has been rooting for the Steelers in almost every Super Bowl from the Chuck Noll days.

And, so, this new book by Brian, which highlights the Great Moments in Pittsburgh Steelers Football is one of the items that is expected to be available all 52 weeks every year and in fact all 365 days each year except in LEAP YEAR where the Steelers add an extra day for your book reading pleasure.

Amazon, Kindle, Barnes & Noble and other online sites in the US and overseas carry this book and it will add to your year-round football experience especially in the off-season. Once you get this book, it is yours forever unless, of course you give it away to one of the many Pittsburgh Steelers fans, who will be in awe of your new possession.

Reading this book is like reliving the last game, the last football season, and / or all the seasons before last season without ever having to get on or off a plane. Seeing a game in Heinz Field is an exhilarating adventure. I know of the experience. This book will help you relive the phenomenon over and over. Besides the great read, with this book in your hand at your private venue, such as your Sun Room or Man-Cave, or "Ma'am Cave," there is no limit on the hours for book-tailgating. Moreover, there is no charge, as long as you have stocked up on the proper snack and beverage victuals before the read.

The book examines more than just great moments. There are some moments that are not so great in every team's football seasons and the Pittsburgh Steelers offer no excuses for those times. Your author shows the bad with the good to get the proper perspective for those great moments in Pittsburgh Steelers football that we are living now.

Not all Pittsburgh coaches for example, are named Tomlin, Cowher, or Noll, so not all games are in the W-column; but most are. However, all teams from 1933 to the present, no matter who the coach is, were Steelers tough, nonetheless. That means they all fought hard for wins for the good of the team and the fans.

Opening with its first story at the very beginning of Football as a sport in America, this book goes all the way to Coach Mike Tomlin, who has stood in time for 11 years changing the record books for Pittsburgh and pushing the win record well over 500.

This book is written for those of us who love Pittsburgh Steelers football as played in many of the great American venues over the years. After discussing the origins of football and then the origins of pro-football, the book first tells the story of the first Pittsburgh Pirates Football Game in 1933 and it tells the story of the first Steelers game eight years later. It then advances to the games, the victories and losses, and onward to the great immortal Pittsburgh coaches of historical fame—Mike Tomlin, Buddy Parker, Bill Cowher, and Chuck Noll.

This book is all about the great moments in Pittsburgh Steelers Football. It touches every aspect of the historical and mythical Pirates/Steelers Football Teams. It tells exhilarating stories about the 16 head coaches and the 85 seasons worth of great games. The book stops every now and then, and it takes the reader on a side excursion in time to learn about a particular event or a great player.

The player list begins with great players from the immortal list such as John Stallworth, Jack Ham, Jerome Bettis, Hines Ward, Franco Harris, Rod Woodson, Mel Blount, Le'Veon Bell, Antonio Brown, Ben Roethlisberger, and of course the inimitable Terry Bradshaw, a great QB with four Super Bowl Rings. Bradshaw is the greatest Steeler of all time. He matches his talent with an outstanding personality and does not toot his own horn.

These stops will add substantially to your reading enjoyment. These Pro Bowlers and others have made Steelers Patriots Football a bright light experience for the program's many years and many fans.

In my role as Editor in Chief of Lets Go Publish! and a die-hard Steelers' fan, I predict that you will not be able to put this book down

You are going to love this book because it is the perfect read for anybody who loves the Pittsburgh Steelers and Steelers smash-mouth football, and who wants to know more about one of the most revered professional athletic teams in all of football.

Few sports books are a must-read but my dad, Brian Kelly's Great Moments in Pittsburgh Steelers Football will quickly appear at the top of Americas most enjoyable must-read books about sports. Enjoy!

Who is Brian Kelly?

Brian Kelly aka Brian W. Kelly, is one of the leading authors in America with this, his 155th published book. Brian continues as an outspoken and eloquent expert on a variety of topics, including the kind of sports that Pennsylvanian's love. Moreover, Kelly also has written several hundred articles on other topics of interest to Americans.

Most of my dad's early works involved high technology. Later, Brian wrote a number of patriotic books and most recently, he has been writing human interest books such as The Wine Diet and Thank you, IBM. His books are always well received. If I could get the pen out of Dad's hand for just awhile, I might be able to write a few books of my own, but my editing chores at Lets Go Publish! always come first.

Brian Kelly's books are highlighted at www.letsgopublish.com. They are for sale at Amazon, Kindle, and Barnes & Noble. The link, Amazon.com/author/brianwkelly, is the best to see the books available from Brian Kelly. Please note that All Kelly books are available at most fine booksellers.

The best!

Sincerely,

Brian P. Kelly, Editor in Chief
I am Brian Kelly's eldest son

About the Author

Brian Kelly retired as an Assistant Professor in the Business Information Technology (BIT) Program at Marywood University, where he also served as the IBM i and Midrange Systems Technical Advisor to the IT Faculty. Kelly designed, developed, and taught many college and professional courses. He continues as a contributing technical editor to a number of technical industry magazines, including "The Four Hundred" and "Four Hundred Guru," published by IT Jungle.

Kelly is a former IBM Senior Systems Engineer. His specialty was problem solving for customers as well as implementing advanced operating systems and software on his client's machines. Brian is the author of 154 other books, including 30 Sports Books, and hundreds of magazine articles. He has been a frequent speaker at technical conferences throughout the United States.

Brian was a candidate for the US Congress from Pennsylvania in 2010 and he ran for Mayor in his home town in 2015. Kelly loves the Steelers and he became a big fan in the 1950's watching NFL games with his dad on Sundays on the 21" Admiral B/W TV.

This is Brian's tenth "Great Moments" book and his third about a professional NFL team. Writing about the Pittsburgh Steelers has been a special treat.

Chapter 1 Introduction to the Book

The Steelers celebrated 80 years of football

Everybody loves the Steelers!

The Pittsburgh Steelers tradition began on July 8, 1933, when they were known as the Pittsburgh Pirates, just like the baseball team. And so, as traditions go the last big celebration for the Steelers was on July 7, 2012. This date celebrated the 80th year after Art Rooney, Sr. purchased his dream NFL franchise for the tidy sum of $2,500. Can you imagine trading in your old Volkswagon today and picking up the Steelers for the original MSRP of $1565, adding about a grand and walking away with the Pittsburgh Steelers. Such a deal.

Art Rooney bought the franchise and the Rooney family has owned and managed the Steelers ever since When Art Rooney passed away on August 25, 1988 in Pittsburgh after a stroke, his son, Dan took over the franchise. Dan Rooney, who succeeded his father and Steelers founder, Art Sr., as team president rose to become one of the most powerful and beloved owners in sports. He passed away on a Thursday in April 2017 at the age of 84.

Under his leadership, since the late 1960s, with the arrival of Coach Chuck Noll. the Steelers transformed from what the pundits called "lovable losers" into a Super Bowl dynasty in the 1970s. Today, Steeler fans and those not so inclined recognize that this great team remains among the most successful and most popular franchises in the game. Many have forgotten that before Dan Rooney hired Chuck Noll, he had offered the position to another Pennsylvania Pride coach, Joe Paterno, whose long-time love for the Nittany Lions forced JoePa to turn down the opportunity.

Long before Dan Rooney passed away, he had brought his son Art Rooney II into the business Art Rooney II is the oldest of Dan Rooney's nine children. He had been named team president in May 2003 Prior to that, he was already serving as vice president and general counsel of the Steelers, and he has served on the board of directors of the Steelers since 1989. Rooney II is also active on many NFL steering boards.

Rooney II controlled a 30% interest in the franchise at the time of his father's 2017 death, Rooney II held a 30% stake in the Steelers He was first in line to inherit most of the 30% share that his dad, Dan Rooney held. This made him the majority owner of the team. He is one of only two third-generation owners in the league, the other being the Giant's John Mara. There is some blood between the Mara's and the Rooney's Mara's brother is married to Rooney's sister, and both owners count actresses Rooney Mara and Kate Mara as nieces. Since

Are we looking at a big change now that one Rooney has total control of the franchise? I would answer that by saying there should be no change other than the change that would be coming regardless of Dan Rooney's passing.

Art Rooney II gave a lot of information earlier in 2018 to the press that gives away where he is on changes for the Pittsburgh Steelers. This year and in the years come to come. Having been the "manager" for years, and coming off a 13-3 regular season, one would expect that he would not be exceedingly harsh in looking at

the team. Reading the lines and between the lines one would conclude that Art Rooney II believes in his heart that there is nothing intrinsically wrong—nothing that needs to change and that many of the team's issues and controversies that had been aired in the press are overblown. Rooney II also suggested that the Steelers defense isn't so bad, especially when you take a look at the state of defenses in the NFL these days. He is a wise man for sure.
The Pundits think he was not completely forthright with them in his prognosis. They think that he knows how badly his team underachieved this season, despite its glowing 13-3 record. They think that Rooney II is not the kind of guy to throw his coaching staff under the bus publicly.

However, the "experts" do expect that Rooney II will step in this offseason to try to fix the things that ail the Steelers and he will work hard to get it right. Of course, every NFL team has something wrong with it, and one must be careful with a 13-3 team, to not dismember it to the point of regret. The pundits have deep concern that the window to win another Super Bowl with Ben Roethlisberger at quarterback is closing, as Big Ben has already discussed retirement, and they believe that the Steelers missed a golden opportunity this year. In other words, the Steelers-loving-press would like the gnarls removed from the organization so that a 42-45 loss in the Division Playoffs goes into the "never can happen again," category.

Art Rooney Senior had a lot of bad years before Chuck Noll came on the scene. Rooney, however, was not Nosterdamus and so he could not predict the future of his $2500 team or that today it would be worth over $2.5 Billion. In other words, Rooney Sr. surely could have never predicted the phenomenal heights that his team—and, for that matter, the NFL—would achieve as the clock on pro football continued to tick through the years.

Art Rooney, Sr.'s team and the city of Pittsburgh have grown together over the course of 80 seasons... (you can add in the five years from 2013 to 2018 in your spare time. But for 80 years, the timing is as follows)

29,220 days...
701,280 hours...
42,076,800 minutes...
2,524,608,000 seconds...

That's a lot of time, folks.

Some Pittsburgh fans love the thought of being with other Pittsburgh fans celebrating the Steelers. In the 8th decade the celebration was another fine Pittsburgh event.

Steelers Unveil 80th Anniversary Celebration Plans

Monday marked the beginning of Pittsburgh's "'The Year of the Fan" events and festivities. by Erin Faulk, Patch Staff | Apr 6, 2012 5:38 pm ET | Updated Apr 6, 2012 5:39 pm ET

In 1982 at the 80th anniversary, the management of the Steelers wanted to give something back and in April 2012, they unveiled a

celebration for this special football season and they called it "The Year of the Fan," Of course, they also put together a nice logo shown above commemorating the 80 seasons (1933-2012).

This was the beginning of a varied range of events and festivities that celebrated the legacy of the team, its players and its fans from the days of the Pirates through the Steelers to 2012. There was even a Steelers Fan Image Season Ticket Design Contest that gave the fans an opportunity to be on the face of Steelers' tickets for the 2012 season.

The fans also got a shot at competing in a 15-second video that highlighted on Steelers.com their three words about, "My Pittsburgh Steelers." Unfortunately, the video is no longer online.

Along with their image on the tickets, the 10 winners also received four tickets to a game, pregame hospitality, on-field pregame field passes, a $100 Steelers gift card and participation in the Terrible Towel twirl on the sidelines before kickoff. It had to be a lot of fun. Look at the tickets above to see some of the happy fans.

Of course, the merchandisers created some new stuff for the event and fans were able to purchase 80th season merchandise at all Steelers Sideline stores and they got a chance to win prizes every half hour, including some of the unique 80th season items.

Some of the stuff like the embroidered patch below was available just last week on ebay for $8.99

Tell me more about this Pittsburgh Steelers Great Moments book.

This book celebrates Pittsburgh Steelers Football; its founding; its struggles; its greatness; and the game of football's long-lasting impact on American life. People like me, who love the team from way back when Buddy Parker was the head coach, will love this book, as we reach back to the founding and up to the 80th anniversary and now as we approach the 90th anniversary of one of the best organizations that has ever played professional football. Thank you, Art Rooney, Dan Rooney, and Art Rooney II.

In defining the format of the book, we chose to use a timetable that is based on a historical chronology. Within this framework, we discuss the great moments in Pittsburgh Steelers Football History, and there are many great moments. No book can claim to be able to capture them all, as it would be a never-ending story, but we sure try. The great moments naturally include a lot of great people, including players and the 16 great coaches that over time would make or break the Pittsburgh Steelers.

A happy Mike Tomlin celebrating in Super Bowl Parade after Steeler's 27-23 win over Cardinals

Even before we get into the meat of Steelers football, we discuss the beginning of football, the first football game in 1869, the first players paid to play, and then on to the beginning of the NFL.

To know the full story of the Pittsburgh Steelers, you have to go through the Pittsburgh Pirates of NFL Football fame. But, there were teams even before Art Rooney's Pittsburgh Pirates.

In the 1920's NFL style pro-football was just firing up and so the precursor team to the Steelers named the Pirates, took ten or more years to come out of the brew that was being concocted in the Pittsburgh region in the 1920's. Thus, the Steelers history traces itself to a regional pro team that was established long before the Pirates and later was joined in the NFL as the Pittsburgh Pirates on July 8, 1933. Art Rooney as previously discussed became the happy owner for $2500 and he gave the team its original name from the baseball team of the same name. This was a common practice for NFL teams looking for name recognition as startups.

The Rooney's were not as clever when they put together a team to play in the what might be called the fledgling NFL back in the 1920's. The team carried the moniker, the "J.P. Rooney's" More formally, they were known as the "James P. Rooney's)". This team was an independent semi-professional team, based in Pittsburgh. It was founded by the same Art Rooney, who is now best known as being the founder of the Pittsburgh Steelers of the National Football League.

This team is considered to be the unofficial beginnings of the modern-day Pittsburgh Steelers. Every team needs a ball park and the J.P. Rooney's played their games at Exposition Park and were doing quite well, with attendance numbers reported as up to 12,000 people in the stands at various games. We'll tell you more about this in its own chapter after we cover the origin of American Football itself.

Art Rooney's "JP Rooney" team were originally known as Hope-Harvey

The Hope Harvey Football Team, 1925 will be Cast in Bronze

New edition in plaster which to be used for the molds in casting a bronze sculpture.

Ray Sokolowski's sculpture depicts the first football team managed by Art Rooney on Pittsburgh's North Side and the only time Art and his 3 brothers played together on a team.

Finished size: 15 in. high x 8 ft. long in single line up configuration.

Ray Sokolowski, Painting & Sculpture, Hope Harvey Football Team Sculpture circa 1925

| 1933 | #1 Forrest Douds | NFLEast | 5th | 3 6 2 | .364 |
| 1934 | #2 Luby DiMeolo | NFLEast | 5th | 2 10 0 | .167 |

With Coach Forrest Douds (3-6-2), the first Pittsburgh Pirates coach, and Coach Luby DiMeolo (2-10-0), the second Pittsburgh coach, the Pirates had a tough time finding the "W" column. In fact, it was not until Coach Walt Kiesling in 1942 that the Steelers had their first winning season. Many of the player names from the Pittsburgh Pirates teams from 1933 to 1940 have slipped into oblivion and it was so long ago that few of those who were alive then are around today to care a heck of a lot.

The members of the Pirates' offensive starting team, which for the most part was the defensive starting team also included the following players:

Pos	Name	Age	Years	Starts	Rushes/Receptions
HB	James Clark	29	Rook	5	76 rushes; 192 yards, 0 TDs
TB	Angelo Brovelli	23	Rook	8	60 rushes; 236 yards, 2 td
					6 catches; 137 yards 0 td
FB	Tony Holm	25	3	9	58 rushes; 160 yards, 0 td,
					2 catches; 13 yards and 0 td
BB	George Shaffer	23	Rook	5	5 rushes; 6 yards, 0 td,
					1 catch; 11 yards and 0 td
LE	Paul Moss	25	Rook	7	13 catches; 283 yards, 2 td
LT	Don Rhodes	24	Rook	5	
LG	Larry Critchfild	25	Rook	10	
C	Cap Oehler	23	Rook	11	
RG	Clarence Jancek	22	Rook	11	
RT	Corrie Artman	26	2	5	
RE	Ray Tesser	21	Rook	10	14 catches; 282 yards, 0 td

The Pittsburgh Steelers have had some of the NFL's greatest players over the years beginning in 1969 when Chuck Noll took over head coaching duties. The Pirates / Steelers before 1969 (Chuck Noll) and the Steelers, 1969 and later played at two completely different levels of competency. completely after 1970. Pre Chuck Noll, the Pittsburgh record was 161-254-19, and Post Chuck Noll, the record was 458-298-2.

The Steelers had to win 93 games from 1969 on just to break even. Today, the team's record from having played 1571 total games, including the playoffs 655-577-21—not too shabby at all. Add to that the league leading 6 Super Bowl Victories shared with Coach Noll (4), Coach Cowher (1), and Coach Tomlin (1) and the Steelers are much more than just a first-class NFL team. They are one of the best.

As you browse through the chapters in this book, in the seasons in which they played, you will find biographical information of some of the top players to wear a Pittsburgh Steeler Uniform rom. You will find players such as the following in these chapters:

Joe Greene*
Jack Lambert*
Mel Blount*
Franco Harris*
Rod Woodson*
Jack Ham*

Mike Webster*
DermDawson
Terry Bradshaw*
Ernie Stautner*
Hines Ward
Jerome Bettis*

Alan Faneca
John Stallworth*
Andy Russell
L. C. Greenwood
Casey Hampton
Donnie Shell

Chapter 1 Introduction 11

Lynn Swann
Carnell Lake
Greg Lloyd
Jack Butler

Rocky Bleier
John Henry
Johnson
Bobby Layne

Mike Wagner*

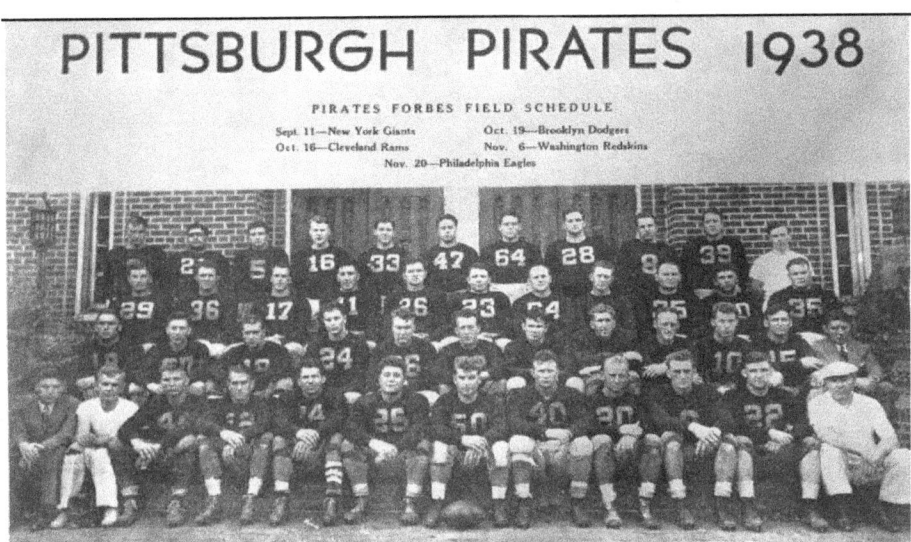

Pittsburgh Pirates Football Team from 1938 above

2017 Pittsburgh Steelers in Color

Chapter 2 Art Rooney & the Pirates

Art Rooney Sr. & well-loved cigar

Is anything easy?

Folks, nothing in life worth having comes easy. Art Rooney loved playing football, coaching football, managing a football team, and of course he absolutely loved owning the Pittsburgh Pirates and then the Pittsburgh Steelers. In May 1933, waiting breathlessly for the repeal of some of Pennsylvania's restrictive business laws, Rooney went for his big dream. He applied for a franchise with the NFL.

He had great chutzpa! His request was granted on May 19, 1933, and his Pittsburgh Professional Football Club, Inc. signed up and joined the National Football League in exchange for $2500 which is not much over $50,000 in today's dollars). For the $2500, Rooney became the owner of an NFL football franchise that today is worth over $2.5 Billion.

The team first was named the Pirates in deference to the baseball club that were the landlords at Forbes Field in Pittsburgh. Forbes was not a given for the Pirate as Rooney had first looked at Greenlee Field, which housed the city's Negro League baseball club.

The bulk of the restrictive PA Blue Laws were not repealed until November's general election, and so the team was forced by law to play its first four home games on Wednesday nights. Analysts reflecting on this scenario saw Rooney's new team as a study in frustration for many years. Between 1933 and 1971, they mustered a winning record just eight times, and they did not make the playoffs until 1947, and then had to wait until after 1971 to repeat. In 1947 they were shut out by in-state rival, Philadelphia.

Art Rooney was not just interested in football. In fact, he shared his love of sports with the Rooney-McGinley Boxing Club, which promoted fights. He also liked handicapping horses and he liked betting on horse races. Rooney liked to have fun. spent a good amount of his time and energy handicapping and placing bets on horse racing, which for the sports entrepreneur was a lifelong hobby.

My dad shared Art Rooney's love of the ponies with me so I know the smiles that one gets when a big one comes in. Rooney is said to have once won a stake of about $250,000 to $300,000, which would be $4.6 to $5.5 million today. He is said to have done it all in just a single 1936 day of betting in his third year of owning the Pirates.

Though nobody can say for sure, speculators suggest that the purchase of the Pittsburgh Steelers was made with other horse race gambling winnings. Unfortunately, the NFL is now focused on being snow white and out of the shade and so Rooney's buying the Pirates as an NFL team is becoming an urban legend.

Meanwhile, the NFL wants to put a lot of distance between the League and the potential for such "shady" early beginnings. Yet, somehow more and more of the individual united states are finding ways to legalize all sorts of betting options to raise revenue.

Rooney did his best to put out a winning product at Pittsburgh but like most new teams in a fledgling industry, there were plenty of obstacles. A few sheckles from gambling on the ponies had to come in handy while trying to keep the business of a pro football team afloat.

During the 1930s, in fact in 1933, the US was in the middle of, or shall we say the depths of the Great Depression. The fan base had to be consistent and the drain of paying the best players had to be manageable to minimize the financial drain from activities in the "depression." Rooney admitted that the team lost nearly $10,000 in 1934 ($182,935 today) when travel expenses were high and when the regular people had a hard time affording an occasional trip to a ball game.

Additionally, some teams had much bigger pockets than others and the better players learned that they could command larger salaries by playing their cards right. Thus, bidding wars for players gave the advantage to more established, well-funded clubs when competing against the newcomers like the Pirates.

Teams like the more seasoned Giants, Bears and Packers for example could buy whatever players they wanted. In 1935, this notion frustrated businessmen that owned smaller teams. Rooney suggested a restriction on the number of players that could be signed by teams that finished at the top of the league. As you will see when we discuss the NFL Draft in later chapters, Rooney's ideas were incorporated into the Draft so that the top teams received later picks. It was and is a good idea. Let's move on to some lighter material

What are the predominate colors of the Pittsburgh Steelers uniforms?

Take a look at the city of Pittsburgh's flag below and you will see that Pittsburgh itself was a major inspiration for the Pirate's uniforms.

And, so the Pirates' first uniforms were gold with black stripes and they were embellished with the city crest. The original stripes were created with felt overlays, and as such they had functional as well as aesthetic value in that they allowed the ball carrier to hold the ball more securely.

When pro football began, owners had a lot of expenses and they saved money in a number of ways. Hiring locals who had an affinity for the city was one way and another was having the offensive players also play a lot of defense. A third way was to hire young talented players who could also earn a coaching alary as player-coaches.

We no longer see player coaches, and rarely do we see two-way players, and even less regularly do we see two-sport athletes. Some may remember Deion Sanders, and some may remember Bo Jackson, two of the last to try two sports. This notion by the way did not save the team any money. Many know that after he gave up football, the very athletic Tim Tebow is now giving baseball a shot. But, when he was playing, football, he played football.

When Rooney was looking for a new coach for the Pittsburgh Pirates, he had his budget clearly in mind when he hired Forrest "Jap" Douds as player and coach. Douds had been a three-time All-American and local legend as a player at Washington & Jefferson College, and he had already been an All-Pro in the NFL. In Pittsburgh's first game ever, against the New York Giants in New

York, the team was well-defeated L (2-23) in front of a crowd of about 20,000. The franchise's first points ever in NFL play came from a safety.

Pirates center John "Cap" Oehler, playing on defense, blocked a punt through the end zone but it was not enough to dig out this lost cause. Rooney had a problem with the first game. He later wrote: "The Giants won. Our team looks terrible. The fans didn't get their money's worth." Art Rooney wanted fans to keep coming back to see a good show. The fans loved him "The Chief," 'til the day he died.

The Pirates secured their first NFL victory one week later, defeating the Chicago Cardinals in a nail-biter W (14–13). This time, there were about 5,000 fans. The Pirates scored their first ever touchdown when Martin "Butch" Kottler returned an interception for 99-yards. The other hero that day was Mose Kelsch, who at 36 years of age was the oldest player in the NFL—four years older even than team owner Rooney. Kelsch was a holdover from the sandlot Majestics. He had a good foot and kicked the extra point that provided the margin of victory in the Pirates eternal game #2. .

In their sixth game of the inaugural season, the Pirates set an NFL record indicating how tough it was to move the ball in that game. The Cincinnati Reds share the record as the teams had to punt 31 times in a scoreless tie. The Bears and Packers matched that mark in a game played on the same day, but it has never been surpassed. Starting in a new league was never expected to bring perfection

It was important to have home attendance to pay the players. The total attendance for their five home games in the inaugural season was around 57,000. To put that number into perspective, that year's Pitt-Duquesne college matchup was watched by around 60,000 fans.

Pro football was not yet the national past-time. The team finished its initial season with a 3–6–2 record, and so Coach Douds was not retained as coach. However, his talents as a player were superior and he stuck it out suiting up each week for two more years .

Rooney always wanted a great coach but had a hard time getting one for the right price. He liked Heartley "Hunk" Anderson, who had replaced Knute Rockne after his death at Notre Dame.

Anderson had recently stepped down as head coach at Notre Dame, and was now available to replace Douds. However, he did not want the job, Heartly did not take the offer nor did Greasy Neale, another great coach, take the job, Neale eventually became head coach for the Philadelphia Eagles and did a fine job for a number of years. Art Rooney was a loveable owner, but he could not find a coach.

Luby DiMeolo, who had been rumored as the leading candidate for the Pirates coaching job prior to the team's first season, agreed to take the job of replacing Douds. He had been captain of the 1929 Pittsburgh Panthers football team on which Jimmy Rooney also starred. DiMeolo hired Jimmy Rooney as an assistant. It was always tough bringing in a non-coach to coach and so after a very poor 2–10 season in 1934, DiMeolo was let go. A lot of early coaches did not make it.

Rooney wanted a good team and like many, he believed that a good player would be a good coach, but it is not always so. The owner went after football legend Red Grange, who had just retired as a player. Rooney hoped to get him to coach the Pirates in 1935.

Grange showed interest but then declined the offer in favor of an assistant coaching position with the better financially endowed Chicago Bears. Rooney settled again. This time he hired Duquesne coach Joe Bach. Bach had good history and was notable as one of Notre Dame's "seven mules," who had blocked for the team's famed "Four Horsemen." In Bach's first season, Pittsburgh doubled its wins to four, but they still did not look very good at 4–8.

Rooney's idea for the NFL Draft took effect in 1936 and this did help distribute the new talent more equitably among all the teams. The Pirates saw little to help their record, however, as the team's first draft pick, William Shakespeare, would never play in the NFL. I could joke and say that he began to write plays for the New York Stage, but you would not laugh, and it would not be true.

Pittsburgh was not very good in the art of the draft and so the franchise would trade their first-round pick multiple times in their first 30 years. The coaches and players always did their best, but they could not get the right formula going. In his second season with the Pirates in 1936, Bach did the best of any coach before him for nine games.

The team became a contender for the NFL's Eastern Division title with a 6–3 record through nine games. However, the season fell apart as the Pirates lost their final three games. Rooney and Bach had disagreements about why there was a collapse and they played the blame game for a while instead of preparing for football.

Though Bach had agreed to remain with the club in 1937, he did not like how it felt on the wrong side of the owner and he opted to say good-by to the Pirates in favor of a head-coaching job at Niagara University. Rooney was a good enough man to release him from his verbal commitment. Rooney later expressed regret for letting Bach leave as he showed the type of mettle that the Pirates needed.

Johnny "Blood" McNally was the next coaching "victim" in the dark seasons when the Steelers were known as the Pirates. He became player-coach in 1937. McNally had been an eleven-year NFL veteran and knew the Pirates since he had played for Pittsburgh in 1934. His nickname gives an idea that he could have been one of the game's most colorful characters. He was. Rooney was a marketeer and he hired "Blood" hoping to increase ticket sales and wins at the same time.

The decision looked great for the first two games but then, the Pirates lost five games in a row, finishing the season at 4–7.

With Blood back, the next season saw the arrival of the franchise's first superstar, Byron "Whizzer" White. The Pirates selected White, the All-America quarterback from the University of Colorado, with the fourth overall selection of the 1938 NFL Draft and offered him an unheard-of salary of $15,000 (around $260,000 today) to join the team.

White declined the generous offer, in order to continue his education through a Rhodes Scholarship at Oxford University. Some "wise" Irish guys would be saying if it were not for Pittsburgh's bad luck, the team would have no luck at all.

However, the Pirates got some luck when White found out he could pick up the $15 grand and defer his start at Oxford until the following January. So, he did a retake and signed the deal. Rooney never had given anybody else such a deal, Whizzer got the league-high salary plus his deal included a share of the gate at exhibition games. And, so overall, White picked up $15,800 (around $270,000 today) for a short season and no regrets.

McNally could only wish for such high earnings. As both coach and player, the "Blood" earned just $3,500 (roughly $61,000 today). The big contract Rooney gave White angered several of his fellow owners and it surely did not help stop the owners from engaging in a bidding war for players.

Though the arrival of White led to much optimism in Pittsburgh, the team did not become an overnight sensation. McNally stated that, "We had calculated on a championship without him, and since we have him it looks like we can't miss." Don't you just love optimists?

White did not disappoint anybody, but he could not carry the team by himself. The Whizzer led the league in rushing with 567 yards on 152 attempts. However, despite Rooney's best of the best wishes, the Pirates were unable to capitalize on White's performance. They looked good with White, but their record was what was disappointing at two wins against nine losses. Pittsburgh had a season-ending string of six straight defeats.

After the season, White sailed on to England and never again played for the Pirates. His education payed off as he would go on to a major career in law ultimately becoming one of the longest serving justices in the history of the U.S. Supreme Court. There were no lawyers who came before him, however who called him Judge Whizzer.

Rooney realized the big money did not work when spent on one star. He began to realize that great coaches make great differences. After seeing the disappointing results of Whizzer White, other than in the court-room. Rooney determined to pursue a star coach so that the whole team would benefit.

So, he offered the Pittsburgh head coaching job to Jock Sutherland, who was a legendary football coach and "national hero." Sutherland had just stepped down as head coach at the University of Pittsburgh. The $13,000+ offer was again "excessive" and a lot more than Sutherland earned at Pitt. At first, Sutherland spurned the offer (due most likely to the disdain in which he held the professional game).

McNally was not fired as the Pirates' coach, because somebody had to do the mundane things. McNally did announce his retirement as a player, however, so he had to be replaced. Pittsburgh was beginning to have a lot of "almosts," in terms of having the right coach at the right time. Pro football for many coaches was not a sure thing while at the same time, college football was booming

McNally's 1939 season was the last for the Pirates as they would become the Steelers the following year. They started poorly with a string of losses. After the third straight loss, which stretched the two-season run of failure to nine games, McNally could not stand his own performance and he tendered his resignation.

Despite compiling a coaching record with the Pirates of just 6–19, Johnny "Blood" McNally would, nonetheless, enter the Hall of Fame in 1963. It was a tough thing trying to get the right formula for success while assuring that the team itself did not go under for excessive expenditures. Art Rooney was not poor by a long-shot, but the Pirates had not yet become a cash cow and so each major financial decision was very important in the early days.

Before the Steeler name came by to add some firmament to the franchise. Blood McNally was replaced by Walt Kiesling. He had been McNally's assistant coach for the previous two seasons, and he was well liked by Rooney. When things got going bad in future years, Rooney would bring Kiesling in to settle things down.

Kiesling took over as head coach while Rooney's Pirates were in their seventh season with less than half of it played. Something was rotten in Denmark, but nobody could figure out what it was. The

Pirates were taking action to improve but maybe too much action. They had just hired their fifth head coach in seven years. How is that good?

Kiesling may have known a lot and may have been OK-good but he was unable to salvage this season. Thus, the team ended 1939 with a worst yet mark of 1–9–1. Pundits would speculate that nobody could have solved this season's ills, even all the bottles of Aspirin managed all at once in all the world.

The season's lone win came in the season's final game against the Philadelphia Eagles, with whom the Steelers shared the league cellar. The Eagles were just as dejected by their poor record as were the Steelers. Both compiled identical 1–9–1 records. The irony for the Eagles was that their season's sole bright spot had been an earlier triumph over the Steelers. The victory broke a winless streak that had extended to nearly fourteen months.

Through the whole of the 1930s, the Pirates never finished higher than second place in their division, or with a record better than .500. It was a wonder that marketeer Rooney was able to keep the franchise afloat. Sometimes it seemed like he could not keep up with it all. We'll come back to this after we discuss the stadiums of Pittsburgh and we look at the first couple seasons of the Pirates / Steelers in detail.

Chapter 3 History of Pirates / Steelers Football Stadiums

The NFL Pittsburgh Pirates used existing stadiums for years

The Pittsburgh NFL franchise dates back to 1933. It has had several home stadiums over the years. For example. for thirty-one seasons, the Steelers shared Forbes Field with the Pittsburgh Pirates from 1933 to 1963. In 1958, though Forbes Field was still the #1 venue, the Steelers started splitting their home games at Pitt Stadium three blocks away at the University of Pittsburgh. They were waiting for Three-Reivers stadium to be built.

From 1964 to 1969, the Steelers played exclusively at the on-campus Pitt Stadium before moving with the baseball Pirates to Three Rivers Stadium on the city's Northside. Three Rivers is remembered fondly by the Steeler Nation as where Chuck Noll and Dan Rooney turned the franchise into a national powerhouse, collecting four Super Bowls in just six seasons and making the playoffs 11 times in 13 seasons from 1972 to 1984. The team also won the AFC title game seven times.

In 2001, the Steelers team moved to Heinz Field for its home games. This was when a new generation of Steeler football greats made Heinz Field a legendary venue with multiple AFC Championship Games being hosted and two Super Bowl championships being achieved.

Heinz Field looks like it is the place to be for pro football in the foreseeable future. The team is planning $2.5 million in short-term renovations at Heinz Field involving an expansion of the Pub 33 food and beverage space inside the FedEx Great Hall. It will include a new outdoor patio area that will be open even on non-game days.

Let's take a look at these four stadiums where the 1933-1939 Football Pirates and later the Football Steelers played. We'll start with Forbes Field

Forbes Field

Like many other ballparks in America, there are a number of pseudonyms by which Forbes Field is recognized. Three of the most widely used are as follows

- The House of Thrills
- The Old Lady of Schenley Park
- The Orchard of Oakland

Forbes Field was built to be a baseball park located at 230 South Bouquet St. in Oakland, adjacent to Schenley Park. In 1909, its capacity was 23,000, increased to 41,000 in 1925 and then in a remodeling, it was reduced to 35,000 (1970).

When the "baseball" park was built in 1909, these were the dimensions:

- Field size 1909:
- Left Field—360 feet (110m)
- Deepest corner—462 feet (141m)
- Center Field—442 feet (135m)
- Right Field—376 feet (115m)]

There was no artificial turf in 1909. Other than an infield mix of a combination of sand, silt, and, clay, the field surface was grass. The Scoreboard like most of the day was hand-operated.

The construction team broke ground for Forbes Field on March 1, 1909. They meant business and were ready for a grand opening less than four months later by June 30, 1909. The facility was shut down for good on June 28, 1970, after a great run, and it was demolished in 1971

Pittsburgh Pirates Major League Baseball team used the field from 1909–1970). Additionally, the Pittsburgh Pirates/Steelers of the

NFL used Forbes Field from 1933–1963. The Philadelphia–Pittsburgh "Steagles" of the NFL) used the facility in its one season of operation in 1943. Other teams used this grand facility over the years. These include the following

- "Card-Pitt" Chicago Cardinals & Pittsburgh compo team (NFL) (1944)
- Pittsburgh Panthers –NCAA 1909–1924.
- Homestead Grays (Negro leagues) 1922–1939
- Pittsburgh Americans (AFL) 1936–1937.
- Pittsburgh Phantoms (NPSL) 1967.

Forbes Field was the third home of the Pittsburgh Pirates Major League Baseball (MLB) team, and the first home of the Pittsburgh Steelers, the city's National Football League (NFL) franchise. From 1933 to 1939, the Steelers went by the name Pirates. The stadium also served as the home football field for the University of Pittsburgh "Pitt" Panthers from 1909 to 1924. John Forbes was a British general, who fought in the French and Indian War, and named the city in 1758.

On June 29, 1909, the Pittsburgh Pirates defeated the Chicago Cubs, 8–1 at Exposition Park. The two teams opened Forbes Field the following day. Fans began to arrive at the stadium six and one-half hours early for the 3:30 pm game. Weather conditions were reported as clear skies with a temperature around 80°.

The Pittsburgh Press wrote about this crowd as follows: "the ceremonies were witnessed by the largest throng that ever attended an event of this kind in this or any other city in the country ... Forbes Field is so immense—so far beyond anything else in America in the way of a baseball park—that old experts, accustomed to judging crowds at a glance, were at a loss for reasonable figures." Records show that this first game was attended by a standing-room only crowd of 30,338.

Forbes Field and Forbes Street, 1909

Though Forbes Field was praised upon its opening, age took its tool. The stadium began to show major deterioration after 60 years of use. The park was the second oldest baseball field in the major leagues league at the time, being used for both baseball, football, and even boxing. Only Shibe Park in Philadelphia was older before it was replaced in 1971 by Veterans Stadium.

The location of the ball park, which initially was criticized for not being developed into more than just a stadium, grew into a "bustling business district" which then led to a lack of parking spaces. Planning always helps in major endeavors.

As Forbes was on the block for demolition, construction began on Three Rivers Stadium on April 25, 1968. A community group did attempt to rescue the legendary Forbes Field structure from demolition, but their efforts failed. They proposed such things as an outdoor stage, apartments and a farmer's market for the site. They did not want to lose such a historic building. They compared Forbes Field to the Eiffel Tower in significance. It did not happen.

Chapter 3 History of Pirates / Steelers Football Stadiums   27

A handsome Forbes Field in its early years.

There are many baseball accomplishments noted in the history of Forbes Field but not as many in football, though many great games were played whenever the field was relined and reacclimated for college and pro football.

On May 25, 1935, for example, at Forbes Field, Babe Ruth hit the last three home runs of his career as his Boston Braves lost to the Pirates, 11-7. His last home run cleared the right field stands roofline, making him the first player to ever do so.

On October 8, 1946, 6 months before his major league debut Jackie Robinson played at Forbes with his African American all-stars against Honus Wagner's all-stars. Additionally, most of the game-action scenes from the 1951 film "Angels in the Outfield" were filmed at this memorable stadium.

On May 28, 1956, Dale Long of the Pirates made history for excellent playing. One author stated that this was the first-ever curtain call in baseball history. Long had come off of a long-ball ripper in that he hit at least one home run in eight consecutive games. This prompted the Pittsburgh fans to cheer for him five minutes.

The University of Pittsburgh's football team moved from Exposition Park into Forbes Field upon its opening in 1909 and played there until 1924 when the University built a stadium on campus, which they named Pitt Stadium. It was just a few blocks away.

Pittsburgh Steelers

As we have discussed previously in this book, Pittsburgh native, Art Rooney founded his NFL team under the name the Pittsburgh Pirates, on July 8, 1933, for $2,500 ($47,262 in present-day terms). The football franchise's first game, against the New York Giants, was held on September 20, 1933, at Forbes Field. The Giants won the game 23-2 in front of 25,000 people. At least it wasn't a baseball game with that score.

Rooney penned this note after the game: "The Giants won. Our team looks terrible. The fans didn't get their money's worth." It is tough to find such honesty in the sports world of today.

The Pirates rebounded from their first loss to gain their first ever franchise victory a week later at Forbes Field, against the Chicago Cardinals. The NFL's Pirates were renamed the Steelers in 1940. Regardless of their name, the Steelers struggled during much of their three-decades of tenancy at Forbes Field. The club achieved its first winning record in 1942; during its tenth season of existence.

On November 30, 1952, the Steelers met the New York Giants at Forbes Field for a snowy afternoon game. Pittsburgh entered the game with a 3-6 record, but went on to set multiple team records, including scoring nine touchdowns, to win the game 63-7. Excited by their team's play, the 15,140 spectators ran onto the field and began to tear the goal posts out of the ground.

The University of Pittsburgh's acquired Forbes Field in 1958 this gave the Steelers some new options. The franchise began to move some of their home games to the much larger Pitt Stadium that year. The Steelers played their final game at Forbes Field on December 1, 1963. The Steelers moved permanently to Pitt Stadium the following season and they left Forbes Field behind for others, but nobody wanted it.

Pittsburgh Panthers game against Washington & Jefferson College – 1915

Demolition of Forbes Field.

You can see chairs being removed from the ballpark, as the scoreboard continued to pay homage to a bygone era.

After opening in 1909, its time had come. The legendary ballpark had seen Babe Ruth hit his last home runs here and Pittsburgh's Bill Mazeroski hit his infamous home run to win the 1960 World Series. The actual home plate from Forbes Field has been preserved in the floor of Wesley W. Posvar Hall. A commemorative plaque mentions the final games played; a double-header against the Chicago Cubs on June 28, 1970. The Pirates won both games, 4-1 and 3-2. Demolition began on July 28, 1971 after two fires severely damaged the structure. The NFL Steelers at the close of Forbes days played at Pitt Stadium and then Three Rivers before Heinz.

Pitt Stadium – University of Pittsburgh Campus

From 1925 to 1999, the University of Pittsburgh had its very own football stadium. It was such a proud and substantial edifice, that even after Pitt acquired Forbes Field, the team continued playing at Pitt Stadium just down the street from Forbes. Additionally, the NFL Pirates and the Steelers played there for a time until Three Rivers Stadium was built and ready for use.

Because people age and new people are born all the time, it is safe to say that most people (except for alumni and Pitt fans) are unaware that Pitt Stadium ever existed. However, the idea is kept alive for those who take the regular Pitt tour. The tour guides have no problem telling the eager listeners that just like fifty is the new forty, the Petersen Events Center is the new Pitt Stadium. Well, not exactly but it is right where Pitt Stadium once stood.

Now, Pitt plays its football off campus in Heinz Field, as do the NFL's Pittsburgh Steelers. For Pittsburgh Panthers fans, it (Heinz) is an amazing facility in which to watch football. However, one big thing is missing. Heinz Field is not on the Pitt Oakland campus. Nonetheless, this does not affect the great venue now housing the NFL's highly successful Steelers.

Up until 1999, when Pitt Stadium signed off to the ball on the huge crane, Oakland was flooded with people on game day. Pitt Students and others would climb what had been affectionately known as Cardiac Hill to get to a game. Everybody enjoyed a great day on campus by the bookstore in a great stadium.

Some Pitt Alums still lament the change to Heinz for the Panthers as they believe there was a greater tie to school spirit as it was so unavoidable to not be part of the spirit on game day. They have a perception that since Pitt had its own stadium on campus, there was once a different attitude about Pitt football. In other words, they feel that the people cared a lot more. None of this affected the NFL Steelers, whose fans continue to love the great comforts of Heinz Field.

Pitt Stadium at the top of Cardiac Hill – the last game

Pitt Stadium was not unlike other well-built outdoor athletic stadiums, in the eastern United States. Located on the campus of the University of Pittsburgh in the Oakland neighborhood of Pittsburgh, Pennsylvania, the facility opened in 1925. It was the Pitt Stadium.

Thus, it served primarily as the home of the university's Pittsburgh Panthers football team, through 1999. Like other large stadiums, it was put to other uses such as sporting events including basketball, soccer, baseball, track and field, rifle, and gymnastics.

The stadium was a home produce designed by University of Pittsburgh graduate W. S. Hindman and it was built for $2.1 million. There is always a "why" for new stadiums, and this one is answered easily. It was because the seating capacity of the Panthers' previous home, Forbes Field, was seen as being inadequate in light of the growing popularity of college football. College Football was at its peak and former college players were working hard to form pro clubs to permit them to keep playing. f

Pitt Stadium eventually became the second home of the Pittsburgh Steelers, the city's National Football League (NFL) franchise. After the stadium was torn down, the Pittsburgh Panthers shared Three Rivers Stadiums, with the Pirates and the Steelers as of 2000, before moving as did the Steelers to Heinz Field in 2001.

Starting in 1929, the Carnegie Tech Tartans played home games in Pitt Stadium on a split schedule basis with the Panthers. As people grew bigger and fire officials got tougher, by the 1940s, new safety rules from the city fire marshal prohibited temporary bleacher seats on the rim of the stadium and in the track area. Additionally, in order to provide comfort to larger spectators, (Ahem, I resemble that remark), the Department of Athletics also widened seats from 16 to 18 inches (41 to 46 cm), reducing the final capacity of Pitt Stadium to 56,500.

Pitt Stadium's custodians were affected by the rush to AstroTurf in 1970 but the new stuff did not last. SuperTurf was installed in 1984. However, after six years AstroTurf was brought back after dissatisfaction reigned on the field.

In the late 1970s, the original 17 miles (27 km) of wood seating was replaced with metal bleachers. Temporary lighting was installed at Pitt Stadium in 1985 but was firmed up and made permanent before the 1987 season. An automatic scoreboard was later installed at the eastern end of the stadium in 1995. This improvement was followed in 1997 with the installation of the PantherVision videoboard, which allowed fans to see instant replays of the games. Pitt Stadium had reached the modern age, but it was not Heinz and it did not have the modern amenities of Heinz Stadium.

The highest attended game at Pitt Stadium was in 1938, when 68,918 saw the Panthers defeat Fordham 24–13 on October 29.

The NFL's Pirates/Steelers played home games at Forbes Field from their birth in 1933 to 1957. They played their first game at Pitt Stadium in 1942, in an exhibition match for U.S.O. charity against the Fort Knox "Armoraiders." It was played on November 15.

From 1958 to 1963, the Steelers split home games between Forbes Field and Pitt Stadium, knowing some kind of new facility was about to be built. During this interim time, fans were able to purchase season ticket packages for one site or the other.

In 1964, the Steelers began to play home games exclusively at Pitt Stadium, which they continued until moving to the new Three Rivers Stadium in 1970.

Repeat Pic of Pitt Stadium prior to its last game — 1999

A wise man once said that all good things must come to an end. It sure seems to be true. The final game at Pitt Stadium took place on November 13, 1999. For Pitt, it was a great game as the Panthers defeated Notre Dame 37–27. The Panthers took a lot of time to get the great feeling of victory from their hearts. Having the ND win at Pitt Stadium made it even sweeter.

The final touchdown in Pitt Stadium was scored by Kevan Barlow at 7:06 pm, just minutes prior to fans rushing onto the field. This created a bit of a problem for officials as a number of the 60,190 spectators—the largest crowd in 16 years—ran onto the field with nine seconds remaining in the game. They tore down both goal posts and removed pieces of turf.

The final game at Pitt Stadium, where the Panthers defeated Notre Dame, 37-27, on Nov. 13, 1999

The Panthers moved to Three Rivers Stadium, before eventually beginning to use the off-campus Heinz Field in 2001. Demolition of Pitt Stadium began in December 1999. Concrete from the stadium was ground and left on site for use in the Petersen Events Center and student housing which was built at the site. I like preservation of monuments better; but it was nice that Pitt Stadium, at least parts of it, still exists.

Tell us about Three Rivers Stadium, A Pittsburgh City Monument

There was a time when Three Rivers Stadium and its possibilities was one of the main items discussed in the transformation of the Pittsburgh riverfront from an industrial center to a showcase attraction to highlight the city's Golden Triangle. Conceived in the 1950s during Pittsburgh's Renaissance Period, as a replacement for aging Forbes Field, many different designs were debated, some of which were *way to0 expensive* to ever see the light of day.

One interesting design submitted in 1958 envisioned a stadium built on the Monongahela River. The Smithfield Street Bridge that existed, would be replaced by a massive span, complete with adjoining parking and hotel, along with the stadium. The complex would be built entirely above water. The stadium would actually exist on top of the river. Wow! Don't you just love that kind of great thinking?

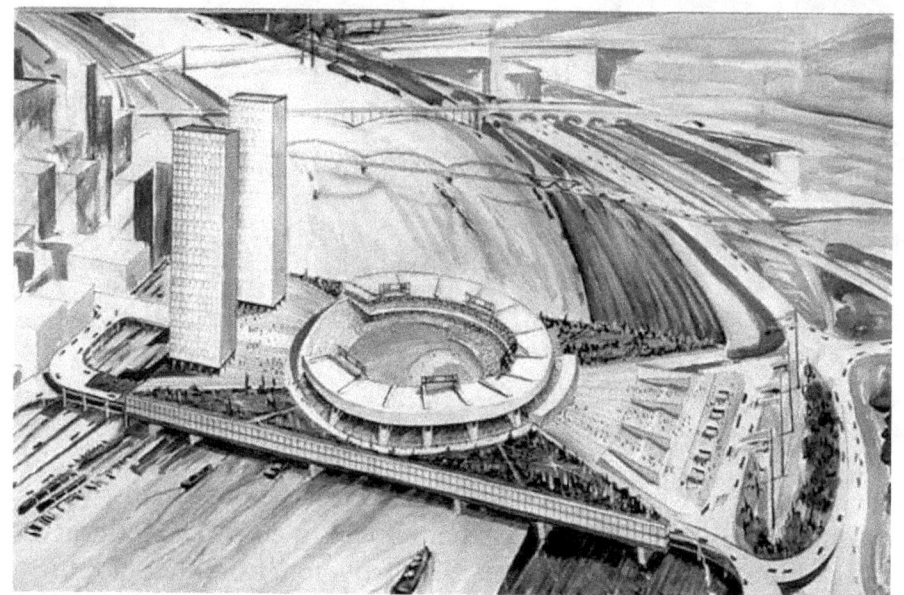
A 1958 proposal submitted for a Pittsburgh stadium built entirely above the Monongahela River.

Eventually, the north shore was chosen as the spot for the new "Pittsburgh Stadium." It would not be over the river. The complex would include hotels, restaurants and a riverfront park to complement the new state-of-the-art multi-purpose stadium. The original stadium prototype shown below, was a bit different from the final design. The original was round with an open end facing the city. Due to cost constraints, this design was modified into the cookie-cutter shape.

Although the hotel and restaurant development never materialized, the stadium that was to be the centerpiece of the north shore renaissance was built. Ground was broken in April of 1968 and construction was completed in June of 1970. In between the groundbreaking and the completion of construction, the structure was given a new name, "Three Rivers Stadium." The Pirates left Forbes Field after sixty-one years and moved into their new home in July 1970. The Steelers eagerly followed the Pirates in the fall.

Original prototype for Pittsburgh Stadium. Open end was closed in the final design.

Three River Stadium was big deal for Pittsburgh

It took two years to complete construction. It took nearly as long to reach a final consensus on a new name. After much deliberation, the agreed upon name was "Three Rivers Stadium."

The new stadium rises from the rubble in 1969.

The Pirates MLB team made playoff appearances in five of their first six seasons at Three Rivers. Manager Danny Murtaugh and "The Lumber Company" captured a World Series title in 1971. Pirate legend Roberto Clemente got his 3000th and final hit during the last home game of the 1972 season. He died in a plane crash shortly after when he was going home to his native Puerto Rico for some rescue work. Pitcher John Candelaria threw the first no-hitter in 1976. The Buccos gained another title in 1979 with Manager Chuck Tanner, Captain Willie Stargell and "The Family".

Three Rivers Stadium lined for baseball--under the lights

The Baseball Pirates of the early 1990s again brought the National League Championship series to the home turf. Manager Jim Leyland and the "Killer Bees", featuring Barry Bonds and Bobby Bonilla. They came up short of the World Series three consecutive years. The 1993 season was the final time the Pirates compiled a winning record at Three Rivers Stadium. Another great Pittsburgh team in a great Pittsburgh venue.

The Steelers also made the most of their new home field, aka Three Rivers. Franco Harris made the Immaculate Reception at home during the 1972 playoffs. This goes down as arguably the greatest play in NFL history. In 1974, Coach Chuck Noll and his gridiron juggernaut captured, that was just five years old, captured the first of four Vince Lombardi Trophies earned during the 1970s. The Steelers also engaged in three epic AFC championship games against the Oakland Raiders (1975) and Houston Oilers (1978 and 1979). It was not difficult for Pittsburgh fans to keep up their love affair with the Steelers.

This montage requires no caption

In what many called home field advantage, these football battles were all fought on frozen turf; perfect Steeler football weather. The Steelers enjoyed adorning the stadium facade with the Roman Numerals IX, X, XIII and XIV as they were the games in which Chuck Noll and a cast of characters brought championship recognition to Pittsburgh. It was not too long that Pittsburgh became known as the "City of Champions". Three Rivers Stadium, an icon to sports fans around the globe, was the place to be. Where else?

A great view of Three Rivers Stadium

Houston Oiler Coach Bum Phillips, after failing in the AFC championship two years in a row, uttered in frustration, "The road to the Super Bowl runs through Pittsburgh." During the 1970s, no truer words were spoken. The Steel Curtain, led by "Mean" Joe Greene, Dwight White, Ernie Holmes, and L.C. Greenwood was adept at stopping all opposing traffic. In the 1975 Pro Bowl, eight of eleven defensive starters were Pittsburgh Steelers!

After Chuck Noll's four Super Bowls, no matter which coach Pittsburgh hired to take Noll's place, and there were only two of them to today, they each brought home a Super Bowl Win – even without Terry Bradshaw, the best of the best

In the 1990s, the Steelers brought the playoff magic back to Pittsburgh under Coach Bill Cowher with an AFC championship win over the Indianapolis Colts in 1995. The team, led by Rod Woodson and Greg Lloyd, did fail to bring home one-for-the-thumb, losing to the Dallas Cowboys in Super Bowl XXX. But Cowher would get his own ring in another few years.

By the turn of the century, the idea of cookie-cutter-type-multi-purpose stadiums like Pittsburgh's Three Rivers Stadium, and Philadelphia's Veterans Stadium and Cincinnati's Riverfront Stadium were no longer financially or aesthetically pleasing to the professional sports world. Unless you are making cookies, the cookie cutter approach is not pleasing.

All good things come to an end. And, so, in February 11, 2001, the 33-year reign of Pittsburgh's Stadium of Champions came to an end. Three Rivers Stadium could not withstand the demolition and it came crashing down in a thunderous, controlled blast to make way for the Pirates PNC Baseball Park and the Steelers Heinz Field.

What began as a heap of rubble in 1963 became another heap of rubble in 2001.

If Pittsburgh could not save Forbes Field, Three Rivers Stadium had no chance to survive—even in its dust.

Pittsburgh natives and football fans and baseball fans loved their stadiums and the games played therein. On the next page, you will see a montage of four stadiums that have occupied the north shore since 1890. Exposition Park stood until 1915. Three Rivers was there from 1968 to 2001. The current stadiums, PNC Park and Heinz Field, were both built in 2000. Each of the stadiums has a rich Pittsburgh sports history.

The Four Ballparks on the River's North Shore

Our thanks to Doug Brendel for creating the four-ballpark image above.

Let's move on to the current stadium for the Pittsburgh Steelers, aka, Heinz Field.

Heinz Field

Heinz Field is owned by the Sports and Exhibition Authority of Pittsburgh and Allegheny County. The stadium was not developed as a baseball field as Forbes Field or Three Rivers Stadium. Instead it was developed as a football stadium by the Pittsburgh Steelers, The Pittsburgh Steelers and the University of Pittsburgh are the prime tenants.

How do you know this is Heinz Field from the outside?

The architect of Heinz Field was HOK Sports and the manager of construction was a joint venture between Hunt Construction Group and Mascaro Construction. The construction of the 1.49 million square feet structure began with a ground breaking on June 18, 1999. The seating capacity for football games is 68,400 seats. The seats are fairly wide at (19-21 inches, all with cup holders).

There is also Club Seating (7,300 seats (20-21 inches wide) and there are Suites offering 1,544 seats (129 suites totaling over 38,000 square feet). There are also three 3 Club Lounges – East and West Club approximately 45,000 square feet; North Club 20,000 square feet

There are 24 women's, 24 men's, and 8 family restrooms. The fixtures include 487 lavatories, 835 water closets, and 204 urinals. Everybody eats and drinks at a game and they buy stuff. At Heinz, there are 47 concession stands with 7 novelty stores.

The stadium is built for two home teams. The Steelers locker room is 6,000 square feet. The Panthers locker room is 4,600 square feet, and both visiting locker rooms are 2,600 square feet.

The stadium also has a Video Board. The Heinz Field video board represents Daktronics' latest generation of 4.4 trillion color HD-16 LED displays, and measures 27' high and 96' wide. The new technology nearly quadruples the resolution of the former Sony video display. There are 800 televisions linked to the main scoreboard that automatically display special notifications about the game in progress.

The turf is a blend of four varieties of Kentucky Bluegrass, covering just over two acres. The soil is a twelve-inch, sand-based rootzone, meeting USGA specifications for particle size. Under the rootzone approximately 40 miles of ¾ inch piping heat the soil. Below the heating system there is a four-inch layer of pea gravel that contains drain pipes that empty into a 22-inch collector pipe that surrounds the perimeter of the field.

To aid in people moving through the stadium, it is equipped with 5 escalators and 9 elevators (2 for freight). There is a facility within the facility called the FedEx Great Hall. This Hall : Located on the ground level of the East side of Heinz Field, the FedEx Great Hall is home to Pittsburgh Steelers and University of Pittsburgh memorabilia, Hall of Fame artifacts, Pub 33, Quaker Steak & Lube, Primanti Brothers, and Papa Duke's Gyros. Throughout Heinz Field, there are 60 murals from area high schools that have won a WPIAL or City League Football Championship.

Great view of the excitement at Heinz Field

To properly close this chapter on the stadiums used by the NFL's Pittsburgh Pirates / Pittsburgh Steelers football franchise, we would like to include a wonderful public piece put together by Stadium Review. It is well done and it sums up the stadium story perfectly. Enjoy! https://stadiumjourney.com/stadiums/heinz-field-s86

Home of the Terrible Towel

One of the NFL's oldest franchises is also one of the most successful, as far as wins and being in the hearts of its fans. Owned by the Rooney family since 1933, the Pittsburgh Steelers are known for stability, community involvement and doing things the Steeler Way. This has resulted in six Super Bowl Championships, eight Super Bowl appearances and eight AFC conference championships.

Since Chuck Noll was hired in 1969, the Steelers have had only two other coaches, Bill Cowher and Mike Tomlin... an unheard-of level of continuity in the NFL. Twenty-two Steelers have been inducted into the Pro Football Hall of Fame, including three coaches and three members of the Steelers' ownership group.

Despite having a later position in the first round of each draft, the Steelers have an enviable record of picking Pro Bowlers on an annual basis. This consistency and stability have led the Steelers to having one of the most loyal fan bases in any professional sport, as generations of Pittsburgh residents have been brought up in the Steeler Way.

Since the team's inception in 1933, the Steelers have called four stadiums home; Forbes Field, Pitt Stadium, Three Rivers Stadium and now Heinz Field.

Now to review some quick Heinz Field facts: The stadium opened in August of 2001, with seating for nearly 65,000 fans. This includes 56,000 "regular" seats, 7,300 club level seats and 1,544 seats within its 129 suites. Unlike many of its northern counterparts, Heinz Field has a natural turf field, albeit with an extensive underground heating system to keep the playing surface from freezing during the brutal Pittsburgh winters.

Heinz Field has several elements that set it apart from most NFL stadiums. The first is the FedEx Great Hall, a shrine to Pittsburgh's long and successful history in the NFL. Amongst the displays are a History of the Terrible Towel; the actual lockers of several Steeler greats, including Franco Harris, Mean Joe Greene and Lynn Swann, a section devoted to the Immaculate Reception, and salutes to each of the six Super Bowl winning teams the Steelers have fielded. A second very obvious feature is the two huge Heinz Ketchup bottles atop the scoreboard. If filled with ketchup, these bottles would hold more than one million ounces of this famous brand of condiment. The bottles "dip and pour" whenever the home team reaches the red zone.

Food & Beverage 5

The food and beverage offerings at Heinz Field reflect the diverse ethnic neighborhoods that make up the Pittsburgh area.
You will find Italian, Greek, German, Polish and Eastern European fare, along with the typical American ballpark standards.

...
You will not experience long waits in line, as there are nearly 50 concession stands set up pretty evenly throughout Heinz Field.

Heinz Field offers a wide selection of beers as well. Craft beers include Redd Apple, Sierra Torpedo, Third Shift, Sam Adams Rebel, Magic Hat #9, Sierra Pale, Blue Moon and Angry Orchard.
...

Imports include Sethwicks, Guinness and Newcastle.

The Steelers merchandise stands are known as Sideline Stores and offer everything you can think of in the gold/black Steeler colors.

Atmosphere 5
Pittsburgh is a city that believes in history and the importance of maintaining tradition, especially with its largely immigrant past. The Rooney family understands that, and the atmosphere they have created at Heinz Field epitomizes it. The Steel City produces little or no steel anymore, but the stadium is largely made of steel. Glass is another important construction element, a salute to PPG, which is headquartered in Pittsburgh. The three rivers of Pittsburgh are its identity, and the stadium provides wonderful views of the

Allegheny. The food offerings also mirror the foods many of its fans enjoy in their ethnic neighborhoods.

The football history and legacy of the Steelers is definitely woven into the atmosphere, as the Great Hall is a celebration of the Steelers bond with the community. While many teams have adopted more contemporary uniforms, the Steelers uniforms have largely remained the same. Why?... it is the Steelers Way and it works. The field? ... there is nothing artificial here... football was meant to be played on grass, and yes in the mud.

Wisely, Heinz Field has chosen to retain the atmosphere that matches its fan base... one that is hard working, largely blue collar and totally devoted to the Steeler Way. By the way, the stadium's address? Art Rooney Avenue. The fans loved the man and wouldn't have it any other way.

Neighborhood 5
The North Shore neighborhood is the home to both Heinz Field and PNC Park. Having two major sports facilities in the area has made the North Shore one of the hottest areas in Pittsburgh for new development. It has excellent access to the downtown business district via numerous bridges spanning the Allegheny River, and two light rail stations have been built in the area in recent years.

In addition to being the sports hub of the Steel City, the North Shore is also home to the Andy Warhol Museum and the Carnegie Science Center. Another recent improvement to the area is the North Shore Riverfront Park and Trail, which serves as the front door to Heinz Field, and also provides docking facilities for those boats dropping off fans for a Steelers, Pirates or Pitt ball game. It is designed for year-round use for joggers, bikers, picnic groups and special events.

The North Shore has always had a strong Steeler influence in its dining and entertainment offerings as Three Rivers Stadium was also in the neighborhood. One of the standards over the years has been the Clark Bar and Grill, which is across the street from the stadiums. A more recent addition is Grille 36, owned by Steeler great Jerome "The Bus" Bettis. One last neighborhood restaurant I can personally recommend is Peppi's, home of the Roethlisburger. Other Steeler-inspired items on the menu include the Joey Porter "bella" steak and the Franco Italian sub.

Fans 5
A person would be hard-pressed to find a more dedicated fan base than the Steeler Nation. They come dressed head to toe in black and gold, wearing steelworker helmets and sit through some of the dreariest weather imaginable with absolutely no complaints. A Steelers game ticket is hard and costly to come by, as the team has sold out nearly every game for the last 30 years.

The fans can have an intimidating effect on the visiting team, as an extremely loud crowd, dressed in black and gold and waving thousands of the famed terrible towels fervently cannot be replicated on a practice field. Another reason for the strong fan base is geographic, as their fans not only come from western Pennsylvania, but the football heartlands of Ohio, as well.

Pittsburgh fans see several teams as their direct rival, not just a single rivalry, as most NFL franchises have. The Bengals, the Browns and the Eagles all fit in this category due to their close proximity, while the Ravens have become a division rival in the past few seasons.

Access 4
Heinz Field is located on the North Shore across the river from downtown Pittsburgh. The parking situation in close proximity to the field is dominated by lots catering to the season ticket holders, and it can be difficult for a single-game ticket holder to find a parking space. Fortunately, there are a number of options available to choose from that can be less expensive than a close-in space and will drop you right outside the stadium.

The stadium is linked to the downtown area by a number of bridges, which are limited to pedestrian access on game days. Parking in the downtown area is much more abundant, especially around the Convention Center and Heinz Hall. It is then an easy walk across the bridge to the stadium. For those who prefer to be let out right at the stadium, you have both land and water options.

Pittsburgh has a wonderful light rail system that has stations in the downtown area, as well as the Station Square area a bit further away. Two stations (Allegheny and Northside) will drop you off immediately outside of Heinz Field. The water option utilizes Pittsburgh's famous three rivers to drop you off right in front of the stadium. Pittsburgh Water Limo shuttles people across the Allegheny River from downtown and docks outside of the stadium. The Gateway Clipper ($10 roundtrip) journeys a bit further, as it comes up the Ohio River from the Station Square complex and drops you off at the same dock.

Another thing you need to be aware of at any NFL stadium is the need to arrive early, due to the stringent security rules relating to what can be brought to the stadium. Fans are discouraged from bringing any types of bags to the game. What you do bring must fit into a clear plastic bag no larger than specific dimensions. (Go to NFL.com for specific details on what can be brought into the stadium.) For those who are smart and travel bag-free, Heinz Field has Express Entry gates located at the Southwest Rotunda and the FedEx Grand Hall. These lines will get you to your seats much faster.

Once inside Heinz Field, you will find a number of escalators and elevators to transport you to the higher seats in the stadium.

Return on Investment 3
Parking immediately outside Heinz Field is reserved for season ticket holders. Parking in the downtown area across the river will cost between $5-$15, and Station Square charges $8 plus $10 roundtrip on the Gateway Clipper up the river to Heinz Field.

Honestly, the most economical way to reach Heinz Field is via the Light Rail System, which goes to all sections of city and has two stations immediately outside the stadium. The train is free on game days. Tickets honestly are a seller's market, due to the decades of sellouts the Steelers have experienced. Expect to pay upwards of $85 even for an upper deck seat. The concession prices are high, but the selection and quality of the foods is far above the standard fare at other ballparks.

Extras 5

One of the best things about Heinz Field is the enforcement of PRIDE, an acronym for Positive Field Experience, Respect for Each Other, Integrity, Dignified Behavior and Excellence on and Off the Field. Steeler fans are amongst the most rabid fans in the NFL, but they do abide to the PRIDE principles, which are strictly enforced The Terrible Towel is an icon of the NFL and deserves its own mention.

The setting of Heinz Field offers just as impressive views of the river and downtown Pittsburgh as its baseball neighbor, PNC Park. The FedEx Grand Hall is an outstanding celebration of Steeler history and tradition that is not to be missed.

The city of Pittsburgh has made a dramatic transformation from its steel mill past. Today it is a city filled with museums, parks and cultural offerings that cannot be seen in just one day. I highly recommend a three-day weekend to fully enjoy the town.

Chapter 4 Pirates Launch First Football Team

#1 Coach Forrest Douds
#2 Coach Luby DiMealo
#3 Coach Joe Bach
#4 Coach John Blood McNally
#5 Coach Walt Kiesling

Year	Coach	League/Conf/Div	Pl	Record	Pct.
1933	#1 Forrest Douds	NFLEast	5th	3 6 2	.364
1934	#2 Luby DiMeolo	NFLEast	5th	2 10 0	.167
1935	#3 Joe Bach	NFLEast	3rd	4 8 0	.333
1936	#3 Joe Bach	NFLEast	2nd	6 6 0	.500
1937	#4 John McNally	NFLEast	3rd	4 7 0	.364
1938	#4 John McNally	NFLEast	5th	2 9 0	.182
1939	#4 John McNally	NFLEast	4th-T	1 9 1	.136

- McNally's record was 0-3 before he resigned

1939 #5 Walt Kiesling → 1–6–1 record in final 8 games of 1939 season

1933-1939 Pittsburgh Pirates Overall Record 22-55-3

Pittsburgh Pirates 1st Football Team – Predates the Steelers

The Pittsburgh Pirates Professional NFL Football Team launched their first football team in 1933 under a different name than we know today. They were the Pittsburgh Pirates named after the Baseball Team and they would keep that name until the 1940 season when they would rename the club to the Pittsburgh Steelers in honor of the steel makers in the town. They played their games at Forbes Field in the Oakland Neighborhood of Pittsburgh, PA from 1933 through to 1939. At that time, for the 1940 season, they became the Pittsburgh Steelers.

Most fans understand the Pirates / Steelers most recent history which includes eight great shots at the big prize --- the Super Bowl and six wins—highest in the NFL. The Pirates / Steelers have been very successful in all games since Chuck Noll took over the team in 1969 and was followed by Bill Cowher and now Mike Tomin. Each of these coaches have at least one Super Bowl and Noll picked up four in his 23-year tenure. With the 1-2 combo of Chuck Noll and Terry Bradshaw and the 1-2 punch of Bill Cowher & Mike Tomlin with QB Ben Roethlisberger, the Steelers put together whatever was necessary together to win six those eight great Super Bowl Outings.

And, there is great news for the future beginning in the fall of 2018 and Super Bowl winning coach Mike Tomlin is coming back as is two-time Super Bowl winning QB, Roethlisberger. This duo plans to take Pittsburgh to another Super Bowl and get another set of those huge rings—making it seven in all.

New England's debut in the biggest championship game came against the Chicago Bears in Super Bowl XX. The Patriots looked great all season, but Raymond Berry's Patriots were overwhelmed by Mike Ditka's Chicago Bears when game action began. From the opening kickoff at the Louisiana Superdome, led by quarterback Jim McMahon the Bears had their way that day with a 49-10 big victory.

The Steelers returned to the Super Bowl at Sun Devil Stadium with Bill Cowers on January 28, 1996 and were beaten 27-17 by the Dallas Cowboys. This was a big disappointment as the Steelers lost their first Super Bowl ever after four wins with Chuck Noll and Terry Bradshaw.

Cowher had the team back on Feb 5, 2006 to pick up a nice 21-10 win in Super Bowl XL against Seattle in Detroit Michigan's Ford Field. This victory gave the Steelers claim to the franchise's first Super Bowl title since the Steelers' dynasty years of the 1970s. Heinz Ward took home MVP honors after catching five passes for 123 yards that included a great 43-yard touchdown pass from Antwaan Randle El.

Cowher retired the next year and on Feb 1, 2009, in Super Bowl XLIII, new coach Mike Tomlin brought another Lombardi Trophy to Pittsburgh, again with a young Benn Roethlisberger at the helm. In this game, James Harrison's interception return turned the tide. The Steelers pass-rushing linebacker dropped into coverage on a hunch and picked off Warner at the goal line and then scooted 100-yards up the sideline for a TD. This completed what was at least a 10-point swing in Super Bowl XLIII. That number is very significant as Pittsburgh won by just four points—but won they did and Tomlin got his first Super Bowl victory. Coach Tomlin is looking for more.

Coach Forrest Douds is responsible for molding the players who showed up for the first camp into the Pittsburgh Pirates. In 1933, Douds did his best to take the raw material and prove to everybody else but the team that the Pirates could win some games. He got three wins out of twelve games in his first and only season with a bunch of NFL old-timers and rookies .

In the Pittsburgh Pirates second season, coach Luby DiMeolo could not match the three wins achieved by Douds but he did pull off two victories during the season.

The most critical time for a new team is in its first several seasons. Even the pundits recognized that the Pirates were not very lucky as they did not have a coach with a mastery of game to lead them to winning seasons. It was not until 1936 that Joe Bach, in his second season with the Pirates brought in a 500 season after winning that magical fourth game in the 1935 season to become the winningest coach for the new Pirates.

Coach Bach and owner Art Rooney had some words and Joe Bach chose to leave the Pirates Organization just when it looked like things would turn for the better. Art Rooney, who was beloved by the fans, reached into his bag of football owner trips and he pulled out a player coach, John Blood McNally, who was like the three coaches before him, supposed to bring a winning team to Pittsburgh.

It was not happening and in McNally's third year, he could not stand his own performance and he stepped down with an 0-3 record shortly after the season began. Rooney went into his bag of tricks again and came up with Assistant Coach Walt Kiesling who managed one win for the rest of the year giving the Pittsburgh Pirates a combined 1-9-1 record the year before they became the Pittsburgh Steelers.

The Steelers spent their first thirty years almost winning and then in 1969, Chuck Noll took the job of head coach and life for Pittsburgh fans has gotten really good since then.

Let's take a look now at the team selected by Pittsburgh Pirates coaches and how the team did under coach Forrest Douds in their first year as a football team.

1933 Forrest "Jap" Douds, Coach #1

Most Pittsburgh fans know about the great record from Chuck Noll through Mike Tomlin, but few know about the thirteen coaches that preceded the current Pittsburgh success legacy. A quick look would show that the success of the Pittsburgh Pirates / Steelers was never a constant until recently. There was a very long period of time, from the inaugural 1933 season until the Chuck Noll era, where the team from Pittsburgh were at worst, a laughingstock and at best, lovable losers. In many ways, if it were not for Art Rooney's lovefest with football, the team may not have survived.

Having said that. Even during these dark ages, there were still important figures. The first of course is the first person to coach the team that would ultimately become the Steelers.

<<< Jap Douuds
Some pundits suggest that the word "captaining" than coaching is a more appropriate word for Forrest "Jap" Douds, who led the Pittsburgh Pirates in year one. Douds was the man charged with getting the team ready for their first season of the then 13-year-old National Football League. At the time, there were only ten teams, and until Art Rooney showed the NFL the money, Pittsburgh was not one of those cities.

It took Art Rooney just two-and-a-half months after he got the franchise for $2500, during the Great Depression, that he latched on to Douds, just 28 years old, to lead the team at least through year one. Back then a coach was not necessarily a coach as we know it. Douds came in as a player and a coach and a player. A look at the Pittsburgh Media Guide and you will see Douds listed as a tackle from 1933 to 1935. He was surely a great player with little experience to back it up as a coach.

He was a great football player from the first day he touched the weird oval shaped ball. As an All-Star lineman and linebacker at nearby Rochester High School, he led his team to two county championships. Rochester with Douds carrying the load also won a state title with a 33-0 whooping of Monessen in 1920. As one might expect, Douds received many accolades for his play such as being inducted into the Beaver County Hall of Fame in 1976. His success carried over into college, attending Washington and Jefferson and becoming a three-time All-American.

He would not consider a 3-6-2 record with the Pirates as a stellar performance, but nonetheless it tied the franchise low of losses in a season until the Steelers went through a season with just four losses in1942. Four games into the season, the team was a respectable 2-2, with a thrilling inaugural victory over the Chicago Cardinals, and a fine 17-3 defeat of the Cincinnati Reds two weeks later. Even after the Pirates first game, which was to Art Rooney's chagrin, a 23-2 loss to the New York Giants, commissioner Joseph Carr remarked to Douds that the team had the chance to build a "fine foundation."

Douds would only last one season as coach, the first of many to be replaced in the team's carousel-like revolving door of coaches until settling on Chuck Noll in 1969. As previously discussed Luby DiMeolo took over in 1934, being replaced by Joe Bach in 1935, for two years. Little is known about Douds other than what is written here.

He died in August of 1979 at 74, just five months before the Steelers would hoist their fourth Lombardi Super Bowl.

Jap Douds never got to directly be a part of the success Chuck Noll earned from 1969-on, but he got to see the firsts. The first team under "The Chief," the first points in franchise history – a safety by John Oehler – and the team's first victory. It may not have necessarily been a "fine" foundation, but it was the first one. Jap Douds is the only person in Pittsburgh Pirates / Steelers history who can say that.

The 1933 Pittsburgh Pirates football team competed in their first season of Professional National Football League (NFL) football. They were led by Forrest Dowds in his only year as head coach. In this first year in which a Pirates team took the field in a pro game, this Pirates team finished with a losing season record of 3-6-2, winning three games, losing six, and tying two. They failed to qualify for the playoffs for the first time

By the time July came Forrest Douds had the Pirates ready to play football at home in the season opener at Forbes Field.

In the Pirates first ever season and "home" opener on Wednesday, Sept 27, the Douds squad lost in a L (2-23) blowout against the New York Giants at home in Forbes Field, Pittsburgh, PA. On Sept 27 at home, the Pirates got their first win v the Chicago Cardinals W (14-13). On Oct 4, my wedding anniversary, at home, the Boston

Redskins beat the Pirates L (6-21). Then, on Oct 11, the Pirates beat the Cincinnati Reds W (17–3) at home in Forbes Field.

On Oct 15, at Green Bay, the Packers smothered the Pirates L (0-47) in City Stadium. On Oct 22, at Cincinnati, the Pirates tied the football Reds T (0–0) in Redland Field. On Oct 29 at Boston's Fenway Park, the Pirates defeated the Redskins W (16–14). Then, on Nov 5, at Brooklyn's Ebbets Field, the Pirates tied the football Dodgers T (3–3).

On Nov 12 at home, the Brooklyn Dodgers walloped the Pirates L (0-32). On Nov 19 at Philadelphia, the Eagles drubbed the Pirates L (6-25) in the Baker Bowl. Then, on Sunday December 3 at New York, in the final game of the season in the Polo Grounds, the Giants pounded the Pirates L (3-27) to wrap up the season.

Top Pirates Players Bernard Patrick Holm

1933-1936 QB & Punter.

Bernard Patrick Holm (May 22, 1908 – July 15, 1978), nicknamed Tony Holm, was a professional American football player. In his four seasons in the NFL he played punter and quarterback. In 1933 he became the first quarterback for the now Pittsburgh Steelers. He was born in Birmingham, Alabama. Holm played college football for Wallace Wade's Alabama Crimson Tide football teams, earning All-America honors in 1929. "Wade's big express-train fullback, Tom Holm, is in the south all of what Al Marsters and Chris Cagle are in the east. His greatest game was in a 33–13 loss to Georgia Tech.

1934 Luby DiMeolo, Coach #2

The 1934 Pittsburgh Pirates football team competed in their second season of Professional National Football League (NFL) football. They were led by Luby DiMeolo as the second Pirates coach in his only year as head coach. In this second year in which a Pirates team took the field in a pro game, this Pirates team finished with a losing season record of 2-10-0, winning two games, losing ten, and tying none. The team failed to qualify for the playoffs for the second time

This was a miserable 2–10 season, in which the Pirates were shut out in 6 games and only scored more than 10 points in 2 games.

One point of interest of the season was the arrival of John McNally, who we will see again later. He arrived for one season from the Green Bay Packers. Unfortunately, this All-Pro and future Hall of Famer did not have much of an impact for the Pirates before returning to the Packers for the next season.

The Pirates were getting ready to look spiffy. The team introduced their "jailbird" uniforms this year. While these uniforms are now worn by the Steelers as throwbacks (although with the current colors), this was the only year the Pirates wore them. Why? Opposing teams constantly needled the Pirates for looking like convicts.

Top Steelers Players Johnny 'Blood' McNally

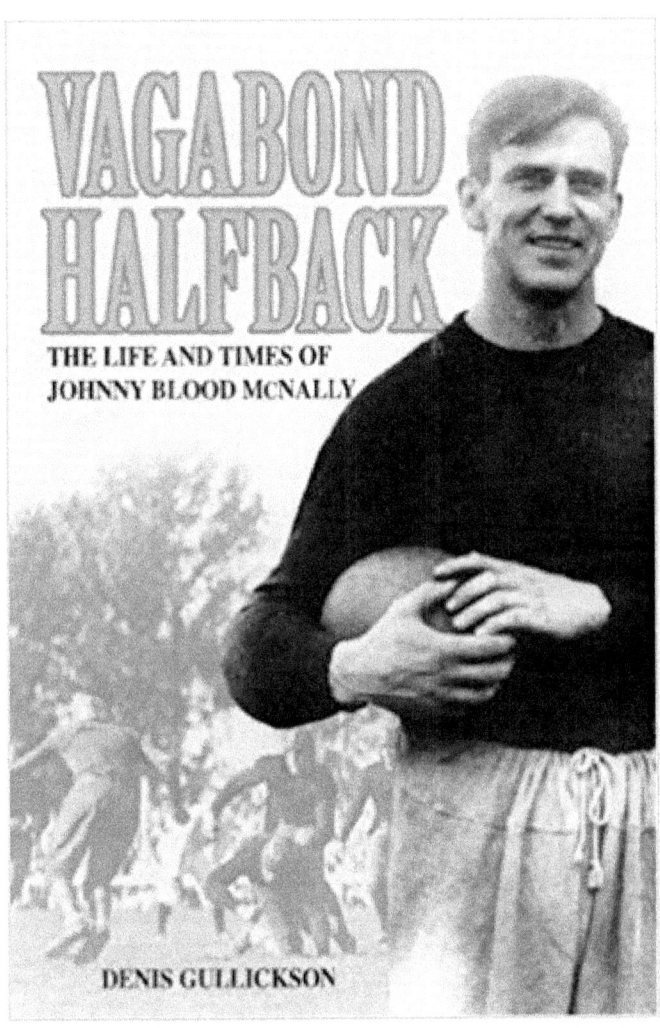

McNally was a player (1934, 1937-39), and Coach (1937-39) John "Blood" McNally played 14 seasons in the NFL with five different teams, including two stints with the Pittsburgh Pirates. He served as both a player and coach from 1937-39 for the Pirates and was considered possibly the best receiver in the NFL during his playing days.

Games of the 1934 season

In the Pirates second season and "home" opener on Wednesday, Sept 27, the DiMeolo-led Pirates squad shut out the Cincinnati Reds W (13-0) at Forbes Field. Then on Sept 16 at home, the Pirates were beaten by the Boston Redskins L (0-7). On Sept 26, at home, the Philadelphia Eagles shut out the Pirates L 0-17). Then, in a close match at home v the New York Giants, the Pirates went down L (12–14).

On Oct 7, At Philadelphia, the Pirates beat the Eagles W (9-7). On Oct 10, at home, the Chicago Bears crushed the Pirates in a Shutout L (0-28). At Boston on Oct 14, the Redskins manhandled the Pirates L (0–39). At NY on Oct 21, the Giants beat the Pirates L (7-17).

At Brooklyn on Oct 28, the Dodgers belted the Pirates L (3–21). At Detroit on Nov 4, the Lions slammed the Pirates L 7–40. Then, on Nov 11, at St. Louis, the Gunners beat the Pirates L (0–6). In the season finale, on Nov 18, the Brooklyn Dodgers whooped the Pirates L (0–10) to close out the season.

1935 Joe Bach, Coach #3

The 1935 Pittsburgh Pirates football team competed in their third season of Professional National Football League (NFL) football. They were led by Joe Bach as the third Pirates coach in his first of two seasons as head coach. In this the Pirates third year, this Pirates team finished with a losing season record of 4-8-0, winning four games, losing eight, and tying none. It was the most games the team had won in a single season. The team failed again to qualify for the playoffs (3rd time).

This was a miserable 4–8 season but better than the prior two. The team responded well to coach Bach on the field and there was hope. They had fired former coach Luby DiMeolo after completing the '34 season with a 2-10 record. They brought in the Duquesne head coach, John Bach, who improved their record to 4-8, and stayed until after the next season before returning to coach in college.
In the Pirates third season and "home" opener on Sept 13, 1935, the Bach-led Pirates squad beat the Philadelphia Eagles W (17-7) at Philadelphia. On Sept 22, the Pirates took it big time on the chin against the New York Giants L (7-42). On Sept 29, at home, the Pirates were beaten by the Chicago Bears L (7-23). At Green Bay on Oct 6, the Packers whipped the Pirates L (0-27).

On Oct 9, the Pirates were beaten in a close match against the Philadelphia Eagles L (6-17). On Oct 20, the Pirates nipped the Chicago Cardinals W (17–13). Then, on Oct 27, Pittsburgh shut-out the Boston Redskins W (6–0). The Brooklyn Dodgers beat Pittsburgh on November 3 L (7-13)

Chapter 4 The Pirates Launch First Football Team   63

In an away game at Brooklyn, the Pirates defeated the Dodgers on Nov 10, W (16–7). Surviving a real trouncing like the Packers often deliver, the Pirates were defeated on Nov 24, by Green Bay L (14-34). On Dec 1, at Boston, the Pirates lost a close match against the Boston Redskins L (3-13). At New York on Dec 8, the Pirates were shut out by the Giants L (0-13) in the season finale.

1936 Joe Bach, Coach #3

The 1936 Pittsburgh Pirates football team competed in their fourth season of Professional National Football League (NFL) football. They were led by Joe Bach as the third Pirates coach in his second and last of two seasons as head coach for the Pirates In this the Pirates fourth year, this Pirates team finished with a break-even season record of 6-6-0, winning six games, losing six, and tying zero. It was the most games the team had won in a single season. Bach had the potential to be a Pittsburgh hero. The team failed again to qualify for the playoffs (4th time).

In this, Joe Bach's second go at it, the team finished the season with the franchise's best record yet, at 6-6. The Pirates played almost all of their home games at Forbes Field in Pittsburgh, Pennsylvania, except for one that was played at Point Stadium in Johnstown, Pennsylvania.

In the Pirates fourth season and "home" opener on Sept 13, 1936, the Bach-led Pirates squad shut-out the Boston Redskins W (10-0) at Boston. On Sept 23, the Pirates made it wo wins in a row with a close match against the Brooklyn Dodgers W (10–6). For three in a row from Joe Bach's boys, on Sept 27, the Pirates beat the New York Giants W (10–7). On my wedding anniversary again on Oct 4 (long before I was married), the Pirates lost to the Chicago Bears L (9-27).

Then, on Oct 14, the Pirates brought their record to 4-1 with a nice shutout win over the Philadelphia Eagles W (17–0). At Chicago on Oct 18, the Bears beat the Pirates convincingly, L (7-26). Then on Oct 25 at Green Bay, the Pirates got whooped again by a very tough

Packers team L (10-38). On Nov 1, the Pirates became 6-2-0 with a nice win over the Brooklyn Dodgers W (10–7).

Playing twice in one week was unusual but on Nov 5, the Pirates played at Philadelphia and beat the Eagles W (6–0) and then Pittsburgh made it to Detroit in time to play Detroit on Nov 8 where they were smashed by the Lions L (3-28). On Nov 15, the Pirates lost to the Chicago Cardinals L (6-14). Then, in the last game on Nov 29, at Boston, the Pirates were manhandled by the Redskins L 0-30 and so the season ended at 6-6 in the best year yet for the NFL Pirates.

1937 John Blood McNally, Coach #4

The 1937 Pittsburgh Pirates football team competed in their fifth season of Professional National Football League (NFL) football. They were led by John Blood McNally as the fourth Pirates coach in his first of three seasons as head coach. In this, the Pirates fifth year, this Pirates team finished with a break-even season record of 4-7-0, winning four games, losing seven, and tying zero. The team failed again to qualify for the playoffs (4th time).

The team hired John McNally as the fourth head coach after John Bach stepped down during the offseason. McNally was a former player, who played halfback for the Pirates during the 1934 season. His team finished with a not so excellent 4-7 record however, Nonetheless, McNally was welcomed back the next season.

In the Pirates season and "home" opener on Sept 5, 1937, the McNally led Pirates squad beat the Philadelphia Eagles W (27-14) in Forbes Field. On Sept 19, the Pirates made it two wins in a row with a nice shutout win (21-0) at Brooklyn against the Dodgers. For three in a row from Joe Bach's boys, on Sept 27, the Pirates beat the New York Giants W (10–7).

On my wedding anniversary again on Oct 4 (long before I was married), the Pirates lost to the Chicago Bears L (9-27). In a close match on Sept 36, at home, the New York Giants beat the Pirates the L (7-10) On Oct 4, at home, on my wedding anniversary, the Chicago Bears shut out Pittsburgh L (0-7)

Then on Oct 10, at Detroit, the Lions edged out the Pirates L (3-7). On Oct 17, at Washington, the Redskins defeated the Pirates L (20-34). On Oct 24, in a tough contest, the Chicago Cardinals beat the Pirates L (7-13) Coming back from five losses in a row, the Pirates beat Philadelphia at home in Forbes Field W (16-7)

At NY on Nov 7, the Giants shut-out the Pirates L (0-17). Then, on Nov 14 at home, the Pirates beat the Washington Redskins W (21-13). In the season finale, on Nov 21, the Brooklyn Dodgers beat the Pirates in a shutout L (0-23).

1938 John Blood McNally, Coach #4

The 1938 Pittsburgh Pirates football team competed in their fifth season of Professional National Football League (NFL) football. They were led by John Blood McNally as the fourth Pirates coach in his second of three seasons as head coach. In this, the Pirates fifth year, this Pirates team finished with a losing season record of 4-7-0, winning four games, losing seven, and tying zero. The team failed again to qualify for the playoffs (5th time).

Though his record was not very good, the 1938 Pirates welcomed back John Blood McNally as head coach. This year was worse than his first as he coached the team's second 2-win season in 3 years, as they placed last (fifth) in the NFL Eastern Division.

This team also welcomed one of the Steelers' best players during their tenure as "the Pirates" (1933-1939). Art Rooney signed college phenom Byron "Whizzer White for one season. White was given a huge salary in his contract. White payed back the Pirates by leading the league in rushing that year. He became the first player to do so while playing for a losing team. He stayed just one year and in 1939 he was overseas pursuing his studies overseas. White liked the NFL money and it did not take him long to return to football as a Lion in 1940.

The Pirates lost their first game of the season on September 9, 1938 at Detroit at the hands of the Lions L (7-16). The next two losses were first against the New York Giants on Sept 11 at home L (14-27) and then a loss to the Philadelphia Eagles L (7-27) on September 16. The only two wins of the season came back to back, first on Sept 23 @ Brooklyn in a nice win v the Dodgers W (17-3). The second was at New York against the Giants W (13-10). From October 9 until December 4, the Pirates did not win a game. Their losses for the remainder of 1938 were as follows

Game	Date	Home?	Opponent	Score
6	October 9, 1938	Yes	Brooklyn Dodgers	L 7-17
7	October 23, 1938	Away	Green Bay Packers	L 0-20
8	November 6, 1938	Yes	Wash Redskins	L 0-7
9	November 20,1938	Away	Philadelph Eagles	L 7-14
10	November 27,1938	Away	Wash'ton Redskins	L 0-15
11	December 4, 1938	Yes	Cleveland Rams	L 7-13

1939 John Blood McNally, Coach #4 (0-3)
1939 Walt Kiesling, Coach #5 (1-6-1)

The 1939 Pittsburgh Pirates football team competed in their sixth season of Professional National Football League (NFL) football. They were led by John Blood McNally as the fourth Pirates coach in his third and last of three seasons as head coach. Additionally, as an assistant for the first three games and as head coach when McNally resigned, this was Walt Kiesling's 1st year. His record after McNally's resignation was 1-6-1 In this, the Pirates seventh and last year of existence, the team finished with a losing record of 1-9-1 in an eleven-game season. The team failed again to qualify for the playoffs (7th time in a row).

The Pirates brought John McNally back for his third year to begin the season. However, finishing 1938 with a 2–9 record, Pirate's owner Art Rooney chose to help him out by signing Walt Kiesling during the offseason to assist with coaching. Despite this, the Pirates experienced their worst season yet, placing last in the league with an overall 1–9–1 record. The team just barely got a number in the win column. The win did not come until Week 11, when they beat the they beat the Philadelphia Eagles W (24-12) It was their first win at home in 9 games at Forbes Field (Week 10, 1937).

On October 29, in the seventh game of the season, Pittsburgh tied the Cleveland Rams T (14-14). Then on Nov 26, against the Eagles, the Pirates won their only game W (24-12) in the season finale.

The rest of the games (all losses) are shown in tabular form below

Game	Date	Home?	Opponent	Score
1	Sept 14, 1939	Away	Brooklyn Dodgers	L 7-12
2	Sept 24, 1939	Yes	Chicago Cardinals	L 0-10
3	October 2, 1939	Yes	Chicago Bears	L 0-32
4	October 8, 1939	Yes	New York Giants	L 7-14
5	October 15, 1939	Away	Wash'ton Redskins	L 14-44
6	October 22, 1939	Yes	Wash'ton Redskins	L 14-21
8	November 6, 1939	Away	Brooklyn Dodgers	L 13-17
9	November 19, 1939	Away	New York Giants	L 7-23
10	November 23, 1939	Yes	Phil'delphia Eagles	L 14-17

That's all she wrote for the Pirates

The facts from this chapter summary are from bleacherreport.com

As discussed, Pittsburgh's original team nickname was the "Pirates," named after the baseball team. At the time, Major League Baseball was the only national sports game that mattered in the United States. It was truly the "National Pastime" and was considered a part of everyday life.

Professional football was basically still in its infancy and was more regarded as a violent, bloody scrum with few highlights and basically a boring affair. College Football had already gotten beyond that. Even though the forward pass was legalized in 1906, few teams threw the ball except in times of desperation, so the running game and subsequent pile-ups dominated the pro football landscape.

Because of baseball's popularity, many pro football teams named themselves the same (or similar) nickname as their baseball counterparts (i.e. Cubs-Bears) taking on the assumption that fans of the diamond would inherently become fans of the gridiron. Since tickets sales were the lone source of revenue for clubs back then, team association was critical to survival.

At the conclusion of the 1939 season and after years of futility trying to win a game on the field as well as win a few sheckles at the gate, along with five head coaches in just seven seasons, Art Rooney wanted a new start and he decided a new nickname was in order.

We will pick up with the 1940 season and Coach Walt Kiesling in due time. First, we will go through some general football history. The next chapters begin with the beginning of football, including its most primitive times in history and they then break into a quick snapshot of the history of the Pittsburgh football organization through 2018. After this we will go back to the detail of each season from 1940, the first year after the Pirates and the first year of the Steelers to the 2017 season, which is the last season played at the time this book was originally written.

Enjoy the ride folks! I know that I will.

Chapter 5 The Evolution of Modern Football

Lots of playing before playing became official

The official agreed upon date for the first American-style football game is November 6, 1869. It would be sixty-four years after this that the Pittsburgh Pirates would win their first game ever in the NFL against the Chicago Cardinals W (14-13). It would be about one hundred-six years after the first game in 1869 for the Pittsburgh Steelers to beat the Minnesota Vikings W (16-6) in Super Bowl IX in 1975 for their first Super Bowl win.

From the first game to the first NFL season in 1920, American football kept changing for the better. If you can find a replay of a game from the early era someplace in the heavens, you would find its replay would not look much like football as we know it. But, it was not completely soccer or rugby either.

Before the first "football" game, teams were playing a rugby style "fuszball" similar to that played in Britain in the mid-19th century.

At the time in the US, a derivative known as association football was also played. In both games, a football is kicked at a goal or run over a line. These styles were based on the varieties of English public-school football games. Over time, as noted, the style of "football" play in America continued to evolve.

On November 6, 1869, the first intercollegiate formal football game in America featured Rutgers and Princeton. Before the teams were even on the field it was being plugged as the first college (intercollegiate) football game of all time. Most of the popular NFL teams of today were being formed after the turn of the century.

The first game of intercollegiate football was a sporting battle between two neighboring schools on a plot of ground where the present-day Rutgers gymnasium now stands in New Brunswick, N.J. Rutgers won that first game, 6-4. Even the scoring was different back then.

There were two teams of 25 men each and the rules were mostly rugby-like, but different enough to make it very interesting and enjoyable.

Like today's football, there were many surprises; strategies needed to be employed; determination exhibited, and of course the players required physical prowess.

Chapter 5 The Evolution of Modern Football   71

1st Game Rutgers 6 Princeton 4 College Field, New Brunswick, NJ

Before we begin to focus solely on the Steelers, the next several chapters will describe the origins of football, the origin of the football, and how the NFL grew out of something that became known as American football that was first played on college campuses.

Chapter 6 The First American College Football Game

Early American Football

We can all read Walter Camp's books about how the rules of American football came about. We can also learn a lot from the writings of the day. However, since nobody alive today was alive way back when, it is safe to say that nobody actually knows. But from all the accounts, we do have a pretty good idea.

There are a lot of guessers and some wrong readers out there because nobody from November 1869, of which I am aware can refute anything via an eye-witness account. So, there are a lot of great stories, some duplicated many times over. Some are right on the money and others are inexact. We'll do our best to bring you the story as it really happened in this book.

Once the first College football game was played, the next major game to be played was the first professional football game. Though there were dribs and drabs of pro football being played by a number of famous coaches such as Knute Rockne, it took a while for professional football to take off.

In these pre-Steelers football chapters that eventually get us to the first pro-football game, it helps to know that the facts in this section come from a book written by your author that sells much better in England than it does in the US. Its title is *The Birth of American Football*. The modified excerpts within this book help set the stage for a proper introduction of professional football, the NFL, and the road to Super Bowl XLIII, a game won by our very own Steelers.

It has been almost 150 years since the first American College Football game. Therefore, it helps to recall the old schoolroom exercise of whispering into a person's ear a little passage and thirty students later seeing what comes back. The good news is that the further back that you get from the time of Walter Camp, the stories are all similar and there are fewer and fewer of them.

Camp had all the future rules in his head!

Eventually, in the 1870's, shortly after the very first recognized collegiate football game in America, the great Walter Camp began to get really interested and he wrote a lot of football history and football rule books. These are trusted implicitly today by most experts as the defining moments in American football.

One of the few things about early football that we do know with reasonable certainty is that professional football as we understand it, was non-existent until long after collegiate football was established. It can also be said with certainty that if it were not for the colleges and Walter Camp, in particular, there probably would be no American football today at any level. Of course, more than likely there would still be rugby and soccer.

We also know that there was a great gifted athlete who played every sport imaginable including soccer and rugby, and then American football. His name is Walter Camp. He is universally recognized as the Father of American Football.

There is some irony in putting this out as a two plus two equals four story, however. You see, Walter Camp, as noted, widely considered the most important figure in the development of American football, was not playing organized football when the first football game took place in 1869. So, who gave them their football rules. Voila, a conundrum!

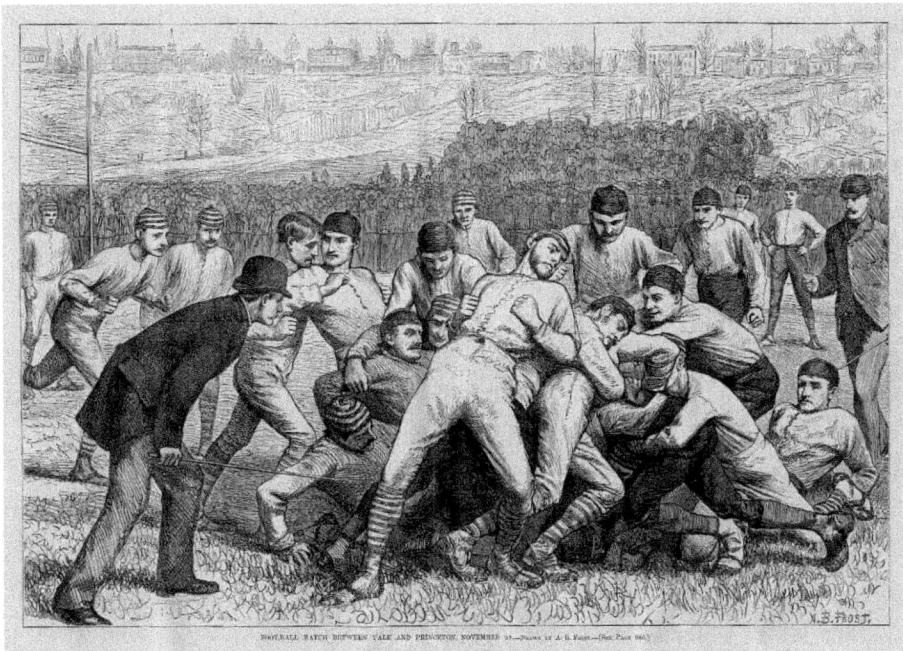

1879 Football Game Depiction

As a youth, we know that Camp excelled in sports such as track, baseball, and association football, and after enrolling at Yale in 1876, he earned varsity honors in every sport the school offered. But, what about 1869, which is the consensus origin date for the beginning of American football in the US?

Many apologists have written about this period from 1869 onward as if it were the beginning of American football that, at the time was played only at the collegiate level. In essence, the true beginning of college football was in fact, the beginning of American football. However, the rules of the game began more as rugby rules than football rules but over the years, changes were made. Today, no other country plays the type of football played in America. America created its own game of football and it is unique.

There were other rough games out there at the time and they still exist across the world. One might conclude that football was unnecessary as those who played soccer and rugby could be maimed or killed in a contest without needing Camp's American football rules.

Scenes from one of first football games

Chapter 6 The First American College Football Game

Considering that the centennial of the US was approaching in 1869, the year of the first game, some feel there was a need to create a game besides the American past-time of baseball, that was a cool-weather sport. Yes, there was soccer and rugby, but these have a European or English heritage, from whom America had declared independence about 100 years prior. England for the most part owned the rules of soccer and rugby for some time.

Nonetheless, historians trace the roots of American football to early versions of rugby football and association football. Both games have their origin in varieties of football played in Britain in the mid-19th century, in which a football is kicked at a goal or kicked over a line. These varieties of style in England were based on the various English public school football games.

It helps to be reminded in this story that our nation's birth date is July 4, 1776 and so 1869 was just 93 years from the founding.

There are lots of stories about the evolution towards American football, and this part of this discusses many ideas supplied by Walter Camp for the transition. American football resulted from several major modifications from association football and rugby football, most notably the rule changes instituted by Camp at Yale University and as a Hopkins School graduate. To repeat Camp is significant as he is attributed as being the designated "Father of American Football."

One of the changes not attributed to Walter Camp was the shape of the ball. As you will see, the forward pass did not become legal until 1906 and so the spherical shape of modern footballs was not required until passing became a bigger part of the game.

The football was evolving steadily from the first game. But, it was not completely perfected until 1935. The ball used in the very first game was round, like a soccer ball and like early rugby balls. It was tough to carry, and awkward to throw. In 1874, in a McGill and Harvard game, they used a ball that looked like a watermelon. Over time, balls became more plum-like and easier to throw. The problem was that pigs' bladders, not balloons were used and they by definition were inexact. We refine this study of the ball later in this section before we look at Patriot's season summaries, so please hang on. For now, know that Walter Camp was not involved in determining the ball per se.

Among these important changes to rugby that Camp brought into American football were the introduction of the line of scrimmage, and the down-and-distance rules. He also introduced the notion of legal interference, which today is called blocking. Camp was the rules guy but before he went to Yale, like most New Englanders of the day, he played soccer, which was the preferred cool-weather fall sport of the day. He did not play much rugby football until his time at Yale University from 1876 to 1881.

Camp was not the first person to play football—any kind of football—be it soccer, rugby, or Harpastum. Some joke that Adam and Eve may have played football with a round fruit. Most of us would hope it was an orange or a grapefruit.

A sport called Harpastum and others

You can go back through history and find sports that had some of the roughness and rudiments of soccer, rugby, and American football but the games they played were not very rule-based.

In a "sport" called ***Harpastum***, a form of ball game played in the Roman Empire, for example, the Romans enjoyed their own form of football.

There have been many forms of traditional football that have been played throughout Europe and beyond since the beginning of mankind.

We have already discussed the possibility that there may have been nicht-verboten round or oval fruits in the Garden of Paradise used for football.

From the beginning of antiquity, knowing man's propensity to exercise, have fun and use various shaped balls in so doing, if not in the garden, then one can bet it was not long after Paradise that ancient forms of football abounded. See pic of ***Harpastum*** next page.

Many of these ancient matches would involve handling of a ball and scrummage-like formations. Several of the oldest examples of football-like games include the Greek game of *Episkyros* and the Roman game of *Harpastum* (both pictures on opposite side of page).

Over time many countries across the world developed their own national football-like games. For example, New Zealand has Ki-o-rahi, Australia has Marngrook, Japan has Kemari, China has Cuju, Georgia has Lelo Burti, and the Borders have Jeddart Ba' and Cornwall Cornish have Hurling.

The pictures in this section of balls and balls in play are interesting and make the point. Left to right, Ki-o-rahi ball, Marngrook ball, and a snap of a game of Kemari in process. None of these forms appear to have a direct link to American football but they surely are forerunners.

A traditional kī-o-rahi ball. Marngrook (possum skin football). A game of Kemari

In football-story-telling, there is also an often-told story about a ship in 1586, almost 100 years after Columbus, in which the men from the ship wanted to play a little sport. The ship was reportedly commanded by an English explorer named John Davis. The young crew would go ashore to play a form of football with the Inuit (Eskimo) people in Greenland. There are other later accounts of an Inuit game played on ice, called Aqsaqtuk.

This game had a similarity to football in that each game, which was called a match, began with the two teams facing each other in parallel lines. The objective was to kick the "ball" through each other team's line and then kick it at a goal. Moving along in time, it is recorded from 1610 that William Strachley from Jamestown Virginia, an English Colonist, wrote the account of a game played by Native Americans. They called the game Pahsaheman.

Though there are stories of Native Americans playing games, a variety of American football historians agree that the game has its roots from the traditional football games played all over Europe in villages, towns, and schools for centuries before Columbus.

The scuttle on those is that the early games appear to have had much in common with what has been called "mob football" from England. There were typically no uniforms or coaches nor hard and fast rules.

In the 19th century, intramural games of rugby, soccer, and association football began to be played on American college campuses. There were no rules committees and no Walter Camp at the time and so each school played its own variety of football with its own rules.

Princeton University students, for example, are reported to have played a game called ball-own, as early as 1820.

Harvard had its own tradition known as "Bloody Monday," which began in 1827. This was all about a mass ballgame between the freshman and sophomore classes. In 1860, both the town police and the college authorities agreed the Bloody Monday had to go. There was too much blood for the good of the game.

The gendarme would not permit "football" for well over twelve years. Then the game was played again. Dartmouth had its own version, which they called "Old division football." Its rules were first published in 1871, though it is said they played the game from the 1830's.

There were commonalities in all these games Yet, they remained largely "mob" style games, with huge numbers of players on the "field" or whatever makeshift was available. All players were on the field at the same time. There was a little rhyme and some reason as the objective seemed always to be to advance the ball into a goal area, quite often by any means possible and necessary.

There were no complicated rules as the games were played for sport—just for fun. Rules were simple, and so without protection by rules, violence and injury were common. There was supposedly no beer drinking at the games, but plenty was consumed shortly thereafter by the young adult participants.

Yes, to be sure, the games were often heated as no group wanted to lose. Some games were actually violent. Yet, afterwards, sometimes after beating each other to a pulp, both squads normally would choose to gather together from their rivalry for some post-game revelry that often included the singing of songs, awarding of small prizes, and of course lots of beer-drinking.

There is an old football / rugby saying that parallels the US Las Vegas slogan: "What happens on the pitch, stays on the pitch. "This is an oft-quoted rugby truism.

Take away the violence!

The brutality and frequent bloodshed of these mob-style games led to widespread protests and there were many separate decisions from cities and schools to abandon the games. Yale, for example, under pressure from the city of New Haven, banned the play of all forms of football in 1860. Eventually, because of popular pressure, the games would be brought back in one form or another.

From 1854 to 1882, there was a variant of the mob football style that was once again played at Yale in the form of bladderball. The objective, of this "game" was to gain control of an oversized inflatable ball and bring it through the gates of the residential college represented by another on-campus intramural team.

As one would expect, this game was eventually banned by school authorities for a number of reasons, not the least of which was alcohol fueled violence. The violence and the alcohol were most often precipitated by the game. Revival games were played in 2009 and 2011, and very briefly, in 2014. The revivals are most often scripted though the grog surely flows.

Eventually, the informality of the matches gave way to formality as bona fide institutions began to sponsor collegiate level teams. The 1869 college football season is recognized as the first season of intercollegiate football in the United States, though at the time, there were only two teams in the league – Rutgers and Princeton.

The rules were not refined and so the teams used "agreed-upon improvised rules" resembling soccer and rugby as much as the modern American sport. 1869 is considered by historians as the inaugural college football season.

This 1869 football season consisted of only two total games and as noted, there were just two teams – Rutgers University and Princeton University; The first game was played on November 6 at Rutgers' campus, and the second was played on November 13 on the Princeton's campus.

1869–1875

As noted, the November 6, 1869 football game between Rutgers and Princeton, which by the way was then known as the *College of New Jersey,* was played with a round ball. The rules were provided by Rutgers captain William J. Leggett. They were based on the Football Association's first set of American football rules.

Rutgers Scarlett Knights practice 1869

Walter Camp did not write the first set of rules, but he made them all better. These rules were an early attempt by those who had studied football in England's public schools, to codify the rules and create what hopefully would become a universal and standardized set of dictates for the game. Let me posit an analogy of the *evolution* of American Football Rules.

I remember back in the late 1980's when Windows 2.0 came out and it was a major improvement on DOS and the prior Windows. I am sure if the hardware were capable then, the Bill Gates led Microsoft team would have built Windows 10 or Windows 11 instead of going through all the iterations to make the program better over the next thirty years. But, for lots of reasons, they could not.

Rules changes work well through an iterative process of testing new rules, introducing them to the "game," and then removing objectional parts. In the process, some rules are enhanced; others eliminated; while still other rules are added.

The 1869 football games bore little resemblance to the American game, which would be developed slowly in the following decades through the continual work of Walter Camp and others. Nonetheless, it is still regarded as the first game of Intercollegiate American Football.

Think of the mob playing this first game at a Rutgers field. It could have been worse. Two teams of 25 players lined up and attempted to score by kicking the ball into the opposing team's goal. Throwing or carrying the ball was not allowed, but there was plenty of physical contact between players. The first team to reach six goals was declared the winner. Rutgers won by a score of six to four.

A rematch was played at Princeton a week later under Princeton's own set of rules. There was a major difference in the rules of this game as a team was awarded a "free kick" when any player caught the ball on the fly. This feature had been adopted from the Football Association's rules. The fair catch kick rule has survived through our modern American game.

Princeton won the second game with home field advantage by a score of 8–0. More teams began to play each other in 1870. Columbia was next to join the series and then by 1872 several other schools began to field intercollegiate teams, including Yale and the Stevens Institute of Technology.

Chapter 7 Moving Closer Towards American Football

Nothing happens overnight

Soon after the early football changes, in the late nineteenth and into the early twentieth centuries, more game-play type developments were introduced by college coaches.

The list is like a who's who of early American College Football. Coaches, such as Eddie Cochems, Amos Alonzo Stagg, Parke H. Davis, Knute Rockne, John Heisman, and Glenn "Pop" Warner helped introduce and then take advantage of the newly introduced forward pass.

In later chapters, we will look at the enhancements attributed to these football greats.

We have learned that American College football as well as professional football, were introduced prior to the 20th century. Pro football remained ragtag until 1920 when the American Professional Football Association was formed. Fans were lured into watching again and again once they saw the game played. How could we not love American football?

American college football grew in popularity even after the beginning of professional football. It became the dominant version of the sport of football in the United States. It was this way for the entire first half of the 20th century. For many fans, it still is this way.

There are pro football fans who do not enjoy college football and vice versa.

Bowl games made the idea of football even more exciting in the college ranks. Rivalries grew and continued, and the fans loved it! This great football tradition brought a national audience to college football games that still dominates the sports world today.

Edgar Allan Poe – No kidding!

In researching this section, I found that some players with some great names played football in the early years. For example, Edgar Allan Poe was an All-American for Princeton in 1889. Additionally, in 1889, first-year players were permitted to wear numbers representing their names in college football games.

This particular Edgar Allan Poe was also a great historical figure. He served as Attorney General of the State of Maryland from 1911 to 1915. Born in Baltimore, Poe was named for his second cousin, twice removed, the celebrated author & poet, Edgar Allan Poe, who died in 1849.

What number is he?

Another interesting tidbit on the formation of football is that teams played without uniform numbers. Nonetheless somehow the players were identified. Just two years after Penn State as well as Notre Dame formed their teams and played their first official football games in 1887, the first All-America team was named in 1889.

There is some scuttle about that, for Walter Camp and some others with mostly Eastern College roots were accused of picking players from the big Eastern Colleges almost exclusively and so there were few All Americans at Notre Dame or Penn State or Alabama in the early years.

Seventeen years after the first all-American for example, W. T. (Mother) Dunn was Penn State's first All-American in (1906). He was named by Walter Camp. He was both a linebacker and a center. The next All-American for PSU was Bob Higgins, the long-time PSU football coach who, as an End, gained the honor both in (1915 & 1919). The PSU football program has produced 88 consensus all-Americans in total. Notre Dame has 90. Alabama has 68.

Notre Dame had two All-Americans in 1913—Knute Rockne, an End, and Gus Dorais, a quarterback. By 1913, the forward pass was legal and that is how ND was winning its games in this undefeated season.

As touched on briefly in this section. in 1889, numbers to identify individual players were permitted but not recommended. It took until 1915 that they were recommended. But, it wasn't until 1937 that numerals were required on both the front and back of game jerseys. In 1967 this rule was further modified to require numbering according to position, with offensive players ineligible to receive forward passes if they were assigned numbers in the 50-79 range.

Pro football came from American college football

There is no denying that the greatest college football players more often than not eventually find their fortunes in professional football. Pro football can be traced back to 1889, just a few years after Penn State and Notre Dame rolled out their programs, and just before Alabama got in the game.

It was 1892, when William "Pudge" Heffelfinger signed a $500 contract to play for the Allegheny Athletic Association against the Pittsburgh Athletic Club. He is reportedly the first player to be paid for playing football.

Twenty-eight years later, the American Professional Football Association was formed. This league changed its name to the National Football League (NFL) just two years later.

Eventually, the NFL became the major league of American football. Originally, pro football was just an unaffiliated sport played in midwestern industrial towns in the United States. Yet, professional football eventually became a national phenomenon.

We all know this because from August to February, in America, every year, many of us are glued to our TV sets or chained to our seats in some of the most intriguing pro-football stadiums in America—mostly on Sundays.

The end of football?

Football was never a game for the light of heart. You had to be tough physically and tough mentally to compete. Way back in 1906, for example complaints were many about the violence in American football. It got so bad that universities on the West Coast, led by California and Stanford, replaced the sport with rugby union rules.

At the time, the very future of American college football, a very popular sport enjoyed by fans nationwide was in doubt. The schools that eliminated football and replaced it with Rugby Union believed football would be gone and Rugby Union would eventually be adopted nationwide.

Soon other schools followed this travesty and made the switch. Eventually, due to the perception that West Coast football was an inferior game played by inferior men when compared to the rough and tumble East Coast, manhood prevailed in the West over the inclination to make the game mild.

The many tough East Coast and Midwest teams had shrugged off the loss of the few teams out West and they had continued to play American style football.

And, so the available pool of Rugby Union "football" teams to play remained small. The Western colleges therefore had to schedule games against local club teams and they reached out to Rugby Union powers in Australia, New Zealand, and especially, due to its proximity, Canada. America at the time was almost exclusively playing American football.

American football OK without the West

The famous Stanford and California game continued as rugby. To make it seem important. The winner was invited by the British Columbia Rugby Union to a tournament in Vancouver over the Christmas holidays. The winner of that tournament was rewarded with the Cooper Keith Trophy. Nobody in the American football America cared. Eventually the West Coast came back to American-style football ala Walter Camp.

Nonetheless the situation of injury and death in football persisted and though there was a lot of pushback, it came to a head in 1905 when there were 19 fatalities nationwide. Nobody wanted this.

President Theodore Roosevelt, a tough guy himself, is reported to have threatened to shut down the game nationwide if drastic changes were not made. Sports historians however, dispute that Roosevelt ever intervened with any wielded power.

What is certified, however, is that on October 9, 1905, the President held a meeting of football representatives from Harvard, Yale, and Princeton. The topic was eliminating and reducing injuries and the President, according to the record, never threatened to ban football.

The fact is that Roosevelt lacked the authority to abolish football but more importantly, he was a big fan and wanted the game to continue. The little Roosevelts also loved the sport and were playing football at the college and secondary levels at the time.

This was over 110 years ago, a century plus. That is why they say football was an even more brutal sport then, than some believe it is today. There are accounts of games that left dozens of dead on college and prep school gridirons. Though I have the reference, I cannot find any of the games in which such carnage may have occurred.

Many in the country were asking for action from politicians. With the very existence of the sport in jeopardy, President Theodore Roosevelt, who actually loved the sport, entered the fray and urged the schools noted above to institute some radical reforms that according to observers at the time saved the sport and gave another birth to the modern game of American football.

On the next page is a picture of a Teddy's Nephew being carried off the field after an injury in the brutal game of football.

There are those who went as far as calling the turn of the 20th century America's football gridirons killing fields. College games drew tens of thousands of spectators and had even more fan appeal than professional baseball, the national pastime.

Baseball was a gentle sport compared to football. American football in the early 1900s was lethally brutal. It was a grinding, bruising sport that required major physical contact on each play. In 1905, the forward pass was still illegal and, so it was sheer brute strength that was required to move the ball.

One of the Roosevelt offspring carried off after injuring his ankle.

Huge players were permitted to lock their arms in mass formations and they would use their unprotected helmetless heads as battering rams. Gang tackles routinely buried ball carriers underneath a ton and a half of "tangled humanity."

Football players fought like gladiators

There was little in the way of protective equipment. Apparently, nobody had ever thought of pads and helmets. Players would often sustain gruesome injuries such as wrenched spinal cords, crushed skulls and broken ribs that were sometimes so severe they pierced their hearts. It did not go unnoticed.

The Chicago Tribune wrote a piece that in 1904 alone, the year before Roosevelt's involvement. there were 18 football deaths and 159 serious injuries, mostly among prep school players. It was sad.

A look at tangled humanity

TR as a college undergraduate; Theodore Roosevelt Collection, Harvard College Library

There were obituaries of young pigskin players on a near-weekly basis during the football season. The carnage appalled America. Everybody loved the sport but not the maimings. The Newspapers did not take it easy on the game. Editorials called for the outright banishment of college and high school football.

Football was often compared to the Roman Gladiators: "The once athletic sport has degenerated into a contest that for brutality is little better than the gladiatorial combats in the arena in ancient Rome," opined the Beaumont Express. The sport had reached such a crisis that one of its biggest boosters—President Theodore Roosevelt—got involved.

Roosevelt's glasses gave away his nearsightedness. But, as a youth in college he did not wear them. This, however, was more than enough to keep this tough man from making the Harvard varsity squad, Yet, he was always a vocal exponent of football's contribution to the "strenuous life," both on and off the field.

When "Teddy" was New York City police commissioner, he helped bring back the old Harvard-Yale football series after it had been canceled for two years following the violent 1894 clash that was labeled "the bloodbath at Hampden Park."

He believed that the football field was more or less a proving ground for the battlefield. This was validated by the performance of his fellow Rough Riders who were mostly former football standouts. "In life, as in a football game," he wrote, "the principle to follow is: Hit the line hard; don't foul and don't shirk but hit the line hard!"

Teddy Roosevelt liked football

In 1903, the president told an audience, "I believe in rough games and in rough, manly sports. I do not feel any particular sympathy for the person who gets battered about a good deal so long as it is not fatal." Unfortunately, in 1904-1905, football injuries were too often fatalities, and it was not improving.

Yes, even the President knew that football had become fatal, and he acknowledged that it needed reform if it were to be saved. With his son, Theodore Jr. who had begun to play for the Harvard freshman team, he had a major league paternal interest in reforming the game as well.

Roosevelt was the guy to negotiate with the foot-ballers for sure. He was straight from having negotiated an end to the Russo-Japanese War. He sought to end violence on the football field as well as the battlefield. Using his "big stick," the gentleman known as the "First Fan" brought the necessary parties together—especially those from the premier collegiate football powers of the day—Harvard, Yale and Princeton—to the White House on October 9, 1905.

Roosevelt made no threats. But, he did urge them to curb excessive violence and set an example of fair play for the rest of the country. The schools responded with a heartfelt and effective press release condemning brutality and pledging to keep the game clean.

Ironically, Roosevelt, in taking on the problem of football fatalities, learned that real war may be even easier to gain peace than getting this new American sport to clean up its act. Fatalities and injuries continued and in fact increased during the 1905 season. In the freshman tilt against Yale, the president's son was bruised, and his nose broken—some say quite deliberately. This would not do. Yet, it continued

The following week, Harvard's entire varsity were ready to leave the field of play against Yale, after their captain was felled by an illegal hit on a fair catch. His nose was broken and bloodied. Union College halfback Harold Moore suffered a cerebral hemorrhage and died the same afternoon after being kicked in the head while attempting to tackle a New York University runner.

THE TWELFTH PLAYER IN EVERY FOOTBALL GAME.

It was a grim and savage season and it finally ended. There was work to be done. The Chicago Tribune saw the senseless deaths as a "death harvest," The football season had brought about 19 player deaths and 137 serious injuries. Newspaper artists had a field day creating "cartoons" of figures such as the Grim Reaper on a goalpost surveying a twisted mass of fallen players. It was similar to the cartoon on the prior page.

It was so tough that some tough schools such as Stanford and California switched to rugby while Columbia, Northwestern and Duke dropped football all together. Harvard president Charles Eliot, who considered football "more brutalizing than prizefighting, cockfighting or bullfighting," warned that Harvard would be next. This would be a totally crushing blow to the college game and the Harvard alum, President Roosevelt who worked every day in the Oval Office.

Helmet testing was quite animated in the early 1900's

Roosevelt appreciated the need for men to play men sports and he captured his views in a letter to a friend. He stated that he would not permit the Harvard College president Elliott to "emasculate football," and that Roosevelt hoped to "minimize the danger" without football having to be played "on too ladylike a basis." Roosevelt was a tough man and, so he again used his bully pulpit. He urged all parties from the Harvard coach to other leading football authorities to quickly adopt radical rule changes. He invited other school leaders and football aficionados to the White House in the offseason for productive discussions.

Good rules made football even better

Many good rules were put forth at an intercollegiate conference, which would become the forerunner of the NCAA. The "radical" rules were approved for the 1906 season. They would have a very positive effect on the game and eventually would substantially reduce injuries.

The rules legalized the forward pass, abolished the dangerous mass formations, created a neutral zone between offense and defense and doubled the first-down distance to 10 yards, to be gained in three downs. The rule changes did not completely eliminate football's dangers, but fatalities declined—to 11 per year in both 1906 and 1907—while injuries fell sharply. A spike in fatalities in 1909 led to another round of reforms that further eased restrictions on the forward pass and formed the foundation of the modern sport.

So, the rule changes were good. There were others such as the notion of reducing the number of scrimmage plays to earn a first down from four to three in an attempt to reduce injuries. The LA Times reported an increase in punts in an experimental game and thus considered the game much safer than regular play. Football lovers did not accept many of the new rules because they felt they were not "conducive to the sport." There was a period when rapid rule changes interfered with coaching strategies as a favored play in early season might be illegal before the season ended.

Because nobody wanted players injured or killed in a game, on December 28, 1905, to be sure the rules were put out for 1906, a group representing 62 schools met without the president in New York City to discuss the proposed major rule changes to make the game safer. From this meeting, the Intercollegiate Athletic

Association of the United States, later named the National Collegiate Athletic Association (NCAA), was formed.

The forward pass is legalized

One particular rule change that was introduced in 1906 was devised to open up the game and thus reduce injury eventually gained favor with the coaches, players, and fans. This new rule introduced the legal forward pass. Though it was underutilized for years afterwards, this proved to be one of the most important rule changes in the establishment of the modern game. Those coaches, such as Eddie Cochems, who adopted the pass early, had a major advantage in winning games.

Because of these 1905-1906 reforms, mass formation plays in which many players joined together became illegal when forward passes became legal.

Chapter 8 Origin of the Oval-Shaped Sports-Ball

The coming of the sports-ball!

One of my great curiosities in researching this book is who would have ever thought of using an oval ball shaped like today's modern football? Secondly, why don't we all know that answer?

To answer the question, I got some help from the people at Inventors-Handbook as surely the oval football was a key invention for the game of football.

Please note that the folks from the Inventor's handbook have a different interest than I, in pursuing this information. They use the invention of the football as a reason why inventors should patent their works while I was merely interested in learning who the inventor was and how he came about inventing the football.

The invention of the *football,* the ball used in the popular team game is not necessarily attributed to one inventor. But most historians agree that one English shoe maker is more than likely responsible for the way footballs looks today.

This description is not for the faint of heart, and in fact, there is a death reported in this account.

Early footballs were essentially pig's or other animals' bladders which were inflated by the power of the human lungs (blowing hot air into them). They were then tied and sealed, much like balloons would be sealed – knotted at the end.

As a result, they were often plum, or pear shaped, and not round, depending on the size of the individual animal's bladder.

Before the invention of football as we know it, balls were often prone to exploding while in use. This led to shoemakers selling leather cases to protect the inflated bladders. Shoes and boots makers used leather on a daily basis and were the most appropriate people to be able to sew the ball's leather cases around the bladder.

You may ask why rubber was not used instead of animal bladders. It took a while to be able to work rubber into all the uses we have today. Rubber was invented in 1839 by Charles Goodyear. He accidentally dropped Sulphur and white latex from a rubber tree onto a hot stove. This resulted in the formation of a dark elastic substance which came to be called vulcanized rubber, and the rest is history but not yet for football.

Until the 1860's, football, soccer and rugby were all played with a plum or pear-shaped ball made of leather, encasing an inflated animal bladder.

In Europe, the first proper football invention is attributed to two shoemakers: Richard Lindon and William Gilbert who invented round and oval shaped balls. Lindon is credited for inventing the rubber inflatable bladder.

In 1849, at the age of 33, Lindon, who worked just in front of the rugby school in Rugby England, was constantly asked to create footballs for the school's boys.

As a shoemaker, he was regularly receiving leather supplies for making shoes and, so he used some of this supply to also create balls for the boys' teams by covering the pig's bladders with leather.

Both Lindon and his wife worked at the craft and prepared the balls when requested. Because she was not a craft shoemaker and yet wanted to help with the many orders, Lindon's wife took on the additional responsibility of inflating the bladders by blowing air into them.

This was not as simple and innocuous as it sounds. In many ways, it was downright dangerous as many bladders were infected, having originated from diseased pigs.

It was around 1862 that Lindon had begun looking for an alternative to inflated pig's bladders that would be safer than the current practice. For his wife, those efforts came way too late. She eventually died by falling ill from inflating too many infected pig's bladders.

Lindon invented an inflatable inner tube made of natural rubber, instead of the existing animal bladders. Because of the newly understood pliability of rubber, the shape of the football was able to be molded to the shape of a perfect round sphere.

His first prototype was made from such a rubber inflated tube covered with 7 strips of leather, stitched at the end with "bottoms" on both sides. The ball was almost spherical. This design gained popularity and became the one he used for all of the "footballs" that he sold.

Lindon's Brass Pump Invention

Since he found inflating the rubber that he used too hard to do by hand, Lindon also invented a brass pump, inspired by a simple ear syringe. This could be used to inflate his footballs without the need to blow them up with one's mouth. Thus, he is also credited not only for the invention of the football but also for the invention of the air pump. Until his death, Lindon had never patented the bladder, ball or air pump, which he invented. Yet, these were key inventions for football. The moral of the story for the invention people is that he could have made a ton of money, which could have been passed on to his family on his death if he had only patented his invention.

The shape of the football

On October 5, in 2012, Jimmy Stamp of Smithsonian Magazine wrote an expose on how the "pigskin" for modern football got its shape. "How Did the Pigskin Get Its Shape?"

Stamp put forth that even though American football may have evolved from soccer and rugby, the football was never truly designed; it just sorta happened.

Like the shoemaker's invention, Stamp also points out that the "pigskin" is not made of pig skin or pig's bladders but is, in fact, made from cowhide, aka leather, and not the tanned skin of a pig.

He cites that the shape is mysterious, but we know it is because of the inexact shape of the original pig's bladder. He asks, "If the sport evolved from soccer and rugby, how and when did the football gain its distinct shape – technically known as a prolate spheroid?" Stamp answers:

"Well, it turns out that the football was never truly designed, it just sorta happened." This fact comes from one Henry Duffield, a man who happened to be a spectator at the Princeton and Rutgers American Football Game in 1869, which as we know is considered the first intercollegiate game ever:

"The ball was not an oval but was supposed to be completely round. It never was, though — it was too hard to blow up right. The game was stopped several times that day while the teams called for a little key from the sidelines. They used it to unlock the small nozzle which was tucked into the ball, and then, the players took turns blowing it up. The last man generally got tired and they put it back in play somewhat lopsided."

This would surely indicate that the football that bounces erratically all over a field and can fly through the air in a perfect spiral is not, in fact, the product of a grand design. According to Stamp, it is simply the result of a leaky sphere and some lazy inflators.

Rugby balls had been constructed long before this game but for some time, the round ball dominated the scene in soccer style / association football. The rugby balls were always in the shoemakers for repair because of their pointy ends.

In 1879, Thomas Sherrin, from Australia took the point off the ends of the rugby balls and made his own design. His nephew noted that "He made a ball and created the ball that had less pointy ends. It was still able to bounce unpredictably but it was a little more consistent in its movement." Sherrin also made leather punching bags.

Stamp wraps up his Smithsonian article with an interesting summary:

"Initially, football was a very different game – or perhaps I should say games. There were kicking games and running games, but as those two games began to merge together, as rules began to standardize, the ball began to slightly stretch out in order to accommodate more types of use. The unique shape of the ball was somewhat formalized in the early 20th century and that form was exploited to great success when the forward pass was introduced to football in 1906."

Chapter 8 Origin of the Oval Shaped Sports Ball 105

PHONE—4641 Central   FACTORY : 32 and 34 Wellington Street COLLINGWOOD.

T. W. SHERRIN

Largest Manufacturer and Exporter of High-class Athletic Goods in the Commonwealth

Awarded Prize Medal and First Order of Merit, Adelaide International Exhibition 1881; awarded First Order of Merit, Melbourne Industrial Exhibition, 1879-80; Diploma of Merit, Centennial Exhibition, 1888-89.
(Under the patronage of the Victorian Government)

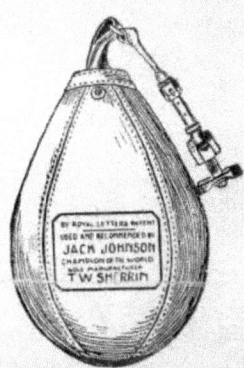

DICK LEE

Champion Goal Kicker of the Victorian Football League, seasons 1907-8-9, 159 Goals, performed with T. W. Sherrin's Kangaroo Brand Footballs, with the assistance of a shield scientifically cut by Sherrin for Lee's injured shin, without which he would have been unable to complete season 1909.

Sherrin's Patent Punching Balls and Boxing Gloves, 30s., 25s., 21s., used and recommended by all champions.

Jack Johnson, Champion of the World, say they excel all others he has ever used, both in England and America.

Caution.

In consequence of the inferior class of sporting goods being placed before the public, and in many cases represented as T. W. Sherrin's make, I wish to caution all athletes, when ordering, to see that the name T. W. Sherrin and the Kangaroo Brand are plainly stamped thereon.

SHERRIN'S Famous "Kangaroo" Brand Match II Footballs are the only Balls ordered by the VICTORIAN FOOTBALL LEAGUE for all semi-final and final matches they are also used by all the leading Clubs in the Commonwealth.

AUSTRALASIAN FOOTBALL COUNCIL

Mr. T. W. Sherrin.   Melbourne, 17th February, 1909.

Dear Sir,—During the contests, held in celebration of the Jubilee of the game, at the Melbourne Cricket Ground in August last, in which teams from New Zealand, New South Wales, Queensland, South Australia, Tasmania, Victoria and West Australia competed, the only footballs used were those of your manufacture. I heard nothing but praise of the excellence of your workmanship, and it must give you much satisfaction to know that your goods command everywhere the highest reputation.—
Yours faithfully,   (Signed), E. L. WILSON, Secretary.

To be obtained at all the Leading Sporting Goods Dealers in Australasia.   Be sure and ask for

Sherrin's "Kangaroo" Brand

Chapter 9 The Birth of Play with Pay

"PUDGE" HEFFELFINGER Guard

When you look at the records of the college teams in the early years of their sports programs, you find they did not always play other colleges. Sometimes they played associations such as the Frankford Athletic Association, a precursor of the Pirates / Steelers, and sometimes, they played high school powerhouses and they did not always win those games. Football was no different in its growth as a respected sport than other sports.

It was very popular with the many athletic clubs that proliferated in the late 19th century. Just like high school teams and prep schools and junior colleges, full four-year colleges often played athletic clubs from their area to get a good football game on a Saturday afternoon. When the pros fired up, Sunday was the only day of the weekend that was available.

These clubs were formed to compete against one another, but they had no problem saying yes to play Notre Dame or Penn State, or Alabama or any great college team of the day. Soon, the players were making real money.

The first documented professional football player was Pudge Heffelfinger. He broke the bank on November 12, 1892, when he received $500 for just one game with the Allegheny Athletic Association. There were no easy ways to record information other than pencil and paper back then, so a lot of stories and their history did not make the newspapers and, so they are lost forever. The Pudge Heffelfinger story is the exception.

It is a safe bet that many other athletes played for money but managed to keep their earnings a deep secret. In 1893, the Pittsburgh Athletic Club signed one of its players to a contract to play for the entire season. By 1896, several of the clubs from the Pittsburgh area were openly professional.

For years after college football took off, there were attempts by graduates and coaches and others to create leagues with rules and better opportunities for players and fans. The first documented attempt came in 1902 with a Pennsylvania league known as the National Football League (NFL) with no relationship to the modern-day league. A lot of the action in these endeavors came about in Pennsylvania and then later, Ohio.

John Rogers, who owned the Philadelphia Phillies baseball team, founded a football team called the Phillies in 1901. This prompted another man with some extra change in his pocket, Ben Shibe, who owned the Philadelphia Athletics to create another new team in 1902. The baseball rivals tried to get other teams to join with them to compete for a self-proclaimed "football world championship." Great ideas, however, are easier to conceive than to implement.

There was just one taker, a promoter in Pittsburgh. Out of nowhere, the National Football League was conceived, and it got a bump start. It was also a bumpy start. The three teams enjoyed being THE National Football League and they went ahead and played each other in a round-robin tournament.

The beauty of a "league" without rules is that each team, though each finished with a 2-2 record, could claim the national championship. Who could cast aspersions on three teams with equal records?

I surely do not want to make light of this effort as many of the best football players of the day participated in this league, as did three well-known baseball Hall of Famers who happened to love the emerging sport of football. Christy Mathewson, ace pitcher for the New York Giants played halfback and punter for the Pittsburgh Stars. Connie Mack, manager of the Athletics baseball team also managed the Athletics football team, and Rube Waddell one of the best left-handed pitchers in history, was a reserve lineman for Mack's squad.

Waddell put his weight in each pitch and it was enough weight for him to change sports at will, and block for the backs in this pro-league or tackle as many opponents' backs as may have made the mistake of running his way.

Think about how exciting those days had to be. There was no real NCAA and there was no real NFL to tell the players or the organizers that they needed to behave one way or another. Nobody said they had to wear stuff under their eyes during games or that they could not have a beer after practice. There was no bureaucracy with which to deal.

Nothing good happens overnight. Nothing worth having in life is easy. And, so players and investors with a lot of chutzpah chose to face the difficulties and they took up the challenge of making football, which was beginning to be very successful in American colleges, into a professional sport. Players, other than twenty-year old college kids could compete and could earn a few dollars on Sunday after they passed the hat.

The "NFL" three teams played a yearly football tournament in New York in 1902 and 1903. It was dubbed the "World Series of Football." With less than 2000 tickets sold for each game, there wasn't much evidence that there was much money to be made by running a football team. But, somehow Baseball teams were making it; but then again, baseball teams played a lot more games.

Baseball teams played games every day for six months, and that produced enough revenues that teams could afford to travel from New York to Chicago, Boston to Cincinnati, or St. Louis to

Philadelphia. The pageantry of college football drew fans in droves, and it wasn't unusual for crowds of 60,000 to see a matchup between rival schools when they could book a big stadium. That helped colleges pay to build their own stadiums and eventually pay coaches handsomely.

It was tough to do when everybody had to reach into their pockets in order to be able to put something into their pockets from pro-football. The pro game did not draw the numbers of college games with ardent fans. It was just a passing interest, so teams were forced to minimize costs in whatever ways they could.

There was no concentration on player safety in the early days so that cost nothing. The best way to reduce expenses was to limit team travel. Consequently, big entrepreneurs, who knew how to make a buck, were not stepping quickly into unorganized pro-football so they could make a killing. There was no killing to be made.

There was not much of an incentive for a nation-wide league of professional football teams in the 1910s. It made more sense to stay closer to home, with teams sponsored by local businessmen, whose chief interest was promoting their company. If local businesses were not gaining sales, they too would have abandoned pro-football in its infancy, in a heartbeat.

Over the next few years, the center focus of pro football moved from Pennsylvania to central Ohio. By 1905 there were at least seven pro teams playing in Ohio. They had great names such as the Massillon Tigers and the Canton Bulldogs. There was no really organized league, so these were independent teams. They had to fend for themselves. Though some were more successful than others, they all faced the same challenges.

Pro football needed to be profitable

Prior to television and the phone technology revolution. fans looked upon football as a great form of entertainment, even better, say some, than movie theatres. World War I soured a lot of people on life and everybody in the second decade of the twentieth century needed a pick-me-up. Football and the movies often lifted their spirits.

Nonetheless, it was tough for pro football teams to generate revenues without really good players. Since such players cost pro-teams big money, it became tougher for small football enterprises to make ends meet. Besides player raiding, steadily rising salaries made it difficult for many teams who wanted to win games and not be also-rans, to continue operating.

Finding and signing players was tough enough; but keeping them was even tougher. There were no rules for players having to stay with a team and their major opponents would often snatch players by offering bigger paydays. The poorly financed teams just as today did poorly in the standings.

There were also issues with what were known as "ringers." Knute Rockne was a ringer in his day. There were lots of other college athletes who either coached or played while still enrolled in school. The pros were offering them comparatively big bucks to move out and join them. Certain teams with lots of cash were "stockpiling" college stars to make sure their teams won. If your team could not afford the going rate, your team's talent level was at a major disadvantage.

Cooperation of the teams without a formal league framework could have resolved most of these issues in the twenty-years from 1900 to 1920 but it did not happen. The teams were more concerned about winning than cooperating.

Chapter 10 When Pro Football Was Unorganized

ORIGINAL NATIONAL FOOTBALL LEAGUE

1902
Pittsburgh Stars

Former college players and coaches wanted to keep playing football

There were no million-dollar players in the professional football ranks at the beginning of the twentieth century, but there were a lot of players and coaches who wanted to play football and hoped to get paid to play their favorite sport. Just like there are social clubs, dart clubs, shuffleboard clubs, rod and gun clubs, and a host of other clubs, before the NFL pro football league, there were a lot of athletic clubs that focused on football as it was evolving into American football.

The current NFL compiled a brief snapshot of what was going on in these early football days from 1900 to 1909 and then the Football Hall of Fame continued their work from 1910 to 2012. It is nice work and I hope the Hall of Fame picks it up again and keeps it current.

We thank these groups for putting together this very brief compendium that takes us through the Early Pro Football period right up until the formation of a league that lasted, the NFL. And, so the rest of this chapter is courtesy of the NFL and the Pro football Hall of Fame:

1900
William C. Temple took over the team payments for the Duquesne Country and Athletic Club, becoming the first known individual club owner.

1902
Baseball's Philadelphia Athletics, managed by Connie Mack, and the Philadelphia Phillies formed professional football teams, joining the Pittsburgh Stars in the first attempt at a pro football league, named the National Football League. The Athletics won the first night football game ever played, 39-0 over Kanaweola AC at Elmira, New York, November 21.

All three teams claimed the pro championship for the year, but the league president, Dave Berry, named the Stars the champions. Pitcher Rube Waddell was with the Athletics, and pitcher Christy Mathewson a fullback for Pittsburgh.

The first World Series of pro football, actually a five-team tournament, was played among a team made up of players from both the Athletics and the Phillies, but simply named New York; the New York Knickerbockers; the Syracuse AC; the Warlow AC; and the Orange (New Jersey) AC at New York's original Madison Square Garden. New York and Syracuse played the first indoor football game before 3,000, December 28. Syracuse, with Glen (Pop) Warner at guard, won 6-0 and went on to win the tournament.

1903
The Franklin (Pa.) Athletic Club won the second and last World Series of pro football over the Oreos AC of Asbury Park, New Jersey; the Watertown Red and Blacks; and the Orange AC. Pro football was popularized in Ohio when the Massillon Tigers, a strong amateur team, hired four Pittsburgh pros to play in the season-ending game against Akron. At the same time, pro football declined in the Pittsburgh area, and the emphasis on the pro game moved west from Pennsylvania to Ohio.

1904

A field goal was changed from five points to four. Ohio had at least seven pro teams, with Massillon winning the Ohio Independent Championship, that is, the pro title. Talk surfaced about forming a state-wide league to end spiraling salaries brought about by constant bidding for players and to write universal rules for the game. The feeble attempt to start the league failed. Halfback Charles Follis signed a contract with the Shelby (Ohio) AC, making him the first known black pro football player.

1905

The Canton AC, later to become known as the Bulldogs, became a professional team. Massillon again won the Ohio League championship.

1906

The forward pass was legalized. The first authenticated pass completion in a pro game came on October 27, when George (Peggy) Parratt of Massillon threw a completion to Dan (Bullet) Riley in a victory over a combined Benwood-Moundsville team. Arch-rivals Canton and Massillon, the two best pro teams in America, played twice, with Canton winning the first game but Massillon winning the second and the Ohio League championship.

A betting scandal and the financial disaster wrought upon the two clubs by paying huge salaries caused a temporary decline in interest in pro football in the two cities and, somewhat, throughout Ohio.

1909

A field goal dropped from four points to three.

1909 Shibe Park Opened. It became Connie Mack Stadium, Philadelphia

1912
A touchdown was increased from five points to six. Jack Cusack revived a strong pro team in Canton.

1913
Jim Thorpe, a former football and track star at the Carlisle Indian School (Pa.) and a double gold medal winner at the 1912 Olympics in Stockholm, played for the Pine Village Pros in Indiana.

1915
Massillon again fielded a major team, reviving the old rivalry with Canton. Cusack signed Thorpe to play for Canton for $250 a game.

1916
With Thorpe and former Carlisle teammate Pete Calac starring, Canton went 9-0-1, won the Ohio League championship, and was acclaimed the pro football champion.

1917
Despite an upset by Massillon, Canton again won the Ohio League championship.

1919

Canton again won the Ohio League championship, despite the team having been turned over from Cusack to Ralph Hay. Thorpe and Calac were joined in the backfield by Joe Guyon.

Earl (Curly) Lambeau and George Calhoun organized the Green Bay Packers. Lambeau's employer at the Indian Packing Company provided $500 for equipment and allowed the team to use the company field for practices. The Packers went 10-1.

1920

Pro football was in a state of confusion due to three major problems: dramatically rising salaries; players continually jumping from one team to another following the highest offer; and the use of college players still enrolled in school. A league in which all the members would follow the same rules seemed the answer.

An organizational meeting, at which the Akron Pros, Canton Bulldogs, Cleveland Indians, and Dayton Triangles were represented, was held at the Jordan and Hupmobile auto showroom in Canton, Ohio,

The meeting was on August 20, 1920. Just seven men, including legendary all-around athlete and football star Jim Thorpe, met with the purpose as noted above of organizing a professional football league. The meeting led to the creation of the American Professional Football Conference (APFC), the forerunner to the hugely successful National Football League.

The APFA began play on September 26, with the Rock Island Independents of Illinois defeating a team from outside the league, the St. Paul Ideals, 48-0. A week later, Dayton beat Columbus 14-0 in the first game between two teams from the APFA, the forerunner of the modern NFL.

The teams were from four states-Akron, Canton, Cleveland, and Dayton from Ohio; the Hammond Pros and Muncie Flyers from Indiana; the Rochester Jeffersons from New York; and the Rock Island Independents, Decatur Staleys, and Racine Cardinals from Illinois.

Hoping to capitalize on his fame, the members elected Thorpe president; Stanley Cofall of Cleveland was elected vice president. A membership fee of $100 per team was charged to give an appearance of respectability, but no team ever paid it. Scheduling was left up to the teams, and there were wide variations, both in the overall number of games played, and in the number played against APFA member teams.

Four other teams-the Buffalo All-Americans, Chicago Tigers, Columbus Panhandles, and Detroit Heralds-joined the league sometime during the year. As noted, on September 26, the first game featuring an APFA team was played at Rock Island's Douglas Park. A crowd of 800 watched the Independents defeat the St. Paul Ideals 48-0.

A week later, October 3, the first game matching two APFA teams was held. At Triangle Park, Dayton defeated Columbus 14-0, with Lou Partlow of Dayton scoring the first touchdown in a game between Association teams. The same day, Rock Island defeated Muncie 45-0.

By the beginning of December, most of the teams in the APFA had abandoned their hopes for a championship, and some of them, including the Chicago Tigers and the Detroit Heralds, had finished their seasons, disbanded, and had their franchises canceled by the Association.

Four teams-Akron, Buffalo, Canton, and Decatur-still had championship aspirations, but a series of late-season games among them left Akron as the only undefeated team in the Association. At one of these games, Akron sold tackle Bob Nash to Buffalo for $300 and five percent of the gate receipts. It was the first APFA player deal.

1921

At the league meeting in Akron, April 30, the championship of the 1920 season was awarded to the Akron Pros. The APFA was reorganized, with Joe Carr, of the Columbus Panhandles named president and Carl Storck, of Dayton secretary-treasurer. Carr moved the Association's headquarters to Columbus, drafted a league constitution and by-laws, gave teams territorial rights, restricted player movements, developed membership criteria for the franchises, and issued standings for the first time, so that the APFA would have a clear champion.

The Association's membership increased to 22 teams, including the Green Bay Packers, who were awarded to John Clair of the Acme Packing Company.

Thorpe moved from Canton to the Cleveland Indians, but he was hurt early in the season and played very little.

A.E. Staley turned the Decatur Staleys over to player-coach George Halas, who moved the team to Cubs Park in Chicago. Staley paid Halas $5,000 to keep the name Staleys for one more year. Halas made halfback Ed (Dutch) Sternaman his partner.

Player-coach Fritz Pollard of the Akron Pros became the first black head coach.

The Staleys claimed the APFA championship with a 9-1-1 record, as did Buffalo at 9-1-2. Carr ruled in favor of the Staleys, giving Halas his first championship.

1922

After admitting the use of players who had college eligibility remaining during the 1921 season, Clair and the Green Bay management withdrew from the APFA, January 28. Curly Lambeau promised to obey league rules and then used $50 of his own money to buy back the franchise. Bad weather and low attendance plagued the Packers, and Lambeau went broke, but local merchants arranged a $2,500 loan for the club. A public nonprofit corporation was set up to operate the team, with Lambeau as head coach and manager.

The American Professional Football Association changed its name to the National Football League on June 24. The Chicago Staleys became the Chicago Bears.

The NFL fielded 18 teams, including the new Oorang Indians of Marion, Ohio, an all-Indian team featuring Thorpe, Joe Guyon, and Pete Calac, and sponsored by the Oorang dog kennels. Canton, led by player-coach Guy Chamberlin and tackles Link Lyman and

Wilbur (Pete) Henry, emerged as the league's first true powerhouse, going 10-0-2.

Thank you to the NFL and to the Football Hall of Fame for these facts about the formation of the NFL.

Chapter 11 NFL's Fast Start from 1920 Set the Stage for the Steelers

1920 American Professional Football Association (1920 - 1922) Consisting of 12 Teams:

Canton Bulldogs	Dayton Triangles
Cleveland Indians	Akron Professionals
Rochester Jeffersons	Rock Island Independents
Massillon Tigers	Muncie Flyers
Decatur Staleys	Racine Cardinals
Hammond Pros	Buffalo All-Americans

NFL growth: One thing right after another

Americans, and in fact the whole world sports community, know that the National Football League today is a multi-billion-dollar enterprise. Few know the early history provided by the NFL et al in Chapter 8. We just learned that its origins as the American Professional Football Association were much humbler than today's millionaire players and billionaire players and luxury-box stadiums with capacities of over 100,000 fans.

Pro-football lovers look back at the league's inaugural 1920 campaign, which we know featured its birth in an Ohio auto dealership. They see strange teams such as Decatur and Muncie and the crowning of a champion that was not immediate as today in the middle of the Super Bowl Field. Instead, it took four months after the last snap was taken to get it right—back in 1921.

As promising as the pro-football scenario was in 1920, even though things looked good for the future of the pro sport, just like today, College Football dominated. Pro football remained completely overshadowed by the college game. This was tough for team owners, as we discussed. Most were in it for the profits and there were few to none.

The owners were almost literally bleeding cash because of soaring player salaries and intense bidding wars as they poached players from other squads. The owners of these independent pro teams desired a strong league using the baseball model which had worked for so long. They wanted to gain more control over the sport—and their finances. A fully functional NFL was right around the corner and it would eventually provide this stability.

As we learn in exploring the early days of American football, everything was changing to comply with Camp's rules and others—even the field size. Yes, even the field size in early American football was changing regularly but by 1920, the size had stabilized. The gridiron dimensions were the same in 1920 as today. However, the game of professional football was much different. Back then, there were no Johnny Unitas's, Charley Conerly's, Norm Van Brocklin's, Bart Starr's, Joe Namath's, Tom Brady's. Carson Wentz's, Terry Bradshaw's or Ben Roethlisberger's.

The Quarterback slot on the offense was often a running position. Forward passes were rare. Even things we take for granted today were prohibited. Can you imagine that coaching from the sidelines was not permitted?

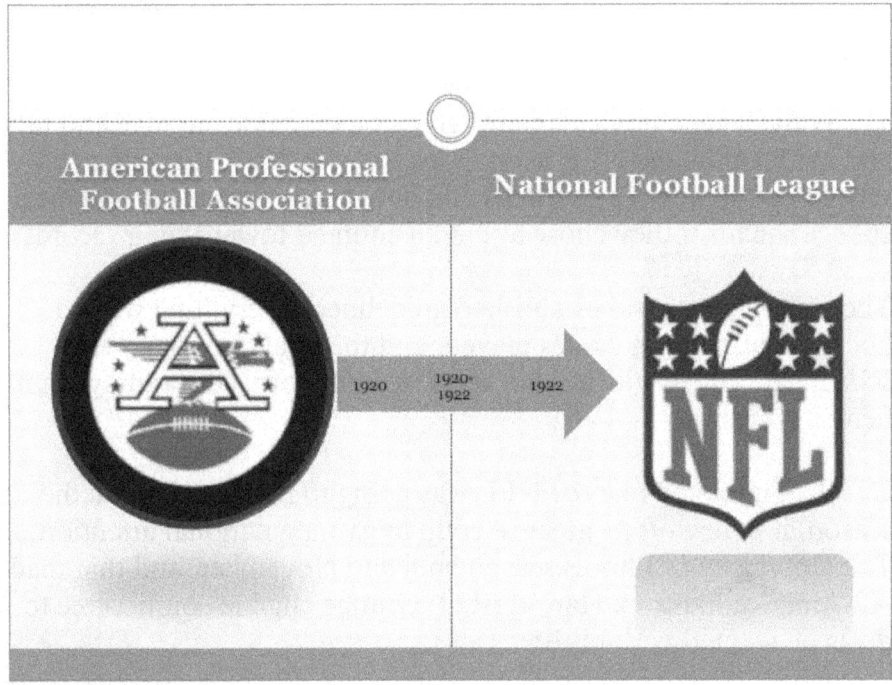

When the pass was legalized in 1906, it still was not like today. It was not readily accepted by "real teams." Established coaches in the elite Eastern schools like Army, Harvard, Pennsylvania and Yale did not embrace the pass. It was also a gamble. You had to be pretty darn good to not lose more than the potential gain.

Here are some of the stipulations. Passes could not be thrown over the line on five yards to either side of the center. An incomplete pass resulted in a 15-yard penalty, and a pass that dropped without being touched meant possession went to the defensive team. According to Kent Stephens, a historian with the College Hall of Fame in South Bend, "Because of these rules and the fact coaches at that time thought the forward pass was a sissified type of play that wasn't really football, they were hesitant to adopt this new strategy."

Each athlete played on both offense and defense. The late great Chuck Bednarik was the last consistent two-way player in the NFL, Bednarik played center and linebacker for a franchise-record 14 seasons with the Eagles from 1949 to 1962. In 1920, just about every player competed on both offense and defense. Money was so tight that the great coach of the Bears, George Halas carried equipment, wrote press releases, sold tickets, taped ankles, played and coached for the Decatur club. Having two platoons would cost twice as much.

Today the league has a standard 16-game schedule, all nice and tidy and made up by the NFL itself. Back then, in 1920, the teams scheduled their own opponents and could play nonleague and even college squads if they chose and it all counted toward their records.

There simply were no established guidelines. Everything was ad hoc—the number of games played, and the quality of opponents scheduled. The league did not even maintain official standings in its fledgling years.

By 1925, it looked like the NFL was going to make it. Late in the season, it pulled off its greatest coup in gaining national attention. The University of Illinois season ended in November, and that made All-America halfback Harold (Red) Grange eligible conflict-free to do as he wanted with his life.

Grange signed a contract to play with the Chicago Bears. On Thanksgiving Day, a crowd of 36,000, which was the largest in pro football history at the time watched Grange and the Bears play the Chicago Cardinals to a scoreless tie at Wrigley Field. At the beginning of December, the Bears hit the jackpot when they went out on the road playing all around the country in 12 days.

They actually played eight games in 12 days, in St. Louis, Philadelphia, New York City, Washington, Boston, Pittsburgh, Detroit, and Chicago. A crowd of 73,000 watched the game against the Giants at the Polo Grounds.

This helped assure the future success of the troubled NFL franchise in New York. The Bears then played nine more games in the South and West, including a game in Los Angeles, in which 75,000 fans watched them defeat the Los Angeles Tigers in the Los Angeles Memorial Coliseum. Owners, players, and coaches were ready to do anything to make sure the new league was a success.

In 1930, the league had changed its whole complexion, literally. Dayton was one of the NFL's original franchises. In 1930, it became the last of the NFL's original franchises when it was purchased by William B. Dwyer and John C. Depler, and the whole team was moved to Brooklyn, and renamed the Dodgers. They were a football team, nonetheless even with the Dodgers name. The Portsmouth, Ohio Spartans also entered the league at the same time. Things were changing rapidly

Other things were happening such as the Packers edged the Giants for the title, but the most improved team was the Bears. George Halas retired as a player and replaced himself as coach of the Bears with Ralph Jones. Jones refined the T-formation by introducing wide ends and a halfback in motion. He also brought in rookie All-America fullback-tackle, the great Bronko Nagurski.

Anybody would still play anybody. The Giants whooped a team of former Notre Dame players coached by Knute Rockne 22-0 in a successful match before 55,000 at the Polo Grounds on December 14. This was a charity game as the proceeds went to the New York Unemployment Fund to help those suffering because of the Great Depression. The easy victory helped the NFL's credibility with the press and the public. Everybody likes an act of kindness.

Carl Storck takes over the NFL as 2nd commissioner

In 1939, as the league was moving closer to 20 years in operation, Joseph Carr, who had been NFL president since 1921, died in Columbus on May 20. Carl Storck was named acting president of the NFL on May 25. Technology was about to help the NFL. The first televised NFL game saw NBC broadcast the Brooklyn Dodgers v Philadelphia Eagles game from Ebbets Field to the approximately 1,000 TV sets that were known to be in the New York Area.

Championships were beginning to be a big thing in pro-football as Green Bay defeated New York 27-0 in the NFL Championship

Game, December 10 at Milwaukee. This was the first year that NFL attendance exceeded 1 million in a season, reaching 1,071,200.

Pro Bowl gave football an All-Star Game

In 1939, The New York Giants defeated the Pro All-Stars 13-10 in the first Pro Bowl. It was played in Chicago at Wrigley Field on January 15. The NFL also decided to change the format of the field, but not the dimensions. Each field would need just a paint job. The inbounds lines or hashmarks were moved from 15 yards away from the sidelines to nearer the center of the field-20 yards from the sidelines.

Funny things were happening that were unexpected. For example, Brooklyn and Boston merged into a team that played home games in both cities and was known simply as The Yanks. Additionally, George Halas rejoined the Bears late in the season after service time with the U.S. Navy during World War II. He took over much of the coaching duties, but he kept the prior coaches throughout the season. Steve Van Buren of the Philadelphia Eagles led the NFL in rushing, kickoff returns, and scoring.

Rookie quarterback Bob Waterfield led Cleveland to a 15-14 victory over Washington in the NFL Championship Game,

At the end of World War II, after the Japanese surrender, 638 players had served in the Armed forces and 21 of them had died in action.

After the 1942 Pro-Bowl game, during the war period, the game was not played again until 1951. This classic contest was revived. On January 14, the American Conference defeated the National Conference in a nail-biter 28-27.

More rules were passed including some we might think were in the rulebook forever. For example, no tackle, guard, or center would be eligible to catch a forward pass.

The 1951 NFL Championship Game was televised coast-to-coast for the first time The Rams defeated the Browns 24-17.

Ted Collins sold the New York Yanks' franchise back to the NFL in 1952 and a new franchise was awarded to a group in Dallas after it purchased the assets of the Yanks on January 24. The new Texans went 1-11. This of course was not too good for the new owners. At the end of the season the franchise was canceled. It was the last time than an NFL team would fail.

The Pittsburgh Steelers abandoned the Single-Wing for the T-formation, the last pro team to do so. The Detroit Lions won their first NFL championship in 17 years in 1952 defeating the Browns 17-7 in the title game, played before New Year's on December 28.

In 1953 the Old Yanks came back to life again as a Baltimore group headed by Carroll Rosenbloom got the franchise and the holdings of the defunct Dallas organization. The new team became The Baltimore Colts. It was the product of the largest trade in league history, acquiring 10 players from Cleveland in exchange for five. In a cosmetic name change, American and National conferences were changed to the Eastern and Western conferences.

Another major happening was that the immortal great Jim Thorpe died on March 28. Mauch Chunk, Pennsylvania agreed to terms with Thorpe's widow to build a memorial and change the Town's name to Jim Thorpe. Thorpe's bones are buried in this beautiful memorial, which I visit every year on my annual visit to this wonderful town where Sean Connery and Richard Harris tipped a few in the filming of the Molly Maguires.

In 1956, the NFL Players Association was founded to give players a bigger voice in what was going on in the NFL. In 1959, the immortal Vince Lombardi was named coach of the Green Bay Packers and Tim Mara of New York Giants fame passed away.

The NFL was so successful, it spawned the AFL

The American Football League (AFL) was formed as a major professional American football league in 1960 and it was very successful. It was a lot of fun watching all the new teams in action.

The teams included the Dallas Cowboys, Houston Oilers, New York Jets, Kansas City Chiefs, Boston Patriots, and even John Madden's Oakland Raiders. It operated for ten seasons from 1960 until 1969, when it merged with the older National Football League (NFL), that had been established in the 1920-1922 period.

The first AFL-NFL World Championship Game in professional American football was dubbed retroactively as Super Bowl I. it had been referred to in some contemporaneous reports, including the game's radio broadcast, as the Super Bowl. The name stuck. It was played after the 1966 season on January 15 at Los Angeles Memorial Coliseum. In this game, NFL Green Bay Packers defeated the AFL champion Kansas City Chiefs by the score of 35–10.

John Madden is still a people's favorite at 83 years of age. He was hired by Al Davis when the AFL was in its prime as the linebackers' coach for the AFL's Oakland Raiders. This was in 1967 and the league would last only two more seasons. He helped the team reach Super Bowl II that season. A year later, after Raiders head coach John Rauchleft, John Madden stepped in to become the Raiders' head coach. This made Madden professional football's youngest head coach at the age of 32.

Former Raiders coach Dennis Allen in interviews noted that John Madden was arguably the best Oakland Raiders coach in the history of the team. His Raiders reached but lost five AFC Title games in seven years. This left the Raiders with the same image that the Dallas Cowboys had previously had—as a team unable to "win the big one."

Despite a 12–1–1 mark in 1969, for example the team lost 17–7 to the Kansas City Chiefs in the final American Football League championship game. The next year, the Raiders would be in the AFC Division of the NFL as the AFL lost its identity.

Was the AFL Any Good? See Super Bowl III

Super Bowl III was the third AFL–NFL Championship Game in professional American football, and the first to officially bear the name "Super Bowl". It was not AFC v NFC. It was the last interleague Super Bowl and the AFL did not win either of the first two games.

This game was played on January 12, 1969, at the Orange Bowl in Miami, Florida. Everybody over five years old at the time remembers Broadway Joe Namath, cocky as can be, making a prediction that the AFL's Jets would win the game.

This game is still regarded as one of the greatest upsets in American sports history. The heavy underdog American Football League (AFL) champion New York Jets, led by former Alabama QB Joe Namath defeated the National Football League (NFL) champion Baltimore Colts by a score of 16–7. I was a senior in College at the time. What a great football game. I watched it from pre-game through post-game.

This was the first Super Bowl victory for the AFL. Though the AFL had been in existence ten years, before the start of this game, most sports writers and fans had written off the AFL teams as being less talented than every one of the NFL clubs. There were few who expected anything less than the Colts to whoop the Jets by a wide margin.

Baltimore had posted a 13–1 record during the 1968 NFL season before defeating the Cleveland Browns, 34–0, in the 1968 NFL Championship Game. The Jets finished the 1968 AFL season at 11–3, and defeated John Madden's great Oakland Raiders, 27–23, in the 1968 AFL Championship Game. Darryl Lamonica had a poor game and Kenny, the Snake, Stabler, who took Oakland to Super XI had just joined the Raiders.

After beating the Raiders and despite the hype saying the Jets did not have a shot, Joe Namath was undaunted. This unafraid Jets quarterback made an appearance three-days before the Super Bowl at the Miami Touchdown Club and brashly guaranteed a victory. The Jets could not have been more pleased with the prediction and they backed up Broadway Joe's words by controlling most of the game. They built a 16–0 lead by the fourth quarter off of a touchdown run by Matt Snell and three field goals by Jim Turner.

Colts quarterback Earl Morrall threw three interceptions before being replaced by the great Johnny Unitas, who then led Baltimore to its only touchdown during the last few minutes of the game.

With the victory, the Jets remain the only winning Super Bowl team to only score one touchdown (either offensive, defensive, or special teams). Namath, who completed 17 out of 28 passes for 206 yards, was named as the Super Bowl's Most Valuable Player, despite not throwing a touchdown pass in the game or any passes at all in the fourth quarter. The recap of the game is not as exciting as its reality.

And that, my friends, is how the NFL got to where it is today.

Chapter 12 After the Pirates, Steelers History

Forbes Field served as the Pirates/Steelers home for most of the franchise's first thirty years.

Why don't we rename the team for good luck?

Art Rooney was a great football player who became a dedicated football manager / orchestrator. If he had been a coach longer, he would have had all he needed to know what it took to create a great team. Rooney was also a businessman and a marketeer, and these characteristics helped him keep the Pittsburgh franchise alive to fight another day.

Rooney was not a copycat as he had so many great original ideas that it bugged him that he might use anything that was a copy of anybody else's marketing idea. He began to dislike the copycat "Pirates" moniker that he had "stolen" from the Baseball Pirates. It did nothing to make his team unique. Instead it confused fans who liked baseball as well as football that the same Pirates played football in the fall and baseball in the spring. Yet, real fans knew there were two different sports and two different teams with one name.

After handling all the objections about why he should have a team with a copycat name, Art Rooney let his creative juices flow as he chose to change it. In early 1940, Rooney decided that he had had enough of the copycat Pirates moniker.

He worked with the Pittsburgh Post-Gazette to run a contest to find a new name for the old Pirates football team. Former coach Joe Bach led the naming panel. Bach and company selected the name *Steelers* from amongst the many entries. The new name paid homage to the city's largest industry of producing steel. Steel was a tough metal and the Steelers were to always be a tough team with enough mettle to handle the rigors of the NFL.

It's unclear who deserves credit for suggesting the name (which was already being used by at least one local high school team),but it appears there were a total of twenty-one "winners". Each winner received a pair of season tickets to the upcoming season, a prize with a value of about $5 ($88 today).Among them were Joe Santoni, a local restaurateur, who received a pair of season tickets as a prize, and Margaret Elizabeth O'Donnell, the girlfriend (and eventual wife) of the team's business manager, Joe Carr.

The first entrant who suggested "Steelers" was Arnold Goldberg, who was the sports editor for the Evening Standard of Uniontown, Pennsylvania. Other suggestions were Wahoos, Condors, Pioneers, Triangles, Bridgers, Buckaroos and Yankees, along with such steel-centric possibilities as the Millers, Vulcans, Tubers, Smokers, Rollers, Ingots and Puddlers. It was a great idea and a lot of fun for Pirates people. Rooney liked the fans to have a lot of fun on the Steelers.

Walt Kiesling continued to be Rooney's coach for 1940, after finishing up for McNally in 1939. The Steelers were accustomed to slow starts and 1940, name change and all, would be no different. Their slow start for the season was 0–2 even before the team fell at home by a score of 10–3 to a Brooklyn Dodgers squad coached by local hero Jock Sutherland.

It was the legendary coach's first professional victory after leaving Duquesne University in 1939. He had taken the head coaching position for the Dodgers spurning a similar offer from Rooney and the Pirates. His rejection made the loss a little more bitter for Rooney.

Rooney simply got sick of losing but he was not a coach. Over its seven years, the Pirates were 24–62–5 and had lost around $100,000 of mostly Rooney's money. Art Rooney was also concerned about getting quality players in the forthcoming seasons as the ongoing war in Europe was likely to spread and a military draft was likely.

Despite all that, Rooney did not want to sell his team and cut his losses and he said "no" quite a few times to offers that could have made him rich. But, enough became enough and even great men change their minds.

You have read enough already in this book that you know from the Steelers inception and let me suggest the Eagles were in the same boat, both squads were horrible each year. The pundits called the Eagles and the Pirates / Steelers, the bottom-feeders in the division.

As a result of loathsome teams, the very financial lifeblood of every NFL club was in danger – ghastly paid attendance. Both franchises were in trouble monetarily.

In March of 1940, the word was leaking out that the Steelers had offers from various groups in Boston, the West Coast, and Cincinnati. When it got too much after the first year operating as the Steelers, in December 1940, Rooney changed his mind to save his money and he sold the Steelers to Alexis Thompson.

Thomson was not much of a sportsman. He was a 26-year-old, Yale-educated heir to a steel fortune and an entrepreneur living in New York. To Thompson, the cost of the non-profitable franchise was not an issue if it was not a lot of work, and if he could have fun—a very important criterion for a 26-year-old.

He really wanted the Pirates or, so he thought. He had gone after Rooney for several months to get him to sell the franchise. When it was all settled, Rooney picked up a reported $160,000 ($2.8 million today).

This price was less than the $225,000 ($3.9 million today) that the Detroit Lions had gone for but then again, the Lions at the time had an enviable record and they had won an NFL championship.

Rooney needed the cash big time, but he also needed an affiliation with pro football for his spiritual side. He wasted no time taking half of his windfall proceeds and he bought a 50% interest in the Philadelphia Eagles from his buddy, Bert Bell.

The Eagles at the time, were owned by Art Rooney's good friend, Bert Bell. Bell had helped Rooney when he was considering negotiations with Thompson to make sure the sale of the Steelers was a good deal. Thompson had earlier offered to purchase Bell's franchise.

Swapping teams was an unheard of "deal."

In an unusual management maneuver, Rooney, Bell and Thompson contrived a scheme in which they pooled the rosters of the two PA teams. Rooney wanted to own a team without going broke and Bell would like to keep most of the team while getting some cash. To split the players management conducted a mini-draft in order to distribute the talent on both squads among both teams. The two impresarios hoped the big changes for both teams would result in better play. Thompson just went along, and he brought his wallet.

There were 51 players signed by the Steelers and Eagles at the end of the 1940 season. They were shuffled between the Steelers and the Eagles. In this transaction, Rooney & Bell picked up eleven players from the 1940 Steelers: ends George Platukis, Walt Kichefski and John Klumb; tackles Clark Goff and Ted Doyle; guards Carl Nery and Jack Sanders; and backs Boyd Brumbaugh, John Noppenberg, George Kiick and Rocco Pirro.

In exchange, Thompson's team gained seven players: ends Joe Carter and Herschel Ramsey, tackles Phil Ragazzo and Clem Woltman, guard Ted Schmitt, and backs Joe Bukant and Foster Watkins, all of whom had played for Bell's 1940 Eagles the prior year.

Thompson had the financial resources to hire Greasy Neale, whom Rooney had earlier pursued to coach the Pirates, to conduct this player swap as well as to assist him with the draft which took place the day after the deal with Rooney was finalized. Once he was released from his contract with Yale, Neale became head coach of Thompson's new Eagle's team.

Thompson vowed to make Pittsburgh into a winner and he paid very handsomely for new head coach Greasy Neale. In the Jan. 17, 1941 issue of the *Pittsburgh Post-Gazette*, it was reported that the club would receive its third nickname. "The local eleven would henceforth be renamed as the "Pittsburgh Iron Men," the article stated.

Thompson renamed the team while in attendance at the owner's meeting in Chicago. They were not the only Thompson changes. The entrepreneur made it known that his recently acquired club was about to relocate to Boston, but part of the agreement of the sale was that the team would play in Pittsburgh for at least one more season. Thompson did not like being inconvenienced in any way. Boston would be the most convenient locale for him.

Rooney didn't want his hometown to be without pro football so he and his buddy, Bert Bell decided that after the Iron Men would leave the steel city for Boston, the Eagles, half-owned by both men, would play home contests on both sides of the state and would be renamed as the "Keystoners." Thankfully, this was unnecessary as the two sages convinced the youngster that there was a better way for him to get what he wanted.

It helps to recall that Thompson was just a 26-year old kid with a lot of money and little experience. He really was unsure of what he wanted out of the deal, but he eventually knew what he did not want. He did not like long trips.

He set up his business shop in New York City but planned a football operations office in Pittsburgh. His timetable said that March 1, 1941 was the day. While Thompson appeared to be having misgivings, so was Rooney. He complained to anybody who would listen about a five-hour cross-state daily commute from Pittsburgh to Philadelphia –and then back to Pittsburgh. Both Thompson and Rooney were looking for something that would not happen by itself.

March came and went, and Thompson did not seem to really care about opening a Pittsburgh office. Like Rooney's grumblings, Thompson was showing signs of distance fatigue. He commented that he preferred to transfer team operations closer to home as well as his work. After tasting New York and Pittsburgh, he concluded that Philadelphia would be much more convenient to his lifestyle.

He figured that it was just as easy for a novice to make a start in one city as it would be in another, so why should it not be convenient for the person's lifestyle. Having enough money to spare helped Thompson do whatever he wanted.

He saw the less than two-hour drive from New York City to Philly as being much more favorable than the long haul to Pittsburgh. Thompson was hoping to cut more than half of the 368-mile trek to Pittsburgh from his itinerary. So that is the setup. Rooney wanted to be in Pittsburgh and Thompson wanted to be in Philadelphia. Rooney had part ownership in Philadelphia and Thompson owned Pittsburgh. Seems like there was room for a deal.

Rooney knew Thompson preferred Philadelphia and Thompson knew that Rooney preferred Pittsburgh. When some of your friends ask you if Pittsburgh and Philadelphia once swapped teams, this is the backdrop for that strange happening. Rooney contacted Thompson and made an offer. It was accepted. There would be a team swap—of sorts.

The date was Thursday April 3, 1941. Rooney made an announcement that that the Eagles would move to Pittsburgh and that the Iron Men would relocate to Philadelphia. Everything was swapped except uniforms: players, equipment, front office, and coaches without any exchange of money at all.

The fact that they already had an equitable mini-draft that preceded this helped both owners know that the swap was as fair as it could be. From this moment in April, until as late as 1945, Pittsburgh was officially owned by the "Philadelphia Football Club, Inc." Now, you know why!

With the swap, Rooney renamed the Iron Men back to the Steelers. Officially, the renamed team (Iron Men) never played a single game as the Iron Men and Rooney never spent a single season in Philadelphia. The affable Bert Bell became head coach of the Steelers and Rooney served as general manager. Once the swap was completed, there was no Boston move . It was no longer necessary and the Keystoners simply went into the bucket where ideas that

Chapter 12 After the Pirates, Steelers History

never come to fruition are stored. From that point on, Thompson owned the Eagles and the Bell / Rooney duo owned the Steelers.

It was not too long for Rooney to begin to regret his decision to sell the team that he had founded. He loved football. This swap of teams is still unprecedented in football, but it was real, and the machinations involved helped Art Rooney get back a Pittsburgh team.

Rooney was alerted as to the possibilities when he observed that Thompson had not yet established a local office for his team, as he had announced he would do by March 1. Like other offers you've heard about during the years, Rooney made an offer that Thompson could not refuse and now you know the rest of the story.

For two other people, who were not trying to make their personal lives better, the swap and the mini-draft, etc. would seem like a farce. But for Rooney and Thompson, it was an unexpected gift from heaven,

The rationale for the swap was that two owners out of three wanted a change for the better in their personal lives, that would be impacted by a big change in their business circumstances. This entire strange turn of events took place during the off-season and so if you were alive and not into pro football organizations at the time, you might have missed it.

The Steelers never actually missed a single game in Pittsburgh, though they almost played games in Boston or Philadelphia. Since nothing really changed despite ownership realignments, The NFL still considers the Rooney reign at Pittsburgh as unbroken. The transaction, after the fog cleared amounted Bert Bell selling the Eagles off and purchasing half-interest in the Steelers. Pundits with a sense of humor have termed this strange happening, the "Pennsylvania Polka.

What about the Steagles?

Though Pittsburgh had a team and so did Philadelphia in 1941, the owners had swapped teams. Pittsburgh's players were those drafted by Philadelphia and Philadelphia's players were those drafted by Pittsburgh in the unique owner-sponsored mini draft that had already occurred at the end of the 1940 season.

Neither Rooney nor Bell wanted a losing team; but their combined finances had not improved any more than when Rooney owned Pittsburgh by himself. So, to get a better team, Rooney and Bell conducted a coaching search seeking "one of the top men of the coaching profession."

Pete Cawthon was the favorite candidate. He was interviewed for the job. Cawthon had recently left Texas Tech after a successful 12-year run. "Buff" Donelli was also in consideration. He was the head coach for the Duquesne University's football team. Duquesne was a University with Pittsburgh roots.

In the end, Bell, who knew how to coach but had always delivered poorly on wins, declared himself head coach of the team. That was not looked upon by many as a coaching upgrade as Bell had coached the Eagles to five straight losing seasons. Nonetheless, Bell was an owner and he loved the idea of being the Pittsburgh coach. This move had the advantage of eliminating the necessity for the owners from having to make promises to a new coach, when the US was about to enter a big war, and all bets on teams surviving would be off.

Walt Kiesling, who had been the Steelers coach the previous season, stayed on as Bell's assistant. The Steelers did not do well in the past and under Bell it looked like there would be more of the same. Bell agreed to step down only if Rooney could convince Buff Donelli from Duquesne to take over the team, but Rooney could not pull it off in time.

Donelli and Rooney were later able to work out a nice deal with the Duquesne administrators that permitted Donelli to keep his head coaching job at Duquesne, with the idea that he would be permitted to coach the Steelers in his "spare moments.".

The time split was that Donelli would coach Pittsburgh in the morning and the Duquesne in the afternoon. He would spend Saturday coaching on the sidelines for the Dukes and Sunday coaching the Steelers. Sometimes out of the box thinking is good. Sometimes, not. At least Bert Bell would be off the sidelines if they pulled this off and at the time, that was good.

The NFL, however, did not like the deal at all. This highly unusual situation did not sit well with new NFL commissioner Elmer Layden (for whom Donelli had played when Layden was the coach at Duquesne). Layden believed that it was "impossible, physically and mentally, to direct two major football teams at the same time."

Donelli stepped down as coach at Duquesne to ameliorate Layden. But, he retained the title of athletic director at the school and his schedule changed little, if at all. It was a ruse. He continued to attend all of Duquesne's practices and games and continued to be acknowledged as the coach, if not in title.

Donelli was more active as a coach under these circumstances than anybody would have thought possible. He replaced the single-wing offense the Steelers had employed since their founding with his "wing-T", which was a variation on the T formation. Change, even good changes, are seldom good for a team's short-term record right as the changes are made. When he got the reins, he coached the Steelers to five straight losses, even while his college team, which had been using his system for years, flourished.

In early November 1941, Donelli faced a big dilemma: Duquesne was scheduled to play Saint Mary's College of California on the same weekend the Steelers had a contest in Philadelphia. Layden, representing the NFL, ordered Donelli to appear on the sidelines in Philly. Donelli chose to stick with the undefeated college squad and stepped down as head coach of the winless Steelers. What a bummer.

The Steelers' now had an obvious coaching position vacancy and because he was a great friend of the Steelers, the job was again handed over to Kiesling. In Kiesling's second game of this second stint as the Steelers' leader, he led the team to a victory over Jock Sutherland's Brooklyn Dodgers.

This was a big victory for Pittsburgh because of Sutherland's prior snub. The Steelers struggled getting anything real together with this one and only victory in a 1–9–1 season. It matched the team's worst record to date. Looking for other bright spots, this was the Steelers first campaign in which they were never shut out.

Art Rooney was quite a quip and he made a lot of statements that were highly quotable. Some pundits have characterized the most enduring event of the 1941 season as an off-hand remark that Rooney made to a reporter during the team's training camp. Art Rooney, representing the owners' interests was visiting camp and quipped to a reporter, "They look like the Steelers to me—in green jerseys." Rooney was well aware of the struggles Pittsburgh had in making the grade over the years. So, this "jab" was taken as a reference to the club's poor performance throughout its existence.

You know the story of lining up twenty grade schoolers and giving the first one a line to remember and then hearing the line after being filtered by twenty ears and minds and mouths later. It was never the same. Well, the Rooney snide remark would morph into the slogan "Same Old Steelers. This eternal jab was applied by fans as a sort of unofficial team motto throughout the team's consistent struggles over the subsequent thirty years, trying to make something of themselves.

Nobody was joking about the prospects of the US entering a World War, however. Within weeks of the end of the 1941 season, America entered World War II. Nothing was as important as the war effort. America and all businesses and all sports endeavors and entertainment mechanisms were focused on America winning the big war. This war affected everything in the nation, including of course, the NFL and all of its teams, though some teams more than others.

The military draft was not as necessary as the government thought as most "boys" who were surely men, such as my father and his five brothers enlisted or tried to enlist to help the American war effort. Such patriotism was last seen in World War II, and of course the Revolutionary War of Independence. Of course, there were also a large share of American heroes in Korea and Vietnam.

The Congress wanted to make sure there were enough GIs available to defeat the enemy and so they made enlistment in the service obligatory for those who qualified. The Selective Training and Service Act of 1940 had already instituted conscription in late 1940. However, the NFL was not significantly impacted until after the United States joined the war big-time following Pearl Harbor attack December 7, 1941.

Because no potential soldier knew their status for the coming year, Rooney and Bell lobbied to delay the 1942 NFL Draft due to the uncertainty of the war situation, but they were overruled by their fellow owners as it looked like full deployment was not going to occur in 1942.

The Steelers had the first overall pick, due to their last-place showing the previous season. They chose Virginia halfback "Bullet" Bill Dudley the first pick. They then rounded out the football draft by choosing as many married players as possible with an eye toward the likelihood those players might avoid the military draft, at least for the upcoming season. Everything was "iffy" and businesses still needed to survive—even those providing entertainment to the masses such as the NFL.

Pittsburgh lost several players who had filled key roles the previous year to the military, including quarterbacks Johnny Patrick and Rocco Pirro, leading runner Art Jones and budding tackle Joe Coomer. The team's first-round pick, Bill Dudley was very iffy, like many young men who intended as well to join the military rather than play football.

Yet, when Dudley enlisted in September 1942 there was such a backlog of recruits that his induction was delayed by a few months. So, he chose to sign with the Steelers for $5,000 ($74,888 today) while he waited to be called. For Dudley it was a better deal than working as a waiter or washing cars.

Pittsburgh began the season not knowing how they could ever finish it. After a slow start, losing their first two games, the 1942 squad then had a fire lit under them as they awaited a resolution of their own Selective Service Status and their own enlistments.

This team was a lot tougher than prior Steeler teams. They won seven of their next eight contests. Nothing is ever sure even if great effort is expended. Pittsburgh finished their 1942 season with a loss to the vaunted Green Bay Packers to put a sour cap on an otherwise nice 7–4 season. This was like a revival for Pitt as it put them in second place in the NFL Eastern Division right behind the Washington Redskins. The Skins went on to capture the league title.

From 1933 to 1942, in all those ten years of Pittsburgh pro football,.1942 was the first winning record the club had ever recorded. Dudley became the second Steeler to lead the league in rushing with 696 yards on 162 attempts.[102] The "triple-threat" back also snagged 35 passes for 438 yards and he could also punt the ball and he achieved 18 punts.

In terms of comparison to other stars in the league, he was runner-up to Green Bay's Don Hutson for the Joe F. Carr Trophy which was a big deal at the time. It was awarded to the NFL's most valuable player.

Still concerned about the war and its impact on NFL players, at the annual league meeting held on the same weekend as the 1942 NFL Championship Game, the league's owners discussed canceling the entire 1943 season. There were a number of issues and of course there was the major issue of player availability due to the war, and there was concern about whether it would be good for the country to have such a season of entertainment in which strong men would participate.

Instead they chose to delay the decision, along with the college draft, until the following April. At the April meeting roster sizes were reduced from 33 to 25 players. Additionally, the Cleveland Rams announced that they would suspend operations for the season since the team's two top executives were serving in the military. Of course, Teddy Roosevelt was always a great football advocate and he wanted football to continue in the WWI period. Like his cousin, Franklin Roosevelt liked sports also but was not necessarily fascinated as much by football.

His boyhood love of baseball helped make it no surprise that Roosevelt would come to baseball's defense when the question arose soon after the Japanese attack on Pearl Harbor. Should the "national pastime" be suspended when the United States became fully engaged in World War II.

As expected, the President declared that professional baseball should continue. And so, it did, throughout the war, even though most of its players, including some future Hall of Famers, traded their baseball cleats for combat boots and hoped that their prowess on the field would not be missed during their time in service.

To Play or Not to Play?

In the late 1930s and early 1940s, America was in love with baseball, a welcome respite from the Great Depression and the war clouds forming over Europe. But many of the big stars of the 1920s and 1930s had already retired by the time fans bade a tearful farewell to the fatally ill Lou Gehrig, even as the stars of the 1940s and 1950s were emerging. Roosevelt voted "play ball."

The National archives tell the story of Roosevelt's love for the national past-time during the war, but they say little about football. However, one just need go back to 1933 after Roosevelt first took office to see what he thought about football. He was not the first president to use sports analogies to help explain his political and economic agenda. The following quote gives FDR's perspective on sports. It was made at a press conference on April 19, 1933—just six weeks after he took office— He likened himself to a football quarterback when he responded to a question about his administration's evolving policy on inflation:

"It is a little bit like a football team that has a general plan of game against the other side. Now, the captain and the quarterback of that team know pretty well what the next play is going to be, and they know the general strategy of the team; but they cannot tell you what the play after the next play is going to be until the next play is run off. If the play makes ten yards, the succeeding play will be different from what it would have been if they had been thrown for a loss. I think that is the easiest way to explain it."

The people loved the image of FDR as a quarterback and the notion became a popular metaphor in political cartoons and presidential ephemera. Seen on the next page is an example—a postcard made by Hilborn Novelty Advertisement entitled, "Our President."

Note that the picture on the page above shows FDR's head superimposed over a football player's body. The player is aptly given the number 32, for the 32nd president:

Moving along with the Steeler's struggles during the war, their roster continued in 1943 to be decimated throughout the off-season. By late May, they were down to just five players under contract who would be available to play in the upcoming season. Rooney and Bell reached out to Alexis Thompson's Philadelphia Eagles to discuss the possibility of combining the two squads in 1943.

They agreed and submitted a proposal to the League. At a league meeting in June, the Chicago Bears and the Chicago Cardinals sprung a similar request of their own. The league owners were concerned about the effect on league standings and voted down the two mergers believing that a combination of team resources would gain an unfair advantage.

Rooney and Bell were better negotiators than coaches. They then lobbied the Chicago clubs to withdraw their request, which they eventually agreed to do. After a contentious debate the owners then voted by a narrow 5–4 margin to allow the Steelers and Eagles to merge operations for the upcoming season and retain their own players thereafter.

Once they gained approval, the name of the team was officially the Eagles, but it was to have no city designation. The folks began to call it the Phil-Pitt "Steagles.". The club did its best to get along and it split its home dates between the two cities with four games played in Philadelphia and two in Pittsburgh. Walt Kiesling shared coaching duties with Eagles coach Greasy Neale, who was to become one of the greatest Philadelphia coaches of all time.

In terms of how they played football, the Steagles adopted the T formation, shown to be effective by the Chicago Bears. Many of the Steagles players were those men who had been classified 4-F by the Selective Service. This meant that they were judged as unfit for military service for reasons that would not inhibit them from playing football. Common ailments were ulcers, perforated eardrums and poor eyesight or hearing.

One of the problems the owners did not necessarily expect was that co-coaches Neale and Kiesling disliked each other intensely. In order to avoid coaching together, they split coaching responsibility along the lines of offense and defense. This accommodation presaged the rise of the modern offensive and defensive coordinator positions that are near universal in the modern game of football.

The Steagles team had a winning season in their only year of existence, with a 5–4–1 record. It was the first winning record in the Eagles' history, and just the second the Steelers had enjoyed. They missed the playoffs and the team disbanded into their original franchises immediately upon the season's end. Pittsburgh still needed some help after 1943 but the Eagles were able to get by after the dissolution of the Steagles.

Card-Pitt

Philadelphia stayed separate from further temporary mergers. However, Pittsburgh still was looking for player help. In 1944, the Steelers merged again. This time, the partner team was the Chicago Cardinals. The combined team was known in the 1944 season as "Card-Pitt."

Of course, the nick-namers were out in force and so the team was informally known as the "Car-Pitts" or "Carpets." They played like an old wet carpet that year and were winless through the entire season. The Steelers separated from the Cards for the 1945 season and Pittsburgh won two games, 2–8. But in 1946, things seemed like they would go back to "normal." Dudley was back from the war for the 1946 season and he had not lost his skills. He became league MVP. The rest of team did no better than in the past, however, and the Steelers had a tough time down the stretch, finishing at 5–5–1.

Chapter 13 The 1940's & 1950' Same Old Steelers

Vintage Pittsburgh Pirates / Steelers

A few signs of brilliance

The Steelers showed some signs of brilliance in the later 1940's, though it was not a recurring theme. They made the playoffs for the first time in 1947, tying for first place in the division at 8–4 with the Eagles. There was a tie-breaking playoff game at Forbes Field, which the Steelers lost 21–0. The playoff game between the Eagles and the Steelers in 1947 was an anomaly and never happened again.

Top Steelers Players Johnny Clement

Halfback, Quarterback... In 1960, the American Football league formed and their eight team league was very successful. The NFL began merger talks and by 1970, the NFL expanded to include all the former AFL teams.

The Steelers and Eagles were placed in different conferences after the 1970 merger so the 1947 game was the only time that the two major Pennsylvania cities played each other in the NFL playoffs. Steelers Quarterback Johnny Clement, who was one of few people to ever wear number "0" actually finished second in the league in rushing yardage with 670.

That would be Pittsburgh's last playoff game for 25 years. In the 1948 off season, coach Jock Sutherland died. The team struggled through the season (one quarterback, Ray Evans, threw 17 interceptions to only five touchdowns) and finished 4–8. The team once again faded down the stretch in 1949 after a strong start, ending with a 6–5–1 record.

In 19480, Pittsburgh drafted Bobby Layne but for some reason could not keep him. Layne did not want to play for the Steelers, because they were the last team in the NFL to use the single-wing formation, so his rights were quickly traded to the Chicago Bears. That was followed up in 1950 with a 6–6 season, and consecutive losing seasons in 1951 (4–7–1) and 1952 (5–7).

After a 6–6 season in 1953 and 5–7 season in 1954, the Steelers drafted Johnny Unitas in 1955. Having watched Unitas and Charley Conerly of the Giants as a kid, I know that Unitas could have helped a lot. However, Johnny Unitas was cut by the Steelers in training camp. He was a great QB and later became a Super Bowl hero for the Baltimore Colts. Unitas for Pittsburgh was the good luck that the team was seeking for a long time, but they refused to recognize it.

On the way through the 1950's the Steelers suffered another two losing seasons before a 6–6 campaign in 1957 in the first season for coach Buddy Parker. Another highlight of 1957 showed the growth of inclusiveness in football as Pittsburgh hired the first NFL African American coach, Lowell Perry to coach the pass catching crew. He became the Steelers receivers coach.

From day one Pittsburgh home games were played almost exclusively at Forbes Field, The Steelers began to play at Pitt Stadium from 1958 through 1969. From 1958 to 1963, the Steelers split home games between Forbes Field and Pitt Stadium. Season tickets were less expensive, but the packages were for just half the games. Fans were able to purchase season ticket packages for one site or the other. In 1964, Pittsburgh began to play home games exclusively at Pitt Stadium, which they continued until they moved into the new Three Rivers Stadium in 1970.

I can remember pictures of Bobby Lane, the QB with no facemask as a kid on football cards. Early in the 1958 season the Steelers traded for Layne, who had led the Detroit Lions to two NFL championships.

Here's what happened back then. After the second game of the 1958 season, Pittsburgh Steelers coach Buddy Parker, formerly of Detroit, arranged a trade on October 6 that brought Layne to the Steelers. This was Pittsburgh's second chance with the great Bobby Layne.

During his eight seasons in Detroit, after being traded by Pittsburgh, the Lions won three NFL championships and Layne played in four Pro Bowls. Layne made first team All-Pro twice, and at various times led the league in over a dozen single-season statistical categories.

Following the trade, Layne played five seasons with the Pittsburgh Steelers. Though he made the Pro Bowl two more times, he never made it back to the playoffs, and the team's best finish was second in the conference in 1962. Nonetheless, the results of Layne being with the Steelers were immediate. The Steelers went 7–4–1 for the best record in nine years, though they still missed the playoffs by two games.

The Steelers finished above .500 again with a 6–5–1 record in 1959. After a 5–6–1 season in 1960, Rudy Bukich took over the starting QB job during the 1961 season but fared no better. Pittsburgh finished 6–8.

What happened in the 1960s?

Bobby Layne was back as the full-time starting quarterback position and running back John Henry Johnson had the best season of his career with 1,141 yards (second in the NFL). Pittsburgh did a lot of work on their defense also, picking up Clendon Thomas from the Los Angeles Rams. Clendon led the Steelers with seven interceptions. Ernie Stautner anchored the defensive line. The Steelers had their best season ever, finishing 9–5. They got a second place in the division, and a spot in the Playoff Bowl, The Steelers lost the playoffs in a good show, 17–10, to the Detroit Lions.

After a 7-4-3 season in 1963, with Ed Brown as the QB replacing Bobby Layne, the next few years were total disasters. Over the last four years of the decade, the Steelers never finished higher than 5–8–1 (1966), with the team using eight quarterbacks between 1965 and 1969.

Showing how deep the troubles were, and how unlucky the Pirates were in cashing in from home-growns born in their own back-yard, you will find this hard to believe. Western Pennsylvania had long been an area producing fine quarterbacks, but the Steelers could not manage to keep them home. .They somehow all slipped away.

The great Johnny Unitas, for example, was a native of Pittsburgh. The great George Blanda also came from the Pittsburgh area, but the Steelers never signed him. The nearby town of Beaver Falls produced Babe Parilli and later Joe Namath. Both became stars in the AFL with the Patriots and the Jets respectively. The Steelers did sign another future Hall-of-Famer, close-by Ohio native Len Dawson, but would let him go as well, before he began a great career with the Kansas City Chiefs. Jack Kemp, a Los Angeles native, was also on the Steelers' roster before being cut.

Finally, the Steelers hit Gold and black of course when they signed Terry Bradshaw in 1970. By the time Western Pennsylvania had also produced future Hall-of-Famers Joe Montana, Dan Marino and Jim Kelly, Bradshaw and his teammates have long since turned the Steelers from what was often called a laughingstock into one of the NFL's most successful and beloved franchises of all time.

Chapter 14 Three Great Coaches – Noll, Cowher, & Tomlin, 1969 >>>

1970s: The Steel Curtain

Nobody has magic as magic does not really exist but even the great Alabama coach Bear Bryant believed that a little luck always helped out in football games. For many years, the Steelers had a talent void, but they also had bad luck in games and in knowing which draftees and new trades to keep for the team.

The good news in the Steelers story is that the team eventually forgot how to lose, and they forgot how to play consistently poor football. The Pittsburgh Steelers are a modern-day phenomenon. And, the luck began to change the year I graduated from college—1969.

Pittsburgh luck did begin to change for the better with a single act. The management team hired coach Chuck Noll in early 1969, though he too won only a single game in his first season. The Steelers worst since 1941). As noted previously in this book, Joe Paterno had turned down the job before it was offered to Noll. Chuck Noll was nothing short of fantastic as a coach.

Dan Rooney was the Pittsburgh executive who turned Pittsburgh around. It was his role to develop a winner out of what existed in the Steelers organization in the 1960's.

One must look back as we have been doing in this historical section to the thirty odd years before Dan Rooney took over the reins of the Steelers. It was no secret that Pittsburgh was looked upon as perennial losers. Dan's father, Art Rooney, was beloved by all, but he had done a terrible job of running the Steelers. Though Art Rooney loved football, his real passion and interests were in boxing and horse racing. To him, the Steelers were little more than a hobby.

It is easy to know why. Back when the senior Rooney bought the Steelers in 1933, pro football was a novelty. There were no guarantees and there was very little money in the game. There was no TV revenue, and attendance depended more on the weather than the talent on your team.

Boxing and horse racing on the other hand for Art Rooney, were real and he was good at making a buck at both. These "sports" were much more lucrative than pro football, and so it is very understandable why Art Rooney concentrated his efforts on those sports.

But all that changed for the Rooney family and for Pittsburgh, when Dan Rooney took control of the team in the late 1960s. One of his first moves was to hire Chuck Noll as the team's coach.

Joe Gilliam, Terry Bradshaw & Terry Hanratty Pittsburgh QBs
Terry Bradshaw won four Super Bowls for the Steelers, repeating as champions twice.

Chuck Noll figured out how to draft the new college talent and he also knew how to make great football players from this talent. He brought in "Mean" Joe Greene in 1969, Terry Bradshaw and Mel Blount in 1970, Jack Ham in 1971, Franco Harris in 1972, and Mike Webster, Lynn Swann, John Stallworth, and Jack Lambert in 1974.

According to the NFL Network, 1974 is the best draft class in the history of the NFL. Webster, Swann, Stallworth, & Lambert all were future Hall of Fame inductees, and all four won four Super Bowl Championships. This group of players formed the base of one of the greatest teams in NFL history. Terry Bradshaw is still around as a TV sportscaster still showing the chutzpah of a great man and a great field general. Nothing great happens overnight. In 1971, for example, with Chuck Noll as his coach. Bradshaw threw 22 interceptions during a 6–8 season. He learned quickly under Noll and became one of the greatest ever.

Three Rivers Stadium became the Steelers' home in 1970.

The Immaculate Reception

Rookie Franco Harris joined the Steelers in 1972. It was not long before he was viewed as a talented veteran rather than a greenhorn rookies. While proving himself, he helped prove that Pittsburgh was something as he ran for 1,055 yards and scored 11 touchdowns in his first season. Pittsburgh finished 11–3 in 1972. Chuck Noll's Steelers, with that rascal QB, Terry Bradshaw came in first place in the AFC Central, and they made the big-time NFL playoffs for the first time since 1947.

<<< Franco Harris pic in 2009.

The Steelers were feeling their oats after their fine 1972 season, and they began 1973 with an 8–1 start.

They forgot their bravado at the end of the season and encountered a losing streak that cost them home games during the playoffs. They lost a tiebreaker to Cincy for first place in the division at 10–4.

Then, they found themselves on the road to Oakland for the first round of the playoffs and they were beaten L (14-33). The new Chuck Noll Steelers would never forget that bitter taste of defeat.

There was this thing in the seventies in Pittsburgh known as the **Steel Curtain**. It seemed to appear overnight, and among other things, it meant the Steelers could no longer lose big games and would not take little games lightly. The Steel Curtain came mostly from Chuck Noll's selections in the 1974 NFL draft. With the Steel Curtain, the Steelers were enabled to reach the top for the first time. They were Super Bowl Champions in 1974. Who would ever have thought that of Art Rooney and Bert Bell's old Pirates.

As good as he was, Terry Bradshaw was not as perfect in his early years. And, so the guy we may hail today as the best Steeler ever, was benched in 1974 for poor performance early in the season and Chuck Noll replaced his star with Joe Gilliam, who was a pretty darn good quarterback. Eventually, Pittsburgh stuck Bradshaw back into the starting lineup when Gilliam did not win favor with Chuck Noll for a number of reasons.

After so many poor seasons there were those who saw a 10-3-1 season as inadequate for the Steelers in 1974. Nonetheless, they did finish 10-3-1, and with that record, they walked away with the division title. Their new guy, just with a season or so of vintage, "Mean" Joe Greene won Defensive Player of the Year honors.

After whooping the Buffalo Bills and the Oakland Raiders with relative ease in the AFC playoffs, the Steelers met the Minnesota Vikings in New Orleans for Super Bowl IX. It was their first big dance and they were all looking for big rings and fat cigars. The new Steelers did not relate at all to the guys who once were the laughingstocks of the NFL.

The game was not E-Z. It was a defensive struggle. The Steelers managed the only score in the first half. It was a safety when the Steel Curtain sacked the legendary Fran Tarkenton in the end zone.

In the second half, the Steelers scored a real touchdown after a fumbled kickoff and then clinched this close match with a late Larry Brown TD. The Steelers defense gave up little and won 16-6. The Steelers had finally earned an NFL league championship after 42 years of futility. Whatever the Steelers had suffered from 1933 onward, they found the cure that day, when they won Super Bowl IX. It would not be their last trip to glory.

Pittsburgh under Chuck Noll and Terry Bradshaw were like Bill Belichick and Tom Brady but before their time. They led the team to an 11-game winning streak the next year. They had read their own press clippings and they knew they were on the mark. Their stats showed they meant business as the team gave up no more than twenty points in just two games. Try to score on the Steelers, I dare you.

The Steelers got all the accolades. Mel Blount got the award for AFC Defensive Player of the Year; Franco Harris ran for 1,246 yards (second behind O.J. Simpson), and Lynn Swann caught 11 touchdown passes from the inimitable Terry Bradshaw. Even the pundits credited Terry Bradshaw with being much better than his performance of previous seasons. He was un-stoppable and his passes had destiny written on them. He claimed 2,055 passing yards, 18 TDs, and only nine interceptions. His Steelers finished 12–2. It was the best record in the AFC.

In the playoffs, Pittsburgh was ready for anything. They first whooped the Baltimore Colts 28–10 in the first round, and then they came back after surviving a late scare from the Oakland Raiders in a game in which Lynn Swann suffered a concussion, only to win 16–10 in the AFC Championship. Pittsburgh was no laughingstock.

After so great a season and playoffs, the Steelers were in their second straight Super Bowl. This time, the opponent was the "vaunted" Dallas Cowboys in Miami. It did not begin as Art Rooney would have scripted. The Steelers were down 10–7 in the fourth quarter, and they needed to begin some action to win the game. So, they did!

Roy Gerela kicked two field goals and Terry Bradshaw threw a 64-yard touchdown pass to Lynn Swann to put Pittsburgh in the lead for good. The Cowboys did come back with a touchdown, as the immortal Roger Staubach was no slouch and he knew how to win games. But, Tom Landry's Dallas could not claim the cigar as Staubach threw a last-second interception that sealed a 21–17 win for the Steelers.

In this game, even the walking wounded performed well as Lynn Swann, who had returned not 100% from his injuries, racked up four receptions for 161 yards and a TD in this great Super Bowl victory, earning him the title of game MVP. How about that?

The Steelers were on their way to greater things, but even as talented and as determined Pittsburgh had become, they had not become invincible. Every now and then, but not too often, things slowed down. The Steelers experienced odds even they could not overcome. But, none of their future battles were ever as bad as the odds they faced in their startup period in the 1930's, 1940's, 1950's, 1960's and into the 1970's. The Steelers had arrived and like Rocky Marciano, they would either be contenders or champions but nothing in between. They would punch their opponents arms so hard and so long, that eventually they would score and win the game.

Now, after this great Super Bowl victory. The Steelers had become two-time defending champions. Nonetheless, they got off to a rough start in 1976, losing four of their first five games. The team regrouped and, based on their powerful defense, won their last nine regular season games, five of which were shutouts.

For the third consecutive year, a Steelers player (this time Jack Lambert) won the AFC Defensive Player of the Year award. Pittsburgh finished 10–4 and blew out the Colts 40–14 in the divisional playoffs. In the AFC Championship, an injury-plagued Steeler team lost 24–7 to their perennial playoff nemeses and eventual Super Bowl champions, the Raiders with the late great Kenny the Snake Stabler as QB and John Madden at the helm. .

Pittsburgh's 1977 season was a relative disappointment. Bradshaw was off the mark and threw more interceptions than touchdowns. Fullback Rocky Bleier had only half as productive a season as he did in 1976, and the famed Steel Curtain defense gave up nearly twice as many points. The team still won the division at 9–5 but lost 34–21 to the Denver Broncos in the divisional playoff. Nonetheless, the Steelers were still headed for greater things.

Pittsburgh kicked off their 1978 season with controversy. During mini-camp after the draft, they were caught wearing shoulder pads in violation of league rules. One might simply call that rule violation, stupid. It did not matter what fans thought. The NFL was tough in assuring its rules were kept, whether the rules made sense to the teams or not.

Pittsburgh paid the price by losing a draft pick the following year for the infraction. The Steelers were at their best for the whole season with just two losses. They posted a 14–2 regular season record, best in the NFL. In the playoffs, the Steelers blew away the Denver

Broncos and Houston Oilers by a combined score of 67–15 en-route to an engagement in Super Bowl XIII.

The Super Bowl was more or less a rematch with the Cowboys. It is considered by many pundits to be one of the greatest Super Bowls of all time. Terry Bradshaw was almost perfect, throwing for four touchdowns. However, the Cowboys did not retreat and stayed in the game. One of the things that kept the Cowboys alive was a Steelers fumble and a Dallas recovery for a touchdown by Mike Hegman.

After Swann and Harris scored touchdowns 19 seconds apart in the fourth quarter, the Cowboys countered with scores of their own by Billy Joe Dupree and Butch Johnson to pull within four points with 22 seconds left. The Steelers recovered the Dallas onside kick and pulled off a 35–31 win. Terry Bradshaw was honored as the game MVP. The Steelers grabbed their third Lombardi Trophy -- Super Bowl Championship.

The 1979 season was Bradshaw's best, but it was the last season of the Steel Curtain dynasty. Let's enjoy recounting this great season. Bradshaw threw for over 3,700 yards and 26 touchdowns. John Stallworth snagged a ton of passes for 1183 yards receiving. The Steelers finished 12–4, once again tops in the AFC Central. In the playoffs they pounded the Dolphins 34–14 and the Oilers 27–13, and they met the Los Angeles Rams in their fourth Super Bowl engagement in the 1970's

The Rams were part Steeler and they understood the Steelers organization, having a number of ex-Steelers staff members in their team setup. Thus, they knew the Steelers play book – basic plays, audibles, and even silent hand signs. With this advantage, they played the Steelers hard for three quarters. Bradshaw had some issues before the fourth quarter, throwing three interceptions. However, he made up for it somewhat with two long touchdown passes in the second half (one to Swann and one to Stallworth). The Rams couldn't recover from this bombardment and Pittsburgh won their fourth Super Bowl 31–19.

Right after the nineteen-seventies, the Steelers would suffer what pundits have referred to as a decade of decline. It took a long while for the Steelers to climb out of this hole. It was a big rip in a steel curtain that basically disappeared during this time. Still, it was not as bad as their early years, especially the time when the Steelers were known as the Pirates.

Players get older and they are not as good as they age, and many choose to retire when their time comes. The Steelers were hit with the retirements of all their key players from the Super Bowl years, with Rocky Bleier after the 1980 season, "Mean Joe" Greene and L. C. Greenwood after the 1981 season, Lynn Swann and Jack Ham after 1982, Terry Bradshaw and Mel Blount after 1983, Jack Lambert and Franco Harris after 1984 and John Stallworth after 1987. Not only were these great names gone but the replacements did not measure up to the same job level that once had been done.

Moving through the 1980s

The big-win seasons from the 1970's were over as the Steelers finished the 1980 season at 9-7, and 1981 at 8-8. The dynasty had ended. Chuck Noll decided to change the defense to a 3-2 to handle the league's new pass-oriented rules. In the strike shortened 1982 season, the Steelers did well at 6-3 but lost in the playoffs when Kellen Winslow caught two touchdowns in the 4th quarter of their first playoff game, a 31–28 loss to the San Diego Chargers.

Bradshaw was out most of the 1983 season (his last). Cliff Stoudt was the QB in lieu of Bradshaw. picking up the reins behind center. Franco Harris ran for 1,007 yards in his last season in Pittsburgh. Harris would play for Seattle in his final year. Keith Willis recorded a career-best 13 sacks.

The streaky Steelers lost four of their last five regular season games, but their team record was 10–6 and it was good for a division title. The Steelers finished the regular season with an emotional victory against the New York Jets in the last football game ever played at Shea Stadium. Bradshaw, finally returned from injury, and he led the Steelers with two touchdown passes. Unfortunately, he left the game in the first half after hearing a "pop" in his elbow when making the final pass of his NFL career, a touchdown. After this win, the

Steelers quickly were eliminated from the playoffs with a 38–10 poor showing against the Los Angeles Raiders.

The Steelers' 9–7 record in 1984 somehow was good enough for another division title. Though they got nine victories, and got to play for the AFC Championship, they lost the AFC Championship to Dan Marino's Dolphins. Marino was another one of those Pittsburgh guys that the Steelers let through their grasp. Marino was a Pittsburgh native, who starred for the Panthers and whom the Steelers passed up in the 1983 Draft. The Dolphins won 45–28. 1985 through 1987 were poor years by anybody's standards with records of 7-9, 6-10, and 8-7 respectively and no playoffs during the period.

Bubby Brister became the new Steelers QB. Despite Brister at the helm, the 1988 season was the worst for the Steelers in twenty years, with a 5–11 record. 1989 was a bit brighter at 9-7 with Pittsburgh winning five of its last six and a Wild Card playoff win over Houston 26-23 in OT, In the divisional playoffs John Elway came back for the Broncos in a nail biter and secured the one-point win over the Steelers, 24-23.

Chuck Noll's teams were playing respectably but they were not knocking league opponents dead as they had in his early years with the squad. But, the Pittsburgh teams were all respectable and very unlike the 30's, 40's, 50's and 60's.

The Steelers finished positive at 9–7 in 1990 and their defense led the way at #1 in the league in terms of yards allowed. The secondary was key, led by the superb play of Rod Woodson. The secondary was particularly effective v touchdowns—just 9, while intercepting 19. The Steelers intercepted 24 in total as a team).

The 1990 season ended as another disappointment however as the squad lost twice in three weeks to the Cincinnati Bengals, and they lost the last game of the season, which is always a downer, on the road to the Houston Oilers.

This devastating loss took them out of the playoff picture. Brister lost his full-time starting job in 1991 to Neil O'Donnell, who pundits would say showed some flashes of brilliance. However, the rest of the team could not keep up with his brilliant moments and faltered to a 7-9 finish. Chuck Noll said good-by to the Steelers at the end of 1991

Chuck Noll Calls it Quits.

On December 26, 1991, the Chuck Noll Era came to a close. It could be called the end of an era, for it was for sure. Steelers head coach Chuck Noll announced that he would be retiring after 23 years at the helm, most of them great. Looking back, Noll was the 14th head coach in the Steel City as of 1969. He did not have a free ride, but he was a cut above all other coaches at the time in the NFL and in college More importantly, Noll was ready to win; he knew how to bring many wins home; and he did.

They say it is always better to replace a poor manager than a good manager. Noll had no problem like that. Some would say that almost everybody before him stunk the house out. He had his work cut out for him with the fans as every new guy brought a new list of fan expectations. Nobody likes to lose. He did not have to do much to be better than his predecessors as the Steelers had only enjoyed 8 winning seasons in 36 years of existence. Noll' job was to make them a legitimate contender to the throne.

We have a saying in Pennsylvania that "Nothing happens overnight in Scranton." It's true and it applies to more than Scranton. It took Chuck Noll three seasons of losing while working very hard for him to turnaround a team that knew one of its jabs was being the "laughingstock of the NFL."

How did Noll do what nobody else could do without a change in ownership? His big key to success was picking up good players through the draft. He had an eye for football talent, and his determination to get the best helped Chuck Noll mold one of the greatest dynasties in the history of the NFL. As we have already recounted Noll's story, you may recall that it all began with linebacker "Mean Joe" Greene, the future Hall of Famer, who became a centerpiece to a defense that became known as "The Steel Curtain."

Don't forget Terry Bradshaw, one of the best ever and of course Franco Harris, a great player who would never quit. Noll worked his new team from the cellar to the heavens with four Super Bowls in the 1970's. After the slowdown in the 1980's Noll decided it was time to call it quits.

His decision to retire came after a 7-9 season in '91 as he realized the time had come. Even with the 80's being a bit disappointing by most standards, nothing could take away from the 4-time championship decade of the 70's. He would forever be a legend in Pittsburgh and beyond as the only head coach at the time to guide a team to four Super Bowl titles in one decade. Generations to come will remember and know the name Chuck Noll and it will be held in similar regard as Curly Lambeau, George Halas, and Vince Lombardi as he stands alongside them at the Hall of Fame in Canton, Ohio. Chuck Noll put a smiley face on Steeler fans for 23 years

Bill Cowher replaces Chuck Noll

Bill Cowher put in fifteen good years with the Steelers and though he was not as immediately impressive as Chuck Noll, he was one heck of a fine coach. When Chuck Noll, retired at the end of the 1991 season. Pittsburgh found the Kansas City Chiefs defensive coordinator Bill Cowher, a native of the Pittsburgh suburb of Crafton.

Cowher led the Steelers to the playoffs in each of his first six seasons as coach, a feat that had only previously been accomplished by legendary coach Paul Brown of the Cleveland Browns. One of those playoff appearances, 1965 took the Steelers to the Super Bowl. Yancey Thigpen had amassed 1,307 receiving yards and Willie Williams had seven interceptions. The Steelers' 11–5 record once again won them the division and a first-round bye. As in 1994, the Steelers dominated in the divisional playoff with a 40–21 win over the Buffalo Bill.

Next it was the Indianapolis Colts in the AFC championship. There were four lead changes, tin the game and the very last lead change was when Bam Morris scored a one-yard touchdown with 1:34 remaining. Colts quarterback Jim Harbaugh threw a "hail mary" that was dropped by Aaron Bailey in the end zone. The Steelers narrowly won this gateway to the Super Bowl, 20–16, and went on to play the Dallas Cowboys in Super Bowl XXX.

O'Donnell's three interceptions contributed heavily to the Steelers' 27–17 loss. Seeing the displeasure of the fans, Super Bowl XXX was O'Donnell's last game as a Steeler. He signed with the New York Jets as a free agent in the offseason.

Close but no cigar

Mike Tomczak was the play caller in 1996. The Steelers also picked up Notre Dame great, Jerome Bettis, aka the "Bus," from the St. Louis Rams. The Bus loved action and he produced when asked. He ran for 1,400 yards in his first year in a Steeler uniform. In 1996, a late-season bumbling was hurting the Steelers Super Bowl chances, but their 10–6 record still won them the division. Pittsburgh won their wild-card playoff game handily (42–14 over the Colts), but lost too easily, 28–3, to the New England Patriots in the divisional playoff—even before the Belichick dynasty. Cowher was determined to bring s few more of those huge rings to Pittsburgh.

Kordell Stewart sat out a few years before getting the nod in 1997 as the starting QB.

Tomczak simply failed to impress the team and the fans. Stewart did impress fans, however and he was the talk of the NFL. In his first full season, he clicked for 3,000 passing yards and 21 touchdowns. Bettis pulled a Bettis as he was always superlative whenever called upon to carry the load. He chalked up another 1,000-yard rushing season, and Thigpen collected his own 1,000 yards receiving to boot. The Steelers once again won the AFC Central. Their 11–5 record was good enough this year to give the squad a first-round playoff bye.

The New England Patriots had come out of a similar set of poor performance years in which they suffered win blights after coming over from the AFL. However, owner Robert Kraft, Ray Berry, Bill Parcells, Pete Carrol and ultimately Bill Belichick more than turned around the Patriots franchise and built a dynasty like Pittsburgh. In

1997, as the Patriots were emerging to their own eventual greatness, Pittsburgh narrowly won a 7–6 defensive struggle against the Patriots in the divisional playoff.

This set the stage for an AFC Championship showdown at Three Rivers Stadium against the Denver Broncos. Kordell Stewart was on his game. He scored early, going for 33 yards with one of his well-known scrambles, but the Broncos did not stand still. They exploded in the second quarter (aided by two questionable interference calls). The Steelers mounted a great late comeback, but it was put down and the eventual Super Bowl champion Broncos went on to win a close battle 24–21.

Jerome Bettis was a hard-nosed ball carrier who fit the Steelers style of play.

Bill Cowher had his nose pressed against the glass of the big championship scenario but could not get through soon enough to suit him so that he could smoke one of those huge cigars. The scent of the glass and the dream of the rings and the big cigars had to be like great Jockey Mike Smith helping the great horse "Justify" gain the scent of the Preakness finish line after collecting the Derby trophy in 2018.

It looked like the Steelers would be back in the playoffs for most of the 1998 regular season, especially after going 7-4 in their first eleven games. But two losses to the Cincinnati Bengals and a loss on Thanksgiving to the Detroit Lions kept the Steelers out of the playoffs. Again.

Please let me entertain you with a recount of the Thanksgiving game against the Detroit Lions in 1998, which is most known for the infamous coin flip call before overtime was played. It was a big deal.

The Flip

It was a 16–16 game at the end of regulation. Captain Jerome Bettis was asked to call "heads" or "tails" as the ref flipped the coin in the air. Bettis stammered while making the call, and referee (Phil Luckett) stated "the Steelers called heads; it's tails." This caused an uproar from Bettis and the Steelers, as replays seemed to show that Bettis clearly called "tails." Replays tell the truth but what if Bettis called heads and tails. Then, what, a re-flip probably?

Contrary to many press reports, Referee Luckett did not make a mistake in this incident. At least he could justify his call. A week after the game, the tape was enhanced by local Pittsburgh TV station KDKA-TV and Bettis is clearly heard saying "hea-tails." A sideline microphone enhancement also clearly had Bettis telling Coach Bill Cowher that (Bettis) had said "hea-tails." Seems to me like it should have been a void toss if there is such a thing in the NFL rule book.

It is tough for any fan to believe that gibberish or a stuck tongue should determine the fate of an important football game. Nonetheless, the call stood, and the Steelers never got to touch the ball again and went on to lose 19-16. They would lose their next four games and would end up finishing 7-9. Their lack of heart after being so close gave them their poor finish. Cowher had yet to win his Super Bowl. His big cigar ash-tray was still unused.

There were team issues in 1999 with Stewart being benched and Tomczak coming back in to start and the team finished 6-10 reflecting the lack of decision making. In the 2000 season, the last one at Three Rivers Stadium, Kent Graham was given a chance to start at quarterback. Stewart came back in—hopefully to save the day but he did not. The Steelers failed to make the playoffs for the third consecutive season under Bill Cowher. The Steelers did win their final game at Three Rivers Stadium by defeating the Washington Redskins 24–3, ending the season with a 9–7 record. In an unusual move, the NFL formally apologized to the team three times for missed or blown calls in games against Cleveland, Tennessee, and Philadelphia that may have contributed to the team's losses.

In 2001, the Steelers lost to New England after a 13-3 record. Zereoue, filling in for Bettis, scored two touchdowns in the divisional playoff against the defending Super Bowl champion Baltimore Ravens. The Steelers won 27–10. Pittsburgh then hosted its fourth AFC championship game in eight years—this one against New England. Jerome Bettis was back off the injury list for the game After the Patriots jumped to a two-TD lead, the Steelers tried a third-quarter comeback with rushing touchdowns by Bettis and Zereoue. Kordell Stewart did his best but was picked off in each of the final two drives. The eventual Super Bowl champs, the Patriots won the game 24–17.

The Steelers were thinking that Stewart was incapable of winning big games with a nasty tendency to throw interceptions at the worst times. This cost him his starting job once in the 2002 season. The Steelers then called upon Tommy Maddox, who had won the XFL MVP after the league's only season. He became the Steelers starting quarterback. Maddox lost only three games as the Steelers finished 10–5–1, tops in the new AFC North division. (Stewart, who made a short comeback after Maddox was injured later in the year, was cut and later resurfaced with the Chicago Bears.)

Looking for a path to the Super Bowl, Cowher's Steelers came back to win the Wild Card v Cleveland, 36-33 and then in the divisional playoff, v Tennessee. With a field goal kicker for the Titans getting three chances to win the game, the third was the charm and so the Steelers bit the dust in a 34–31 loss –another disappointing end to the season for the Steelers. 2003 gave the Steelers a 6-10 record and got them nowhere.

In 2004, Ben Roethlisberger joined the team from Miami University of Ohio. He was a great find immediately. The Steelers went 15-1. As a result of this dominant season, the Steelers received home field advantage throughout the AFC playoffs. They squeaked through the Divisional Playoffs beating the Jets 20-17, and then they were back in the AFC Championship, against the dynasty-driven Patriots, losing 41–27. Cowher was a great coach, but this defeat marked the fourth time in ten years that the Steelers had lost the conference title game at home under Bill Cowher. The fans were talking but the talk would not last too long. Cowher had enough too.

The Steelers were looking for the Super Bowl all the way in 2005 after too many close calls. Using the Chuck Noll method of building a team, the Steelers were careful in the NFL draft. They first selected TE Heath Miller from the University of Virginia. They also picked Florida State CB Bryant McFadden, Northwestern University OG Trai Essex, Georgia University WR Fred Gibson, and Temple University LB Rian Wallace. One never knows how well college athletes will perform but these were good picks.

Like the years before but especially in 2005, the Steelers were over-ready to make a post-season run. Nobody was telling anybody to take it easy and see where the chips might fall. However, injuries to Jerome Bettis and Duce Staley caused Willie Parker to become the Steelers' starter at running back. Parker did well in two convincing wins against the Tennessee Titans (34–7) and Houston Texans (27–7) to open the season.

The Steelers had a tough time as did most teams with Bill Belichick's New England Patriots with his Tom Brady-driven offense. After a good season start, the Patriots were next. Despite all the preparedness the Steelers squad went through, the visiting New England Patriots handed Ben Roethlisberger his first regular-season loss as the Steelers lost the much-hyped rematch of the 2004 AFC Championship Game 23–20. Pittsburgh, however, did not hang up their spikes for the season.

Just two weeks later, Pittsburgh came back and beat the San Diego Chargers 24–22. The Chargers were wearing their throw-back uniforms. The victory came on a 40-yard field goal by Jeff Reed. This win proved costly as Big Ben Roethlisberger suffered an injury when he was hit on his left knee by the helmet of Chargers rookie lineman Luis Castillo.

Due to Big Ben's injury, Tommy Maddox was named starter for their next home game against the Jacksonville Jaguars. He got the practice snaps. The Steelers struggled throughout the game, as Maddox threw two interceptions through regulation. At the end of the game, it was a tie at 17 going into OT. Maddox threw an interception in OT to Jags DB Rashean Mathis. He returned it into a pick-six, 41 yards for a touchdown. The Steelers fell, 23–17. That was that. However.

Maddox's off-field arguments with head coach Bill Cowher cost him his No. 1 back-up spot on the team. Roethlisberger healed quickly and was able to play in their next road game against their division rival, the Cincinnati Bengals. Despite winning 27–13, his left knee had some issues. Roethlisberger fought through the pain in the Steelers' 20–19 Monday Night victory over the Baltimore Ravens but reaggravated his knee injuries.

Charlie Batch was named the starter until Ben was better. He helped the team with wins over the struggling Green Bay Packers (20–10 on the road), and against their rust belt rival, the Cleveland Browns (34–21 at home). During the Browns game, wide receiver Hines Ward set the Steelers record for most career receptions (543), breaking John Stallworth's mark of 537. Batch broke his hand in the game, which sent him right to the sidelines.

Tommy Maddox was given the starting nod for their road game against the Ravens, but again, he showed his inability to win games as the Steelers fell in overtime 16–13. After Roethlisberger's came back, Pittsburgh twice. The first game was against the then-undefeated Indianapolis Colts (7-26 on the road) and the next was at home against the resurgent Bengals (31–38). Pittsburgh recovered from these stumbles to win their last four regular-season games (21–9 vs. Bears, 18–3 @ Vikings, 41–0 @ Browns, and 35–21 vs. Lions) to clinch the sixth and last seed in the AFC playoffs.

During the last game of the regular season in Pittsburgh, the Steelers fans gave Jerome Bettis a standing ovation when he was taken out of the game in the fourth quarter by Bill Cowher. Bettis was a mainstay. It was the last game in Pittsburgh for Bettis, as he announced his retirement after the Steelers' ultimate victory when they "breezed through" the playoffs and won Super Bowl XL. Bettis finished the game with 41 yards rushing and 3 TDs and gave the team a boost after the Lions had taken a 14–7 first quarter lead.

In the Playoffs, Pittsburgh first beat the Bengals 31-17 at Paul Brown Stadium. Then, on Sunday, January 15, at the RCA Dome in Indianapolis, they beat the #1 seeded Colts, defeating them 21–18 after a strange fourth quarter, which included a call reversal that turned a crucial Troy Polamalu interception into an incomplete pass. The reversal helped give the suddenly alive again Colts offense another chance to win.

Jerome Bettis committed an unlikely fumble for him on the Colts 1 with just over a minute remaining, Colts cornerback Nick Harper sped downfield toward what would have been a game-winning touchdown. However, he was tripped up by none other than the Steelers quarterback Ben Roethlisberger in a shoe-string tackle, preventing the game-winning touchdown for the Colts.

The Steelers D then held their ground. It marked the first time that a sixth seed would get to play in a Conference Championship game. In the third playoff game, the Steelers won their 6th AFC Championship at INVESCO Field at Mile High in Denver, Colorado, taking out the Broncos 34–17. QB Roethlisberger was right on and completed 21 out of 29 passes, 2 of which were touchdowns. He also ran for another as he led the team to a great victory. As noted, this win marked the first time that a sixth-seeded team would get to play in the Super Bowl.

QB Ben Roethlisberger at Steelers Super Bowl XL parade in downtown Pittsburgh

At one time in the 1970's, the Steelers expected trips to the Super Bowl, and they expected to win. This was their first trip to the Super Bowl since the 1995 season, when they had lost. But, they did not lose this time. Instead, they played tough and won. They defeated the Seattle Seahawks 21–10 in Super Bowl XL on February 5, 2006, at Ford Field in Detroit, Michigan.

The game had been hyped by the press as a homecoming for Detroit native Jerome Bettis. There were a lot of records reset in this game as it was a great day for the Pittsburgh Steelers. Willie Parker set the record for longest run from scrimmage for the Steelers (75 yards), there was the longest interception return (76 yards by Seahawks CB Kelly Herndon), and the Steelers executed the first touchdown pass by a wide receiver (thrown by Antwaan Randle El to Hines Ward on a reverse).

Hines Ward, the MVP of Super Bowl XL

The Steelers came from nowhere to win this Super Bowl. They year before they were 15-1 and this year they were lucky to be in the playoffs.

They become the first 6th-seeded team, since the NFL changed to a 12-team playoff format in 1990, to go to the Super Bowl and then win the game. They are also the first NFL team to win 9 road games in a season. Roethlisberger became the youngest QB to ever win a Super Bowl.

After this game, they successfully tied with the San Francisco 49ers and the Dallas Cowboys for the most Super Bowl titles with five. Five would still be the record today with New England holding its part with 5 victories. However, somewhere between then and now, Pittsburgh upped the ante with another Super Bowl Victory for Mike Tomlin in Game XLII.

Willie Parker in 2006.

Super Bowl Fatigue

There is often a letdown after a major life achievement. It happened for sure to the 2006 Pittsburgh Steelers. Of course, after a Super Bowl win, the idea of a repeat is prevalent as mostly the same team that won the game is on the field again the next season.

The Steelers thus hoped to improve on their 11–5 record from 2005 and they tried to defend their Super Bowl XL championship.

However, it did not happen, and they unexpectedly finished 8–8 in 2006 and they did not even make it to the playoffs. Bill Cowher had gotten his Super Bowl and so he felt OK in stepping down from the top coaching spot when he did not get a repeat. Cowher was ready to go on with the rest of his life.

In 2016 in an interview with Rolling Stone, Bill Cowher came clean with why he retired. It was not a big secret for those who knew him well; but he clearly spelled out his reasons in the interview, giving an honest answer about why he walked away from football after 2006.

Cowher initially had said the usual about wanting to spend more time with his family after 15 seasons as coach of the Steelers. He offered that the time restrictions and years in the spotlight had become too much.

"I didn't really like where I was going with myself," Cowher said. "I'd walk around a lot with my head down. Wouldn't make eye contact. I felt like a little bit of a prisoner. You'd go into hotels and you don't go down to the lobby because you'd get recognized. It's just not a good place to be."

Cowher admitted that he "had the best job in the National Football League." He said that he did not mind the hours, but he did not like the lifestyle. "I won a championship and I just felt like I got to the point where I couldn't go anywhere. It's like living in a fishbowl. Honestly, it's what it is. I look at what I have now, and it's living normal." Bill Cowher does not regret his new life. In 2007, Mike

Tomlin, another fine coach took over for Bill Cower and eventually he got his Super Bowl. Some continue to say to Mike, "Now what?"

Mike Tomlin New Steelers Coach gets and keeps the job

Since the time of Chuck Noll, unlike many pro teams, the Steelers have retained coaches for more than ten years. I have written a number of "Great Moments" books and my style is always to put forth an attractive front cover that includes all of the coaches that ever coached the team in a baseball/football card format with a few other great sights, such as a view of the home stadium.

I first put all of the coaches in football card format even if they never were in a football card ever in their lives. I have a great book designer, Michele Thomas, from Wilkes-Barre, PA on my team. Michele takes everything I give and asks for more and comes up with the most wonderful covers I have ever seen. I bet you like this Pittsburgh cover that she designed with all sixteen Pittsburgh Steelers coaches highlighted.

Unlike Pittsburgh, many other teams have over thirty coaches, whose baseball card images we must squeeze onto the front cover. That's about twice as many coaches as Pittsburgh has had in its history. Somehow, my designer, Michele, always gets all the coaches needed on the front cover, and she does a great job in doing it.

We know that Chuck Noll coached for twenty-three years. That is a long time. There is something to say about coaches at the helm for over a decade. The great Bill Belichick has 18 years right now with the Patriots and the Patriots are tied with the Cowboys and the 49ers for the second-most Super Bowl victories (5) in history. The Steelers are in first place of course with six (6) Super Bowl wins.

Additionally, of the last three Steeler coaches from 1969 to today each have brought the team a Super Bowl victory, with Chuck Noll, of course leading all coaches with four (4) big wins.

With Mike Tomlin as the new Steelers coach in 2007, the Steelers improved upon their 8–8 record from Bill Cowher's last season in 2006, to finish with a record of 10–6, and a win the AFC North Division.

Mike Tomlin had been the Minnesota Vikings' defensive coordinator, was hired by the Pittsburgh Steelers for 2007, making him the first black head coach in the team's 74-year history. Tomlin was hired for approximately $2.5 million a year under his first contract. He is still at the helm, hired as the Steelers' third coach in 38 years, following Chuck Noll (23 seasons) and Bill Cowher (15 seasons).

Though Tomlin already brought the team a Super Bowl victory, there are those who want more from him and from Pittsburgh, and want the "more" faster, and they would be willing to let Mike Tomlin go to get what they want. My own opinion is that it would be tough to find any coach in the NFL who has won a Super Bowl. Many coaches secretly think they already made it if they get to get beaten in a Super Bowl. Sometimes fans get the change they ask for and it is not good.

The 2007 season marked the 75th anniversary of Steelers football. It was a great year for the Steelers and Mike Tomlin and it featured what the pundits called two notable playoff rematches. The first was against the New England Patriots on December 9. This was the first regular season game v the Pats since 2005, when Pittsburgh lost at home on a last-second Adam Vinatieri field goal 23–20.

This year's (2007) 34–13 loss was also the Steelers' first visit to Foxboro, Massachusetts since 2002. The second rematch was against a different team, going back to when the Steelers defeated the Seattle Seahawks 21–0 in week 5 on October 7. This was the teams' first meeting since the Steelers' 21–10 victory in Super Bowl XL 20 months earlier and it was the Steelers' and Seahawks' first meeting in Pittsburgh since 1999 as well as the Seahawks' first-ever visit to Heinz Field.

The Pro Bowl was a big deal for Pittsburgh in 2007 as the Steelers were honored to send six of their best players. Two Steelers started, the game. Two others were selected to the reserve squad, and two were not able to play due to injury.

1. 7 Ben Roethlisberger – Quarterback (reserve)
2. 39 Willie Parker – Running back (injured, did not play)
3. 43 Troy Polamalu – Strong safety (injured, did not play)
4. 66 Alan Faneca – Offensive guard
5. 92 James Harrison – Outside linebacker
6. 98 Casey Hampton – Defensive tackle (reserve)

Super Bowl Win # 6 in 2008

There was a bad omen starting the 2008 season when the Steelers lost Alan Faneca. When his contract ran out, he signed with the New York Jets. Feeling great about Big Ben Roethlisberger, the Steelers inked their star franchise QB to an eight-year, $102 million contract, the largest in franchise history. The team also grabbed Rashard Mendenhall, running back from Illinois, with the 23rd overall pick in the 2008 NFL Draft as well as top wide receiver prospect, Limas Sweed of Texas with the 53rd overall pick. The Steelers were preparing for what's next.

An injury to Willie Parker made his future production questionable so Mendenhall was drafted to be the next Steelers running back of the future. The season went well with 12 wins and four losses—all to strong opponents, the Philadelphia Eagles, the New York Giants, the Indianapolis Colts, and the Tennessee Titans. The team's record cinched them a first-round bye and home advantage through the playoffs. Mike Tomlin would accept no failing acts.

James Harrison excelled. He was voted as the 2008 AP Defensive Player of the Year with a terrific regular season performance of 16 sacks (fourth in league) and 7 forced fumbles (first in the league). Troy Polamalu also had a great season, with seven interceptions, a tie for second in the league.

James Harrison in 2008.

When the Steelers beat San Diego 35-24 in the divisional round, of the playoffs, they moved on to face their AFC North rival Baltimore in the conference championship. The Tomlin squad soundly defeated them, 23-14. Thus, the Steelers made it to their seventh Super Bowl.

Their opponent was the Arizona Cardinals, a team that had not appeared in any league championship since 1948.

The Steelers engaged against the Arizona Cardinals in Super Bowl XLIII on February 1, 2009 at the Buccaneers' Raymond James Stadium. By halftime, the Steelers were creating distance at 17–7.

Arizona was having a tough time both by the Steelers and the officials. They had been nailed by penalties, in particular three personal fouls.

Despite their bad fortune, they managed to get ahead of Pittsburgh when WR Larry Fitzgerald scored a 63-yard touchdown, bringing the score to 23–20. But Pittsburgh came back when Santonio Holmes smashed in a 6-yard TD in the final two minutes.

With that, the game ended 27–23 and the Steelers claimed their sixth championship, becoming the first team ever to win six Super Bowls since the start of the Super Bowl era. That record still stands.

Steelers defenders Troy Polamalu (left) and Ryan Clark(right) at the Super Bowl XLIII victory parade in Pittsburgh.

In 2009, though the Steelers got off to a good 6-2 start, they finished slow at 9-7 and missed the playoffs. In 2010, Ben Roethlisberger had some big issues that affected the team. He was accused of unwelcome advances to a woman in a bar and was suspended for six games, which was later reduced to four games while the NFL sorted out the matter.

Dennis Dixon and Charlie Batch filled in as the starting QB. Despite dire predictions, the Steelers had a great season beginning with a win v Atlanta in the season opener in OT 15–9 and a win at Tennessee in game 2. By the time Roethlisberger came back, the Steelers were 3-1 and were no worse for the wear.

After a bye week #6, Big Ben was given a standing ovation by Steelers fans and he delivered a nice 28–10 win over the Browns.

On Nov 14, the Steelers lost at home to nemesis Tom Brady and the New England Patriots 39–26. They then won 4 in a row. They finished winning 2 and losing one game to close out the season very positively.

The finish was 12-4, winning the AFC North division, and winning the AFC's No. 2 seed in the playoffs. In their first postseason game at home against Baltimore, the Steelers made a second half rally and beat the Ravens 31–24. They then defeated the Jets 24–19 in the AFC Championship to earn the right to play in Super Bowl XLV.

In this Super Bowl against the Green Bay Packers in 2010, Pittsburgh fell behind 21-3 and then fought back to make the score 21–17. After Rashard Mendenhall fumbled in the 4th quarter, Green Bay scored making it 28–17. Pittsburgh came right back with a 25-yard pass to Mike Wallace and a 2-point conversion making the game 28–25.

Green Bay took time off the clock on their next drive and then scored a Field Goal making the tally 31–25. Pittsburgh needed a TD on its final drive but came up empty. With this game, the Steelers tied the Dallas Cowboys for most Super bowl appearances with eight. (The Patriots now have ten) Mike Tomlin took them right to the edge of the big cigar payoff, but again, the ashtray stayed empty.

The Steelers are a great team under Noll, Cowher, and Tomlin. Under Mike Tomlin, the squad pulled off another great 12-4 season in **2011**. On the way to the Super Bowl, however, injuries began piling up. Ben Roethlisberger was sidelined with a foot injury and Charlie Batch was scheduled to start in Week 5 against Tennessee.

Despite what was supposed to be, however, Ben Roethlisberger played, and he was terrific. He threw for 5 touchdowns in a 38–17 win. After easily winning that game, he returned to action as

Pittsburgh beat Jacksonville at home 17–13 and then won in Arizona 32–20 for their first encounter since Super Bowl XLIII.

The Steelers set a franchise record in the latter half of the game as Roethlisberger threw a 95-yard TD pass to Mike Wallace. The next week, Pittsburgh returned home to face Tom Brady and the New England Patriots. In a spectacular defensive effort, in which Pittsburgh held Brady to a season-low 198 yards passing, the Steelers beat the Patriots 25–17.

With a 12-4 record, the Steelers were in a Wild Card game at Denver against the 8-8 Broncos. The Broncos were led by Tim Tebow, and they quickly and unexpectedly gained a 20-6 halftime lead. Despite an interception, Big Ben brought the Steelers back to tie the game 23-23 following a Willis McGahee fumble.

The game went into OT. On the opening play, the Steelers lined ten men at the line of scrimmage, leaving the field behind them all but uncovered; Tebow recognized the opportunity and lofted a pass caught by Demaryius Thomas. Thomas outran two Steelers defenders for the winning touchdown. Tomlin again had the Steelers at the precipice of a championship season, but the big cigar ashtray remained clean. .

In **2012** The Steelers had a tough year with a record of 8–8. It was their first non-winning season since 2006. The games were close but there were few cigars as the 2012 Steelers set a new NFL record for the most games decided on the last play, with 6. The team finished looking forward to 2013. **2013** was not so hot. The Steelers had another poor season at 8-8 in 2013. It was the first season since 1999 that the Steelers would miss back-to-back postseasons.

In **2014**, the Steelers made a fine comeback from their 8-8 record from each of their previous two seasons They clinched a playoff berth for the first time in three years with their week 16 victory over the Kansas City Chiefs. They took the AFC North division title, but then could not keep it going as they lost to the Baltimore Ravens in the Wild Card round of the playoffs by a score of 30–17. T

The Steelers became the first team in NFL history to have a 4,500-yard passer, 1,500-yard receiver and 1,300-yard rusher in the same season. But the championship eluded them again. The Steelers are a great team. A little bit of Bear Bryant luck and they would have more Lombardi Trophies for sure.

2015 was another fine year for Pittsburgh, and this time the Steelers went deeper into the playoffs. They won the last AFC playoff spot, finishing tied with the New York Jets with a 10–6 record. The Steelers won the tiebreaker over the Jets based on their better record vs. common opponents. The Steelers defeated the Cincinnati Bengals in a tight match W (18-16) in the Wild Card round but lost to the eventual Super Bowl champion Denver Broncos in another tight game in the Divisional round L (16-23). Tomlin was getting the team there but not closing the deal. No Cigar!

In **2016**, with an 11-5 record, Pittsburgh improved on its 10–6 record from 2015. Le'Veon Bell made his career first playoff appearance with the Steelers in the 2016–17 playoffs. The Steelers defeated the Dolphins in the Wild Card round and then they defeated the Kansas City Chiefs in the Divisional round before they lost to the new dynasty. the eventual Super Bowl champion New England Patriots, 36–17, in the AFC Championship Game. This was the Steelers' first appearance in the AFC Championship Game since the 2010–11 NFL Season.

2016 would be the final season under the ownership of the immortal Dan Rooney, a great Pittsburgh Steelers leader who died on April 13, 2017. His son Arthur Joseph Rooney II (born September 14, 1952) is the current owner of the Pittsburgh Steelers of the National Football League (NFL). Rooney II is the eldest of nine children of longtime Steelers chairman Dan Rooney. He is the grandson of Steelers' founder "The Chief", Art Rooney, Sr. He was named team president in May 2003.He has been associated with the Steelers all of his life. Prior to serving as president, he served as vice president and general counsel of the Steelers, and he has served on the board of directors of the Steelers since 1989.

In **2017**, The Steelers had their best regular season since 2004 with a record of 13-3. They clinched the AFC North division title for the second consecutive season with a 39–38 nail-biter win over the Baltimore Ravens in Week 14, and they grabbed a first-round playoff bye for the first time since 2010 with a 34–6 win over the Houston Texans in Week 16.

In the Divisional Round, unexpectedly, the Steelers lost to the Jacksonville Jaguars by a score of 45–42 after they had fallen behind 28–14 at halftime. The pundits and the fans were not happy as they accused the Steelers of looking past the Jaguars and anticipating a rematch with the New England Patriots. That 13-3 record however is tough to argue with and Mike Tomlin has been pretty successful in bringing winning seasons to Pittsburgh Pennsylvania. Tomlin and the Steelers look like they are ready to claim another Super Bowl sometime soon. We'll see!

I feel it in my bones. Who would you put up against an already-great coach such as Mike Tomlin to lead the Steelers in the future. From my eyes, if Tomlin can take the pressure and he sure seems like he can, he needs to stay as the Pittsburgh Steelers man on the scene.

Chapter Summary

You may recall that we got to this point of the story of the Steelers first by discussing in detail the Pirates seven years from 1933 to 1939. That set us up for talking about the Pittsburgh Steelers. In the last several chapters.

From the Pirates, we took a breather to help the fanbase understand pro-football and how, while baseball was the acknowledged American past-time, pro-football NFL-style was the next logical step after college football. As you may recall, we put forth a number of chapters that began with the beginning of football as a sport in college and the rules put forth by Walter Camp.

We also went back in prehistoric times to show the football games played by primitive man, and we showed how the oval football came to being on the way for pro football becoming a bona fide sport like baseball in America. From there, of course we began to look at the history of the Pittsburgh Pirates / Steelers and then we detailed the Pirates seasons. Now, as a good tale should take us, we are ready to continue with the detail beginning with the team after the Pittsburgh Pirates. Of course, I am talking about the 1940 Pittsburgh Steelers. Coming up in the next chapter is their first season in detail on the way to 2018.

Chapter 15 The Pittsburgh Steelers Seasons 1 to 3; 1940-1942

#5 Coach Walt Kiesling
#6 Coach Bert Bell
#7 Coach Aldo Donelli

Year	Coach	League/Conf/Div	Pl	Record	Pct.
1940	#5 Walt Kiesling	NFLEast	4th	2 7 2	.273
1941	All coaches	NFLEast	5th	1 9 1	.136
• Art Rooney convinced Bell to resign- 0-2 record					
• Aldo Donelli took over 5 games record 0-5					
• Walt Kiesling came back & finished year at 1-2-1					
1941	#6 Bert Bell	NFLEast	5th	0-2-0	.136
• Shared with coaches #5,6 (0-5)					
1941	#7 Aldo Donelli	NFLEast	5th	0-5-0	.136
• Shared with coaches #5,6 (0-5)					
1941	#5 Walt Kiesling	NFLEast	5th	1-2-1	.136
• Shared with coaches #6,7 (2-0-2)					
1942	#5 Walt Kiesling	NFLEast	2nd	7 4 0	.636

1940 Pittsburgh Steelers Game when Dan Rooney was the 8-yr-old Water-Boy

After an inglorious seven years as the Pittsburgh Pirates, Art Rooney decided that it was time for a name change. And, so after a radio naming contest, the Pittsburgh Pirates became the Pittsburgh Steelers. Everything else was the same except the name. e

We know that the Steelers were founded in 1933 as the Pirates by Art Rooney. Rooney had established a semi-pro football team called the Hope-Harvey Majestics which competed in the Western Pennsylvania Senior Independent Football Conference, so he was not new to football. The team would win two titles in the early 1930s before he bought the Pirates/Steelers franchise.

Pennsylvania had become a hotbed for football, especially the college game. College football was very popular as pro football found its way. The PA state "blue laws" that were designed to help promote religious practices on Sundays got in the way of professional recreation as the Sabbath was set aside as a day of rest. There were many restrictions from shopping to restaurants to alcohol to athletic events. Because pro football played its games on Sundays, this made it especially tough to own such a team in the state of Pennsylvania.

In the spring of 1933, some blue laws were repealed and so it looked like pro football would be a good bet for Rooney, who also liked to bet on the ponies, and so he got the team franchise from the NFL for $2500.00 . Because the blue laws would not be voted on until November, the first four Pirate home games were played on Wednesday nights.

For the next seven years, the Pirates were perennial loser and usually made the cellar its habitat. In fact, in 1940 for the next 33 years or so, the Steelers carried the same reputation as a losing team. The club had a winning record only eight times and never came close to a championship. From player signings to draft selections if there were a good way to do it, Pittsburgh had not figured it out. They were literally horrid—and so were their coaching choices. They were appalling in just every way possible.

Once, in 1938, two years before the Pirates became the Steelers, their head coach took his job so lightly that Johnny Blood missed the team train home after a road game. On his return back to Pittsburgh, he stopped off in Chicago to see his former team, the Packers, play against the Bears. While he was at the game, a sportswriter recognized Johnny and asked Blood why he wasn't with his team. Blood gave the moral equivalent of a huh? As he said Pittsburgh was not playing on that weekend. By the time the words left his mouth, league scores were announced over the stadium loudspeaker. One score that was announced was Philadelphia 14, Pittsburgh 7.

The Steelers were not the original name of the team as noted, they were the Pirates. Baseball ruled the times as the national past-time so pro teams piggy backed on the success of the town's baseball team and picked up the same name to get the fans in the park. The notion was that fans of the diamond would inherently become fans of the gridiron. Tickets sales were the lone source of revenue for clubs back then, so having a good team association was critical to survival.

Nonetheless Art Rooney did not like the name Pirates and it had brought him no luck for seven years. He'd had his seven years of bad luck and wanted some good luck for a change. So, at the end of the 1939 season, sick of needing a head coach every year (five head coaches in 7 seasons) Rooney decided to start anew with a new team nickname.

The Pittsburgh Post-Gazette ran a promotion in 1940 to rename the team and after dozens of fans chose the "Steelers," Rooney made his decision. The winning person in the drawing was Margaret O'Donnell. Of course, the new handle for the Steelers was chosen in respect to the area's production of steel and the industry as a whole. After all the fun of creating a new name for the team, it was soon time for Pittsburgh's new Steelers to play football in the fall of 1940.

1940 Walt Kiesling, Coach #5

The 1940 Pittsburgh Steelers football team competed in their eighth season of Professional National Football League (NFL) football and their first using the moniker "Steelers.". They were led by Walt Kiesling as the fifth coach in his second of three seasons as head coach. Kiesling's assistant coaches were Wilbur "Bill" Sortet and Hank Bruder. Both assistants also played on the team.

In this, the Pirates/Steelers eighth year, this Steelers team finished with a break-even season record of 2-7-2, winning two games, losing two, and tying two. The new Steelers team failed again to qualify for the playoffs.

The Steelers began the season with two ties. In the season and "home" opener on Sept 2, 19407, the Kiesling-led Steelers squad tied the Chicago Cardinals T (7-7) On Sept 15, the Steelers made it two ties in a row at home in Forbes Field against the New York Giants T (10-10). At Detroit on Sept 22, the Steelers got their first win ever under the name Steelers against the Lions W (10-7). At home again on Sept 29, the Steelers lost their first game of the season—this was against the Brooklyn Dodgers L (3-10).

In the second of six losses in a row, on Oct 6, at home, the Steelers were whooped by the Washington Redskins L (10-40) at Forbes Field. At Brooklyn on Oct 13, the Steelers were shut out by the Dodgers L (0-21) At New York, on Oct 20, the Steelers were shut out by the Giants L (0-12). At Green Bay on Oct 27, the Packers beat the Steelers L (3-24)

On Nov 3, in the last game of the six-game losing streak, at Washington, the Redskins pounded the Steelers L (10-37). On Nov 10, at home, the Steelers defeated the Philadelphia Eagles W (7-3). Then wrapping up the Season, Kiesling's Steelers lost its final game of 1940 at Philadelphia to the Eagles L (0-7).

1941 Bert Bell, Coach #6
1941 Aldo Donelli, Coach #7
1941 Walt Kiesling, Coach #5

Year	Coach	League/Conf/Div	Pl	Record	Pct.
1941	All coaches	NFLEast	5th	1 9 1	.136

- Art Rooney convinced Bell to resign- 0-2 record
- Aldo Donelli took over 5 games record 0-5
- Walt Kiesling came back & finished year at 1-2-1

Year	Coach	League/Conf/Div	Pl	Record	Pct.
1941	#6 Bert Bell	NFLEast	5th	0-2-0	.136

- Shared with coaches #5,6 (0-5)

Year	Coach	League/Conf/Div	Pl	Record	Pct.
1941	#7 Aldo Donelli	NFLEast	5th	0-5-0	.136

- Shared with coaches #5,6 (0-5)

Year	Coach	League/Conf/Div	Pl	Record	Pct.
1941	#5 Walt Kiesling	NFLEast	5th	1-2-1	.136

- Shared with coaches #6,7 (2-0-2)

1941 was a strange year for Pittsburgh long before the Pearl Harbor attack in December. The new name for the Pittsburgh football team was only one of many things Art Rooney grappled with in 1941. Among others was that the Philadelphia and Pittsburgh franchises went through what can be seen as an off-season team swap. Additionally, for a time. Bert Bell became the coach of the Steelers. Bell had been owner of the Eagles until Pittsburgh was sold to Alexis Thompson, a 26-year old well-to-do entrepreneur, and to stay in football Art Rooney bought half of the Eagles.

Eventually, Bert Bell (former Eagles owner) and Art Rooney together owned the Steelers and Alexis Thompson owned the Eagles There is a more detailed version of the big team swap in the Post Pirates chapters in this book. To reread this information, please go to Chapter 12.

When instead of owning the Eagles together, Art Rooney and his buddy Bert Bell owned Pittsburgh together, Rooney was not very anxious for Bert Bell to become the head coach Pittsburgh. Rooney wanted Aldo Donelli, a one-time football star and great coach at Duquesne to take the reins.

Bell, who owned half the team in 1941 after Rooney had sold out, insisted on being the coach. Bell made a concession that he would give up coaching only if Rooney were to talk Aldo Donelli into coaching the team. Rooney got the job done but it was convoluted. So, Bell is the first listed coach in 1941 and Donelli is second listed before Kiesling at third.

Bert Bell took Pittsburgh to its first two losses and then he stepped down in favor of Aldo Donelli, whose deal was that he could continue to coach at Duquesne while coaching at Pittsburgh. This complete story is also told in Chapter 12. The NFL did not like it one bit.

Donelli did no better than the worst coaches ever for the Pirates. He lost five of five games with the team. Walt Kiesling, who had been serving as assistant coach all along in 1941, took over as head coach and he more or less mopped up the season by winning two games, losing none, and typing two. Donelli was given a choice when

Duquesne and the Steelers had a common play/travel date. Rather than quit Duquesne for Pittsburgh as the NFL suggested, Donelli quit his Pittsburgh job with an 0-5 record. It was a strange year all around.

In the offseason, Art Rooney needed cash and he sold the whole Pittsburgh team to Alexis Thompson team and then re-acquired (more or less) the team with his buddy Bert Bell in a bizarre series of transactions which has come to be referred to as the "Pennsylvania Polka". The Pittsburgh roster consisted of many players who had played for the Philadelphia Eagles the previous year, who had joined the Steelers as a result of the ownership moves.

Bert Bell became half-owner of the team in the off-season as Art Rooney sold out, bought half of the Eagles and then the Eagles and Pittsburgh swapped teams. Bell named himself the head coach. After starting the season with two straight losses, Aldo "Buff" Donelli was brought in. As noted, Donelli was acting concurrently as head coach at Duquesne University, and when the team's schedules prevented him from fulfilling both roles, he stepped down as the Steelers' coach in favor of Walt Kiesling. To get more of this story, see Chapter 12.

The 1941 Pittsburgh Steelers football team competed in their ninth season of Professional National Football League (NFL) football and their second using the moniker "Steelers.". They were led by Walt Kiesling as the fifth coach in his third of three seasons as head coach. Kiesling's assistant coaches were Wilbur "Bill" Sortet and Hank Bruder. Both assistants also played on the team.

In this, the Pirates/Steelers ninth year, this Steelers team finished with a poor record of 1-9-1, winning one games, losing nine, and tying one The Steelers team failed again to qualify for the playoffs.

The Steelers began the season with seven losses spread over two coaches. In the season opener on Sept 7, 1941, the Bell-led Steelers squad were defeated in a close match by the Cleveland Rams L (14-17). At home on Sept 21. The Eagles defeated the Steelers in another close match. L (7-10). Then, on Oct 5 at home in Forbes Field, the Steelers were pummeled by the New York Giants L (37-10) in Aldo Donelli's first game with the Steelers. On Oct 12, at home, the Steelers lost to the Washington Redskins L (20-24).

At New York on Oct 19, the Giants prevailed L (28-7). At Chicago on Oct 26, the Bears dominated L (7-34). Then, on Nov 2, at Washington, the Redskins beat the Eagles L (3-23). Then, on Nov 9, at Philadelphia, the Eagles tied the Steelers T (7-7)

On Nov 16, at home in Forbes Field, the Walt Kiesling led Pittsburgh Steelers won their only game of the year against the Brooklyn Dodgers W (14-7). The Steelers under Kiesling would lose their second-last and last games of the year. On Nov 23, the Green Bay Packers walloped the Steelers L (7-54) at Forbes Field. On Nov 30, at Brooklyn, the Dodgers drubbed the Steelers L (7-35) closing out the season with a big loss.

1942 Walt Kiesling, Coach #5

The 1942 Pittsburgh Steelers football team competed in their tenth season of Professional National Football League (NFL) football. They were led by Walt Kiesling who returned for another seasons as head coach. The team improved substantially on its previous season result of 1–9–1 with a record of 7–4–0. This was good enough for 2nd place in the NFL East. This was the franchise's first ever winning record. The Steelers did not make the playoffs, but their name was mentioned a few times this season.

The Steelers began the season with two losses. In the season and home opener at Forbes Field on Sept 13, 1941, the Kiesling-led Steelers squad were defeated by the Philadelphia Eagles L (14-24). At Washington on Sept 20., the Redskins defeated the Steelers by two TDs, L (14-28) Then, on Oct 4, my wedding anniversary, at home in Forbes Field, the Steelers defeated the New York Giants W (13-10) for the first win of the 1942 season. At Brooklyn on Oct 11, the Steelers shut out the Brooklyn Dodgers W (7-0)

At Philadelphia on Oct 18, the Steelers shut out the Eagles W (14-0). Walt Kiesling had the Steelers looking like a real team. On Oct 25, at home, the Steelers lost to the Washington Redskins L (0-14). Then, on Nov 1, at New York, the Steelers defeated the Giants W (17-9). On Nov 8, @ Detroit, Steelers thumped the Lions W (35-7).

Then, on Nov 22, the Steelers whooped the Chicago Cardinals W 19-3 at home in Forbes Field. Then, at home again on Nov 29, the Steelers defeated the Brooklyn Dodgers W (13-0). Not being able to win the season finale, the Steelers put up a fine battle at Green Bay on Dec 6, against the Packers L (21-24).

Top Steelers Players Bill Dudley

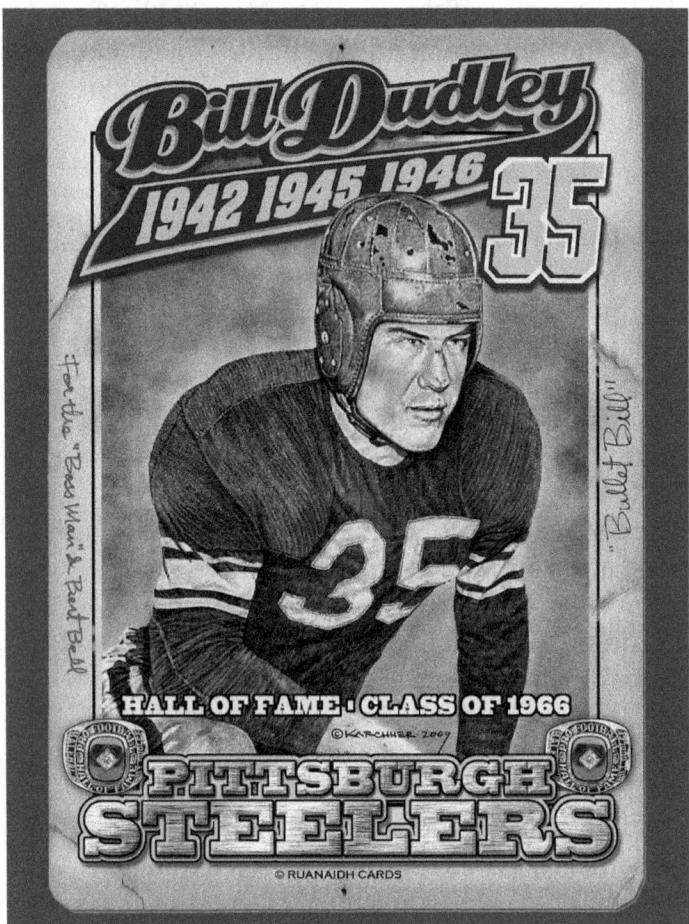

Dudley was a halfback (1942, 1945-46) Elected to hall of fame 1966
Bill Dudley nicknamed "Bullet Bill", was a first-round draft pick of the Steelers in 1942 and finished his rookie season as the league's leading rusher with 696 yards, earning him all-league honors. In 1946, he became the NFL's first player to lead the league in four distinctly different statistical categories, including rushing, punt returns, interceptions and lateral passes attempted. That same year he was named the NFL's Most Valuable Player. Dudley was a two-time All-NFL selection during his nine-year career.

Chapter 16 1943 Steagles; 1944 Card-Pitt

Coach #5 Walt Kiesling

Pittsburgh & Philadelphia = Steagles
Year Coach   League/Conf/Div Pl   Record Pct.
1943 #5 Walt Kiesling   NFLEast   3rd   5 4 1   .550
1943 Greasy Neale co-coach from Philadelphia Eagles0

Chicago Cardinals & Pittsburgh = Card-Pitt
Year Coach   League/Conf/Div Pl   Record Pct.
1944 #5 Walt Kiesling   NFLEast   5th   0 10 0 .000
1944 Phil Handlers co-coach from the Chicago Cardinals

Philadelphia & Pittsburgh Combined Team aka, Pitt-Phil; Steagles

The Philadelphia and Pittsburgh teams were forced to merge because both had lost many players to military service during World War II. The league's official record book refers to the team as "Phil-Pitt Combine", but the fans unofficially referred to this combination Pitt-Phil team as the "Steagles." Despite its never being registered by the NFL, the Steagles has become the enduring moniker for the team that played the 1943 season.

Our deepest thank you to Pennlive.com and author Aaron Kasiniz for this fine summary of the 1943 Steagles. Lots of other great prose is available on Penn Live.

Steagles legacy: Eagles, Steelers merged in 1943 to form a team of misfits that kept the NFL afloat

Updated on September 21, 2016 at 10:11 AM Posted on September 21, 2016 at 9:00 AM

By Aaron Kasinitz
akasinitz@pennlive.com

A star wide receiver on one of the more significant teams in NFL history was blind in one eye. The center was partially deaf. And another key lineman helped construct parts for the atomic bomb weekdays during the season before heading to practice at Fairmount Park in West Philadelphia each night.

When the Eagles and Steelers merged to form the Steagles in 1943, the team's goal was to keep the NFL afloat and help capture normalcy on the homefront as war raged in Europe. But it wasn't easy, said Matthew Algeo, a radio journalist who authored "Last Team Standing: How the Pittsburgh Steelers and Philadelphia Eagles -- The 'Steagles' -- Saved Pro Football." The jumbled squad didn't include the type of highly-paid, uber-athletic stars fans see today, Algeo said.

And before the modern-day Eagles (2-0) and Steelers (2-0) square off Sunday at Lincoln Financial Field, Algeo wants people to keep that in mind. He wants football fans to understand the 1943 Steagles were unlike any other team to enter the record books.

"Most of these guys were there because they were not able to serve in the military," Algeo said. "A lot of them were classified 4F, which was unfit for military service. A lot of them had ulcers, perforated eardrums."

Somehow, though, the Steagles and the NFL thrived during World War II. The NFL's first merged squad posted a 5-4-1 record in its only season of existence, finishing one game back of first place in the Eastern Division.

And they helped steady the NFL in a time of flux.
The league lacked players in 1943, because so many joined the military. The Steelers only had seven under contract for the season before joining forces with the Eagles, Algeo said. That's why the NFL owners decided the Steelers and Eagles should merge, despite the tension it caused in the Keystone State.

The Steagles didn't get along at first, as competitive tempers overwhelmed the desire for unity. Not to mention, the two co-head coaches, tasked with promoting camaraderie, couldn't stand each other when the season began.

Eagles coach Greasy Neale wanted to follow George Halas' lead by using the innovative T-formation. He hoped to play with a quarterback who could chuck the ball downfield.
Steelers coach Walt Kiesling, meanwhile, thought it was unmanly to throw passes and run fakes.

Even the two fanbases had lingering reservations. The Steagles played four home games in Philadelphia and just two in Pittsburgh. Plus, the team wore green and white uniforms instead of black and gold.

"Pittsburghers who supported the Steelers in the old days have the right to complain over the way Philadelphia hogged the merger," Pittsburgh Press sports editor Chester L. Smith wrote in a 1943 column.

But one thing helped ease the strain: The Steagles won games. They jumped out to a 2-0 start and finished with a 4-1-1 record at home. The Steagles led the league in rushing, according to Pro Football Reference, while Tony Bova, the receiver blind in an eye, had a team-best five touchdown catches.

As the season wore on, the two coaches smoothed over their relationship by separating responsibilities. Neale took over as coach of the offense and Kiesling directed the defense. Both wound up in the Pro Football Hall of Fame.

And, for one season, they helped an odd combination of players find a semblance of stability and success.

"If the Steagles had been a terrible team, I think I would have found much more dissent from Steelers fans about the merger," Algeo said. "Once fans realized that this was a winning team, they kind of changed their attitude and became very supportive."

The growing fandom was a trend around the league, Algeo said. During World War II, many Americans on the home front had to work long hours and spend six days a week in factories. Most everyone, however, had Sundays off. And with worry looming over American families, football provided an outlet.

The league might have folded if the Steelers and Eagles hadn't joined forces to form an eighth team, Algeo said. Yet NFL attendance rose during the war.

"It provided entertainment on those Sunday afternoons, especially in the fall after baseball ended, because there was nothing else to do," Algeo said. "All the trolleys ran to all the ballparks. At the time, the NFL teams used Major League ballparks. So, all this helped the league survive."

The Steagles players weren't just contributing to the war efforts with their play on the field, though. Steelers owners Art Rooney and Bert Bell and Eagles owner Alexis Thompson required their players to work in wartime industries during the week.

Philadelphia was a hub for shipyards, while Pittsburgh produced much of the steel used in World War II. Offensive guard Ted Doyle worked in Pittsburgh and constructed parts for the atomic bomb, though he didn't know it at the time, Algeo said.
The work schedules and distance between teammates created logistical problems.

But the Steagles made things work. According to Algeo, the team was able to use a field in Philadelphia's Fairmount Park for night-time practices. It had lights because a Negro League baseball team played games there.

The late practices allowed Steagles players time to get to the field after working from about 7 a.m. to 3 p.m., Algeo said. Some from Pittsburgh rode the train across the state regularly. It took some finagling, but the Steagles remained on firm ground. They had to. Owners knew the NFL could face a downward spiral if the league suspended play for a significant amount of time during the war.

"People don't remember this, but another league came into existence in '46: The All-America Football Conference. That's who gave us the Baltimore Colts and the San Francisco 49ers," Algeo said. "The [NFL] came very close to suspending operations for a year or two during World War II, and if they had, it would have been much more difficult to defeat the rival leagues that came up after.

"So, I don't think it's an exaggeration to say that by merging the Eagles and Steelers, they were keeping the league alive. The NFL really, really saved itself during WWII."

The challenges facing the Steagles stood out to Algeo when he covered a reunion event in 2003 for NPR. Not a huge football nut, Algeo said he always considered himself a moderate Eagles fans and wanted to explore the history of the merged franchises.

By the time he published the book in 2006, Algeo had interviewed the nine living members of the Steagles. Ten years later, none are left. Al Wistert, an all-pro tackle, died in March at the age of 95. He was the last remaining Steagle.

And as he looks back on his research, Algeo's biggest takeaway wasn't simply that the team revived the NFL or lifted American morale during a devastating war.

It's that many of the players who accomplished those things were the ones unallowed to make an impact through more conventional wartime methods.

"These guys were not able to contribute in the military, but in some small way, they were able to contribute by keeping this game alive," Algeo said. "It was a tough game. It was a tough game, especially for some of the guys with disabilities. They deserve a lot of respect."

-- @AaronKazreports

1943 Steagles starting line-up Back row (left to right): *unknown*, back (#11); Ben Kish, back (#44); Ernie Steele, halfback (#37) Middle row: Roy Zimmerman, quarterback (#7) Front row (left to right): Larry Cabrelli, end (#84); Bucko Kilroy, tackle (#76); Ed Michaels, guard (#60); Ray Graves, center (#52); Elbie Schultz, guard (#71); Vic Sears, tackle (#79); Bob Masters, end (#31)

1943 Walt Kiesling, Pittsburgh Steelers Coach #5
1943 Greasy Neal Philadelphia Eagles co-coach

The 1943 Pittsburgh Steelers football team competed as a combined team along with the Philadelphia Eagles in their eleventh season of Professional National Football League (NFL) football. This was the first and last time Pittsburgh and Philadelphia would combine their resources to be able to field a team, though the Pirates combined with the Chicago Cardinals again in 1944.

The combined team was led by co-coaches Pittsburgh Coach Walt Kiesling and Philadelphia Coach Greasy Neale. Neither coach would be demoted and so both were used throughout the season. In order to keep conflicts to a minimum between the two coaches,

Neale took over as coach of the offense and Kiesling directed the defense. The team had a nice record of 5-4-1 and they tied for second.

The Steagles began the season with two wins. In the season and home opener at Shibe Park in Philadelphia, on October 2, 1943, the Steagles shut-out the Brooklyn Dodgers W (17-0) At home again in Shibe Park, Philadelphia, on Oct 9, the Steagles defeated the New York Giants W (28-14). On Oct 17, the Steagles lost their first game of 1943 to the Chicago Bears in a rout L (21-48) at Wrigley Field. Then, in New York on Sunday, Oct 24, the Giants defeated the Steagles L(42–14) at the Polo Grounds before 42,681.

On Oct 31, the Steagles belted the Chicago Cardinals W (34–13) at home in Forbes Field before 16,351. On Nov 7, the Washington Redskins tied the Steagles at Shibe Park T (14–14) before 32,694. On Nov 14, in a close match at Ebbets Field, the Brooklyn Dodgers defeated the Steagles L (7-13) before 7,613.

Then, at Forbes Field, on Nov 21, in a one-point nail-biter, the Steagles defeated the Detroit Lions W 35–34 before 23,338. On Nov 28, the Steagles defeated the Washington Redskins W (27–14) at Griffith Stadium before 35,540. In the final game ever for the Steagles team, on Dec 5, in a tough match, the Steagles fell to the Green Bay Packers L (28-3) at Shibe Park in Philadelphia before 34,294. And, so the Steagles record was then superimposed in Philadelphia and Pittsburgh as if the he original teams played the games of 1943.

1944 Chicago Cardinals & Pittsburgh Steelers Merger

Card-Pitt was another temporary merger of two NFL teams to form one on a temporary basis. It was the second time the Pittsburgh Steelers were involved in such a Merger. We have just discussed the 1943 Steagles.

This new temporary team was created by the temporary merger of two National Football League (NFL) teams, the Pittsburgh Steelers and the Chicago Cardinals, during the 1944 season. Pittsburgh still did not have enough players or enough money to get players and the war was still taking its toll on the Steelers organization. The Cardinals merger request the prior year had been turned down the prior year and like Pittsburgh, their existence was hanging on a thread.

So, as noted, it was the second such merger for the Steelers, who had combined with the Philadelphia Eagles in 1943 to form the "Steagles". The arrangement was made necessary by the loss of numerous players to World War II military service and was dissolved upon completion of the season.

The war ended before the start of the 1945 season, and both teams resumed normal operations. Card-Pitt finished did not have the success of the Steagles and finished with a 0–10–0 record in the Western Division. This led sportswriters to derisively label the team the "Car-Pitts", or "carpets". The Associated press through the NFL, recently put out an article about what happened in 1944 and we have provided it with a thank you to the NFL below: Enjoy.

Merged 1944 Cardinals-Steelers team brought memories, not wins
From nfl.com: / Associated Press
Published: Jan. 25, 2009 at 05:33 p.m.
Updated: July 26, 2012 at 08:28 p.m.

TAMPA, Fla. -- They wore hand-me-down jerseys, the little rips and tears widening with every loss. The holes at quarterback and kicker were more obvious.

The brief World War II merger of the Steelers and Cardinals might have helped the NFL, but it sure didn't benefit anyone who spent that season shuttling to home games in Pittsburgh and Chicago.

"We were terrible," said former lineman Chet Bulger, now 91. "You'd get beat so bad, you'd cry."

Walt Kiesling Co-Coach Coach of Card-Pitt

Long, long before the franchises reached any Super Bowl, they teamed together in 1944 to create a much different legacy.

At 0-10, the ragtag outfit was outscored by an average of three touchdowns per game, threw a league-record, 41 interceptions and set an NFL mark that still stands for the worst punting.

Their nickname seemed inevitable: *the Car-Pitts*. As in, every team walked right over them.

"That was true," recalled Vince Banonis, who played two games while on weekend furlough as a Navy lieutenant. "We got massacred every week."

Beset by fights, fines and suspensions in a rough-and-tumble era, there was hardly a Ben Roethlisberger or Larry Fitzgerald among them. Their lone ace, Johnny Grigas, threw away his leather helmet and skipped town before it was over.

About one hour before the wrap-up, a 49-7 rout by the Chicago Bears at Forbes Field, the Car-Pitts discovered Grigas already was on a train.

The former Holy Cross star left a note for his hotel roommate. "This is the end," Grigas wrote, saying he didn't care to finish up on a frozen field.

"I thought he'd gone to become a priest," Bulger said. "He'd had enough."

So had many of the guys. Most of them came from the Chicago Cardinals -- they were in the midst of a 29-game losing streak, and only the merger kept them out of the record book for consecutive defeats by a single franchise.

A few guys straggled over from the Steelers. They had joined Philadelphia in 1943 as the "Steagles" after military service left both teams short-handed, but the sides broke apart when the season ended.

"They were at each other's throats, the way I heard it," Banonis said.

In April 1944, the NFL suddenly found itself with 11 teams when the Cleveland Rams rejoined the league and the Boston Yanks also entered. That caused scheduling problems, so commissioner Elmer Layden, one of the original "Four Horsemen of Notre Dame," asked Steelers owner Art Rooney and Cardinals boss Charles Bidwill if they'd be interested in a merger.

The patriarchs of the families that still own the franchises agreed. A few months later, the combined club went off to training camp in Waukesha, Wis.

"We were all sitting there on the porch the first day," Bulger said. "We're all just looking at each other. These were guys you'd tried to beat up before. Finally, one of the co-owners, Bert Bell, says, 'You're going to have to get together.'"

Finding a nickname for the team was a little more challenging.

At the outset, there were several: the Chi-Pitts, the Card-Pitts and Cardinals-Pitt, among them.

A 3-0 loss to Sammy Baugh and the Washington Redskins in an exhibition game gave the Car-Pitts hope. They lost the opener to the Rams 30-28 on a late touchdown, then actually won one week later -- too bad for them, the 17-16 victory over the New York Giants came in an exhibition game, a frequent occurrence during the war.

From there, it got real bad in a hurry.

Team management fined three players for "indifferent play" after a 34-7 loss to the defending champion Bears.

None of their quarterbacks could run the popular T-formation, and the famed "Notre Dame box" didn't work, either. Military commitments caused chaos with the roster, and replacements signed off the sandlots showed up in Pittsburgh for practice.

"It was an odd year," Bulger said. "We got all mixed up." Especially when it came to kicking. They averaged only 32.7 yards per punt.

"Everybody tried to punt. We all tried in practice," Bulger said. "We couldn't find anyone."

Co-coaches Phil Handler of the Cardinals and Walt Kiesling of the Steelers were at a loss. Kiesling had been a Hall of Fame lineman, but he wasn't nearly so successful as a coach. Many years later in Steelers camp, he cut a young quarterback named Johnny Unitas.

Art Rooney also thought Kiesling spent too much time around the horse tracks in Chicago. "He studies the Racing Form more than he does the playbook," Rooney once said.[Rooney would know!]

The next week, after the Giants whacked the Car-Pitts 23-0, it was clear this merged team was brutal.

"The Card-Pitts played the role of a red plush rug this afternoon as the undefeated Giants paraded over and past them," the Chicago Tribune reported.

Then came a wild brawl with the Redskins, with Gil "Cactus Face" Duggan among the players ejected once police restored order. There were two losses at their other home field, Comiskey Park in Chicago, and that final rout by the Bears. Overall, the Car-Pitts were outscored 328-108.

For Bulger and Banonis, the good times came later. The rugged two-way linemen played together in 1947 on the last Cardinals team to win the NFL championship, and Banonis won two titles with the Detroit Lions in the early 1950s. Bell also made out well, later becoming commissioner.

Banonis, now 87 and in a wheelchair, will root for the Cardinals in Super Bowl XLIII (When this article was written]. During a telephone interview from his home in Southfield, Mich., Banonis began singing the team fight song from long ago.

"Hail Chicago Cardinals, crimson and white," he belted.

Told of Banonis' performance, Bulger laughed.

"He was always singing these Lithuanian songs," Bulger said. "Oh, what a football player he was."

After nine years in the NFL, Bulger coached and taught for 30-plus years at De La Salle Institute in Chicago. The school named its main athletic field for him, and he continues to help with its fundraising efforts.
And he keeps rooting for his old team.

"I'm still a Cardinal, always a Cardinal," he said. "I can't see too well anymore, but I'm going to get up real close to the TV to watch that game. Maybe we'll win that Super Bowl. Wouldn't that be something?"

1944 Walt Kiesling, Coach #5
1944 Phil Handler, Coach of the Cardinals

The 0-10-0 record gave few in Pittsburgh anything to cheer about, but it helped Art Rooney and Bert Bell get by one more year before post-war operations could begin again as the team moved to a normal program.

1944 Card-Pitt

The 1944 Pittsburgh Steelers football team competed as a combined team along with the Chicago Cardinals in their twelfth season of Professional National Football League (NFL) football. This was the first and last time Pittsburgh and Chicago would combine their resources to be able to field a team.

The combined team was led by co-coaches Pittsburgh Coach Walt Kiesling and Cardinal Coach Phil Handler. The team had the worst record possible for a ten-game season – 0-10-0. They came in last place.

The Card-Pitt began the season with a loss at home and continued losing for the rest of the season.

In the season and home opener at one of the home fields, Comiskey Park in Chicago, on September 24, 1944, the Car-Pitts gave up the game in the last minutes L (28-30) What came next was nine straight losses for the ten-game season as shown below in list form. The games were all losses so there is not much to say..

1 September 24, 1944 Cleveland Rams L 28–30
2 October 8, 1944 at Green Bay Packers L 7–34
3 October 15, 1944 at Chicago Bears L 7–34
4 October 22, 1944 at New York Giants L 0–23
5 October 29, 1944 at Washington Redskins L 20-42
6 November 5, 1944 Detroit Lions L 6–27
7 November 12, 1944 at Detroit Lions L 7–21
8 November 19, 1944 Cleveland Rams L 6–33
9 November 26, 1944 Green Bay Packers L 20–35
10 December 3, 1944 Chicago Bears L 7–49

Chapter 17 Five Coaches from 1945 through 1956

Coach #8 Jim Leonard
Coach #9 Jock Sutherland
Coach #10 John Michelosen
Coach #3 Joe Bach
Coach #5 Walt Kiesling

Year	Coach	League/Conf/Div	Pl	Record	Pct.
1945	#8 Jim Leonard	NFLEast	5th	2 8 0	.200
1946	#9 Jock Sutherland	NFLEast	3rd-T	5 5 1	.500
• Bill Dudley – Joe F. Carr Trophy (MVP)					
1947	#9 Jock Sutherland	NFLEast	2nd	8 4 0	.667
• Lost Eastern Divisional Playoff (Eagles) 21–0					
1948	#10 John Michelosen	NFLEast	3rd-T	4 8 0	.333
1949	#10 John Michelosen	NFLEast	2nd	6 5 1	.542
1950	#10 John Michelosen	NFLAmerican	3rd-T	6 6 0	.500
1951	#10 John Michelosen	NFLAmerican	4th	4 7 1	.375
1952	#3 Joe Bach	NFLAmerican	4th	5 7 0	.417
1953	#3 Joe Bach	NFLEastern	4th	6 6 0	.500
1954	#5 Walt Kiesling	NFLEastern	4th	5 7 0	.417
1955	#5 Walt Kiesling	NFLEastern	6th	4 8 0	.346
1956	#5 Walt Kiesling	NFLEastern	4th-T	5 7 0	.500

1945 Jim Leonard, Coach #8

#8 Jim Leonard

The 1945 Pittsburgh Steelers football team competed in their thirteenth season of Professional National Football League (NFL) football. They were led by Jim Leonard in his first and only year as head coach. It would be facetious to say that the team improved substantially on its previous season result of 0-10-0, but it did with an almost as poor record of 2-8-0. The Steelers did not make the playoffs.

Pittsburgh began the season with two losses. In the season and home opener at Forbes Field on September 26, 1945, Leonard-led Steelers squad were defeated by the Boston Yanks L (7-28). In the next outing at Forbes Field, on Oct 7, the New York Giants beat the Steelers L (6-34). On Oct 14, the Washington

Redskins shut out the Steelers L (0-14). Then, on Oct 21, at New York, the Steelers defeated the Giants for the first win of the year,

On Oct 28, the Boston Yanks beat the Steelers at home L (6-10). Then, on Nov 4, the Steelers were pounded by the cross-state Philadelphia Eagles L (3-45). The second and last win of the year came on Nov 11 at home against the Chicago Cardinals in a shutout W (23–0).

At Philadelphia on Nov 18, the Eagles beat the Steelers for the second time this season, L (6-30). On Nov 25, at Chicago, the Bears beat the Steelers L (7-28). In the season finale at Washington on Dec 2, the Redskins shut out the Steelers L (0-24) to wrap up the season.

1946 Jock Sutherland, Coach #9

<< Jock Sutherland circa 1945

The 1945 Pittsburgh Steelers football team competed in their fourteenth season of Professional National Football League (NFL) football. The team improved substantially on its previous season result of 2-8-0, breaking even at 5-5-1. The Steelers did not make the playoffs, but they responded to Jock Sutherland's style and after this season, there was a glimmer of hope for the future.

Pittsburgh began the season with a win followed by a tie. The team was off to a good start. In the season and home opener at Forbes Field on September 20, 1946, the Sutherland led Steelers squad defeated the Chicago Cardinals W (14-7). In the next outing at Forbes Field, on Sept 29, the Steelers tied the Washington Redskins T (14-14). Then, on Oct 6, the Steelers lost their first game—to the NY Giants L (14-17) .

On Oct 13, the Steelers picked up a milestone win (#3) against the Boston Yanks at Forbes Field W (16-7). The second loss for the squad came quickly when the two weeks later on Oct 20, at Green Bay, the Packers beat the Steelers L (7-17. On Oct 27 at Boston, the Steelers ripped the Yanks apart W (33-7), dominating the game. Another win came in Week #7 on Nov 3 at home against the Washington Redskins W (14-7).

On Nov 10, at Detroit, the Lions beat the Steelers, L (7-17) On Nov 17, Philadelphia came to town and the Steelers beat the Eagles W (10–7). After what would have been a winning season, Sutherland's squad lost its last two games by close margins to finish at 5-5-1. The first of the two losses was L (0-7) on Nov 24, at the New York Giants L 7–0. The final game was even closer on Dec 1, @ Philadelphia where the Steelers were beaten by the Eagles by just three points L(10–7).

1947 Jock Sutherland, Coach #9

The 1947 Pittsburgh Steelers football team competed in their fifteenth season of Professional National Football League (NFL) football. The team improved again on its previous season result of 2-8-0, breaking even at 8-4-0. The Steelers made the playoffs. This record tied for the lead in the Eastern Division and qualified the Steelers for the franchise's first playoff berth. It was the Steelers' only postseason appearance before 1972. Jock Sutherland had moved mountains, but it was his final year as head coach; he died the following April.

Because he was such a good coach and he died so suddenly, I made some Internet inquiries and I found that Sutherland planned to stay at Pittsburgh and that sure would have been a shot in the arm for the sad-sack Steelers at that time.

He was on a scouting trip for the Steelers in April 1948, when Sutherland was found in his car in Bandana, Kentucky. He was experiencing confusion and was then taken to a hospital in Cairo, Illinois. It was serious. He was initially diagnosed with "nervous exhaustion," as his illness was sudden. He was then flown back to Pittsburgh for further treatment.

He underwent an exploratory surgery to determine whether he was suffering from a hemorrhage or a tumor. Sutherland died in Pittsburgh on April 11, 1948, following the surgery to remove a malignant brain tumor. RIP.

In the season and home opener at Forbes Field on September 21, 1947, the Sutherland led Steelers squad defeated the Detroit Lions W (17-10). In the next outing at Forbes Field, on Sept 29, the team suffered a big letdown and they were pummeled by the LA Rams L (7-48). They played much better on Oct 5 at Washington against the Redskins but lost by one-point L (25-27). The team fought their way back into the win column in their fourth season game on Oct 12, at Boston, beating the Yanks W (30–14).

On Oct 19, the Steelers whooped the Eagles W (35–24). Then, at NY on Oct 26, the Steelers defeated the Giants W (38–21). On Nov 2, after the trip to Green Bay, the Steelers beat the Packers W (18–17). It was another win at home on Nov 9 against Washington's Redskins W (21–14)

At home on Nov 16, the Steelers prevailed v the New York Giants W (24–7) On Nov 23 at Chicago, the Steelers smashed the Bears L (49-7). On Nov 30, there was a letdown at Philadelphia and the Eagles beat the Steelers in a shutout L (0-21). For the first season in while, the Steelers finished with a win. This time it was on Dec 7 at home against the Boston Yanks W (17–7). 8-4 was one of the best seasons ever. The team made the playoffs.

In the Playoffs, the Steelers replayed the Philadelphia Eagles who were also having a great season. At 2:00 PM on Dec 21, in 39-degree weather before 35,729 fans the Steelers were not able to move the ball and lost the contest L (0-21). The Eagles scored once in each of the first three quarters. The first was a Van Buren 15 yd pass reception from Thompson with a Patton PAT. The second was a Ferrante 28 yd pass reception from Thompson and a Patton PAT. The third score in the third quarter was via Pritchard's 79-yard punt return followed by another accurate Patton PAT.

1948 John Michelosen, Coach #9

The 1948 Pittsburgh Steelers football team competed in their sixteenth season of Professional National Football League (NFL) football. The team was adapting to the replacement coach for Jock Sutherland, John Michelosen who was in his first of four seasons. . Their record went south from last year's result of 8-4-0, to 4-8-0. The Steelers did not make made the playoffs.

In the season opener at Washington on September 26, 1948, the Michelosen- led Steelers squad suffered a defeat in a very close match against the Redskins L (14-17) . In the next outing at Forbes Field, on Oct 3, the team put it together to whip the Boston Yanks W (24-14). They brought their record above 500 with win # 2 at Forbes Field on Oct 10, against the Washington Redskins W (10–7). Then on Oct 17, the Steelers were beaten at Boston by the Yanks L (13–7).

At New York, on Oct 24, the Giants beat the Steelers L (27-34). This was followed by another loss on Oct 31 at home in Forbes Field against the Philadelphia Eagles L (7-34). On Nov 7, at home the

Steelers hammered the Green Bay Packers W (38–7). Then, on Nov 14, Pittsburgh was beaten by the Chicago Cardinals L (7-24).

At Detroit on Nov 21, the Lions beat the Steelers L (14-17). At Philadelphia on Nov 28, the Eagles shut out the Steelers L (0-17). At home in Forbes Field on Dec 5, the Steelers beat the New York Giants W (38–28). Then, in the season finale, on Dec 12, at Los Angeles, the Rams whipped the Steelers L (14-31) to close out the season for the Steelers.

1949 John Michelosen, Coach #9

The 1949 Pittsburgh Steelers football team competed in their seventeenth season of Professional National Football League (NFL) football. The team was led by John Michelosen in his second of four seasons. Their record improved from last year's result of 4-8-0, to better than 500 at 6-5-1. The Steelers finished second in the NFL Eastern Division and though a bit closer, the team did not make the playoffs in 1949.

In the season and home opener in Forbes Field on September 26, 1948, the Steelers squad played well and defeated the New York Giants W(28-7). In the next outing at Forbes Field, on Oct 3, the team played an OK game but lost to the Washington Redskins L (14-27). On Oct 8, at Forbes Field, the Steelers beat the Detroit Lions W 14–7. In another win, on Oct 16, at New York, the Steelers beat the Giants W (21–17)

On Oct 23, at home, the Steelers beat the New York Bulldogs W (24–13). Then, on Oct 30, the Steelers took it on the chin from the Eagles in a blowout L (7-38) . At Washington, on Nov 6, the Redskins overpowered the Steelers L (14-27). At home in Forbes on Nov 13, the visiting Los Angeles Rams tied the Steelers T (7–7). At Green Bay on Nov 20, the Steelers powered by the Packers W (30–7). At Philly on Nov. 27, the Eagles doubled the score v the Steelers and beat us L (17-34). On Dec 4 at Chicago, the Bears put it all together to beat the Steelers L (21-30). Then, on Dec 11, at New York in the final game of the season, the Steelers whipped the Bulldogs W 27–0. It was a great way to end the season.

1950 John Michelosen, Coach #9

The 1950 Pittsburgh Steelers football team competed in their eighteenth season of Professional National Football League (NFL) football. The team was led by John Michelosen in his third of four seasons. Their record diminished result of 6-5-1, to a dead even 6-6-0. better than 500 at 6-5-1. The Steelers finished tied for third in the NFL Eastern Division and though just a not a lot further from the playoffs, the team would have to wait at least one more year to get there as it would not be this year.

Top Steelers Players Ernie Stautner

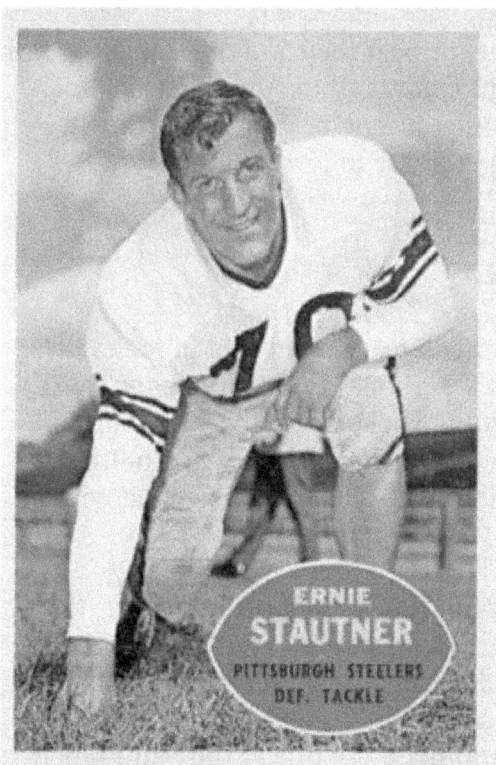

Defensive Tackle (1950-63)
Elected: 1969
Ernie Stautner, considered one of the toughest players in league history by his teammates and opponents, was a nine-time Pro Bowl selection as he anchored Pittsburgh's defense for 14 seasons. He captured the NFL's Best Lineman Award in 1957 and was named all-league four times. Showing his gritty and hard-working attitude, Stautner missed just six games during his 14-year career despite having numerous broken ribs, shoulders, hands and a nose. The Steelers honored him by retiring his No. 70 jersey in 1964 following his retirement, and he remains the only Steeler to have received that honor.

Games of the 1950 season

In the season and home opener in Forbes Field on September 17, 1950, at 2:00 PM, the Steelers squad could not get the job done and were beaten by the New York Giants L(7-18). In the next outing at Detroit, Sept 24, the team played a tough game but lost to the Detroit Lions L (7-10). On Oct 1, at Washington, the Steelers beat the Redskins W (26-7). In another loss, on Oct 7, at home in a night game, the Browns beat the Steelers, L 17–30

On Oct 15 at New York, the Steelers beat the Giants W (17–6). On Oct 22, in the afternoon, the Steelers lost to the Eagles L (10–17). Then, on Oct 29 at Cleveland, the Browns thumped the Eagles L (7–45). At Philadelphia on Nov 5, the Steelers edged out the Eagles W 9–7. On Nov 12, the Eagles beat the Baltimore Colts W (17–7). The team then had a bye week.

On Nov 23, at Chicago, the Steelers beat the Cardinals W 28–17. On Dec 3, the Washington Redskins beat the Pittsburgh Steelers L (7–24). Wrapping up the season with a nice win, on Dec 10, the Steelers defeated the Chicago Cardinals at home in Forbes Field W (28–7).

1951 John Michelosen, Coach #9

The 1951 Pittsburgh Steelers football team competed in their nineteenth season of Professional National Football League (NFL) football. The team was led by John Michelosen in his last of four seasons. Their record diminished from a prior result of 6-6-0, to 4-7-1. The Steelers finished fourth in the NFL Eastern Division with no chance for the playoffs.

In the season and home opener in Forbes Field on October 1, the Steelers tied the New York Giants on Oct 1, 1951, T (13-13). In the next outing on Oct 7, at Green Bay, in a nail-biter tough match, the Packers edged out the Steelers L (33-35). On Oct 14, at home in Forbes Field, the Steelers lost another close one to the San Francisco 49ers L (24–28) On October 21, at Cleveland, the Browns shut out the Steelers giving Pittsburgh its third loss in a row.

At Chicago on Oct 28, the Steelers beat the Cardinals W (28–14). Then, on Nov4, at home, the Philadelphia Eagles beat the Steelers L (13–34). On Nov 11, the Steelers whooped the Green Bay Packers at Forbes Field W (28–7). Then, on Nov 8,the Washington Redskins beat the Steelers L (7–22)

At Philadelphia on Nov 25, the Steelers beat the Eagles W (17-13). Then, on Dec 2, at New York, the Giants shut out the Steelers L (0–14). At home on Dec 9, the Steelers were defeated by the Cleveland Browns L (0–28). Wrapping up the season on Dec 16 at Washington, the Steelers beat the Redskins W (20–10).

1952 Joe Bach, Coach #3

Bach

The 1952 Pittsburgh Steelers football team competed in their twentieth season of Professional National Football League (NFL) football. The team was led by Joe Bach in the first year of his second stint as Coach of the Steelers. Bach was the coach of the Pirates in 1935 & 1936. He returned to the franchise to replace coach John Michelosen. Their record improved from a prior result of 4-7-1 to 5-7-0. 6-6-0, to 4-7-1. The Steelers finished fourth in the NFL Eastern Division with no chance for the playoffs.

This season was noteworthy in that it was the last year the Steelers used the single-wing formation on offense, switching to the T formation the following year. The Steelers were the last NFL team to use the single-wing as their primary offensive formation.

In the season and home opener in Forbes Field on September 28, 1952, the Steelers were defeated by the Philadelphia Eagles L (25-31). In the next outing at home in Forbes Field on my wedding anniversary, Oct 4, in a one-point matchup, the Cleveland Browns defeated the Steelers L (20-21). At Philadelphia on Oct 12, the Steelers lost another close game to the Eagles L (21-26). Then, on 4

Oct 19, at home in Forbes Field, the Washington Redskins beat the Steelers L (24-28).

At Chicago on Oct 26, the Steelers defeated the Cardinals W (34–28). At Washington on Nov 2, the Steelers prevailed over the Redskins by one point, W (24023). On Nov 9, at home in Forbes Field, the Detroit Lions outplayed the Steelers L (6-31). At Cleveland on Nov 16, , in another one-point match, the Browns beat the Steelers L (28-29).

On Nov 23. At home in Forbes Field, the Steelers defeated the Chicago Cardinals W (17–14) At home on Nov 30, the Steelers shellacked the New York Giants W (63–7). At San Francisco on Dec 7, the Steelers beat the 49ers W (24–7). In the season finale at Los Angeles, the Rams beat the Steelers L (14-28).

1953 Joe Bach, Coach #3

The 1953 Pittsburgh Steelers football team competed in their twenty-first season of Professional National Football League (NFL) football. The team was led by Joe Bach in the second year of his second stint as Coach of the Steelers. Their record improved from a prior result of 5-7-0 to 6-6-0. The Steelers finished fourth in the NFL Eastern Division with no chance for the playoffs.

In the season opener at Detroit on September 27, 1953, the Steelers were defeated by the Lions L (21-38). In the next outing at home in Forbes Field on Oct 3, the Steelers beat the New York Giants W (24-14) At home on Oct 11, the Steelers won their second game in a row v the Chicago Cardinals W (31-28). Them on Oct 17, at Philadelphia, the Eagles beat the Steelers L 23–7

On Oct 24, the Steelers beat the Green Bay Packers W (31–14). At home in Forbes Field on Nov 1, the Philadelphia Eagles pounded the Steelers L (7-35). At Cleveland on Nov 8, the Browns beat the Steelers L (16-34). At New York on Nov 15, the Steelers beat the Giants W (14–10).

At home in Forbes Field on Nov 22, the Cleveland Browns defeated the Steelers L (16-20). At Forbes Field in another home game on

Nov 29, the Washington Redskins beat the Steelers L (9-17). At Chicago on Dec 6, the Steelers defeated the Cardinals W (21–17). Then, to wrap up a 500 season, on Dec 13, at Washington the Steelers beat the Redskins W (14–13).

1954 Walt Kiesling, Coach #5

The 1954 Pittsburgh Steelers football team competed in their twenty-second season of Professional National Football League (NFL) football. The team was led by Walt Kiesling in the first year of his third stint as Coach of the Steelers. Their record declined from a prior result of 6-6-0 to 5-7-0. The Steelers finished fourth again in the NFL Eastern Division with no chance for the playoffs.

In the season opener at Green Bay on September 26, 1954, the Steelers defeated the Packers W (21-20). In the next outing at home in Forbes Field on Oct 2, the Steelers whooped the Washington Redskins W (37-7). At Philadelphia on Oct 9, the Steelers were beaten by just two points by the Eagles L (22-24). At home in Forbes Field on Oct 17, the Eagles beat the Cleveland Browns W 55–27 in a shootout.

At home in Forbes Field on Oct 23, the Steelers beat the Eagles W 17–7. At Chicago on Oct 31, the Cardinals beat the Steelers L (14-17). Then, on Nov 7, the New York Giants beat the Steelers L (6-30). Then at Washington on Nov 14, , the Redskins beat the Steelers in a close match L (14-17).

At home in Forbes Field on Nov 20, the San Francisco 49ers smothered Pittsburgh L (3-31). At home again on November 28, the Steelers beat the Chicago Cardinals W (20–17). At New York on Dec 5, the Giants outplayed the Steelers L (3-24). In the last game of the season on Dec 12, at Cleveland, the Browns squashed the Steelers L (7-42).

1955 Walt Kiesling, Coach #5

The 1955 Pittsburgh Steelers football team competed in their twenty-third season of Professional National Football League (NFL) football. The team was led by Walt Kiesling in the second year of his third stint as Coach of the Steelers. Their record declined from a prior result of 5-7-0 to 4-8-0. The Steelers finished in sixth place in the NFL Eastern Division with no chance for the playoffs.

In the season and home opener on September 26, 1955, the Steelers defeated the Chicago Cardinals W (14-0). In the next outing at Los Angeles on Oct 2, the Steelers beat the Rams in a one-point match L (26-27). The Steelers then won their next three games. At home on Oct 9, the Steelers beat the New York Giants W (30-23) At home in Forbes Field on Oct 15, the Eagles beat the Philadelphia Eagles W (13-7). The third win in a row came at New York as the Steelers beat the Giants on Oct 23, W (19-17).

At 4-1 and knocking them dead one at time, the Steelers hit bottom as they closed out what would have been a fine season with seven losses in a row.

At Philadelphia on Oct 30. The Eagles shut out the Steelers L (0-24). At Chicago, on Nov 5, the Cardinals won L (13-27). At home in Forbes Field on Nov 13, 1955, the Detroit Lions beat the Eagles L (28-31).At Cleveland on Nov 20, the Browns lambasted the Steelers L (14-4).

At home in Forbes Field, on Nov 27, the Washington Redskins beat the Steelers L (14-23). On Dec 4, the Cleveland Browns beat the Steelers L (7-30) in Forbes Field. Then, to wrap up the season, the Steelers lost their seventh game in a row—this one at on Dec 11 at Washington v the Redskins L (17-28).

1956 Walt Kiesling, Coach #5

The 1956 Pittsburgh Steelers football team competed in their twenty-fourth season of Professional National Football League (NFL) football. The team was led by Walt Kiesling in the third and final year of his third stint as Coach of the Steelers. Their record improved slightly from a prior result of 4-9-0 to 5-7-0. The Steelers finished in fifth place in the NFL Eastern Division with no chance for the playoffs.

In the season and home opener on September 30, 1956, the Steelers defeated the Washington Redskins W (30-13). The Steelers then lost three in a row. In the next outing at home in Forbes Field, on Oct14, the Steelers were beaten by the Philadelphia Eagles L (21-35) then at

New York, on Oct 9, the Steelers were thumped by the New York Giants W (10-38).

At Cleveland on Oct 28, the Steelers beat the Browns W (24–16). Then, at home in Forbes Field on November 4, the New York Giants beat Pittsburgh L (14-17). At Philadelphia on Nov 11, the Eagles beat the Steelers L (7-14). Then at home on Nov 18, the Steelers beat the Chicago Cardinals W (14–7).

At Chicago on Nov 25, the Cardinals beat the Steelers L (27-38). At home in Forbes Field on Dec 2, the Steelers beat the Los Angeles Rams W (30–13). At Detroit on Dec 9 the Lions scorched the Steelers L (7-45). In the season finale at Washington on Dec 16, the Stealers shut out the Redskins W (23–0).

Chapter 18 Coach Buddy Parker, 1957 to 1964

Coach #11 Buddy Parker

Year	Coach	League/Conf/Div	Pl	Record	Pct.
1957	#11 Buddy Parker	NFLEastern	3rd	6 6 0	.500
1958	#11 Buddy Parker	NFLEastern	3rd	7 4 1	.625
1959	#11 Buddy Parker	NFLEastern	4th	6 5 1	.542
1960	#11 Buddy Parker	NFLEastern	5th	5 6 1	.458
1961	#11 Buddy Parker	NFLEastern	5th	6 8 0	.429
1962	#11 Buddy Parker	NFLEastern	2nd	9 5 0	.643

- Lost Playoff Bowl(Lions) 17-10 exhibition game

1963	#11 Buddy Parker	NFLEastern	4th	7 4 3	.607
1964	#11 Buddy Parker	NFLEastern	6th	5 9 0	.357

1957 Pittsburgh Steelers Football Team

1957 Buddy Parker, Coach #11

The 1957 Pittsburgh Steelers football team competed in their twenty-fifth season of Professional National Football League (NFL) football. The team was led by Buddy Parker in the first of his eight years as coach of the Steelers. Their record improved slightly from a prior result of 5-7-0 to 6-0-0. The Steelers finished in third place in the NFL Eastern Division with no chance for the playoffs.

For the first time, the Steelers' yellow helmets sported uniform numbers. Pittsburgh would use these uniforms through the 1961 season.

In the season and home opener on September 29, 1957, the Steelers defeated the Washington Redskins W (28-7). The Steelers then lost to the Cleveland Browns on Oct 5, L (12-23) In the next outing at home in Forbes Field, on Oct13, the Steelers beat the Chicago Cardinals W (29-20). Then, at New York, on Oct 20, the Steelers were hammered the New York Giants in a shutout L (0-35).

At home in Forbes Field, the Steelers shut out the Philadelphia Eagles W (6–0). At Baltimore on Nov 3, the Steelers beat the Colts W (19–13) At Cleveland, on Nov 10, the Browns shut out the Steelers L (0-24). On Nov 24 at home in Forbes Field, the Green Bay Packers defeated the Steelers L (10-27).

At Philadelphia on Dec 1, the Eagles beat the Steelers in a very close match L (6-7). At home in Forbes Field, the Steelers beat the New York Giants W (21–10). At Washington on Dec 15, the Redskins beat the Steelers L (3-10). Wrapping up the season, at Chicago, on Dec 22, Pittsburgh beat the Cardinals W (27–2).

1958 Buddy Parker, Coach #11

The 1958 Pittsburgh Steelers football team competed in their twenty-sixth season of Professional National Football League (NFL) football. The team was led by Buddy Parker in the second of his eight years as coach of the Steelers. Their record improved slightly from a prior result of 6-6-0 to 7-4-1. The Steelers finished in third place in the NFL Eastern Division with no chance for the playoffs.

In the season and home opener on September 28, 1958, the Steelers were defeated by the San Francisco 49ers L (20-23) The Steelers then were pounded by the Cleveland Browns on Oct 5, L (12-45). In the next outing at home in Forbes Field, on Oct23, the Steelers beat the Philadelphia Eagles W (24-3). Then, at Cleveland, on Oct 19, the Steelers were defeated by the Browns L (10-27).

At New York, on Oct 26, the New York Giants beat the Steelers L (6-17). At home in Forbes Field on Nov 2, the Steelers beat the Washington Redskins W (24–16). At Philadelphia on Nov 9, the Steelers beat the Eagles W (31–24). On Nov 16, at home in Forbes Field, the Eagles whipped the New York Giants W (31–10).

At Chicago, on Nov 23, the Eagles beat the Cardinals W (27–20). On Nov 30, at home, the Eagles beat the Chicago Bears W (24–10). Then, at Washington, on Dec 7, the Washington Redskins tied the Pittsburgh Steelers T (14–14) In the season finale on Dec 13, at home in Forbes Field, the Steelers beat the Chicago Cardinals W (38–21).

Top Steeler Players Bobby Layne

Layne was a great quarterback (1958-62)
Elected: 1967
Bobby Layne played five of his 15 NFL seasons with the Pittsburgh Steelers. He helped provide the Steelers with some of their finest seasons up to that point. Prior to Pittsburgh, Layne was a two-time All-NFL selection and was the league's scoring champion in 1956. His last-second touchdown pass won the 1953 NFL title game for the Detroit Lions.

1959 Buddy Parker, Coach #11

The 1959 Pittsburgh Steelers football team competed in their twenty-seventh season of Professional National Football League (NFL) football. The team was led by Buddy Parker in the third of his eight years as coach of the Steelers. Their record declined slightly from a prior result of 7-4-1 to 6-5-1. The Steelers finished in fourth place in the NFL Eastern Division with no chance for the playoffs.

In the season and home opener on September 26, 1959, the Steelers defeated the Cleveland Browns W (17-7). The Steelers then were beaten by the Washington Redskins on Oct 4, L (17-23). In the next outing at Philadelphia, on Oct 11, the Steelers were beaten by the Philadelphia Eagles L(24-28). Then, at Washington, on Oct 18, the Steelers defeated by the Redskins W (27-6).

At home in Forbes Field on Oct 25, the New York Giants beat the Steelers L (16-21). At Chicago on Nov 1, the Cardinals beat the

Steelers L (24-45). Then at home in Forbes Field on Nov 8, the Detroit Lions tied the Steelers T (10–10). At New York on Nov 15, the Steelers beat the Giants W (14-9).

At Cleveland, on Nov 22, Pittsburgh beat the Browns W (21–20). Then, at home in Forbes Field, on Nov 29, the Steelers pounded the Philadelphia Eagles in a shutout W (31-0). On Dec 6, at Chicago, the Bears defeated the Steelers, L (21-27). At the end of an OK season, the Steelers needed a win to get over 500. They got it at home in Forbes Field on Dec 13, by overpowering the Chicago Cardinals W (35-20).

1960 Buddy Parker, Coach #11

The 1960 Pittsburgh Steelers football team competed in their twenty-eighth season of Professional National Football League (NFL) football. The team was led by Buddy Parker in the fourth of his eight years as coach of the Steelers. Their record declined slightly from a prior result of 6-5-1 to 5-6-1. The Steelers finished in fifth place in the NFL Eastern Division with no chance for the playoffs.

Top Steelers Players
John Henry Johnson

Fullback (1960-65) Elected: 1987 Originally drafted by the Pittsburgh Steelers in 1953, John Henry Johnson spent his first eight years in the NFL outside of the Steel City. However, Johnson enjoyed his finest seasons with the Steelers. In both 1962 and 1964, Johnson became the first Steeler to eclipse the 1,000-yard rushing barrier. After retiring in 1966 from the Houston Oilers, Johnson's 6,803 career rushing yards ranked him fourth at the

time among the NFL's all-time top ground gainers behind only Jim Brown, Jim Taylor and Joe Perry
Games of the 1960 season

Games of the 1960 season

In the season and home opener on September 10, 1960, the Steelers defeated the Dallas Cowboys W (35-28). The Steelers then were beaten by the Cleveland Browns on Sept 25, L (20-28). In the next outing at home in Forbes Field, on Oct 2, the Steelers were beaten by the New York Giants in a two-point game L(17-19). Then, at St. Louis, on Oct 98, the Steelers defeated the Cardinals, W (27-14). The Cardinals had moved from Chicago.

At Washington on Oct 16, the Steelers tied the Redskins T (27–27). On Oct 23 at home in Forbes Field, the Steelers lost to the Green Bay Packers L (13-19). On Oct 30 at Philadelphia, the Eagles beat the Steelers L (7-34). On Nov 6 at New York, the Giants beat the Steelers L (24-27).

On Nov20 at home, the Steelers beat the Cleveland Browns W (14–10). Then, at home in Forbes Field, on Nov 27, the Steelers beat the Washington Redskins W (22-10). On Dec 4, the team had a bye week. Then on Dec 11, at home in Forbes Field, the Steelers beat the Philadelphia Eagles W (27–21). Then, in the season finale, on Dec 18 at St. Louis, the Cardinals smashed the Steelers L (7-38).

1961 Buddy Parker, Coach #11

The 1961 Pittsburgh Steelers football team competed in their twenty-ninth season of Professional National Football League (NFL) football. The team was led by Buddy Parker in the fifth of his eight years as coach of the Steelers. Their record declined slightly from a prior result of 5-6-1 to 6-8-0. The league upped the # of games per season for each team from 12 to 14. The Steelers finished in fifth place in the NFL Eastern Division with no chance for the playoffs.

In the season and home opener on September 17, 1961, the Steelers lost to the Dallas Cowboys L (24-27). The Steelers then were beaten by the New York Giants on Sept 24, L (14-17). In the next outing at

Los Angeles, on Oct 1, the Steelers were beaten by the Rams L (14-24). Then, at Philadelphia, St. Louis, on Oct 8, the Steelers defeated the Eagles L (16-21).

At home in Forbes Field on Oct 15, the Steelers shut out the Washington Redskins W (20–0). At home again in Forbes Field on Oct 22, the Cleveland Browns beat the Steelers L (28-30). At home on Oct 29, the Steelers beat the San Francisco 49ers W (20–10). On Nov 5 at Cleveland, the Steelers beat the Browns W (17–13).

At home on Nov 12, the Steelers smothered the Dallas Cowboys W (37–7). At New York, on Nov 19, the Giants hammered the Steelers L (21-42). Hen at Forbes Field, the Steelers beat the St. Louis Cardinals W (30–27). On Dec 3, at home in Forbes Field, the Philadelphia Eagles beat the Steelers L (24-35). At Washington, on Dec 10, the Steelers beat the Redskins W (30–14). On Dec 17 at St. Louis, the Cardinals shut-out the Steelers L (0-20).

1962 Buddy Parker, Coach #11

The 1962 Pittsburgh Steelers football team competed in their thirtieth season of Professional National Football League (NFL) football. The team was led by Buddy Parker in the sixth of his eight years as coach of the Steelers. Their record improved substantially from a prior result of 6-8-0 to 9-5-0. The league upped the # of games per season for each team from 12 to 14 in 1961. The Steelers finished in 2nf place in the NFL Eastern Division and lost the playoff bowl, thus coming in third place.

This was the best season ever for the Pirates. With 14 games to play, they did very well and made the playoffs. In the season opener at Detroit on September 16, 1962, the Steelers lost to the Detroit Lions by a ton of points L (7-45). This loss must have motivated the Steelers to never be so embarrassed again. The Steelers picked up the pace and beat the Dallas Cowboys in a tight match on Sept 23, W (30-28). In the next outing at home in Forbes Field, the New York Giants edged out the Steelers L (27-31). The Steelers picked up the pace again and brought their record to 500 for the season by defeating the Philadelphia Eagles W (13-7).

At New York on Oct 14, the Steelers in the end, overpowered the Giants W (20-17). Then at home in Forbes Field, the Cowboys would not die, and Pittsburgh went down L (27-42). Still not having shaken out all the season losses by Oct 28, the Cleveland Browns thumped the Steelers L (14-41). In the first game against the new team, the Minnesota Vikings on Nov 4, the Steelers prevailed W (39-31).

At St Louis, the former other Chicago team, the Cardinals, took it on the chin from Pittsburgh W (26–17). Then, on November 18, the Steelers beat the Washington Redskins in a close call W (23-21). At Cleveland, on Nov 25, the Browns outmuscled the Stealers L (14-35).

Getting into the really cold months, on Dec 2, at home in Forbes Field, the Steelers got the best of the St. Louis Cardinals W (19-7). At Philadelphia, on Dec 9, Pittsburgh beat the Eagles W (26-17). Then, in the season's swan song game, on Dec 16, at Washington, the Steelers outplayed the Redskins W (27-24)

Top Steelers Players
Clendon Thomas
Both a halfback and defensive back. (born December 28, 1935 in Oklahoma City, Oklahoma. Thomas was a football halfback and Defensive back for Pittsburgh in the 1960's.

In college, Clendon was a great athlete for the Oklahoma Sooners under coach Bud Wilkinson. He was the Sooners scoring leader during both the 1956 and '57 seasons. He also was the nation's leading scorer in 1956.

In the 1958 NFL Draft, Thomas was selected by the Los Angeles Rams in the second round. He played for the Rams for four seasons before being traded to the Pittsburgh Steelers where he played for another seven years and finished his career. He was selected to the Pro Bowl after the 1963 NFL season.

1963 Buddy Parker, Coach #11

The 1963 Pittsburgh Steelers football team competed in their thirty-first season of Professional National Football League (NFL) football. The team was led by Buddy Parker in the seventh of his eight years as head coach of the Steelers. Their record improved substantially from a prior result of 9-5-0 to 7-4-3. The Steelers finished in 4th place in the NFL Eastern Division and did not qualify for the playoffs.

In this fine season, the Steelers won seven games, and lost four, with three games ending in a tie. As noted, the Steelers finished in fourth place in the NFL Eastern Conference. It was also their final season of splitting home games between Forbes Field and Pitt Stadium before moving all of their home games to Pitt Stadium for the next six seasons.

Because tie games were not included in NFL standings at the time, the Steelers had a chance to play in their first ever NFL Championship Game if they had defeated the New York Giants in the season finale, but they fell 33-17. The Steelers luck was always an issue and it was about ten years at the time away from changing permanently for the good.

For the first time in 1963, the Steelers wore their trademark black helmets with their logo on one side of the helmet. They had used the logo previously on yellow helmets, but 1963 was the first season in which their now-signature look was used full-time in the regular season. The Steelers were preparing for great seasons to come. Buddy Parker had given them a good taste for how sweet winning could be.

This season came after the best season ever for the Steelers. It was one of the team's best seasons by itself, but a season in which they would not make the playoffs, was not a Super Bowl season, indeed.

Top Steelers Players Andy Russel

Linebacker Andy Russell was one of the few Steelers from the pre-Chuck Noll era to hang around for the team's first Super Bowl victory. He and a pair of Jacks in Ham and Lambert became the gold standard for linebacker play in the NFL

A seven-time Pro Bowler, Russell's legacy hasn't stood the test of time like Ham and Lambert. Nonetheless, I'm sure he takes solace in the fact that he was able to earn two Super Bowl victories after enduring quite a bit of losing earlier in his career.

In the season opener at Philadelphia on September 15, 1963, the Steelers tied the Eagles T (21-21).The Steelers picked up the pace and smothered the New York Giants in a shutout match on Sept 23, W (31-0). In the next outing at home in Forbes Field, the Steelers defeated the St. Louis Cardinals W (23-10). The Steelers let down a bit in game 4 and the Cleveland Browns prevailed L (23-35).

At St. Louis, on Oct 13, the Cardinals won a nail-biter against Pittsburgh L (23–24. On Oct 20, the Steelers outplayed the Washington Redskins in a tough match. W (38–27). On Oct 27, the Steelers got by the Dallas Cowboys W (27–21) in a tough one. At Green Bay, on Nov 3, the Packers got the best of the Steelers L (14-33).

At home at Pitt Stadium, on Nov 10, the Steelers got the best of the Cleveland Browns W (9–7). Then at Washington, on Nov 17, Pittsburgh defeated the Redskins W (34–28). On Nov 24, at home, the Steelers played the Chicago Bears to a tie T (17–17). Then on Dec 1, the Steelers played another tie v the Philadelphia Eagles T (20–20). At Dallas on Dec 8, the Steelers out played the Cowboys for the win W (24–19). In the season denouement on Dec 15, the Stealers could not hang on and lost the final game of the season v the New York Giants L (17-33). And, that was that!

1964 Buddy Parker, Coach #11

The 1964 Pittsburgh Steelers football team competed in their thirty-second season of Professional National Football League (NFL) football. The team was led by Buddy Parker in the last of eight seasons as head coach of the Steelers. Their record improved substantially from a prior result of 7-4-3 to 5-9. The Steelers finished in 5th place in the NFL Eastern Division and did not qualify for the playoffs.

I always find it incredulous when a great coach, and quite frankly, Buddy Parker was no slouch, is dismissed after a bad season, especially a season, which before that coach arrived was the norm. Nonetheless, nobody asked my advice so after one bad season, Buddy Parker got his walking papers, and Mike Nixon got the call to move the Steelers on to the heavenly Noll. (You'll soon get this pun…I think.)

The team played all of their home games at Pitt Stadium, and won five games, while losing nine, resulting in a fifth-place finish in the NFL Eastern Conference. Following the season, the Steelers dismissed head coach Buddy Parker and replaced him with Mike Nixon

In the season and home opener in Forbes Field on September 13, 1963, the LA Rams beat the Steelers L (14-26).The Steelers came back in week 2 and beat the New York Giants in a tough match on Sept 20, W (27-24). In the next outing at home in Forbes Field, the Steelers defeated the Dallas Cowboys W (23-17). The Steelers let down a bit in game 4 and the Philadelphia Eagles prevailed L (7-21) On Oct 10, at Cleveland, the Steelers beat the Browns W (23–7).

Then at Minnesota on Oct 18, the Vikings outplayed the Steelers L (10-30). The Philadelphia Eagles beat the Steelers in the rematch game on Oct 25 at Forbes Field L (10-34). At home on Nov 1, the Cleveland Browns beat the Steelers L (17-30) On Nov 8, at St. Louis, the Cardinals beat the Steelers in a close match L 30–34.

On Nov 15, the Washington Redskins shut out the Steelers L (0-30). At New York, on November 22, the Steelers beat the Giants W 44–17. At home in Forbes Field, on Nov 29, the St. Louis Cardinals beat the Steelers in a one-point match L (20–21). At Washington on Dec 6, the Steelers edged out the Redskins W (14–7). In the last act of the 1964 season, at Dallas, on Dec 13, the Cowboys barely beat the Steelers L (14-17).

Chapter 19 Coaches Nixon & Austin 1965 to 1968

Coach #12 Mike Nixon
Coach #13 Bill Austin

Year	Coach	League/Conf/Div	Pl	Record	Pct.
1965	#12 Mike Nixon	NFLEastern	7th	2 12 0	.143
1966	#13 Bill Austin	NFLEastern	6th	5 8 1	.393
1967	#13 Bill Austin	NFLEasternCent	4th	4 9 1	.321
1968	#13 Bill Austin	NFLEasternCent	4th	2 11 1	.179

Without peeking into the 1965 record books first, I offered my short commentary in the last chapter about the wisdom of "firing" or accepting Buddy Parker's resignation. In other words, should a habitually poor performing team that is one coach away from poor performance, fire that coach or make it so he must resign?

The Steelers could not win a game until they hired Buddy Parker and then 8 years later after 5 winning seasons, they forgot about how tough things had been and wanted more from Parker and they wanted Parker to toe the line on decisions made for the good of the team without the bosses.

It was during the 1965 preseason when the team and Parker were at loggerheads. Parker wanted to trade Ben McGee, who later went to two Pro Bowls. Who knows what Parker would have gotten but he did not want to be micromanaged. He knew there was no winning at Pittsburgh until he had arrived.

Dan Rooney, who had taken over many of the operations from his father Art Rooney, Sr., refused to permit the hypothetical trade. Parker offered his resignation, Dan accepted, but asked him to reconsider and said they would discuss the matter in the morning.

Dan discussed it with The Chief (Art Rooney, Sr.), and convinced his father this was the way to go. The next morning when Parker threatened to resign, Dan gladly accepted. It was a bad idea accepting Parker's resignation. The Steelers had no fallback coach.

The team would go 2-12 during the 1965 season with Mike Nixon as their head coach.

Bill Austin who followed Nixon did not put many smiles on the faces of Pittsburgh's fans. The only good thing I can think of is that without Buddy Parker's departure, there might not have been a reason to bring Chuck Noll in for the 1969 season. But, those four years without a seasoned coach were painful for Pittsburgh for sure.

1965 Mike Nixon, Coach #12

The 1965 Pittsburgh Steelers football team competed in their thirty-third season of Professional National Football League (NFL) football. The team was led by Mike Nixon in his first and last season as head coach of the Steelers. Their record declined substantially from a prior result under Buddy Parker of 5-9-0 to 2-12-0 under Mike Nixon. The Steelers finished in 7th place in the NFL Eastern Division and did not qualify for the playoffs.

The team played all of their home games at Pitt Stadium, and won just two games, while losing twelve, resulting in a seventh-place finish. Following the season, the Steelers dismissed head coach Mike Nixon and replaced him with Bill Austin. Chuck Noll was three years away at the time.

In the season and home opener in Forbes Field on September 19, 1965, the Green Bay Packers hammered the Steelers L (9-41). The Steelers lost again and would lost wo more times before they got a win. In week 2, on Sept 26, at San Francisco, the 49ers beat the Steelers L (17-27) In the next outing at home in Forbes Field, the Steelers lost to the New York Giants L (13-23) The Steelers lost their 4th game in a row on Oct 9, at Cleveland as the Browns prevailed L (19-24).

At home in Forbes Field on Oct 17, the St. Louis Cardinals beat the Steelers L (7-20). In as season with two wins, it is not probable that both wins come together but that's what happened in 1965. On Oct 24, at Philadelphia, the Steelers beat the Eagles W (20–14). This win was followed by another nice win on Oct 31, v the Dallas Cowboys W (22–13). That was the end of wins for the year. The next loss was at St. Louis, on Nov 7, 1965 as the Cardinals edged out the Steelers L (17-21).

The Steelers proceeded to finish out the season with six losses. The first was at Dallas on Nov 14, as the Cowboys beat the Steelers L (17-24). At home on Nov 21, 1965 Washington Redskins squashed the Steelers L (3-31). Then on Nov 28, the Cleveland Browns thumped the Steelers L (21-42).

On Dec 5, 1965 at New York, the Steelers were whipped by the Giants L (10-35). At home on Dec 12, the Philadelphia Eagles shellacked the Steelers L (13-47). On Dec 19, 1965 at Washington, the Redskins pounded the Steelers L (14-35) in the season denouement. Steeler fans were thankful, after Buddy Parker's optimism, to finish this season at all.

1966 Bill Austin, Coach #13

The 1966 Pittsburgh Steelers football team competed in their thirty-fourth season of Professional National Football League (NFL) football. The team was led by Bill Austin in his first of three seasons as head coach of the Steelers. Their record improved substantially from a prior result under Mike Nixon of 2-12-0 to 5-8-1 under Bill Austin. The Steelers finished in 6th place in the NFL Eastern Division and did not qualify for the playoffs.

The team played all of their home games at Pitt Stadium, and won just five games but it was three more than in 1965. The team lost eight games, while tying 1, resulting in a sixth-place finish. Following the season, the Steelers were not pleased but kept head coach Bill Austin, more than likely because the team had improved.

Chuck Noll was two years away at the time, but nobody knew it at the time.

In the season and home opener in Pitt Stadium on September 11, 1966, the New York Giants tied the Steelers T (34-34). This was one of those games that should have had a winner and a loser and that is why the NFL eventually found a better solution for ties.

At Pitt Stadium again on Sept 18, the Steelers beat the Detroit Lions W (17-3). In the next outing at home at Pitt Stadium on Sept 25, in Pitt Stadium, the Steelers lost to the Washington Redskins L (27-33) At Washington the next week, on Oct 2, at DC Stadium, since obviously the Redskins and Steelers could not get enough of each other, the "Skins" beat the Steelers again—this time L (10-24)

On Oct 8 at Cleveland, the Browns beat the Steelers L (10–41) at Municipal Stadium. Then, on Oct 16, the Philadelphia Eagles beat the Steelers L(14–31) at home in Pitt Stadium. On Oct 30, at Dallas, the Cowboys overpowered the Steelers L (21–52) in the Cotton Bowl Stadium. Then, on Nov 6 the Steelers edged out the Cleveland Browns W (16–6) at Pitt Stadium.

On November 13, the Steelers whooped the St. Louis Cardinals W (30–9) at home in Pitt Stadium. Then, on Nov 20 the Dallas Cowboys beat the Steelers L (7–20) at home in Pitt Stadium. On Nov 27 at St. Louis, the Cardinals prevailed in a close match L (3–6) in Busch Stadium. This game had a baseball-like score.

On Dec 4 at Philadelphia, the Eagles got by the Steelers L (23–27) in Franklin Field. On December 11 at New York, the Steelers pounded the Giants W (47–28) at Yankee Stadium. In a first-time encounter on Dec 18, Pittsburgh defeated the Atlanta Falcons W (57–33) in a big win in Atlanta Stadium to close the season.

1967 Bill Austin, Coach #13

The 1967 Pittsburgh Steelers football team competed in their thirty-fifth season of Professional National Football League (NFL) football. The team was led by Bill Austin in his second of three seasons as head coach of the Steelers. Their record declined slightly from a prior result of 5-8-1 to 4-9-1 under Bill Austin. The Steelers finished in 4th place in the NFL Century Division and did not qualify for the playoffs.

The team played all of their home games at Pitt Stadium, and won just four games, one less than in 1966. The team lost eight games, while tying 1, resulting in a fourth-place finish in the new division. Following the season, the Steelers were not pleased with the record but retained head coach Bill Austin. Chuck Noll and a big improvement was just one year away but nobody knew it at the time.

In the season and home opener in Pitt Stadium on September 17, 1967, the Steelers shellacked the Chicago Bears W (41-13). At Pitt Stadium again on Sept 24, the St. Louis Cardinals beat the Steelers L (14-28). In the next outing at Philadelphia on Oct 1, the Steelers lost to the Eagles L (24-34). At Cleveland the next week, on Oct 7, the Browns beat the Steelers L (10-21)

On October 15, at Pitt Stadium, the New York Giants beat the Steelers L (24-27). On Oct 22, the Dallas Cowboys beat the Steelers by the same three-point margin L (21-24) Finally after a losing streak of five games, the Steelers won a game against the New Orleans Saints on Oct 29, W (14-10) At home on Nov 5, the Cleveland Browns beat the Steelers L (14-34) At
St. Louis on Nov 12, the Cardinals and the Steelers played to a tie game. T (14-14).

On Nov 19, at New York, the Giants beat the Steelers L (20-28) At home on Nov 26, the Minnesota Vikings beat the Steelers L (27-41). At Detroit on Dec 3, the Steelers outplayed the Lions W 24-14, Then, on Dec 10, at home, the Washington Redskins beat the Steelers L (10-15) In the season closer, on Dec 17, at Green Bay, the Steelers finished off the Packers W (24–17).

1968 Bill Austin, Coach #13

The 1968 Pittsburgh Steelers football team competed in their thirty-sixth season of Professional National Football League (NFL) football. The team was led by Bill Austin in his last of three seasons as head coach of the Steelers. Their record declined again from a prior result of 4-9-1 to a dismal 2-11-1 under Bill Austin. The Steelers finished in 4th place in the NFL Century Division and did not qualify for the playoffs.

The team played all of their home games at Pitt Stadium, and won just two games, two less than in 1967. The team lost eleven games, while tying 1, resulting in a fourth-place finish. Austin was the first coach picked by Dan Rooney, long-time head of the organization who passed away last year. Following the season, Rooney was not pleased with the record and dismissed head coach Bill Austin. Chuck Noll, a big improvement for the Steelers was about to be hired after this season, but nobody knew it at the time.

The Steelers had suffered through thirty-six seasons of off again, on again play with just eight winning seasons. In 1968, they continued their descent in the NFL's basement league, finishing with a league-worst 2–11–1 record and of course the firing of head coach Bill Austin at the end of the season. I like to say that this directly led to the eventual hiring of Chuck Noll. To this date, Austin is the last head coach to be fired by the Steelers.

One of the more interesting aspects of Austin's career is that as we have been forecasting, he was the coach before Noll in Pittsburgh. But, Austin was also the coach before the great George Allen in Washington. One could say he paved the way to greatness in both organizations. Or, one could say that both teams struck gold with the coach who followed him. Either way, it is the truth.

The season is notable in that the Steelers had their last tied game before the NFL adopted the overtime rule in regular-season games in 1974. It came in Week 9 against the St. Louis Cardinals in a 28–28 stalemate; that game actually was the deciding game in the NFL Century Division that season,

In the new division, the Cardinals had swept the Cleveland Browns but finished their season 9–4–1, 1/2 game behind the 10–4 Browns. Since that game, the Steelers have only had two tied games, both happening after the overtime rule took effect.

Additionally, the Steelers lost to the Baltimore Colts at home, 41–7, in Week 3. They Colts went on to play in Super Bowl III, in which they were upset by the AFL's New York Jets. After that loss, the Steelers would go another 40 years before losing to the Colts at home again, winning 12 straight (including three postseason meetings, among them the now-famous 1995 AFC Championship game as well as the 1975 Divisional Playoff Game that saw the introduction of the Terrible Towel, before losing to the now-Indianapolis Colts, 24–20, on November 10, 2008.[1]

In the season and home opener in Pitt Stadium on September 15, 1967, the Steelers lost to the New York Giants L (20-34). At Los Angeles, on Sept 22, the Rams walloped the Steelers L (10-45). In their next outing at Baltimore on Oct 1, the Steelers were routed by the Colts, L (7-41). At Cleveland the next week, on Oct 5, the Browns beat the Steelers L (24-31).

At Washington on Oct 13, the Redskins defeated the Steelers L (13-16). At home in Pitt Stadium on Oct 20, the New Orleans Saints beat the Steelers L (12-16). At home on Oct 27, the Steelers won their first of two games this season, W (6–3). The second win came the next week on Nov 3, at Atlanta as the Steelers whipped the Falcons W (41–21). To some it looked like a big comeback. But, this would be the last win for the year. On Nov 10, at St. Louis, the Cardinals tied the Steelers for the last tie ever in Steelers history before the Overtime rule.

On Nov 17 at home, the Cleveland Browns stomped the Steelers L (24-45). At home on Nov 24, the San Francisco 49ers pounded the Steelers L (28-45). Then, on Dec 1, at home, the St. Louis Cardinals beat the Steelers L (10-20). In the second-last game of this terrible season and, the team lost on Dec 8 at Dallas to the Cowboys L (7-28). At New Orleans on Dec 15, in the last game before Chuck Noll came in to restart the Steelers in 1969, the Saints defeated the Steelers L 14-24

Chapter 20 Coach Chuck Noll I, 1969 to 1982

Coach #14 Chuck Noll

Year	Coach	League/Conf/Div	Pl	Record	Pct.
1969	#14 Chuck Noll	NFLEasternCent	4th	1 13 0	.071
	• Joe Greene – Defensive Rookie of the Year				
1970	#14 Chuck Noll	NFLAFCCentral	3rd	5 9 0	.357
1971	#14 Chuck Noll	NFLAFCCentral	2nd	6 8 0	.429

Summary continued below

1969 PITTSBURGH STEELERS
Bottom Row: Terry Hanratty, Kent Nix, Gene Mingo, Dick Shiner, Paul Martha, Jim Shorter, Bob Campbell, Jon Henderson, Clarence Oliver, Bob Hohn, Andy Russell
Second Row: Head Coach Chuck Noll, Don McCall, Chuck Beatty, Earl Gros, Bobby Walden, Dick Hoak, Erwin Williams, Lee Calland, Warren Bankston, Marv Woodson, Coach John Bridges
Third Row: Coach Max Coley, Doug Fisher, Jon Kolb, Ray Mansfield, Sam Davis, Ray May, Ben McGee, Brian Stenger, Ralph Wenzel, Chuck Hinton, Coach Charley Sumner.
Fourth Row: Coach Bob Fry, Lloyd Voss, Bruce Van Dyke, Clarence Washington, L.C. Greenwood, Jerry Hillebrand, Dick Arndt, Ernie Ruple, John Brown, Joe Greene, Coach Walt Hackett
Fifth Row: Trainer Ralph Berlin, Mike Haggerty, Mike Taylor, Larry Gagner, John Hilton, Don Alley, Bob Adams, J.R. Wilburn, Roy Jefferson, Field Manager Jack Hart, Equipment Manager Tony Parisi

1969 Pittsburgh Steelers Team Picture

Year	Coach	League/Conf/Div	Pl	Record	Pct.
1972	#14 Chuck Noll	NFLAFCCentral	1st	11 3 0	.786
	• Won Divisional Playoffs(Raiders) 13–7				
	• Lost Conference Championship(Dolphins) 21–17				
	• Chuck Noll – AFC Coach of the Year				
	• Franco HarrisOffensive Rookie of the Year				
	• Joe Greene – Defensive Player of the Year				
	• Franco Harris– AFC Offensive Rookie of the Year				
1973	#14 Chuck Noll	NFLAFCCentral	2nd	10 4 0	.714

Lost Divisional Playoffs(Raiders) 33–14

Year	Coach	League/Conf/Div	Pl	Record	Pct.
1974	#14 Chuck Noll	NFL AFC Central	1st	10 3 1	.750

- Won Divisional Playoffs(Bills) 32–14
- Won Conference Championship(Raiders) 24–13
- Won Super Bowl IX (1)(Vikings) 16–6
- Jack Lambert– Defensive Rookie of the Year
- Joe Greene – Defensive Player of the Year
- Franco Harris– Super Bowl MVP

| 1975 | #14 Chuck Noll | NFL AFC Central | 1st | 12 2 0 | .857 |

- Won Divisional Playoffs(Colts) 28–10
- Won Conference Championship(Raiders) 16–10
- Won Super Bowl X (2) (Cowboys) 21–17
- Mel Blount – Defensive Player of the Year
- Lynn Swann – Super Bowl MVP

| 1976 | #14 Chuck Noll | NFL AFC Central | 1st | 10 4 0 | .714 |

- Won Divisional Playoffs(Colts) 40–14
- Lost Conference Championship(Raiders) 24–7
- Jack Lambert– Defensive Player of the Year
- Jack Lambert– AFC Defensive Player of the Year

| 1977 | #14 Chuck Noll | NFL AFC Central | 1st | 9 5 0 | .643 |

- Lost Divisional Playoffs(Broncos) 34–21

| 1978 | #14 Chuck Noll | NFL AFC Central | 1st | 14 2 0 | .875 |

- Won Divisional Playoffs(Broncos) 33–10
- Won Conference Championship (Oilers) 34–5
- Won Super Bowl XIII(3) (Cowboys) 35–31
- Terry Bradshaw – Super Bowl MVP
- Terry Bradshaw – Bert Bell MVP

| 1979 | #14 Chuck Noll | NFL AFC Central | 1st | 12 4 0 | .750 |

- Won Divisional Playoffs(Dolphins) 34–14
- Won Conference Championship (Oilers) 27–13
- Won Super Bowl XIV(4) (Rams) 31–19
- Jack Lambert– AFC Defensive Player of the Year
- Terry Bradshaw – Super Bowl MVP

1980	#14 Chuck Noll	NFL AFC Central	3rd	9 7 0	.563
1981	#14 Chuck Noll	NFL AFC Central	2nd	8 8 0	.500
1982	#14 Chuck Noll	NFL AFC Central	4th-T	6 3 0	.667

- Lost First Round(Chargers) 31–28

Chuck Noll takes over as Steelers head coach

From steelersuk.com

After leading the Steelers to a 2-11-1 season, Bill Austin was fired on December 16, 1968. "We already have several applicants and expect many more when the story gets on the wire," Dan Rooney said at a press conference to announce the vacancy.

Only two names were mentioned during the conference, Joe Paterno, the successful coach at Penn State and Bill Peterson of Florida State.

The Steelers first interviewed Joe Paterno a few days after Penn State won the Orange Bowl. Fortunately, he was thinking more about his pension with the University than professional football. He turned down a projected yearly salary of $70,000 which was over three times what he was receiving at Penn State. After deciding not to join the professional ranks, Paterno was named College Coach of the Year.

The Pittsburgh Post-Gazette suggested there were still nine candidates on the Steelers' list after Paterno declined. The newspaper also stated that after 36 years of failures, whoever the new coach, he will need plenty of help and a free hand to operate. His is not an easy job they remarked.

A few days prior to the new coach being declared, the PPG suggested Bill Petersen was one of the top candidates. Also linked by rumor were Ernie Stautner of the Dallas Cowboys, Nick Skorich of the Cleveland Browns, Walter Michaels of the New York Jets and one, Chuck Noll of the Baltimore Colts.

With just two names on the list remaining, Nick Skorich and Chuck Noll, Dan Rooney woke at 7 am January 27 after a restless night's sleep and made his choice. A decision that would turn a forever bad team into winners. The Emperor would reign over his dynasty in Pittsburgh for over two decades ensuring that he will always be an important part of Steelers' history.

When Noll was finally revealed as the new head coach, reference was made in the PPG to the recommendation of his former head coach at the Baltimore Colts, Don Shula. "Chuck is very thorough. He knows every phase of the game. What is important too, is he has a real good manner with players. Firm, but gets along with them. He commands respect without being dominating. He is a fine young man. I hated to lose him."

Twenty-three years later

On December 26, 1991, Chuck Noll announced that he was retiring. After a 7-9 season and approaching 60, he decided that 39 years in professional football was a goodly time.

After 23 years as the Steelers head coach, coach Noll decided the time was right. "Reminisce?" he suggested in reply to a question. "When we get in rocking chairs, we'll probably do that.

There are things to be done, and I am sure I'll be busy from that standpoint. And I'll miss all the guys. I'll miss the training camps. I'll miss the season. That's going to be tough, but I'm sure you'll help me."

1969 Chuck Noll #14

The 1969 Pittsburgh Steelers football team competed in their thirty-seventh season of Professional National Football League (NFL) football. The team was led by Chuck Noll in his first of twenty-three seasons as head coach of the Steelers. Their record declined again as Noll brought new discipline to the team. It went from 2-11-1 under Bill Austin to 1-13 in Chuck Noll's first try. The Steelers finished in 4th place in the NFL Century Division and did not qualify for the playoffs.

The team played all of their home games at Pitt Stadium, and won just two games, two less than in 1968. The team lost eleven games, while tying 1, resulting in a fourth-place finish.

In the season and home opener in Pitt Stadium on September 21, 1969, the Steelers won their only game of the season W (16-13). The thirteen losses and the one win played by the Steelers are listed below

1 Sept 21, 1969 Detroit Lions Pitt Stadium   W 16–13
2 Sept 28, 1969 at Philadelphia Eagles Franklin Field   L 27-41
3 Oct 5, 1969 St. Louis Cardinals Pitt Stadium   L 14-27
4 Oct 12, 1969 at New York Giants Yankee Stadium   L 7-10
5 Oct 18, 1969 at Cleveland Browns Cleveland Municipal   L 31-42
6 Oct 26, 1969 Washington Redskins Pitt Stadium   L 7-14
7 Nov 2, 1969 Green Bay Packers Pitt Stadium   L 34-38
8 Nov 9, 1969 at Chicago Bears Wrigley Field   L 7-38
9 Nov 16, 1969 Cleveland Browns Pitt Stadium   L 3-24
10 Nov 23, 1969 at Minnesota Vikings Metropolitan Stad. L 14-52

11 Nov 30, 1969 at St. Louis Cardinals Busch Stadium   L 10-47
12 Dec 7, 1969 Dallas Cowboys Pitt Stadium   L 7-10
13 Dec 14, 1969 New York Giants Pitt Stadium   L 17-21
14 Dec 21, 1969 at New Orleans Saints Tulane Stadium   L 24-27

Though Chuck Noll did not set Pittsburgh on fire in his first year, he got 22 more years to turn the Steelers into something special...and he did. Nonetheless, 1969 is credited as the year in which the Pittsburgh Steelers turned the corner from its once-deathbed franchise. It was the first season for Hall of Fame head coach Chuck Noll, the first season for defensive lineman "Mean Joe" Greene and L. C. Greenwood, the first season for longtime Steelers public relations director Joe Gordon, and it was the team's last season in Pitt Stadium before moving into what was then state-of-the-art Three Rivers Stadium.

Although considered the year in which the Steelers turned the corner to a new world of greatness, the results were not immediate. In 1969, after Chuck Noll won his first game, that was it for the season. With the Steelers finishing 1–6 at Pitt Stadium, it marked the last time the Steelers finished the season with a losing record at home until 1999. Thirty years is a long time. Good things were happening for sure/

I bet there was some wise guy who wanted to fire Chuck Noll after the 1969 season. Because the Steelers had such a poor record, they got a great draft pick opportunity. In fact, their luck began to change with a coin toss. Both Chicago and Pittsburgh had 1-13 records. So, there was a coin toss between Art Rooney of the Steelers and George Halas of the Bears to determine who would get to select Louisiana Tech quarterback Terry Bradshaw.

The affable Bradshaw was the consensus #1 selection among NFL teams as the number one pick in the 1970 draft. By modern NFL tiebreaking rules, the Steelers would have automatically been given the first pick anyway, as the Bears' one win came against the Steelers in Week 8. So, the Steelers were lucky twice.

The Steelers were busy making up for Bill Austin's poor tenure with the team in the pre-1969 offseason. The big deal for the Steelers was that they hired former defensive coordinator Chuck Noll from the Baltimore Colts days after his team lost to the New York Jets in

Super Bowl III. Noll was a lot better than persona non grata, but the Colts had lost to an AFL team, and they were thought to be inferior.

Noll became Pittsburgh's 14th head coach in the franchise's history. It had taken 36 seasons to go through the first 13 coaches, If Noll did not have a few less than great years at the end of his career, if he put in another 13 years his one coaching tenure would have equaled the total of all 13 coaches who preceded him. Pittsburgh was finicky with coaches plus they had hired some doozies over the years.

Finally, Pittsburgh hired a coach who could win and would stay and would not pick fights with management that would get him fired. Noll stayed through 1991, establishing coaching stability for the Steelers not seen in any other NFL franchises for the next 46 years. Since Noll's retirement, only Bill Cowher and current head coach Mike Tomlin have served as head coach of the Steelers—just two coaches in the next 26 years. Wow! No wonder Pittsburgh plays consistently good football.

Linebacker Andy Russell is quoted as speaking for all other Steelers present when Chuck Noll assembled the team for their first meeting. He plainly stated his thoughts on why the Steelers had lost so often for so long:

> *"So, Coach Noll's first meeting, I'll never forget the speech he gave," said Russell, who became a highly successful businessman after retiring from football in 1976. "He gets up and says, 'I've been watching the game film since I took the job, and I can tell you guys why you've been losing.' You could have heard a pin drop in that room. He says, 'The reason you have been losing is you're not any good.'" he said, 'I'm going to get rid of most of you.' Five of us made it from that room to the Super Bowl in '74."*

Only a handful of players were carried over from the 1968 squad of which Noll spoke to the 1974 Super Bowl Squad. The ones with the mettle to measure up to Noll's demands were veterans Andy Russell, Rocky Bleier, Ray Mansfield, and Bobby Walden. Additionally,

Dick Hoak, who retired before the 1974 season, became the team's running backs coach and he remained with the team in that capacity through the 2006 season. Bleier, who played his rookie season the year before and later became a major contributor to the Super Bowl championship teams, was fighting in Vietnam during this time and was wounded in combat just before the start of the season. Rocky Bleier is a story in strength and desire. We'll tell some of that as we cover the years in which he played so well for the Steelers.

Top Steelers Players Joe Greene

Defensive Tackle (1969-81) Elected: 1987 The leader of the "Steel Curtain" defense during the 1970s, Joe Greene dominated the NFL during that decade and helped the Steelers to four Super Bowl victories. The team's No. 1 draft pick in 1969, Greene quickly became a presence in the league as he was named the NFL's Rookie of the Year and received the first of his 10 Pro Bowl invitations. He earned All-NFL honors five times and all-conference 11 straight years to begin his career. Greene was twice the league's Defensive Player of the Year and played a critical role in the Steelers' Super Bowl IX victory over the Minnesota Vikings with a pass interception and a fumble recovery

Top Steelers Players   L.C. Greenwood

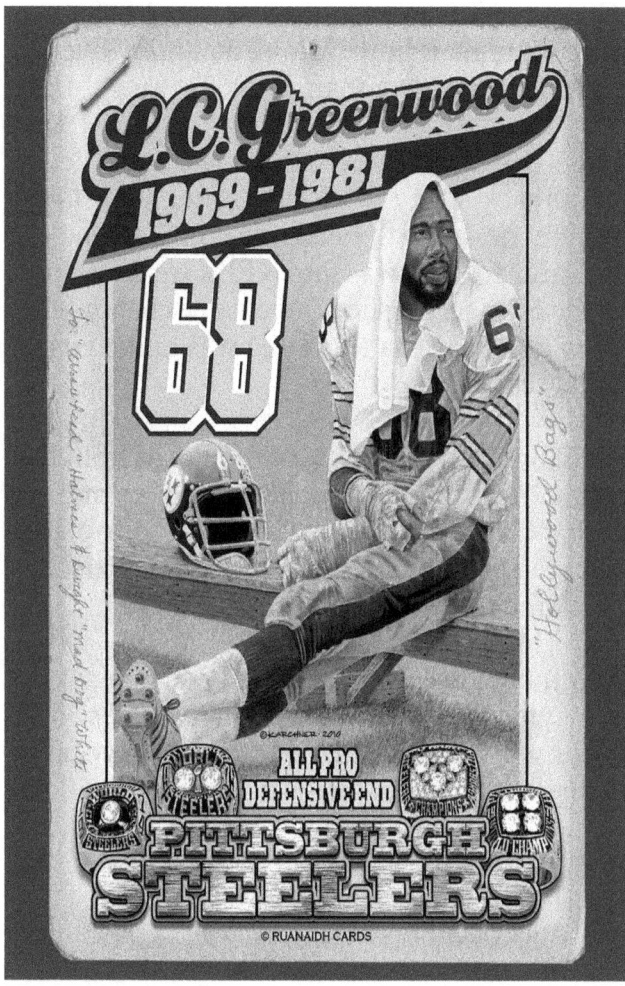

Defensive End
While the Steel Curtain has become synonymous with the likes of "Mean" Joe Greene and Jack Lambert, L.C. Greenwood was another key cog on those dominant defenses.

Sacks weren't a recorded stat in Greenwood's playing days, but he's been credited with 73.5 of them. That total's just five less than the indomitable Greene was credited with for his career.

More importantly, Greenwood saved his best performances for the biggest moments. Unofficially, he recorded five sacks in his team's four Super Bowl wins.

1970 Chuck Noll #14

The 1970 Pittsburgh Steelers football team competed in their thirty-eighth season of Professional National Football League (NFL) football. The team was led by Chuck Noll in his second of twenty-three seasons as head coach of the Steelers. Their record improved again as Noll's system was beginning to click. The record went from 1-13 in 1969 to 5-9 in Chuck Noll's second try. The Steelers finished in 3rd place in the AFC Central Division and did not qualify for the playoffs. The team played all of their home games at Three Rivers Stadium, winning five games, four more than in 1969.

The Steelers began the 70's decade in a new conference and a new stadium with a new quarterback, Terry Bradshaw. After almost 40 years in the NFL, they were moved to the AFC, to complete the merger between the NFL and AFL. It was the NFL's weakest division that season, as the Steelers finished three games behind the division-winning Cincinnati Bengals—a team that was only in its third year of existence that season.

Coach Chuck Noll's rebuilding and reshaping of the squad from the year before continued for 1970. It was not quite ready for prime time. The pundits reported that the greatest change that took place was Chuck Noll's trade of the team's lone superstar, Roy Jefferson. Dan Rooney did not block the trade.

Although Jefferson was among the league leaders in receiving in 1968 and 1969, despite playing for the worst team in football with so-so quarterbacks, he was sent packing after being publicly vocal in criticizing team management. Noll would have no insubordination.

The trade put Jefferson in Baltimore, where he earned a Super Bowl ring. Years later, Jefferson pinpointed what he had done to get traded.

> "I was [in Baltimore] to make a statement. I wanted to show Pittsburgh they'd made a mistake in getting rid of me. I mean, I wasn't a 'yes' man for coach Chuck Noll. If you cursed me, I cursed you back. I messed over the curfew rules a lot and, in training camp, I'd park my car in the coaches' spaces."

> And so, in essence Jefferson was fired for insubordination. Noll would not permit the inmates to run the asylum.

Without Jefferson, there was a big change with Ron Shanklin emerging as a steady receiver for the next few years until John Stallworth and Lynn Swann joined the team in 1974.

As a result of the NFL-AFL merger being finalized for the 1970 season, three teams from the "old" NFL were moved to the newly formed AFC alongside the former AFL teams. The Steelers agreed to be one of them after their archrivals, the Cleveland Browns, volunteered to join the AFL franchises in the AFC.

The Browns mainly joined because of the possibility of an intrastate rivalry with the AFL's Cincinnati Bengals (now known as the Battle of Ohio), largely due to the animosity at the time between Browns owner Art Modell and Bengals owner & coach Paul Brown, who was fired from the Browns by Modell after the 1962 season. The Steelers joined the AFC in order to keep the Browns-Steelers rivalry alive on a regular basis, due to the proximity of the cities of Pittsburgh and Cleveland. All were good reasons.

Another change came after the draft. The Steelers owned the number one selection in the draft after winning a coin toss with the Chicago Bears for the top pick. That's from whence Terry Bradshaw had come.

There were a lot of things happening in Chuck Noll's second year, and it was not all about Noll. For example, the opening of Three Rivers ended the Steelers relatively brief stay at Pitt Stadium, where they had only been playing at a full-time basis for six years. Before that, home games were played at Forbes Field, with a few games being played at Pitt Stadium to take advantage of the larger capacity.

The Steelers later returned the favor of playing in their stadium to the University of Pittsburgh in 2000 when the Pitt Panthers football team moved into Three Rivers for one season as an interim home before Heinz Field was ready in 2001. Pitt would also play their Backyard Brawl games against West Virginia in years Pitt hosted the game during the existence of Three Rivers.

Pittsburgh also upgraded its public presence. WTAE-TV sportscaster Myron Cope joined the Steelers radio network as color commentator for the 1970 season. Cope remained a fixture of the Steelers radio network through the 2004 season. He quickly became beloved by fans due to his enthusiasm and catchphrases behind the announcing booth. In 1975, Cope invented the Terrible Towel, originally conceived as a gimmick in the Steelers playoff game against Baltimore and now, of course, a staple among Steelers fans.

Top Steelers Players Mel Blount

Cornerback (1970-'83)
Elected: 1989
Melvin Cornell Blount, the Steelers' third-round pick in 1970, had superior size, speed, strength and intelligence. His physical style of play is widely credited for changing NFL pass defense rules.
Blount played 14 seasons and 200 regular-season games in Pittsburgh and his 57 interceptions remain a Steelers record. Blount played in five Pro Bowls and was named an All-Pro four times and the NFL defensive MVP in 1975.

Top Steelers Players Terry Bradshaw

Quarterback (1970-'83) Elected: 1989 Terry Paxton Bradshaw was the top-overall pick in the 1970 NFL Draft. Bradshaw led the Steelers to eight AFC Central division and four Super Bowl titles while calling his own plays. Bradshaw was named MVP in Super Bowls XIII and XIV and NFL MVP in 1978. Bradshaw finished his career with 27,989 yards passing and 212 TDs.

The following is from biography.com. Thank you

Bradshaw is the best!

He is a Television Personality, Football Player, Athlete (1948–)

Terry Bradshaw is one of the greatest quarterbacks in NFL history, Terry Bradshaw has spent much of his life playing, reporting and commenting on football.

Born on September 2, 1948, in Shreveport, Louisiana, professional football player Terry Bradshaw was named an All-American while playing for Louisiana Polytechnic Institute. The first player selected in the 1970 NFL draft, Bradshaw went to great success with the Pittsburgh Steelers. During his 14-year NFL career, he helped take his team to the Super Bowl several times and rightfully earned four Super Bowl rings. Following his successful career, he became a leading television personality and analyst for the NFL.

He is a former professional football player on the Pittsburgh Steelers, a television host, an author and an actor. Terry Paxton Bradshaw was born on September 2, 1948, in Shreveport, Louisiana. One of the greatest quarterbacks in NFL history, Bradshaw has spent much of his life playing, reporting and commenting on football. He was named an All-American while playing for Louisiana Polytechnic Institute. The first player selected in the 1970 NFL draft, Bradshaw went to play for the Pittsburgh Steelers.

Like many new players in the NFL, during his first few years, Bradshaw struggled to find his footing with the team. Some people made jokes about his intelligence, calling him "dumb" and the "Bayou Bumpkin," but in the 1974 season he showed his opponents and critics that he was a force to be reckoned with. Bradshaw helped lead the team to a Super Bowl victory over the Minnesota Vikings.

The next year, he and his teammates took on the Dallas Cowboys to win the Super Bowl again. These two teams faced off in 1978 for Super Bowl XIII, with Steelers winning by a narrow margin, 35 to 31. Bradshaw was selected as the Super Bowl Most Valuable Player and the NFL Player of the Year for his accomplishments on the field.

With an arm like a cannon, Bradshaw continued to succeed as quarterback of the Steelers. He won the Super Bowl MVP Award again in 1980 after helping his team defeat the Los Angeles Rams. Unfortunately, he began having difficulty with the muscles in one of his elbows. Bradshaw had surgery to correct the problem, but he returned before he was fully healthy and ended up with permanent damage. He retired after playing just one game in 1983.

Having been a guest commentator for CBS Sports over the years, Bradshaw became one of the network's game analysts. He eventually joined the staff of the show The NFL Today. After 10 years with CBS, Bradshaw jumped ship for Fox Sports in 1994. He became one of the co-hosts and analysts on Fox NFL Sunday. With a sharp strategic mind and a warm sense of humor, Bradshaw has become one of football's most popular commentators.

In addition to his broadcast work, Bradshaw is an author, singer, actor and motivational speaker. He has written several best sellers, including It's Only a Game (2001). A born-again Christian, he has recorded gospel and country music, scoring a Top 10 hit with "I'm So Lonesome I Could Cry," a cover of a song by Hank Williams. Bradshaw has also appeared in several films and television shows, including Failure to Launch (2006) with Matthew McConaughey and Sarah Jessica Parker. In addition, he travels the country each year, giving motivational speeches.

When I was with IBM, and he had first retired, we had these events at golf courses, and the company would arrange to have great people like Terry Bradshaw mingle with us during our rec time. A number of IBMers at the time, reported that Bradshaw played golf in their foursome, and he was as regular a guy as regular can be. I love their stories. Bradshaw is one of us.

Top Steelers Players Rocky Bleier

Heart of a Champion: The Story of Rocky Bleier
BY BRYN SWARTZ, DECEMBER 27, 2008

Rocky Bleier's story is one of the most gripping tales of courage and determination that I have ever heard. Had Bleier been a Philadelphia Eagle, he would probably be my favorite athlete of all time. As it is, he is still one of my heroes, despite playing for a franchise I despise—the Pittsburgh Steelers.

Robert Bleier was born in 1946 but earned the nickname "Rocky" as a baby when his dad used to bring people over to the crib to see his newborn "rock." Someone came up with the nickname, and it stuck.

Bleier played running back and defensive back in high school, earning All-State honors three times on offense and All-Conference twice on defense.

Rocky Bleier

Bleier accepted a scholarship to Notre Dame, where he led the Fighting Irish to the National Championship in 1966. His teammate and quarterback, Terry Hanratty, would later be his teammate on the Pittsburgh Steelers.

Bleier wasn't drafted until the 16th round of the 1968 NFL draft—the 417th overall pick—by the Pittsburgh Steelers. He received very little playing time as a rookie, carrying just six times for 39 yards, and catching three passes for 68 yards, including a 54-yard screen pass. He also returned six kickoffs and two punts.

Bleier was drafted into the United States Army in December of 1968, as his rookie season was ending. He shipped out to Vietnam after five months and served with the 196th Light Infantry Brigade.

On August 20, 1969, Bleier was on a routine patrol in Heip Duic when his platoon was ambushed in a rice paddy, wounding his left thigh. He was also seriously injured when an enemy grenade sent shrapnel into his right leg.

Bleier was sent to a hospital in Tokyo to ensure proper treatment. While recovering from his injuries, he was informed by doctors that he would never play professional football again.

Bleier says he remembers walking the streets late at night, crying because his world was completely turned upside down. As he says, "Playing football was the only thing I knew how to do."

Then something happened that changed Bleier's life forever. He received a postcard from Art Rooney, the owner of the Pittsburgh Steelers. The postcard read "Rock—the team's not doing well. We need you. Art Rooney."

Bleier had a great deal of respect for Art Rooney.

"When you have somebody take the time and interest to send you a postcard, something that they didn't have to do, you have a special place for those kinds of people," he said.

Bleier reported to the Steelers' training camp one year after being wounded. He weighed 180 pounds, having lost 30 pounds in a year. He couldn't even walk without being in pain and, not surprisingly, didn't earn a spot on the Steelers' roster.

Bleier spent two full seasons trying to gain a spot on the active roster and was waived twice by the organization.

But he never gave up. He worked for five to six hours a day to get himself into supreme physical shape.

"Some time in the future you won't have to ask yourself 'what if?'" said Bleier of his hard work habits. "I didn't lose a leg. I didn't lose a foot. I was going to come back and play. That was my desire. I wasn't going to go back and run my daddy's bar."

Bleier finally made the Steelers' roster in 1971. He played in six games, but only on special teams.

"It was enough to get credit for the year," said Bleier.

Bleier played in all 14 games in 1972, but again mostly played on special teams. He carried the ball one time—for 17 yards but fumbled at the end of his run.

He played in 13 of the 14 games in 1973. He carried the ball three times but gained zero yards rushing. He also fumbled twice, meaning he fumbled on three of his first four carries in the National Football League.

And after the season ended, Bleier made the hardest decision of his entire life. He decided to quit professional football.

Then he got a call from Andy Russell, a linebacker for the Steelers, inviting him to a pro football players dinner. Bleier rejected the invitation, telling Russell that he had decided not to come back to professional football.

"You can't quit, Rock. You've got to come back," said Russell to Bleier. "You go back to camp and you make them make a decision as to whether to keep you or cut you. Don't make it easy for them."

Rocky Bleier reported to training camp in 1974.

In 1974, Bleier finally received some playing time at running back. He carried the ball 88 times for 373 yards (4.2 yards per rush) and two touchdowns. More importantly, he only fumbled two times.

The Steelers finished first in the AFC Central Division and won Super Bowl IX, during which Bleier carried the ball 17 times for 65 yards against one of the greatest defensive lines in NFL history—the Purple People Eaters.

Bleier began to earn national recognition for his comeback. He appeared on the cover of Sports Illustrated on June 9, 1975, with the headline, "Rocky Bleier's War: A Pro Football Player in Vietnam."

Bleier made the first 11 starts of his NFL career during the regular season, at the ripe old age of 29.

He rushed for 528 yards and two touchdowns while leading the Steelers to a second consecutive Super Bowl victory. He rushed for 51 yards in the 21-17 victory against the Dallas Cowboys.

The greatest season of Rocky's career occurred in 1976. At an age when most running backs have hung up their cleats for good, Rocky rushed for 1036 yards and five touchdowns (4.7 yards per rush).

He did all this despite not making a single start. He joined teammate Franco Harris as the second set of teammates to each rush for 1000 yards in the same season and earned a reputation as one of the best blocking backs in the league.

Bleier began to show his age in 1977 and 1978. Although he carried 300 times, he gained only 1098 yards. He did score 10 touchdowns, but his 12 fumbles were cause for concern. He did lead the Steelers to a third Super Bowl victory in 1978. His touchdown reception in Super Bowl XIII proved to be the winning score in a 35-31 defeat of the Dallas Cowboys.

Bleier led the Steelers to an unprecedented fourth Super Bowl victory after the 1979 season. He rebounded to set career highs in rushing average (4.7) and receptions (31). He also scored the longest touchdown of his career, a 70-yard romp.

Bleier retired after the 1980 season, at the age of 34. He retired as the Steelers' fourth-leading rusher, with 3865 rushing yards. He scored 30 touchdowns in his 11-year career—25 in the regular season, four in the playoffs, and one in the Super Bowl.

Bleier played in 14 postseason games in his NFL career. His teams won 13 of them. They cemented their legacy as the most dominant dynasty in the history of the National Football League.

Almost 30 years after his final game, Rocky Bleier remains one of the most popular players in the history of Pittsburgh sports. He wrote a book called Fighting Back: The Rocky Bleier Story, which was made into a TV movie in 1980.

Bleier currently tours the United States, talking to high school students as a motivational speaker.

Bleier epitomizes what it means to truly have the heart of a champion. By never giving up, no matter the odds or the enemy, Bleier proved that ordinary people can become extraordinary achievers.

From winning the Purple Heart and the Bronze Star, to finally earning a spot on the Steelers roster, to earning four Super Bowl rings, Rocky Bleier proved that he is truly the definition of success in the 20th century.

Amen!

Games of the 1970 season

In the season and home opener in Three Rivers Stadium on September 21, 1969, the Steelers lost game #1 of the 1970 season to the Houston Oilers L (7-19). At Denver on Sept 27, the Broncos edged out the Steelers L (13-16). On October 3, 1970 at Cleveland, the Steelers lost to the Browns L (7-15). Finally, on Oct 11 at home in Three Rivers Stadium, the Steelers got their first win against the Buffalo Bills W (23–10) At Houston on Oct 18, the Steelers nosed out the Oilers W (7-3)

At Oakland on Oct 25, the Raiders beat the Steelers L (14-31). Then at Three Rivers on Nov 2, the Cincinnati Bengals could not keep up with the Steelers and lost the game W (21–10). On November 8, at home, the Steelers whipped the New York Jets W (21–17). Then, on Nov 15, the Kansas City Chiefs overpowered the Steelers L (14-31). At Cincinnati on Nov 22, the Bengals stomped the Steelers L 7-34).

At home in Three Rivers on Nov 29, the Steelers belted the Cleveland Browns W (28–9). Then, on Dec 6, at Three Rivers in a home game, the Green Bay Packers beat the Steelers L (12-20). At Atlanta on Dec 13, the Falcons prevailed against the Steelers L (16-27). Finishing up a promising but disappointing 1970 season, at Philadelphia on Dec 20, the Eagles beat the Steelers L (20-30) to wrap up the season.

1971 Chuck Noll #14

The 1971 Pittsburgh Steelers football team competed in their thirty-ninth season of Professional National Football League (NFL) football. The team was led by Chuck Noll in his third of twenty-three seasons as head coach of the Steelers. Their record improved again, and the games were better played as Noll's system was clicking in. The record went from 5-9 in 1969 to 6-8 in Chuck Noll's third try.

The Steelers finished in 2nd place in the AFC Central Division and did not qualify for the playoffs. The team played all of their home games at Three Rivers Stadium, winning six games, one more than in 1969. It looked like the Steelers were ready and Chuck Noll thought so too.

Terry Bradshaw , the #1 draftee struggled with turnovers in his second season. He threw 22 interceptions to 13 touchdown passes. Bradshaw is a smart guy and he knew this would not do so I suspect he knew he had to cut off some of the fun and practice his game. Just saying!

The Steelers had just drafted wide receiver Frank Lewis, Hall of Fame linebacker Jack Ham, guard Gerry Mullins, defensive end Dwight White, tight end/tackle Larry Brown, defensive tackle Ernie Holmes, and safety Mike Wagner. They were all key contributors during the Steelers Super Bowl teams of the 1970s.

The problem in 1971 was that nobody knew how great all these guys were but they sure had an inkling. That inkling would begin to flourish as the seasons passed and soon (1974) the Super Bowls would become expected.

Top Steelers Players Jack Ham

Linebacker (1971-82) Elected: 1988 Playing all 12 seasons of his NFL career with the Pittsburgh Steelers, Jack Ham earned All-Pro or All-AFC honors in seven consecutive seasons (1973-79). He also was selected to play in eight straight Pro Bowls and was named the Football News Defensive Player of the Year in 1975. Ham won the starting linebacker job as a rookie and never looked back, playing in five AFC Championship games and three Super Bowls (sat out Super Bowl XIV due to injuries). His interception return against Oakland in the 1974 AFC Championship game that set up the Steelers' go-ahead touchdown, giving the team its first ever championship victory and a berth in Super Bowl IX.

Games of the 1971 season

In the season opener in Chicago on September 19, 1971, the Steelers lost game #1 of the 1971 season to the Chicago Bears L (15-17). At home in Three Rivers on Sept 26, the Bengals were beaten by the Steelers W (21-10). On October 3, 1971 at San Diego, the Steelers beat the Chargers W (21-17). 7-15). Then, on Oct 10 at Cleveland, the Browns beat the Steelers L (17-27) . At Kansas City on Oct 18, the Chiefs whooped the Steelers L (16-38).

On Oct 24, the Steelers beat the Houston Oilers W (23–16).At Baltimore on Oct 31, the Colts beat the Steelers L (21-34). On Nov

7, the Steelers defeated the Cleveland Browns in Three Rivers Stadium W (26–9). At Miami on Nov 14, the Dolphins edged out the Steelers L (21–24). Then, on Nov 21, 1971 the Steelers defeated the New York Giants W (17–13).

On Nov 28, the Denver Broncos overpowered the Steelers L (10-22) At Houston, on Dec 5, the Oilers pounded Pittsburgh L (3-29). At Cincinnati, on Dec 12, the Steelers took down the Bengals W (21–13). In the last game of the 1971 season for Pittsburgh, on Dec 19, at home in Three Rivers, the Los Angeles Rams ripped the Steelers L (14-23). And that was the 1971 season. More to come in 1972.

1972 Chuck Noll #14

The 1972 Pittsburgh Steelers football team competed in their fortieth season of Professional National Football League (NFL) football. The team was led by Chuck Noll in his fourth of twenty-three seasons as head coach of the Steelers. Their record improved phenomenally. The games were well-played as Noll's system was in gear. The record went from 6-8 in 1971 to 11-3 in Chuck Noll's fourth try. They made the playoffs and lost in the AFC Championship game to the Dolphins L (17-21) in a tough match

The Steelers finished in 1st place in the AFC Central Division and were entitled to the Playoffs with their 13-3 record. The team played all of their home games at Three Rivers Stadium. The Steelers were ready, and Chuck Noll thought so too. In another two years, the team would be sized for the big rings and the big cigars and the champagne would be flowing.

Winning their first-ever AFC Central Division title in 1972 made the Steelers understand that they were no longer a laughingstock and in fact were a major force with which to be reckoned. This was the team's third-ever postseason appearance, its first postseason appearance in ten seasons (the Playoff Bowl for third place in the league), and only its second playoff game since 1947.

Top Steelers Players Franco Harris

Running Back (1972-'83) Elected: 1990 Franco Harris is the Steelers' all-time leading rusher with 11,950 yards and all-time leader in rushing touchdowns (91). Harris, the Steelers' first-round pick in 1972, was a big-power back who was on the receiving end of the "Immaculate Reception", which is widely recognized as the greatest play in NFL history. Harris was named Super Bowl IX MVP, after rushing for a then-record 158 yards and a touchdown.

From the pro football hall of fame site re Franco Harris:

"A player should not be measured by statistics alone. He should be measured by something more special, such as the sharing of teammates and fans.

Franco Harris began his pro football career as the Pittsburgh Steelers' No.1 pick and the 13th player selected in the 1972 NFL Draft. For 12 seasons, the 6-2, 230-pounder from Penn State was a big-yardage running back, a key man in the powerful Pittsburgh offensive machine, which also included an outstanding passing attack.

Harris established himself as a future superstar when he became only the fourth rookie in NFL annals to rush for 1,000 yards. He gained additional attention by being on the receiving end of the famous

"Immaculate Reception" pass from Terry Bradshaw that gave the Steelers their first-ever playoff win, a 13-7 victory over the Oakland Raiders. In his 13 seasons, the last of which was spent with the Seattle Seahawks in 1984, Harris rushed 2,949 times for 12,120 yards and 91 touchdowns.

He rushed for 1,000 yards or more eight seasons and for more than 100 yards in 47 games. He also caught 307 passes for 2,287 yards and nine touchdowns. His career rushing total and his combined net yardage figure of 14,622 both ranked as the third highest marks in pro football history at the time of his retirement.

Harris, who was born in Fort Dix, New Jersey, on March 7, 1950, was an All-AFC choice in 1972, 1975, 1976, and 1977 and first- or second-team All-Pro six times. He was selected to nine Pro Bowls. Franco played in five AFC championships – missing a sixth because of injury – and four Super Bowls.

In Super Bowl IX, when the Steelers won their first-ever league title with a 16-6 victory over Minnesota, Harris rushed for 158 yards, compared to just 17 yards rushing for the entire Viking team. He was named the game's Most Valuable Player. Harris held numerous Super Bowl and postseason game records by the end of his career. The most notable included 24 points and 354 yards rushing in four Super Bowls and 17 touchdowns and 1,556 yards rushing in 19 postseason playoff games.

--- End of Top Steeler

This season is famous for the Immaculate Reception, where the Steelers beat the Oakland Raiders in the playoffs 13-7 on a last second touchdown by Franco Harris.

One would say that the rebuilding of the franchise began in 1957 with Buddy Parker but the team took 1965 through 1968 off from rebuilding when it let Parker resign without trying to keep him. Then again, if Parker were still there, perhaps Chuck Noll would not have been hired and the real dynasty would not have begun.

Most would therefore agree that the real rebuilding of the franchise began in 1969 with the hiring of Chuck Noll. In 1972, the rebuilding paid off Noll's fourth year at the helm. Fe w coaches can take over a team and show wins immediately. Noll's Steelers won only one game in his first year in 1969 but the team that showed steady improvement and finally broke through to greatness in 1972 and made the playoffs for the first time since 1947.

The division title was amazing as it was the first in team history, as was the appearance in the AFC Championship game which they lost to the undefeated Miami Dolphins 21-17. It was the first of 8 straight playoff appearances for the Steelers that led to 4 Super Bowl Championships. This is the year in which the Pittsburgh Steelers truly arrived. The four-point difference in the Miami game could have been the difference between Division Champs and Super Bowl Champs in 1972. If only?

But for the best team in football, with six Super Bowl Wins when nobody else has more than five, this was a phenomenal break-out party.

Games of the season

In the season and home opener in Three Rivers Stadium, the Steelers defeated the Oakland Raiders on September 17, 1972 W (34-28). At Cincinnati on Sept 24, the Bengals defeated the Steelers L (10-15). At St. Louis, on Oct 1, the Steelers beat the Cardinals W 25–19. At Dallas on Oct 8, the Cowboys beat the Steelers L (13-17).

On Oct 15, the Steelers beat the Houston Oilers at home W (24–7). Then, on Oct 22, the Steelers pounded the New England Patriots W (33–3) At Buffalo on Oct 29, the Steelers beat the Bills W (38–21). Then on Nov 5, at Three Rivers Stadium, the Steelers slammed the Cincinnati Bengals W (40–17). At home on Nov 12, Pittsburgh beat Kansas City W (16–7).

On Nov 19, at Cleveland, the Browns edged out the Steelers L (24-26). On Nov 26, at Three Rivers Stadium. The Steelers beat the Minnesota Vikings W (23–10). At home in Three Rivers Stadium on Dec 3. The Steelers scorched the Cleveland Browns in a shut-out W

(30–0). At Houston, on Dec 10, in a low scoring game, Pittsburgh defeated Houston W (9–3). In the season finale, on Dec 17, at San Diego, the Steelers pounded the Chargers W (24–2).

Divisional Playoffs December 23, 1972

AFC: Pittsburgh Steelers 13, Oakland Raiders 7

Game summary					
	1	2	3	4	Total
Raiders	0	0	0	7	7
Steelers	0	0	3	10	13

Venue: Three Rivers Stadium, Pittsburgh, Pennsylvania

This Divisional Championship Game began at 1:00 PM on December 23, 1972 at Three Rivers Stadium in Pittsburgh Pennsylvania. It was a packed house of 50,327 at this Steelers home game. After a 13-3 regular season record, the Pittsburgh Steelers overpowered the Oakland Raiders W (13-7).

There are certain key phrases that help people immediately recall a particular game in a particular season. One of these terms is the *Immaculate Reception*. This was a play in which Steelers fullback Franco Harris scored the winning touchdown in a game that was mostly dominated by defense. The contest had remained scoreless throughout the entire first half. Then, things looked like they might open up—but not much.

When the second half began, the Steelers drove 67 yards and took a a 3-0 lead when Roy Gerela split the uprights for an 18-yard field goal. The Pittsburgh defense checked in again and stymied Oakland's attempts to advance.

Two Raiders drives were shut down by Jack Ham's interception and a fumble recovery by Glen Edwards. Then Steelers defensive back

Mike Wagner fell on a fumble by quarterback Ken "the Snake" Stabler (who had replaced injured starter Daryle Lamonica earlier in the game) at the Oakland 35. Five plays later when Gerela kicked another FG—this one was a 29-yarder that gave Pittsburgh a 6-0 lead going into the fourth quarter. The "Snake" responded by leading his team 80 yards to score on a 30-yard touchdown run with 1:13 left in the game. The Steelers had a big mission and little time to accomplish it.

They moved the ball but not very far. They were perhaps one play away from a defeat with a fourth and ten on their own 40-yard line and just 22 seconds left. Terry Bradshaw got the pass off toward running back John "Frenchy" Fuqua. But the pass bounced off Raiders safety Jack Tatum and was caught by Franco Harris, who then ran the rest of the way downfield to score a 60-yard touchdown that gave the Steelers a 12–7 lead with five seconds left in the game.

This play was controversial, as Tatum insisted the ball had bounced off Fuqua, not himself, which would have made the reception illegal under the rules of the time. Replays showing the play were and still are inconclusive as to which player touched the ball (or if perhaps both of them did). So, Franco Harris got credit for an immaculate reception.

Harris was the only offensive star of the game, rushing for 64 yards and catching 4 passes for 96 yards and a touchdown. The Raiders managed just 216 yards total and started 8 of their 12 drives inside their own 22-yard line. Pittsburgh punter Bobby Walden kept the Raiders pinned back the whole game. He averaged over 48 yards per punt on his 6 kicks and set AFC playoff records with punts of 62 and 59 yards. The Steelers advanced in the playoffs to the Conference Championship game

AFC Conference Championship Dec 31, 1972
Miami Dolphins 21, Pittsburgh Steelers 17

Game summary

	1	2	3	4	Total
Dolphins	0	7	7	7	21
Steelers	7	0	3	7	17

Venue: Three Rivers Stadium, Pittsburgh, Pennsylvania

This Conference Championship Game began at 12:00 PM on December 31, 1972 at Three Rivers Stadium in Pittsburgh Pennsylvania. The weather was unusually warm for late December at 67 degrees and partly cloudy There was a packed house of 50,845 at this Steelers home game. After a 13-3 regular season record, the Pittsburgh Steelers were edged out by the undefeated Dolphins by a 4-point margin L (17-21) 7). The Dolphins won all 17 games in 1972.

Miami continued its unbeaten streak as quarterback Bob Griese came back to the starting role. Griese had not started a game since week 5, yet he was mended, and he took over the starting spot and led the team to two touchdowns in the second half.

Things looked good for Pittsburgh as the game got going. Safety Glen Edwards intercepted a pass on the opening drive from veteran signal caller Earl Morrall, who started at QB for the Dolphins. Edwards returned the ball 28 yards to the Dolphins 48. Running back Franco Harris was very active on this drive as he gained 35 yards on 7 carries. Pittsburgh found itself with a third and 2 on the Miami 3-yard line. On the next play, Pittsburgh quarterback Terry Bradshaw fumbled the ball as he tried to run into the end zone, but good luck was on the Steelers side as lineman Gerry Mullins recovered the ball for a touchdown. This gave the Steelers an early 7-0 lead.

Unfortunately for the Steelers, Bradshaw was injured on the play and did not return until the fourth quarter. The Dolphins tied the game after the punter Larry Seiple's faked the punt and pulled off a 37-yard run, setting up Morrall's 9-yard TD pass to fullback Larry Csonka. The score was deadlocked at 7-7 at the end of the first half.

With Bradshaw still mending after his 1Q injury, and not ready to be put back in, Steelers quarterback Terry Hanratty started a second-half drive for the Steelers. He completed passes to John McMakin and Ron Shanklin for gains of 22 and 24 yards, while John Fuqua added 24 yards on a draw play. The team then settled for a 14-yard field goal by Roy Gerela, putting them up 10-7.

At this point, Bob Griese, who had been sidelined with a broken leg for 10 weeks, replaced Morrall and was right on the mark. He threw a 52-yard completion to Paul Warfield on his very first pass attempt. Miami also caught a break on the drive when an offsides penalty against Pittsburgh wiped out an interception by linebacker Jack Ham.

Eventually, running back Jim Kiick finished the 11-play, 80-yard drive with a 2-yard touchdown run, giving the Dolphins their first lead at 14-10. As the third quarter was about to end, Seiple's 33-yard punt gave Pittsburgh a first down on the Miami 48. Franco Harris ran for 7 yards on the first play, but this was followed by two incompletions and Gerela's 48-yard field goal attempt was blocked.

The Dolphins got the ball on the Steelers' 49 after the blocked field goal and put on an 11-play 49-yard drive for the score. They stole a lot of time off the clock as there was just one pass play. Jim Kiick finished it off with a 3-yard touchdown run, giving Miami a 21-10 fourth quarter lead.

Things brightened up a bit for the Steelers when Bradshaw returned to the game for the Steelers' next drive and he quickly led them to a score. The drive started with a 9-yard pass to tight end Larry Brown and followed it up with consecutive 25-yard completions to Al Young and Shanklin. On the fourth play of the possession, he threw a 12-yard touchdown pass to Young, cutting the score to 21-17. Things looked good, however.

The Steelers got the ball back twice before time expired, but Bradshaw did not have the magic. On Pittsburgh's last two drives, he threw interceptions to Miami linebackers Nick Buoniconti and Mike Kolen. The Dolphins were able to become the victors at this point simply by running out the rest of the clock.

1973 Chuck Noll #14

The 1973 Pittsburgh Steelers football team competed in their forty-first season of Professional National Football League (NFL) football. The team was led by Chuck Noll in his fifth of twenty-three seasons as head coach of the Steelers. Their record declined just a bit. The games were well-played as the record went from 11-3 in 1972 to 10-4 this year in Chuck Noll's fifth try. They came in 2nd in the AFC Central Division, made the playoffs for 2 in a row, and lost in the Divisional Playoff game to the Raiders L (14-33). Watch out for next year.

Pittsburgh started the season by tearing up the NFL for eight wins in the first nine games. Unfortunately, at the end of all that winning, a costly three game losing streak put their playoff hopes in jeopardy. With some good play in their last two games the Steelers recovered to win their last two games, settled for a Wild Card berth with a 10-4 record. They lost in the playoffs to the Oakland Raiders 33-14 in Oakland.

The pundits suggest that the 1973 Steelers' pass defense may be the greatest in the history of the NFL. Their defensive passer rating—the quarterback passer rating of all opposing quarterbacks throughout the season—was 33.1, an NFL record for the Super Bowl era.

According to Cold Hard Football Facts, we know the following: Pittsburgh's pass-defense numbers that year were stunning. Opposing passers compiled 164 of 359 (45.7%) for 1,923 yards, 5.36 [yards-per-attempt], 11 [touchdowns] and 37 [interceptions]

The figure that the pundits suggest tops them all is the amazing 37 picks in 14 games. The 2009 Jets, by comparison, allowed a puny 8 TDs in 16 games, but hauled in just 17 picks.

Pittsburgh's all-time best pass defense was an "equal-opportunity unit." Mike Wagner led the team with 8 INT, but 10 other guys recorded at least one pick. It was amazing. There were eleven who owned at least one INT for Pittsburgh that season. The entire starting secondary snagged 24 picks alone, and ironically, Hall of Fame cornerback Mel Blount was last on the list: Wagner (8), safety Glen Edwards(6), cornerback John Rowser (6) and Blount (4). In 1974, it will be the third time in a row for the Steelers to run through the playoffs and let's just say three is the charm.

In the season and home opener in Three Rivers Stadium, the Steelers defeated the Detroit Lions on September 16, 1973 W (24-10). At home on Sept 23, the Steelers slammed the Cleveland Browns W (33-6). At Houston, on Sept 30, the Steelers blasted the Oilers W (36-7). Then, on Oct 7, Pittsburgh beat San Diego's Chargers W (38-21). At Cincinnati on Oct 14, the Steelers suffered their first loss v the Bengals L (7-19).

At home in Three Rivers Stadium on Oct 21, the Steelers beat the New York Jets W (26-14). At home again in Three Rivers Stadium on Oct 28, the Steelers beat the Cincinnati Bengals W (20 13). On Nov 5, at home, Pittsburgh defeated the Washington Redskins W (21 16). At Oakland on Nov 11, the Steelers beat the Raiders W (17-9). Then, on Nov 18 at home, the Steelers lost to the Denver Broncos L 13-23) in the first of three losses in a row.

At Cleveland on November 25 the Steelers lost to the Browns L (16 21). At defending Super Bowl Champions, Miami, on Dec 3, the Dolphins beat the Steelers L (26-30). Back on the winning side, on Dec 9, at home in Three Rivers Stadium, the Steelers hammered the Houston Oilers W (33 7). Then, at San Francisco on Dec 15, the Steelers beat the 49ers in the season finale W (37 14). In the Divisional Playoffs at Oakland as described above, on Dec 22, the Steelers were defeated by the Oakland Raiders L (14 33).

1974 Chuck Noll #14

The 1974 Pittsburgh Steelers football team competed in their forty-second season of Professional National Football League (NFL) football. The team was led by Chuck Noll in his sixth of twenty-three seasons as head coach of the Steelers. Their record improved this year. The games were well-played as the record went from 10-4 in 1973 to 10-3-1 this year in Chuck Noll's sixth try. With six, the Steelers may not have gotten egg-roll, but they got themselves a world championship. They came in 1st in the AFC Central Division, made the playoffs for 3 in a row, and won the Divisional Championship, the Conference Championship, and Super Bowl X. Watch out again for next year.

The '74 team became the first team in Steelers history (42 seasons) to win a league title following one of the franchise's greatest playoff runs ever. It may not have been luck or magic, but it sure seemed that both luck and magic and greatness were involved.

You have heard the story even before we got to 1974 on the season summaries but it is such a good story, let's give it a go again. After Chuck Noll was hired in 1969 as Steelers' Head coach. , Noll signed Defensive Tackle #75 Joe Greene. He then signed Quarterback #12 Terry Bradshaw in 1970. Next came Linebacker #59 Jack Ham and then Cornerback #47 Mel Blount arrived in 1971. Each time the team got better. In 1972, the Steelers signed a fullback from nearby Penn State—Franco Harris.

By 1973, Joe Greene was flanked on the line by Dwight White, Ernie Holmes, and L. C. Greenwood. In the 1974 draft, the Steelers took no time in signing some more talent for the team. Wide Receiver #88 Lynn Swann and #82 John Stallworth, Linebacker Jack Lambert, and Center Mike Webster all became future hall of famers. In retrospect, it can be conjectured that nobody could lose with talent like that. I beg to differ.

The Steelers had some darn good teams before 1969 but never a real championship. They had some darn good players but never a real championship. Buddy Harper might have done it. But, Chuck Noll did it. Can it be that Chuck Noll culled his talent pool to make them the best that they could be while in their own skins?

This season, the Steelers were feeling pretty good after 2 playoff appearances. They were in great shape after finishing the 1974 preseason as the only undefeated team in the NFL. After two straight games, the Steelers scored over 50 points and were 1-0-1.

However, the Steelers still could not manage to beat the Raiders at home. The QB at the time, Joe Gilliam's play continually deteriorated. By Week 7, the Steelers were 4-1-1, which is respectable but not when you want every win to be a win.

So, Noll benched Gilliam for Terry Bradshaw during a win against the Falcons. Bradshaw was one of a kind and still is. He put some Bradshaw oil on the pigskin and won the next two games. But, he was not the savior if he could not keep winning so after a loss in Cincinnati, Noll benched Bradshaw again. This time he was benched in favor of Terry Hanratty (who Noll had selected in the 1969 Draft).

Hanratty blew his chance however, by playing horribly in Cleveland, the Pittsburgh major nemesis from across the water. re . The offense was struggling. Nonetheless, the Steelers were winning and had won those tough games behind a not quite yet mature Steel Curtain defense.

Bradshaw was a little less cocky but still sure of himself when he reentered the Pittsburgh lineup. The Steelers beat the Browns the second time around and they beat the Saints (a game that Bradshaw ran more than he passed). Noll stayed with Bradshaw.

After a loss to Houston, the Steelers would play the most important game of the season in New England. With a win against the Patriots, the Steelers would clinch the AFC Central and they would assure their third straight playoff appearance. But they didn't have to worry. The Steelers dominated the Patriots and then they beat the Bengals and simply awaited the playoffs.

Top Steelers Players Donnie Shell

Safety... Shell was a five-time Pro Bowler between 1978 and 1982, a 4-time All-Pro selection, and was the Steelers team MVP in 1980. He saved several possible six points in Super Bowl XIII and Super Bowl XIV.

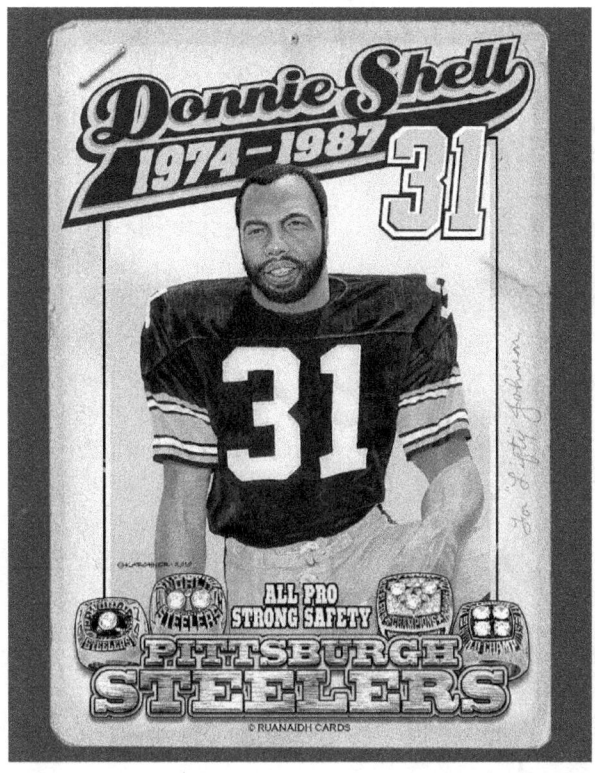

He had been in the top fifteen in balloting for the Pro Football Hall of Fame once before, in 2002 but with no success.] The Professional Football Researchers Association named Shell to the PRFA Hall of Very Good Class of 2013

Shell resides in Rock Hill, South Carolina and was the Carolina Panthers Director of Player Development from 1994 to 2009. With the lone exception of former Steelers safety Mike Logan, who grew up in McKeesport, Pennsylvania just outside Pittsburgh, Shell's number 31 has not been reissued by the team.

He played in 201 games for the Steelers, second only to Hall of Fame Center Mike Webster (who played in 220).

Games of the Season

In the season and home opener in Three Rivers Stadium, the Steelers blanked the Baltimore Colts on September 15, 1974 W (30-0). At home on Sept 22, at Mile High Stadium, the Steelers tied the Denver Broncos in OT T (35-35). At Oakland, on Sept 29, the Steelers took a hit from the Raiders L (0-17). Then, on Oct 6, Pittsburgh beat Houston's Oilers at the Astrodome W (13-7). At Kansas City on Oct 13, at Arrowhead Stadium, whipped the Chiefs W (34-24).

Top Steelers Player Jack Lambert

Linebacker (1974-'84) Elected: 1990 John Harold Lambert was a two-time NFL Defensive Player of the Year, eight-time All-Pro and nine-time Pro-Bowler. He led the team in tackles in every season except his last, when he missed extensive action due to a severe toe injury that forced him to retire. Lambert, the Steelers' second-round draft pick in 1974, was noted for his vicious tackling and is recognized as the premier linebacker of his era.

Games continued 1974

On Oct 20 at home in Three Rivers Stadium, the Steelers beat the Cleveland Browns W (20–16). In a Monday night game on Oct 28 at home in Three Rivers Stadium, the Steelers beat the Atlanta Falcons W (24–17). At home in Three Rivers Stadium on Nov 3, the Steelers manhandled the Philadelphia Eagles W (27–0) in a shutout. Then, on Nov 10 at Riverfront Stadium in Cincinnati, the Bengals beat the Steelers L (10–17). Then at Cleveland Municipal Stadium on Nov 17, the Steelers defeated the Cleveland Browns W (26–16).

In a second Monday Night game for the 1974 Stadium (What did they know?) at Tulane Stadium on Nov 25, the Steelers hammered the New Orleans Saints W (28–7). Then on Dec 1 at home in Three Rivers Stadium, the Houston Oilers beat the Steelers L (10–13). This brought the Eagles record to 8–3–1, which was very respectable. In the two finales second-last and last games of the seasons, on Dec 8, at Schaefer Stadium, in Foxboro, the Steelers defeated the New England Patriots W (21–17). Then, wrapping up the season. On Dec 14 at home in Three Rivers Stadium the Steelers smothered the Cincinnati Bengals W (27–3).

Top Steelers Players Lynn Swann

Wide Receiver (1974-'82) Elected: 2001 Lynn Curtis Swann was the Steelers' first-round draft pick in 1974. Swann filled the highlight reels with his graceful moves and leaping ability. Swann was at his best in the team's biggest games and earned MVP honors for his performance in Super Bowl X when he caught four passes for 161 yards and a TD. Swann finished his career with 336 receptions for 5,462 yards and 51 TDs.

Top Steelers Player John Stallworth

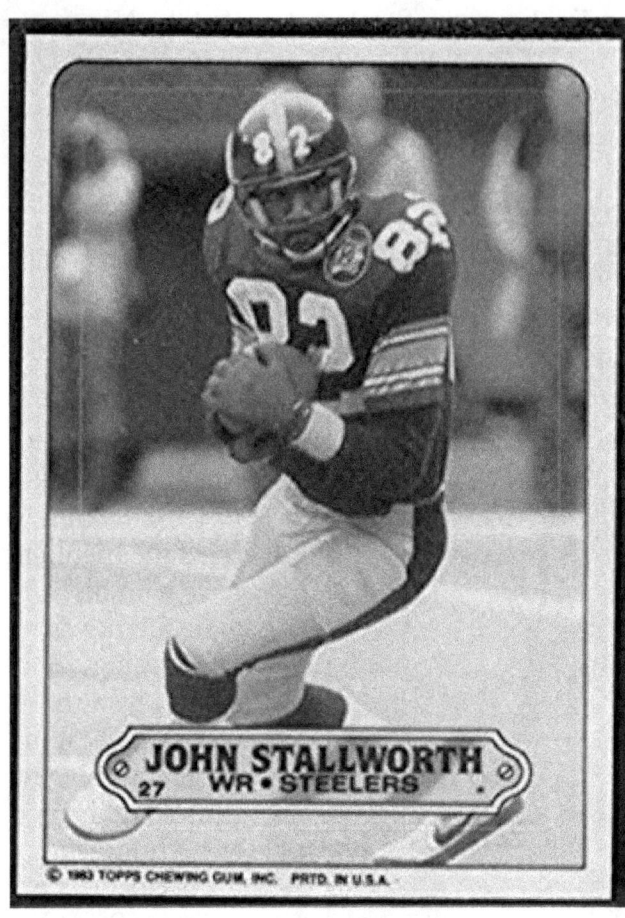

Wide Receiver (1974-'87) Elected: 2002 Johnny Lee Stallworth was the Steelers' fourth-round draft pick in 1974. He had 12 postseason touchdown catches and 17-consecutive postseason games with a reception. Stallworth set Super Bowl records for career average-per-catch (24.4 yards) and for single-game average (40.3), set in Super Bowl XIV. A two-time team MVP, Stallworth retired as the Steelers' all-time leader in receptions (537) yards (8,723) 100-yards receiving games (25) and receiving TDs (63)

Divisional Playoffs

In the Divisional Round Playoff Game, in which Pittsburgh had a 1-1 record the prior two years, the Steelers were slotted to play the Bills. What now? Sports Illustrated's Dan Jenkins had his opinion published. He felt that Pittsburgh was "the only team to reach the playoffs without a quarterback".

However, even without a quarterback, or perhaps Pittsburgh had three quarterbacks, the Steelers would dominate Buffalo and hold O.J. Simpson to 49 yards rushing (it was O.J.'s only playoff game appearance ever).

Top Steelers Players Mike Webster

Center (1974-'88) Elected: 1997 Michael Lewis Webster spent his first 15 NFL seasons in a Steelers uniform. Webster was the leader of one of the most dominant offensive lines of his era. Webster was very durable, missing only six games in his first 16 seasons while playing in 150 consecutive games.

Conference Championship

In the 1974 AFC Championship Game, the Steelers would play an old foe, the Raiders. Each year, the rivalry was escalating: in 1972, the Steelers won in Pittsburgh; in 1973, the Raiders returned the favor in Oakland. However, the Steelers were ready for anything the Raiders could throw at them. Using the new "Stunt 4-3 defense" the Steelers held the Raiders to 29 yards rushing as the Steelers themselves ran for over 200 yards in Oakland.

After a Franco Harris touchdown run, the Steelers clinched their first Super Bowl appearance in club history (and their first league championship appearance). The rings were being sized and the Cigars were being humidor-zed.

Super Bowl IX

In Super Bowl IX, the Steelers and the Vikings had a hard time playing in the rough conditions of the old Tulane Stadium. After many exchanges of punts, the Steelers finally scored a safety on a bobbled handoff by Fran Tarkenton.

And, so, the score at the half was 2–0. The Steel Curtain continually dominated the Vikings. Somebody had thrown more iron ore into the steel formula. While coach Bud Grant tried to run at the strength of the Steel Curtain, the Vikings were shut down time and time again.

The only points Minnesota managed to squeeze off was a blocked punt (the extra point was blocked). After the MVP performance by Franco Harris, the Steelers came away with a 16-6 victory over the Vikings. It was the first league title in Steelers history.

1975 Chuck Noll #14

The 1975 Pittsburgh Steelers football team competed in their forty-third season of Professional National Football League (NFL) football. The team was led by Chuck Noll in his seventh of twenty-three seasons as head coach of the Steelers. Their record improved this year. The games were well-played as the record went from 10-3-1 in 1974 to 12-2 this year in Chuck Noll's seventh try. The Steelers picked up another World Championship. They came in 1st in the AFC Central Division, made the playoffs for 4 in a row, and won the Divisional Championship, the Conference Championship, and Super Bowl X.

This Pittsburgh Steelers team was the second championship team in club history with both championships coming in consecutive years. This Steelers team began the season as defending champions for the first time in their 43-year history. The team was led by a dominating defense and a quick offense, and they won Super Bowl X over the Dallas Cowboys, 21-17. The team posted their best defensive numbers since 1946 and scored more points than any other Steeler team to that point. Bradshaw and company were simply terrific.

Though I suggest it is Bradshaw and the boys, it is clear that John Stallworth made Terry Bradshaw #12, the Pittsburgh QB better every week.

This year was the first time that a division ever had three 10-game winning teams. The Steelers had already beaten the Bengals, and in Week 8, the 6-1 Steelers hosted the 6-1 Oilers. With the game tied in the final minutes, a catch in the end zone by John Stallworth gave them the 24-17 win and placed them at the top of their division.

RB #32 Franco Harris as always, was a standout for the Steelers, rushing for more yards than any other back except for O.J. Simpson. The Steelers topped the league in stats with more wins, more points, and by allowing fewer points than in 1974. Just before beating New York, the Steelers beat the Oilers and the Bengals (a second time) for the AFC Central title. After losing a meaningless game in Los Angeles, the Steelers, with a league best 12-2 record were ready more than for the playoffs.

Games of the Season

In the season opener in San Diego Stadium, the Steelers blanked the Chargers on September 21, 1975 W (37-0). At home at Three Rivers Stadium on Sept 28, the Steelers lost a tough match to the Buffalo Bills L (21-30) At home on Oct 5, the Steelers shellacked the Cleveland Browns W (42-6) at Cleveland Municipal Stadium. Then, on Oct 12, Pittsburgh beat Denver at Three Rivers Stadium W (20-9) At home on Oct 19, the Steelers pounded the Chicago Bears W (34-3).

On Oct 26 at Green Bay, Pittsburgh edged out the Packers W (16–13) at County Stadium. On Nov 2, at Cincinnati's Riverfront Stadium, the Steelers beat the Bengals W (30–24) At home in Three Rivers Stadium. On Nov 9 Pittsburgh beat the Houston Oilers W (24–17). At home on Nov 16 the Steelers smashed the Kansas City Chiefs W (28–3). Then in a Monday Night game on Nov 24, at Houston, the Steelers squashed the Oilers W (32–9) at the Houston Astrodome.

At New York on Nov 30, Pittsburgh defeated the Jets W (20–7) at Shea Stadium. On Dec 7, the Steelers beat the Cleveland Browns at home W (31–17) in Three Rivers Stadium. In a rare Saturday Night game on Dec 13 at home, the Steelers whipped the Cincinnati Bengals W (35–14). Then, in a game that did not matter with the Steelers already tops in the league in wins for the season at 12-1, in the closer on Dec 20 at Los Angeles. The Rams got the best of the Steelers L (3–10) at the Los Angeles Memorial Coliseum.

Divisional Playoffs Dec 27 1975

The Steelers entered the playoffs at 12-2 and were prepared for the 10-4 Baltimore Colts. This game featured great offense and defense from Pittsburgh. The Steel Curtain proved its worth by holding down the Colts, causing their offense stall out in a cold and wet Three Rivers Stadium.

The Curtain caused five turnovers in the course of the game. It was not all Pittsburgh all the time, however. An interception by CB Mel

Blount gave the Steelers a chance to take over. After a touchdown by RB Rocky Bleier, a fumble recovery by LB Andy Russell, it looked like the game was sealed. However, more work needed to be done.

Pittsburgh was trailing 10-7 midway through the third quarter and Baltimore had the ball, third-and-nine just over its own 20-yard line. "I wasn't going to gamble at that point," Colts Coach Domres said. "I called a straight running play so we could then kick the ball on fourth down." As the Colts lined up, however, their Tackle David Taylor suddenly pitched forward—and offside—when his hamstring muscle snapped. Faced with third-and-14, Domres changed his strategy and tried to pass the Colts to a first down.

Domres had been right the first time. Blount, who led the NFL with 11 interceptions, stole the ball from Roger Carr and danced to the Baltimore seven-yard line. From there, Rocky Bleier burst over tackle for the touchdown. Pittsburgh increased its lead to 21-10 midway through the final quarter when Bradshaw hobbled into the end zone from the two-yard line.

Colts QB Bert Jones tried to organize a closing rally. He quickly moved the Colts from their own 12 to the Pittsburgh three. Needing an instant touchdown, as the clock closed on two minutes, Jones wanted to try a quick look-in pass. But as just as he cocked his arm, LB Ham hooked his elbow and knocked the ball loose.

Andy Russell, playing with aching knees, picked up the ball at the seven, after playing the whole game and he saw 93-yards to pay dirt. He began the longest, slowest touchdown run ever witnessed, so slow, in fact, that Jack Ham suggested the referees should have given Russell a penalty for delay of game. The Steelers won, 28-10, and prepared for their rival, the Oakland Raiders.

AFC Championship Game Jan 4, 1976

This AFC Championship game match-was not an exact duplicate of the year before, because this time the Steelers would play in the comfort of Three Rivers and the ice for their joints. The whole week before the game, the weather was terrible in Pittsburgh. But it got worse. The field tarp split during the night, and this caused the sidelines to become became iced over. The effect of the ice was that it narrowed the field for the deep outside passing game of Oakland. So, the bad weather would be in Pittsburgh's favor.

It was a grueling game. After three quarters only 3 points on total had been scored. The number of turnovers (13) was higher than the combined score. This most heated rivalry was ironically stuck in aa deep freeze.

The enmity between the teams had been escalating for four years, and now it was escalating on every play. During the 3rd quarter, Lynn Swann was taken out of the game by a clothesline tackle from Raiders George Atkinson. He had been knocked out and later, was in the hospital.

In the 4th quarter, the Steelers managed to score on a 25-yard run to the outside by #32 Franco Harris. John Stallworth made a key block on two Raider defenders to help pull off the score. Later, a 20-yard pass caught by Stallworth put the Steelers up, 16-7. The game ended when Ken "the Snake" Stabler passed to Cliff Branch, who was brought down by CB Mel Blount. The Steelers were on their way to the Super Bowl again.

Super Bowl X January 18, 1976

Both the Cowboys and the Steelers had previously won Super Bowl victories. This was the first time ever that the game matched two teams that had already won Lombardi Trophies. The pundits kept asking questions about Lynn Swan, who was a victim in the AFC Conference Championship Game. He had received the worst concussion he had ever had.

There was some controversy injected when the Cowboys safety Cliff Harris made a statement that Lynn Swann was not the only Steeler who was challenged.

The game got off to a fast start with the Cowboys scoring quickly on a 29-yard pass to #88 Drew Pearson. The Steel Curtain were back on their heels as they had not previously allowed a first quarter touchdown all year. Swann's presence in the game was quickly noted when he made a leaping sideline catch over Cowboys CB Mark Washington. Later, Swan made another catch that is often repeated by NFL Films as one of the greatest catches in NFL History. Bradshaw threw it deep to Swann who was covered very well by Washington again. However, when the ball was batted, it began to fall. As the ball and Swann were falling, he was able to stick his hands up and grab it with Washington underneath him. What a play.

At the end of the first half, the Cowboys were leading 10-7. The Steelers defense was very challenged by the complicated Cowboy offense. However, the Cowboys had never yet seen a defense quite like the Steelers.

Roger Staubach was sacked seven times for a loss of 42 yards. When the third quarter resumed, Cowboys' safety Cliff Harris began to taunt Steelers kicker #10, Roy Gerela. Jack Lambert, seeing this, ran over and threw Harris to the ground. It became a crucial moment in the game - a huge momentum shift.

Kicker Roy Gerela's ribs were hurting from a game saving tackle he had made earlier in the game and so he was not at his best. , Cliff Harris was mouthing off, and Jack Lambert had seen enough.
The first half of Super Bowl X was not kind to Gerela, the Steelers kicker. After Dallas ran a reverse on the opening kickoff, Gerela found himself as the last Steeler that could stop Thomas Henderson from recording the first kickoff return for a touchdown in Super Bowl history. Gerela made the tackle but paid for it by suffering badly bruised ribs that would affect his kicking for the remainder of the game.

Immediately, Harris began to play the victim, and he lobbied for the official to throw Lambert out. After convincing the official to let him remain in the game, Lambert, in NFL Films broadcaster John Facandae's words used the altercation to "psyche himself into an even higher level of rage. With Joe Greene injured, Lambert became the symbol of Steeler muscle, shifting and rooting through blockers until he found the ball-carrier, which Lambert found 14 times in Super Bowl X."

Eventually things turned a bit for the Steelers as Mike Wagner's pick helped the Steelers to their first lead. Midway through the 4th quarter, ahead 15-10, Pittsburgh struck again deep from their own territory. This was a brilliant, long touchdown pass from Bradshaw to Lynn Swann. However, it came at a cost, as Bradshaw was shaken up and forced to leave the game.

A Dallas touchdown then cut their lead to 4. When #5 Terry Hanratty took over, Chuck Noll made a bold and unusual decision. He turned the game over to the Steel curtain minus Joe Greene. On 4th and 9, the Steelers ran the ball up the middle, giving the ball back to the Cowboys near mid-field. It was clearly the faith Noll had in his defense that caused this decision. With just three seconds left, the Cowboys were not dead yet, but close. They had one last chance and threw a pass into the end-zone.

You never know how the Hail Mary's will go. This one was tipped by Mike Wagner and intercepted by Glen Edwards to end the game. f. The Steelers were Super Bowl champions again. They had beaten the Cowboys, 21-17. The MVP of course was #88 Lynn Swann. At the end of the game, Chuck Noll began to prepare his team in the locker room of the Miami Orange Bowl for the next year. Coaching pro football is definitely a full-time job.

1976 Chuck Noll #14

The 1976 Pittsburgh Steelers football team competed in their forty-fourth season of Professional National Football League (NFL) football. The team was led by Chuck Noll in his eighth of twenty-three seasons as head coach of the Steelers. Their record declined this year from 12-2 in 1975 to 10-4 this year. The Steelers picked up another World Championship. They came in 1st in the AFC Central Division, made the playoffs for 5 in a row, won the Divisional Championship and lost the Conference Championship.

Chapter 20 Coach Chuck Noll 1969 to 1982   287

After two Super Bowl wins in a row, The Steelers looked to become the first team in the Super Bowl era to win three-straight league championships . This years was to have been the first since the 1929–1931 and 1965–1967 -both courtesy of Green Pay.

However, doubt set in big time when the team started the season at 1-4 and then when quarterback Terry Bradshaw was injured in the week 5 loss to the Cleveland Browns. There was a vicious sack by Joe "Turkey" Jones that has since become immortalized in NFL Films as part of the Browns-Steelers rivalry.

Despite the poor start, Pittsburgh would get itself adjusted and perform flawlessly to the playoffs. It was the sheer strength of the Steel Curtain and its dual threat at running back in Franco Harris and Rocky Bleier. Each runner went for over 1,000 yards. This brought the team to a 10–4 finish and they and posted five shutouts. Rookie quarterback Mike Kruczek, in Terry Bradshaw's spot. wound up going 6–0 largely due to the strength of the ground game. This would also stand as an NFL record for best start for a rookie quarterback until 2004—when the Steelers' own Ben Roethlisberger more than doubled that record and went 13–0 as a starter his rookie season. Not bad for a rookie.

In the season opener in Oakland, the Steelers lost to the Raiders on September 12, 1976 L (28-32). At home at Three Rivers Stadium on Sept 19, the Steelers beat the Cleveland Browns W (31-14) At home on Sept 26, the Steelers were edged out by the New England Patriots L (27-30). On Monday, Oct 4, at Minnesota, the Vikings beat the Steelers L (6-17). The fourth loss of five in a row from the onset of the season came on Oct 10, at Cleveland Municipal Stadium, as the Browns nosed out the Steelers L (16-18). There would be no more losses to the playoffs.

On Oct 17, Pittsburgh beat the **Cincinnati Bengals** W (23–6). At New York, on Oct 24, the Steelers shut out the Giants W (27–0) At home at Three Rivers Stadium on October 31, the Steelers overpowered the **San Diego Chargers** W (23–0). At Kansas City on Nov 7, the Steelers Shellacked the Chiefs **W** (45–0). At home, on Nov 14, the Steelers won a close game v the **Miami Dolphins** 1:00 pm NBC **W** (14–3)

At home in Three Rivers Stadium on Nov 21 Pittsburgh beat the **Houston Oilers W** (32–16). At Cincinnati on Nov 28, the Steelers edged out the Bengals **W** (7–3). At home on Dec 5, the Steelers decimated the **Tampa Bay Buccaneers** W (42–0). Then closing out the season, at Houston on Dec 11, the Steelers won against the Oilers **W** (21–0).

Divisional Playoffs Dec 17, 1976

The Steelers were on a roll having gotten the W in their last nine games of the season. They kept it rolling into the Divisional playoffs soundly defeating the Colts 40-14. The Steelers had the game under control from the beginning and ended up with the Division Championship. Significant plays of the game include the following (using short script) .

The scoring was done by P or B but mostly P. It started with Lewis for P taking a 76-yard pass from Bradshaw for a TD. Gerela misfired on the Kick. Pittsburgh mounted another dive and Baltimore's Carr snagged a 17-yard pass from Bert Jones and Linhart got the PAT. Then. P Harrison got in on a one-yard run with a good Gerela kick.

You knew Lynn Swann would get in the action and he began with a 29-yarder from Bradshaw with a Gerela kick. Then when a Pittsburgh drive stalled Gerela kicked a FG to widen the lead to 26-7, Swann then snagged an 11-yard pass from Bradshaw for the score and Gerela got the PAT. W (33-7) Baltimore was not finished as Leaks got in on a one-yard run with a Linhart PAT – score=33-14. The last score was P's Harrison on a 10-yard run and this time a Mansfield kick W (40-14)

In this Divisional game, Pittsburgh gained an NFL record at the time of 524 total yards.

Conference Championship December 26, 1976

The Steelers are not looking for excuses, but they played without their two experienced star running backs with an attack that was mostly ground based or depending on a ground game. In this game, with injuries to both Bleier and Harris in the AFC Divisional Playoff game against the Baltimore Colts sidelining them both for this game, against the Oakland Raiders. The Raiders beat the Steelers 24-7.

Without both of their 1,000-yard rushers, the Steelers lost to the Raiders by a score of 24-7. Even with Pittsburgh coming up short, without whining, we've been told that many Steelers fans—including the Rooney family themselves—consider the 1976 Steelers the best team in franchise history, even better than all six world championship teams.

Jack Lambert, who won 4 Super Bowls with the Steelers between 1974 and 1979, claimed that the 1976 Steelers team was the best team that he ever played for, and subsequently, the loss to the Raiders in the AFC Championship game was the most painful loss of his career. He (Lambert) is convinced that they would have beaten the Raiders and gone on to win that season's Super Bowl had Harris and Bleier both been healthy and available for said AFC Championship game.

The Steelers were getting awards for the 1976 teams as late as 2007. ESPN.com named the 1976 Steelers the greatest defense in NFL history, suggesting that "the 1976 unit was the best (slightly better than the '75 squad). Here's why: "28". That's how many points the Steel Curtain surrendered in the last nine games of the season. That's a total. As a result, Pittsburgh, which started the season 1–4, made it all the way to the AFC Championship Game....

The '76 Steelers didn't have it easy – their opponents had a .528 winning percentage. But they had these guys: Hall of Famers Mean Joe Greene, Jack Lambert, Jack Ham and Mel Blount. And eight Steelers defensive players made the 1976 Pro Bowl team: cornerback J.T. Thomas, defensive end L. C. Greenwood, Greene, Ham, Lambert, defensive back Glen Edwards, safety Mike Wagner, and

Blount." That was one heck of a team—part of a great Steelers tradition.

1977 Chuck Noll #14

The 1977 Pittsburgh Steelers football team competed in their forty-fifth season of Professional National Football League (NFL) football. The team was led by Chuck Noll in his ninth of twenty-three seasons as head coach of the Steelers. Their record declined this year from 10-4 in 1976 to 9-5 this year. The Steelers came in 1st in the AFC Central Division, made the playoffs for their sixth time in a row, and lost in the Divisional Championship to the Broncos L (21-34).

After what the experts consider Pittsburgh's best year ever in 1976, the 1977 Pittsburgh Steelers won a lower total of 9 games yet appeared in the playoffs for their 6th straight season. The Steelers were not as crisp as usual, but they won the AFC Central with a 9–5 record.

They struggled most of the season as their record hovered around .500. Even the Steel curtain seemed to have a little wear and tear allowing 243 points on the season, more than 100 more above the previous season. Lackluster play would catch up with them in the Divisional Playoffs when they were bumped off by the Broncos 34–21 in Denver.

In the season and home opener on Sep 19, in Three Rivers Stadium, the Steelers shut-out the San Francisco 49ers W (27-0). At home again int Three Rivers Stadium on Sept 25, the Steelers were beaten by the Oakland Raiders L (7-16). At Cleveland Municipal Stadium on Oct 2, the Steelers beat the Browns W (28-14). On Oct 9, at Houston, the Oilers beat the Steelers L (10-27) in the Astrodome. Then, on Oct 17, at home in Three Reivers Stadium, Pittsburgh defeated Cincinnati W (20-14).

At home on Oct 23 the Steelers beat the Houston Oilers W (27–10). On Oct 30 at Memorial Stadium in Baltimore, the Colts whooped the Steelers L (14–31). At Denver on Nov. 6, the Broncos beat the Steelers L (7–21) in Mile High Stadium. At home in Three Reivers

Stadium on Nov. 13, Pittsburgh edged out the Cleveland Browns W (35–31). In Three River Stadium on Nov. 20, the Steelers beat the Dallas Cowboys W (28–13).

At New York's Shea Stadium, on Nov. 27 the Jets were defeated by the Steelers W (23–20). At home in Three Rivers on Dec. 4, Pittsburgh beat Seattle W 30–20. At Cincinnati's Riverfront Stadium, on Dec. 10, the Bengals defeated the Steelers L (10-17). Then in the season saving finale, at San Diego Stadium, Pittsburgh barely nosed out the Chargers on Dec 18, W (10–9), finishing the season at 9-5 in first place in the SFC East.

In 1977, the first round of the playoffs was set up differently because of the proximity of the Christmas Holidays. So, the playoffs began on Christmas Eve, December 24, 1977. The full action tournament concluded with the Dallas Cowboys defeating the Denver Broncos in Super Bowl XII, 27–10, on January 15, 1978, at the Louisiana Superdome in New Orleans, Louisiana.

Due to Christmas, the Divisional playoff games in which Pittsburgh played were all held in a span of three days. The AFC playoff games were on Saturday December 24 while the NFC games were held on Monday December 26.

This year also was the only one since the AFL–NFL merger in 1970 that one conference held both of its divisional playoff games on one day and the other conference held both of its games on the other day. In every other season since 1970, the conferences have split their playoff games over the two days. Another last for these playoffs was that it was the last season that the NFL used an eight-team playoff tournament.

Pittsburgh made the playoffs with one of their worst #1 records since making the playoffs for the first time seven years earlier.

AFC East Playoffs: Denver 34, Pittsburgh 21

In Denver's first postseason football contest, linebacker Tom Jackson's 2 interceptions and a fumble recovery set up 17 points, 10 of them in the 4th quarter, as the Broncos defeated the Steelers for the first playoff win in their 18-year history.

Denver scored first after Broncos receiver John Schultz blocked a punt. This set up running back Rob Lytle's 7-yard rushing touchdown. Pittsburgh came back with a 56-yard drive, including Terry Bradshaw's 1-yard rushing touchdown.

In the second quarter, Broncos defensive tackle Lyle Alzado hit Franco Harris, causing a fumble which LB Randy Gradishar recovered and returned 5 yards before he fumbled. Tom Jackson got the second fumble and took it 25 yards to the Pittsburgh 10-yard line.

On the next play, running back Otis Armstrong ran the ball into the end zone to put the Broncos up 14–7. The Steelers came right back with Jim Smith's 28-yard kickoff return to the Steelers 34-yard line. Bradshaw hit John Stallworth for a 21-yarder and Harris went on a 20-yard burst before he finished the drive with a 1-yard touchdown run to tie the game at 14 with 1:41 left in the half.

In the third quarter, the Broncos took it 52 yards to the Pittsburgh 1-yard line, and then lost the ball. They got the ball back quickly after no progress by the Steelers and a punt. They then took the ball 43-yars and went up 21-14 on Craig Morton's 30-yard touchdown pass to tight end Riley Odoms.

Early in the 4th quarter, Pittsburgh managed to come back as Stallworth caught a Bradshaw 48-yar pass setting up a shot quick Bradshaw pass for a 1-yard touchdown toss to TE Larry Brown. The Steelers had scored their last. Denver then took over the game. Jim Turner got the lead (24-21)

Then Jackson intercepted a Bradshaw pass and raced 32 yards to the Steelers 9-yard line, setting up another Turner FG—this on 24-yards, making the score 27-21. When Pittsburgh got the ball back,, Jackson got another pick and he returned it 17 yards to the Steelers 33.

Denver then took to the air, scoring the game clinching touchdown on Morton's 34-yard pass to Jack Dolbin with 1:44 left in the game.

Harris finished the game with 92 rushing yards, 4 receptions for 20 yards, and a touchdown. Morton only completed 11 of 23 passes, but he threw for 167 yards and two touchdowns with no interceptions. It would be a long wait between seasons. Was another Super Bowl in the offing?

1978 Chuck Noll #14

The 1978 Pittsburgh Steelers football team competed in their forty-sixth season of Professional National Football League (NFL) football. The team was led by Chuck Noll in his tenth of twenty-three seasons as head coach of the Steelers. Their record improved big time this year from 9-5 in 1977 to 12-2 in 1978. The Steelers came in 1st in the AFC Central Division, made the playoffs for their seventh time in a row. They won the Divisional Championships, the Conference Championship, and emerged victorious in the Super Bowl for their third Lombardi Trophy.

This 46th season as noted was finished off with a dramatic Super Bowl XIII Victory to become the first franchise in the NFL at the time, to win three Super Bowl titles. Pittsburgh accepts proudly its recognition as the NFL team with the most Super Bowl victories – 6.

It all started with Chuck Noll and then to get the job done a great cast of characters, especially Terry Bradshaw. Quarterback Terry Bradshaw gets major credit for the championship run along with a real comeback in force this year of the team's vaunted Steel Curtain defense. Bradshaw put together the best year of his career in 1988 becoming only the second Steeler to win the NFL MVP award. Ten Steelers players were named to the Pro Bowl team, and four were judged as first-team All-Pros by the AP. Head coach Chuck Noll returned for his tenth season—moving him ahead of Walt Kiesling as the longest tenured head coach in the team's history to that point.

The Steelers had an off year in 1977 coming in to this championship year. They were defending champions of the AFC Central Division, even after a disappointing 9–5 record in 1977. Though Pittsburgh won the Division, the previous season was a difficult one for the team (both on and off the field). The season culminated in a division round playoff loss to the Denver Broncos on Christmas Eve. It was like it was not the Pittsburgh we all know that had taken the field.

The Steelers had some issues with Mel Blount and Jack Ham not signing and that had a negative impact on the 1977 Steelers as the Steel Curtain had a tough time sustaining momentum from challenging offenses. Was Chuck Noll concerned about morale? Noll explained his philosophy of how he motivates players.

When asked, he acknowledged that he liked that he had taken the team to the top and they were Super Bowl winners, but he admitted that football was not his entire life. He never had made a claim to be a motivator. Instead, he said that he and his staff merely select self-motivating players and try to teach them. His hobbies are relaxing and that's what he does when he is not working.

Noll took the time to raise orchids, attend concerts, seek out vintage wines, pilot his own plane and fly his son to Florida on weekends to collect specimens for the saltwater aquarium in their Pittsburgh home. If his players were not ready to play, he would address it but not in Knute Rockne style with a big pep talk. It would mean that the player lost the drive or the love of the team and there would be another player soon to replace them, regardless of talent comparison. No one player was indispensable if not for the team.

Pittsburgh got sick of this 1977 stink of being almost good enough in 1978 The team began its 1978 season with motivation at peak. They grabbed seven straight victories, before losing to the Houston Oilers in prime time on Monday Night Football. They finished the season with a league-best 14–2 record, including a 5-game winning streak to close the season. This record assured them they would play at home throughout the 1978 playoffs.

It was also the best record compiled in the team's history (since surpassed only by a 15–1 mark in 2004). (In 2004, the Steelers were 15-0 in the regular season but could not keep it going. What could have been are powerful words.

The 1978 Steelers team was rated the thirty-fifth best team in the history of the NFL (to September 2015) by FiveThirtyEight, a polling aggregation and statistical service. They have not been slouches in Mike Tomlins last two-years, but the Crown was taken in ono year by the Patriots and the next by the Eagles.

That rating is based upon FiveThirtyEight's proprietary Elo rating system algorithm. Only two Steelers teams were rated higher were the 1975 team at twelfth and the 2005 team one slot ahead of the 1978 team at thirty-fourth. Once Chuck Noll brought his skills to Pittsburgh, Pittsburgh changed for the better and football became a winning sport.

Games of the Season

The NFL extended the season this year, 1978, from 14 games to 16 games. It may make a book that chronicles every game more difficult to write to the volume of games but since every game is exciting, there will be no impact on reading about any individual game. In 2018, as this book was originally written, the season is still set at 16 games with a bye week for a rest mid-season or so.

In the season opener at Buffalo, on Sep 3, the Steelers outplayed the Bills at Rich Stadium W (28-17). At home in Three Rivers Stadium on Sept 10, the Steelers beat the Seattle Seahawks W (21-10). Then at Riverfront Stadium, the Steelers defeated the Cincinnati Bengals W (28-3) At Three Rivers Stadium, Pittsburgh defeated the Cleveland Browns on Sept 24, W (15-9) . On Oct 1, at New York's Shea Stadium, Pittsburgh beat the Jets W (28-17)

On Oct 8 at home, Pittsburgh slugged the Atlanta Falcons W (31–7). Then, on Oct. at Cleveland Municipal Stadium s, Pittsburgh dominated W (34–14). On Oct 23 at home in Three Rivers, in the first loss of the season, Pittsburgh went down in a close match to the Houston Oilers L (17-24). At home again on Oct 29. The Steelers edged out the Kansas City Chiefs W (27–24). Then at Three Rivers Stadium, Pittsburgh beat the New Orleans Saints W (20–14) bringing their season record to a league- leading 9-1

At Los Angeles on Nov 12, , the Rams tagged the Steelers with their second loss of the year at LA Memorial Stadium L (7-10). Then at home on Nov. 19. Pittsburgh nosed out Cincinnati Bengals W (7-6) at Three Rivers Stadium. At San Francisco on Nov 27, the Steelers beat the 49ers W (24-7) at Candlestick Park. At Houston on Dec 3, the Steelers defeated the Oilers W (13-3) in the Astrodome. At home on Dec. 9, the Steelers whipped the Baltimore Colts W (35-13) at Three Rivers Stadium. Then, wrapping it up at Denver, the Steelers got the best of the Broncos on Dec 16 W (21-17) at Mile High Stadium.

1978 Playoffs

Divisional playoffs December 30, 1978

AFC: Pittsburgh Steelers 33, Denver Broncos 10

The Steelers and the Broncos rivalry was turned up another notch, but it was the Steelers who had full control. Pittsburgh dominated the Broncos in the first playoff games by gaining 425 yards of total offense. Denver scored first on a field goal, but it was not long before Pittsburgh responded by driving 66 yards in 8 plays to score on running back Franco Harris' 1-yard touchdown run.

Then on the Steelers' next drive, Harris ran 18 yards to the end zone for his second touchdown. Pittsburgh QB Terry Bradshaw threw two touchdowns in the fourth quarter, a 45-yarder to wide receiver John Stallworth and a 38-yard one to wide receiver Lynn Swann to wrap up the game

In the match, Bradshaw completed 16 of 29 passes for 272 yards and 2 touchdowns, Stallworth had 10 receptions for 156 yards and a touchdown, and Harris rushed for 105 yards and 2 touchdowns. The Steelers were off to the Conference Championship

1978 Conference Championships

January 7, 1979 AFC Championship: Pittsburgh Steelers 34, Houston Oilers 5

Playing at home on a wet, slick, and slippery field was commonplace for Pittsburgh. In this AFC Conference game, the Steelers dominated the Oilers. They forced 9 turnovers and allowed only 5 points. It was a walloping.

The Steelers took the early lead by driving 57 yards to score on when running back Franco Harris went 7 yards to get to the first pay-dirt. Then, linebacker, Jack Ham recovered a fumble at the Houston 17-yard line, which led to running back Rocky Bleier's 15-yard rushing touchdown. Pittsburgh was fired up and Houston was in a chill.

In the second quarter, Oilers kicker Toni Fritsch got a 19-yard field goal to cut the lead to 14–3, Then, the Steelers began to roll again and got 17 points during the last 48 seconds of the second quarter. Amazing.

First, Houston running back Ronnie Coleman lost a fumble. Then, moments later Pittsburgh wide receiver Lynn Swann snagged a 29-yard touchdown reception. Then Johnnie Dirden fumbled the ensuing kickoff, which led to Steelers wide receiver John Stallworth's 17-yard reception.

When the Oilers got the ball back eventually, Coleman fumbled again, and Roy Gerela kicked a field goal to increase Pittsburgh's lead, 31–3. Houston was out of the game from the opening kickoff. At this point, they would never pose a threat for the rest of the game. They turned over the ball 4 times in their 6 second-half possessions.

1978 Conference Championships

January 21, 1979 Super Bowl XIII
Lombardi Trophy

Pittsburgh Steelers 34, Dallas Cowboys 5

Every match between Pittsburgh and Dallas can technically be called a rematch. They are always great football games. This particular rematch was a Super Bowl Rematch.

In the first rematch in Super Bowl history, the Steelers defeated the Cowboys in the Big Game for the second time in four seasons, as Pittsburgh dethroned Dallas to win Super Bowl XIII, 35-31.

After John Banaszak recovered Tony Dorsett's fumble on the game's first drive, the Steelers quickly took a 7-0 lead, as John Stallworth pulled down a nice 28-yard pass from Terry Bradshaw.

After falling behind 14-7, after Bradshaw's 75-yard TD pass to John Stallworth tied the score at 14-14 in the second quarter.

The game progressed and Mel Blount intercepted Roger Staubach, Following the pick, Bradshaw's TD pass to Rocky Bleier gave Pittsburgh a nice 21-14 halftime lead but Dallas was not done for the day.

Dallas got a field goal on the way to the fourth quarter and with Pittsburgh leading 21-17 late in the fourth quarter, Franco Harris broke through on a 22-yard scamper giving the Steelers an 11-point advantage.

Two controversial penalties early in the fourth quarter paved the way for the Steelers to score 14 unanswered points. The game moved quickly after this TD as Pittsburgh got the ball back again. Just 11 seconds after Franco's TD run, Terry Bradshaw fired what proved to be the game-clinching touchdown, pass to Lynn Swann as

The Steelers' had a lead of 35–17 with less than 7 minutes left in the game. The touchdown was Bradshaw's last pass of the game.

Some of the Steelers were already celebrating victory on the sidelines, but the Cowboys refused to give up. On their next drive, Dallas drove 89 yards in 8 plays, including an 18-yard scramble by Staubach on 3rd and 11 and a 29-yard run by Dorsett, to score on Staubach's 7-yard touchdown pass to DuPree.

Then after Dallas' Dennis Thurman recovered an onside kick at 2:19, Drew Pearson caught 2 passes for gains of 22 and 25 yards (the second catch on 4th down and 18) as the Cowboys drove 52 yards in 9 plays to score on Staubach's 4-yard touchdown pass to Butch Johnson. With the ensuing extra point, the Steelers' lead was cut to 35–31 with just 0:22 left in the game. It still felt like it was over. But Staubach kept them going.

The Cowboys' second onside kick attempt was unsuccessful. Bleier recovered the ball, and the Steelers were able to run out the clock to win the game.

Pittsburgh had prevailed in the Super Bowl to become the first NFL team to win three Super-Bowl titles. And, so, on to 1979 with the Noll / Bradshaw dynasty.

1979 Chuck Noll #14

The 1979 Pittsburgh Steelers football team competed in their forty-seventh season of Professional National Football League (NFL) football. The team was led by Chuck Noll in his eleventh of twenty-three seasons as head coach of the Steelers. Their record declined somewhat this year from 14-2 in 1978 to 12-4 in 1978. The Steelers came in 1st in the AFC Central Division, made the playoffs for their eighth time in a row. They won the Divisional Championships, the Conference Championship, and emerged victorious in Super Bowl XIV for and unprecedented fourth Lombardi Trophy.

After winning the Super Bowl, Pittsburgh now had to successfully defend the championship. And they did. They had a nice 12–4 record and they took the game to the Los Angeles Rams in Super

Bowl XIV. The team started strong at 4-0 record. This gave them 12 in a row counting last season's wins.

In six of those games the opponents were held to a touchdown or less. In the playoffs Pittsburgh defeated Miami, 34-14 and then for the second consecutive season beat Houston 27-13, in the AFC championship game. Finally. They whooped the Los Angeles Rams 31-19 in Super Bowl XIV.

With the win, and the Pittsburgh Pirates win in the 1979 World Series, Pittsburgh would be the last city to claim Super Bowl and World Series wins in the same year until 1986 when the New York Mets won the World Series in 7 games over the Boston Red Sox, and the New York Giants won Super Bowl XXI 39–20 over the Denver Broncos.

Games of the 1979 Season

In the season opener at New England, on Sep 3, the Steelers beat the Patriots at Schaefer Stadium W (16-13). At home in Three Rivers Stadium on Sept 9, the Steelers whipped the Houston Oilers W (38-7). Then at Busch Memorial Stadium, the Steelers edged out the St. Louis Cardinals, W (24-21). At Three Rivers Stadium, the Steelers snuck by the Baltimore Colts W (17-13). At Philadelphia's Veterans Stadium, the Eagles showed little respect for their cross-town rival and defeated the Steelers L (14-17). At Cleveland on Oct 7, in a shootout, the Steelers pounded the Browns W (51-35) at Cleveland Municipal Stadium.

At Cincinnati on Oct 14, in one of the few losses this season, the Bengals blasted the Steelers L ((10-34) at Riverfront Stadium. At Three Rivers Stadium, on Oct. 22, Pittsburgh pounded the Denver Broncos W(42–7). At home in Three Rivers Stadium on Oct. 28, the Steelers edged out the Dallas Cowboys W (14–3). Then, at home gain, on Nov. 4 the Steelers crushed the Washington Redskins W (38-7) in Three Rivers Stadium. At Kansas City, on Nov 11, the Steelers outmuscled the Kansas City Chiefs W (30–3) at Arrowhead Stadium.

At San Diego on Nov. 18, the Chargers got the best of the Steelers L (7–35) at San Diego Stadium. At home in Three Rivers Stadium, on

Nov 25, the Steelers nosed out the Cleveland Browns W (33–30) in OT. Then, on Dec 2, at home, the Steelers defeated the Cincinnati Bengals W (37–17). On Dec 10 at Houston's Astrodome, the Oilers edged out the Steelers L (17–20). In the final game of the 1979 regular season, at home, on Dec 16, Pittsburgh shut out Buffalo W (28-0) to close out the 1979 pre-playoff season, The Steelers would be advancing.

Divisional Playoffs December 30, 1979
AFC: Pittsburgh Steelers 34, Miami Dolphins 14

On this day, the defending world champion Pittsburgh Steelers entered the precipice of another world championship and they were as determined as ever to bring all the rings and cigars home to Pittsburgh.

As the Divisional Playoffs got underway, the first quarter saw the Steelers score 20 points while holding the Dolphins to 25 rushing yards. No team at this level of the game are weak. They are all good. Pittsburgh is just better.

In this game, future hall of fame running back Larry Csonka was held to just 20 rushing yards on 10 carries in the final game of his career, while Steelers quarterback Terry Bradshaw pounded the Dolphins throwing for 230 yards and 2 touchdowns.

On the opening drive of the game, Pittsburgh marched 62 yards in 13 plays to score on running back Sidney Thornton's 1-yard touchdown run. On their second possession, the Steelers advanced another 62 yards in 9 plays, 36 of them on carries by Thornton, to score on wide receiver John Stallworth's 17-yard touchdown reception (although the extra point was blocked). And on their third drive, they moved the ball 56 yards to score on wide receiver Lynn Swann's 20-yard touchdown reception.

In the second quarter, the Dolphins moved the ball 63 yards to the Pittsburgh 6-yard line. Then, they lost the ball when a safety blitz by J. T. Thomas forced quarterback Bob Griese to throw a rushed pass.

It was intercepted by linebacker Dennis Winston. Miami soon got another chance to score when Larry Gordon recovered Thornton's fumble on the Steelers 5, but all this resulted in was a turnover on downs. Faced with 4th and 2, Griese tried to connect with tight end Bruce Hardy in the end zone, but Hardy collided with receiver Nat Moore and the pass fell incomplete.

The Steelers picked up a chance to increase their lead even more right before halftime when they tackled Dolphins punter George Roberts on the Miami 21 before he could make a kick. But Matt Bahr's 30-yard field goal was canceled by a Pittsburgh holding infraction, ending the half.

Pittsburgh primarily relied on their rushing game to protect their lead in the second half. They worked through it all even though Miami had the second highest ranked run defense during the season. There was an injury to Thornton in the second half which sidelined him.

The Steelers ended up running the ball 40 times during the game, with Franco Harris gaining 83 yards on 21 carries. Miami finally scored in the third quarter after defensive back Don Bessillieu recovered a punt that bounced into the leg of Pittsburgh blocker Dwayne Woodruff on the Steelers 11-yard line, leading to Griese's 7-yard touchdown pass to Duriel Harris. However, the Steelers responded by advancing 69 yards to score on running back Rocky Bleier's 1-yard touchdown. Harris' 5-yard touchdown in the fourth quarter put the game out of reach.

Larry Csonka is one of the greatest players ever in football. This was his final NFL game, as well as the final playoff game for Bob Griese, who completed just 14 of 26 passes for 118 yards. Griese was sacked 8 times before being replaced by Don Strock with 8:55 left in the fourth quarter. Strock actually ended up with more passing yards, going 8/14 for 125 yards and leading the team 76 yards to their final score on a 1-yard Csonka run. Pittsburgh moved on to the Conference Championship game.

AFC Championship January 6, 1980
Pittsburgh Steelers 27, Houston Oilers 13

The Steelers defense, aka the Steel Curtain was playing at peak. The team held the Oilers to only 24 rushing yards, Additionally, the Steelers were aided by a controversial non-touchdown, which helped the team walk away with a nice 27–13 win.

Many games begin with a lot of flurry that means nothing, The Oilers jumped to a 7–0 lead with just 2:30 into the game when Vernon Perry returned a pick for six after a 75-yards scamper for the TD. Then the teams exchanged field goals, making it 10-3.

The Steelers offense took over with QB Terry Bradshaw completing two touchdown passes—a 16-yarder to tight end Bennie Cunningham and a 20-yarder to steady-eddy wide receiver John Stallworth.

With the Steelers leading 17–10, the controversial play noted earlier occurred. It was in the final seconds of the third quarter after the Oilers had gotten the ball to the Pittsburgh 6-yard line. Quarterback Dan Pastorini threw a pass to Mike Renfro at the back of the end zone. Renfro appeared to have snagged the ball for a touchdown with both feet in bounds before he fell out of the end zone. The Replay team was called in.

TV replays suggested that it was a catch for a touchdown. Despite this, the officials ruled the pass incomplete, saying that Renfro did not have complete control of the ball before going out of bounds. The Oilers then had to settle for a 23-yard field goal.

The Steelers would then take control and put up 10 unanswered points in the fourth quarter to clinch the victory. A 78-yard drive ended with a field goal and running back Rocky Bleier scoring on a 4-yard rushing touchdown added the salt to the wound.

The Steelers were rolling. Running back Franco Harris rushed for 85 yards and he pulled-in 6 passes for 50 yards. Houston running back Earl Campbell, the NFL's leading rusher in 1979, had a tough time getting past the Steel Curtain. Campbell finished the game with just 15 yards on 17 carries. The smiling happy Steelers were going to their next Super Bowl. Just a two-week wait.

The Super Bowl XIV

National Championship Game January 20, 1980
Pittsburgh Steelers 31, Los Angeles Rams 19

Looking at his proud, unassuming face on Sundays with the other prognosticators, Terry Bradshaw stands out as very knowledgeable but the way he handles everything, you would not think he was the phenomenally great football player that he is. Who knows how old he is? Who wants to know? I know that if there were a game with guys his age in it today, I would be voting for Bradshaw's team. I'd even bet on them with my modest means of course.

Well, folks, that same guy in the prior paragraph was once a kid and as a kid, in this Super Bowl, after winning three prior Super Bowls, Terry Bradshaw completed 14 of 21 passes for 309 yards and he outdid himself by setting two passing records as the Steelers became the first team ever to win four Super Bowls. What a team!

Bradshaw was excited as were everybody in the ballpark. So, as long as things were going OK, he did not tighten up. He did not have to tighten up. Despite three interceptions by the Rams, Bradshaw kept his poise and brought the Steelers from behind twice in the second half. The team trailed 13-10 at halftime. Then, Pittsburgh went ahead 17-13 when Mr. Terry hit Lynn Swann with a 47-yard touchdown pass after 2:48 of the third quarter.

Nobody was giving anything up to Pittsburgh. Anything they got, they had to earn. Vince Ferragamo, a fine QB took the next possession to complete the beginning of 15 of 25 passes for 212 yards. In this scenario, he responded with a 50-yard pass to Billy Waddy that moved Los Angeles from its 26 to the Steelers' 24. Ferragamo was looking to get the ball past the goal line.

On the following play, Lawrence McCutcheon connected with Ron Smith on a halfback option pass that gave the Rams a 19-17 lead. Could Pittsburgh possibly lose this Super Bowl attempted win? The answer was forthcoming. On the Steeler's initial set of downs in the 4th quarter, Bradshaw still knew how to pass. He lofted a 73-yard scoring pass to John Stallworth to put the Steelers in front to stay 24-19. What a deal for an NFL team to have Terry Bradshaw and Lance Stallworth able to play catch with each other.

Franco Harris loved to add to the mix. He scored on a 1-yard run later in the quarter to seal the verdict. It began with a 45-yard pass from Bradshaw to Stallworth setting the ball up on the ONE. Harris only needed to get the ball to score.

Bradshaw, was announced as the game's most valuable player for the second straight year. He was as good as it could get. He set career Super Bowl records for most touchdown passes (9) and most passing yards (932). Terry Bradshaw does not look to beat records. He looks to ignore records for or against to get that ball past the goal line as often as possible to assure victory.

Larry Anderson gave the Steelers excellent field position throughout the game with five kickoff returns for a record 162 yards.

There was not a Pittsburgh Steeler on the field or on the bench or in the locker room or in upper management who did not feel that participated in this fine Super Bowl XIV Victory. Pittsburgh would be in the running forever for more Super Bowls.

1980 Chuck Noll #14

The 1980 Pittsburgh Steelers football team competed in their forty-eighth season of Professional National Football League (NFL) football. The team was led by Chuck Noll in his twelfth of twenty-three seasons as head coach of the Steelers. Their record declined this year from 12-4 in 1979 to 9-7 in 1980. The Steelers came in 3rd in the AFC Central Division, and for the first time in nine years, they did not make the NFL playoffs.

The team was defending the Lombardi Trophy, but they did not qualify for the tournament that gave them the right to play.

Every team has a strange year. 1980 was strange for Pittsburgh.

In 1980, the Steelers struggled for the first time in many years. The defense was aging. It was not as effective as it had been in the 1978 and '79 seasons. The team fell from 2nd to 15th in yards allowed. That's a long fall. The Steelers also gave up 313 points, ranked 15th in the league, compared to 262 points (5th in league) the previous season. The Pittsburgh defense able to achieve only 18 quarterback sacks.

One year after a Super Bowl victory and the offense was also showing signs that it was faltering. It was plagued with 42 total turnovers, but it was able to achieve a #6 ranking in total offense, and it did score 352 points.

Despite the team's troubles, the Steelers still had a chance to obtain home field advantage throughout the playoffs. A number of games could have gone either way. They lost several close games, including games against Cincinnati and Cleveland in which they lost despite having large leads in the fourth quarter. Pittsburgh remained in the playoff hunt until week 12. It was a 28–13 loss to Buffalo in week 12 and then a 6–0 loss to Houston that effectively eliminated the team from the postseason.

To many, these two losses marked the end of the Steeler Dynasty. Several key players retired after the 1980 season and the team was never the same again. The 1980 season was the first in which the Steelers did not qualify for the playoffs since 1971. Just remember folks at this point, the Steelers had just won its fourth Super Bowl. Knowing the team has two more Super Bowl victories to its credit needs to give Pittsburgh fans a good feeling from 1981 to 2017, there were a number of other mini-dynasties that brought the Super Bowl total to six.

In the season and home opener in Three River Stadium, on Sep 7, the Steelers beat the Houston Oiler W (31-17). At Baltimore Colts Memorial Stadium, on Sept 14, the Steelers were edged out by the Colts W (20-17). In the first loss of the year, a close match against

Cincinnati in Riverfront Stadium, the Bengals edged out the Steelers L (28-30). Then at home in Three Rivers Stadium, the Steelers shellacked the Chicago Bears W (38-3). At Minnesota Metropolitan Stadium, on Oct 5, Steelers snuck by the Vikings W (23-17). At home in Three Rivers Stadium on Oct 12, the Cincinnati Bengals nosed out the Steelers L (16-17)

At home in Three Rivers on Oct 20, the Oakland Raiders beat the Steelers L (34–45). At Cleveland's Municipal Stadium, the Browns edged out the Steelers L (26–27). At home in Three Rivers on Nov 2, the Steelers got by the Green Bay Packers W (22–20). Then, at Tampa Bay on Nov 9, the Steelers beat the Buccaneers W (24-21). At home on Nov 16, the Steelers beat the Cleveland Browns in Three Rivers Stadium W (16–13).

On Nov. 23 at Buffalo's Rich Stadium, the Steelers were beaten by the Bills L (13-28). At Three Rivers Stadium on Nov. 30, Pittsburgh beat Miami W (23–10). At Houston, on Dec. 4 in the Astrodome, the Oilers shut out the Steelers L (0-6). At home on Dec. 14, the Steelers defeated the Kansas City Chiefs in Three Rivers Stadium W (21–16). At San Diego Stadium on Dec. 22 in the final game of the season, the Chargers beat the Steelers L (17–26).

1981 Chuck Noll #14

The 1981 Pittsburgh Steelers football team competed in their forty-ninth season of Professional National Football League (NFL) football. The team was led by Chuck Noll in his thirteenth of twenty-three seasons as head coach of the Steelers. Their record declined this year from 9-7 in 1980 to 8-8 in 1981. The Steelers came in 2nd in the AFC Central Division and did not make the NFL playoffs for the second year in a row.

After a tough, injury plagued 9-7 season one year after being world champions, the previous year, and then missing the playoffs for the first time since 1971, the Steelers had hoped that their 1980 season was not a harbinger but instead just a small diversion from contending for championships. However, while the Steelers had flashes of their former glory years after starting the season with 2 unimpressive losses, the 1981 season would end at 8-8 record and eventually would be one of the bricks at the beginning of the end of the Steelers great dynasty of the 1970s. For many this realization was tough enough to cause a few tears.

In the season and home opener in Three River Stadium, on Sep 6, the Steelers lost to the Kansas City Chiefs L (33-37). At Miami in the Miami Orange Bowl, on Sept 10, , the Dolphins beat the Steelers L (10-30). In the first win of the year, the Steelers finally looked good against the New York Jets at home W (38-10). In a close match against New England in Three Rivers Stadium, , the Steelers prevailed W (27-21). Then at New Orleans in the Louisiana Super Dome, , the Steelers beat the Saints, W (20-6). Then, at home in Three Rivers Stadium on Oct 11, the got by the Cleveland Browns W (13-7).

At Cincinnati's Riverfront Stadium on Oct. 18, the Bengals beat the Steelers L (7-34). At home on 8 on Oct. 26 Pittsburgh defeated Houston in Three Rivers Stadium W (26–13). At home on Nov 1, the San Francisco 49ers beat the Steelers in Three Rivers Stadium L (14–17). At Seattle's Kingdome, on Nov 8, the Seahawks edged out the Steelers L (21–24). At Atlanta in Fulton County Stadium on Nov 15, Pittsburgh beat Atlanta (34–20).

At Cleveland's Municipal Stadium, the Steelers whooped the Browns, W (32–10). Then, on Nov. 29 at home, the Steelers shut-out the Los Angeles Rams in Three Rivers Stadium W (24–0). On Monday Night Dec 7 at Oakland, in the Alameda County Coliseum, the Raiders beat the Steelers L (27–30). At home on Dec. 13, the Cincinnati Bengals defeated the Steelers in Three Rivers Stadium L (10–17) . In the season finale on Dec. 20 at Houston's Astrodome, the Oilers nosed out the Steelers L (20–21).

1982 Chuck Noll #14

The 1982 Pittsburgh Steelers football team competed in their fiftieth season of Professional National Football League (NFL) football. The team was led by Chuck Noll in his fourteenth of twenty-three seasons as head coach of the Steelers. There was a strike this year and the season was shortened to nine games and the playoff system was redone to accommodate the lack of games. The record improved this year from 8-8 in 1981 to 6-3 in 1980. The Steelers came in 4th in the AFC this special year, and they did make the abbreviated convoluted playoff structure but were taken out in the first round by the Chargers L (28-31).

Makin the playoffs this year was substantially easier than normal, but it is true that the 1982 Pittsburgh Steelers did return to the playoffs after a two-year hiatus. This was also the Steelers 50th Anniversary season. Although the season was shortened as a result of the 1982 strike, the Steelers finished a strong 6–3 record, good enough for fourth in the AFC as a whole. There was no standing for AFC East. Division standings were thrown out as a result of the strike, so the Steelers unofficially finished second in the AFC Central, one game behind defending AFC Champion Cincinnati.

Whereas the 1970's was the dynasty decade, the 1980's was the decade in which the dynasty was disassembled by old age and retirements. The 1982 season is best remembered as the final seasons for a lot of the best players from the 1970.

1982 was the last for Hall of Famers Lynn Swann and Jack Ham and it was the "unofficial" final season of fellow Hall of Famer Terry Bradshaw, who would also miss much of the 1983 season due to injuries before officially retiring. There were some replacements coming in but nothing like the stars of the 1970's.

For example, it was first year of future Hall of Fame placekicker Gary Anderson and the first year of the team using a 3-4 defense, a style still used by the team as of 2017. Having been given a shot at the playoffs by the new structure for the shortened season, the Steelers would nonetheless lose in the first round to the San Diego Chargers. Get out your crying towels folks as this would be the last home playoff game for the Steelers for the next ten years.

Games of the season

So you can see the cancellations during the season, I have presented the game summaries in text form below.

1. at Dallas Cowboys	Texas Stadium	W 36–28
2. Cincinnati Bengals	Three Rivers Stadium	W 26–20 (OT)
3. New York Giants	Three Rivers Stadium	Cancelled
4. at Denver Broncos	Mile High Stadium	Cancelled
5. Philadelphia Eagles	Three Rivers Stadium	Cancelled
6. at Washington Redskins	RFK Stadium	Cancelled
7. Cleveland Browns	Three Rivers Stadium	Postponed
8. Cincinnati Bengals	Riverfront Stadium	Cancelled
9. Houston Oilers	Three Rivers Stadium	Cancelled
10. New York Jets	Three Rivers Stadium	Cancelled
11. at Houston Oilers	Astrodome	W 24–10
12. at Seattle Seahawks	Kingdome	L 16–0
13. Kansas City Chiefs	Three Rivers Stadium	W 35–14
14. at Buffalo Bills	Rich Stadium	L 13–0
15. at Cleveland Browns	Cleveland Municipal	L 10–9
16. New England Patriots	Three Rivers Stadium	W 37–14
17. Cleveland Browns	Three Rivers Stadium	W 37–21

January 9, 1983 Conference Playoff Game
Wild Card: Pittsburgh 28 v. San Diego Chargers 31

Many of the Pittsburgh fans reading this book will use the highlights of the 1982 playoff game shown below as their swan-song story about the greatest dynasty in pro-football as it was beginning to dissipate. Many of the familiar names of the greats from the dynasty were in the game and the Steelers fought valiantly for the win and of course, it was a great game.

The game was played against the Chargers on Jan. 9, 1983 at Three Rivers Stadium. It will go down in history as one of the greatest games of Bradshaw's Hall of Fame career as well as one of the most bitter defeats in Pittsburgh Steelers history.

You may recall that in 1979, the San Diego Chargers went into the AFC Playoffs as the No. 1 seed. However, a loss to the Houston Oilers in the Divisional Round prevented them from even getting a shot at the Steelers in the AFC Championship Game. In 1981 the Chargers had made that step, but they lost in Cincinnati in a game played in temperatures that the pundits would claim "even polar bears would consider on the chilly side." The 1982 San Diego

Chargers were not retired old men and were still explosive offensively, having ranked No. 1 in the NFL in points scored and passing yards.

The Chargers "D" depended upon sacks (19) and takeaways (25) during the course of the nine-game regular season games. The team finished with the same 6-3 record as the Steelers, but they entered the AFC Tournament having won five of their previous six games.

The game began with Steelers linebacker Guy Ruff recovering a Chargers fumble of the opening kickoff in the end zone for a quick touchdown, and then for the next three-and-a-half quarters the game belonged to Pittsburgh QB Terry Bradshaw. At one point he had completed 15 passes in a row. Bradshaw finished the game with 28 completions in 39 attempts for 335 yards, with two touchdowns. On the negative side, the All-Pro QB also threw two interceptions, the second of which served as a turning point in the game.

In the moments just before that turnover, the Steelers held a 28-17 lead with 11 minutes remaining in a game. To that point, the Steelers were in complete control. Facing a tough third down situation, Bradshaw prepared to pass. After escaping the contain of the Chargers pass rush, he had a clear shot to run for the first down. But instead of running, Bradshaw chose to depend on his passing arm once again. Much to the contribution to negative outcome of the game, this pass was intercepted by Jeff Allen and returned to the Steelers 29-yard line. These quick momentum turnarounds need to be addressed immediately when they occur.

In another of the examples of the 1982 Steelers defense being more opportunistic than impregnable, Mel Blount answered with an interception of Dan Fouts, but something else went wrong. The play was brought back by a holding penalty on the Steelers. With new life, Dan Fouts was invigorated. He moved the Chargers offense down the field for a touchdown that came on an 8-yard pass to tight end Kellen Winslow and brought the lead to 28-24—just four points.

After the kickoff and during the next offensive possession, the Steelers were able to grind out a couple of first downs to get close to midfield before, they were stopped, and John Goodson had to come on to punt. In another bad turn of events, instead of what was expected – the pinning of the Chargers deep, Goodson, a barefoot punter, shanked the punt for only 20 yards to the Chargers 36-yard line.

Fouts saw the opportunity and he moved the offense down the field methodically, and with one-minute remaining to play, he threw a 2-yard touchdown pass to Winslow, and the Steelers got nothing other than the sinking feeling of having been eliminated from the Tournament, 28-31. And that was that until the 1983 season.

Chapter 21 Coach Chuck Noll II, 1983 to 1991

Coach #14 Chuck Noll

Year	Coach	League/Conf/Div	Pl	Record	Pct.
1983	#14 Chuck Noll	NFLAFCCentral	1st	10 6 0	.625

- Lost Divisional Playoffs(Raiders) 38–10

Year	Coach	League/Conf/Div	Pl	Record	Pct.
1984	#14 Chuck Noll	NFLAFCCentral	1st	9 7 0	.563

- Won Divisional Playoffs(Broncos) 24–17
- Lost Conference Championship(Dolphins) 45–28
- Louis Lipps – Offensive Rookie of the Year
- John Stallworth – Comeback Player of the Year

1985	#14 Chuck Noll	NFLAFCCentral	3rd	7 9 0	.438
1986	#14 Chuck Noll	NFLAFCCentral	3rd	6 10 0	.375
1987	#14 Chuck Noll	NFLAFCCentral	3rd	8 7 0	.533
1988	#14 Chuck Noll	NFLAFCCentral	4th	5 11 0	.313
1989	#14 Chuck Noll	NFLAFCCentral	2nd	9 7 0	.563

- Won Wild Card Playoffs(Oilers) 26–23
- Lost Divisional playoff(Broncos) 24–23
- Chuck Noll – Maxwell Football Club Coach of the Year

1990	#14 Chuck Noll	NFLAFCCentral	3rd	9 7 0	.563
1991	#14 Chuck Noll	NFLAFCCentral	2nd	7 9 0	.438

1983 Chuck Noll #14

The 1983 Pittsburgh Steelers football team competed in their fifty-first season of Professional National Football League (NFL) football. The team was led by Chuck Noll in his fifteenth of twenty-three seasons as head coach of the Steelers. The season game limit went back to 16 and the playoffs were executed as usual after the strike shortened 1982-season. .The record improved this year from 6-3 in 1982 to 10-6 in 1983. The Steelers came in 1st in the AFC Central this year, and they made the playoffs. But they were taken out in the first round by the Raiders L (38-10).

By the time the 1983 season began, the Steelers had suffered many retirements, and thus they had been forced to adapt to many changes. There was no longer a Steel Curtain. There was no assurance that it could be rebuilt. Joe Greene, L.C. Greenwood, Dwight White and Ernie Holmes had all retired. Moreover, the team had switched from a 4-3 to the 3-4.

The pundits at the time suggested that nothing was as dramatic as what they were about to live through for the first time in a very long time. Life without Terry Bradshaw. Though Pittsburgh's whole team during the dynasty was great, Terry Bradshaw was the difference maker.

In just one more year, Jack Lambert's career would be ended by a dislocated big toe, but at this point in franchise history the most important appendage to the team was Bradshaw's right arm, which had already endured lots of action over the years. More specifically, the part of Bradshaw's arm that gave him the most trouble was his right elbow. If you could put an egg timer display on that elbow, it would be tough to find any time left for the 1983 season.

Sometime in the months that would follow the 1983 NFL season, a doctor would perform surgery on that very valuable elbow, but in September 1983, the medical plan agreed to by the Steelers and Bradshaw called for rest and treatment. Several times over the season, the false hope for Bradshaw's return to the starting lineup would crystallize, but then inevitably it evaporated. Deadlines passed. More deadlines were set. They passed as well. And on and on it went.

The sporting press loved the QB as much as the fans and they had their concerns. They would dutifully attend each practice session from the start of the 1983 season and report the one thing everyone wanted to know, and it usually read like this: Bradshaw didn't throw today. He was viewed to b that important because he was.

Coach Chuck Noll never was one who spent any time worrying – or even talking – about injured players, and so when the Steelers opened their regular season at Three Rivers Stadium against the Denver Broncos and rookie sensation John Elway, it was Cliff Stoudt starting at quarterback and fourth-year pro Mark Malone as the No. 2 QB. Neither were Terry Bradshaw.

The 1983 Steelers were not a bad team on either side of the ball. They had talent, but they also had their flaws. When they turned the ball over and/or were highly penalized they had a tough time coming up with ways and plays that could make up for their faux pas.

When they tried to make things up quickly, such as – three interceptions vs. Green Bay, five interceptions vs. Detroit on Thanksgiving Day, three fumbles and two interceptions vs. Cincinnati, two interceptions combined with 11 penalties in Cleveland – they lost the games decisively. Comebacks were not part of the game plan.

When the Steelers were not beating themselves, the season record shows they were good enough to win 10 games, finish 10-6 and claim the AFC Central Division title--#1 over the 9-7 Cleveland Browns. The clincher for the regular season came against the New York Jets in what was the final NFL game to be played at Shea Stadium. To Steelers fans, this was a game that always will be remembered as Terry Bradshaw's final appearance at quarterback for the Pittsburgh Steelers—even though it was not necessarily supposed to be.

That it would be Bradshaw's last NFL game wasn't known at the time, but what was known was the Steelers needed a hero because they needed a win. The team has started 9-2 but found itself mired in a three-game losing streak at the time bringing the record to 9-5.

They faced back-to-back road trips – at New York and then at Cleveland.

In New York, Bradshaw dragged his 36-year-old right arm out for one grand finale in the media capital of the world. Clearly not himself, Bradshaw still mustered what he had and authored a final great performance.

The ailing QB played two complete series and directed touchdown drives of 77 yards in eight plays and 72 yards in nine plays. He completed 5-of-8 for 77 yards and the two scores – 17 yards to Gregg Garrity and 10 yards to Calvin Sweeney. Above all else, he inspired the team to a great 34-7 win that clinched the division championship and it gave Pittsburgh a second-straight appearance in the playoffs.

Un unfortunately for the Steelers, the coaches, and the loyal fans, Terry Bradshaw's 10th trip to the playoffs would only be as a spectator. He still looked great standing there on the sideline of the Los Angeles Coliseum in his uniform, but the self-described gunslinger had no more bullets and if he did the revolver cylinder had a few issues needing fixing.

Games of the season

In the home and season opener at Three Rivers, on Sep 4, the Steelers were beaten by the Denver Broncos L (10-14). At Green Bay in Lambeau Field, on Sep 18, the Steelers beat the Packers W (25-21). Then at the Houston Astrodome, the Steelers defeated the Oilers W (40-28). At home in Three Rivers Stadium on Sep 25, the Patriots defeated the Steelers L ((28-33). At Three Rivers Stadium, the Steelers beat the Houston Oilers W (17-10). At Cincinnati on Oct 10, , the Steelers picked up a win on the Bengals W (24-14).

On Oct. 16 at home in Three Rivers Stadium, the Steelers scorched the Cleveland Browns W (44–17). At Seattle in the Kingdome, on Oct 23, Pittsburgh prevailed against the Seahawks W (27-21). On Oct. 30 at home, the Steelers beat the Tampa Bay Buccaneers in Three Rivers Stadium W (17-12). Then on Nov. 6 at home the Steelers whipped the San Diego Chargers in Three Rivers Stadium w

(26-3). At Baltimore, Colts Memorial Stadium, on Nov 13, the Steelers won v the Colts W (24-13).

At home on Nov. 20 the Minnesota Vikings beat the Steelers in Three Rivers Stadium L 14–17). At Detroit in the Pontiac Silverdome on Nov 24, , the Lions pounded the Steelers L (3-45). Then, at home on Dec. 4 the Cincinnati Bengals beat the Steelers in Three Rivers Stadium L (10–23). At New York, on Dec 10. The Steelers blasted the Jets at Shea Stadium W (34–7). Then, at Cleveland in the season finale, on Dec 18, in Municipal Stadium, the Browns beat the Steelers L (17–30).

1984 Chuck Noll #14

The 1984 Pittsburgh Steelers football team competed in their fifty-second season of Professional National Football League (NFL) football. The team was led by Chuck Noll in his sixteenth of twenty-three seasons as head coach of the Steelers. .The record improved this year from 10-6 in 1983 to 9-7 in 1984. The Steelers came in 1st again in the AFC Central this year, and they made the playoffs. They defeated the Broncos W (24-17) in the Divisional Round and then in the AFC Championship, they were beaten by the Dolphins W (45-28)

It hurts me to say this but most of the stars from the 1970s were already gone. However, Pittsburgh showed signs of their past glory by putting up a 9-7 record to capture the AFC Central Title again. The highlight of the season was an October 14th win over the 49ers in San Francisco. It was the only loss the 49ers had all season.

Also making it to the highlight reel this year, was WR Louis Lipps who won the Offensive Rookie of the Year. In the playoffs the Steelers stunned the Broncos 24-17 in Denver to earn a trip to the AFC Championship. However, the Steelers season would end with a 45-28 scorching at the hands of the Dolphins in Miami. Though all the fame and glory guys were supposedly gone, Chuck Noll kept the refresher button on and maybe every now and then the new Steelers even surprised Chuck Noll.

In the home and season opener at Three Rivers Stadium, on Sep 4, the Steelers were beaten by the Kansas City Chiefs L (27-37). At New York's Jets-Giants Stadium, the Steelers beat the Jets W (23-17). Then at home on Sep 16, in Three Rivers Stadium, the Steelers defeated the Los Angeles Rams W (24-14). At Cleveland Municipal Stadium, on Sep 23, the Browns defeated the Steelers L (10-20). At Three Rivers Stadium, on Oct 1, the Steelers beat the Cincinnati Bengals W (38-17) At home on Oct 10, the Steelers lost to the Miami Dolphins in Three River Stadium, L (7-31).

At San Francisco's Candlestick park on Oct. 14, the Steelers edged out the 49ers W (20–17). At Indianapolis on Oct. 21 in the Colts Hoosier Dome, the Colts beat the Steelers L (16-17). At home on Oct. 28, the Steelers hammered the Atlanta Falcons in Three Rivers Stadium W (35–10). Then at Cincinnati on Nov. 11, the Steelers lost to the Bengals in Three Rivers Stadium L (20-22) .

At New Orleans in the Superdome, the Saints beat the Steelers L 24-27). At home on Nov 25, , Pittsburgh shellacked the San Diego Chargers at Three Rivers Stadium W (52–24). Then on Dec. 2 at the Astrodome, the Houston Oilers beat the Steelers L (20–23) (OT). At home on Dec. 9 the Steelers beat the Cleveland Browns in Three Rivers Stadium W (23–20). Then, in the last game of the 1984 season, on Dec. 16 at the Los Angeles Memorial Coliseum, the Steelers edged out the Los Angeles Raiders W (13–7). And that was the season.

1985 Chuck Noll #14

The 1985 Pittsburgh Steelers football team competed in their fifty-third season of Professional National Football League (NFL) football. The team was led by Chuck Noll in his seventeenth of twenty-three seasons as head coach of the Steelers. .The record declined this year from 9-7 in 1984 to 7-9 in 1985. The Steelers came in 2nd in the AFC Central this year, but they did not make the playoffs.

To look back The Steelers were close all year long until after the twelfth game. They led the AFC Central most of the season. Sitting at 7-5, after twelve games, there was a breakdown that saw a season ending four game losing streak. It ended the chances of a division title and any playoff hopes. Their 7-9 record was Pittsburgh's first losing season in 14 years. That was a cold glass of water in the face for sure

In the home and season opener at Three Rivers Stadium, on Sep 8, the Steelers pounded the Indianapolis Colts W (45-3) . At Cleveland on Monday Sep 16, the Browns beat the Steelers L (7-17). At home on Sept 23, the Steelers shut-out the Houston Oilers W (20-0) in Three Rivers Stadium W (20-0). Then at home on Sep 30, in Three Rivers Stadium, the Steelers were defeated by the Cincinnati Bengals L (24-37). At Miami on Oct 6 in the Orange Bowl, the Dolphins beat the Steelers L (20-24) . At Dallas, in Texas Stadium on Oct 13, the Cowboys pasted the Steelers L (13-27).

At home on Oct. 20, the Steelers were able to somewhat scorch the St. Louis Cardinals in Three Rivers Stadium W (23–10). At Cincinnati on Oct 27, in Riverfront Stadium, the Bengals prevailed L (21-26). On Nov. 3 at home, the Steelers got the best of the Cleveland Browns in Three Rivers Stadium W (10–9). The maintenance staff was picking up a lot of bit fingernails and teeth-skin after such a close game. On Nov. 10 at Kansas City, in Arrowhead Stadium, the Steelers got by the Chiefs W (36–28). In a slow materializing season, at Houston on Nov 17, in the Astrodome, the Steelers slammed the Oilers W (30–7).

At home on Nov. 24, the Washington Redskins beat the Steelers in Three Rivers Stadium L (23–30). At home again on Dec. 1, the Denver Broncos beat the Steelers in Three Rivers Stadium L (23–31). At San Diego on Dec. 8 in Jack Murphy Stadium , the Chargers overwhelmed the Steelers in a shootout L (44–54). Then at home on Dec. 15, the Steelers beat the Buffalo Bills in Three Rivers Stadium W (30–24). Wrapping up the regular season on Sat. Dec. 21 at New York in Giants Stadium, the Giants beat the Steelers L (10-28).

1986 Chuck Noll #14

The 1986 Pittsburgh Steelers football team competed in their fifty-fourth season of Professional National Football League (NFL) football. The team was led by Chuck Noll in his eighteenth of twenty-three seasons as head coach of the Steelers. .The record declined further this year from 7-9 in 1985 to 6-10 in 1986. The Steelers came in 3rd in the AFC Central this year, but they did not make the playoffs for the second straight season.

In the season opener at Seattle's Kingdom, on Sep 7, the Seahawks ripped the Steelers W (30-0). At home in Monday Night Football on Sep 16, the Broncos beat the Steelers in Three Rivers Stadium L (10-21). At Minnesota in the HHH Metrodome, the Vikings beat the Steelers L (7-31). Then at Houston's Astrodome, on Sep 28, the Steelers defeated the Oilers W (22-16). At home on Oct 5, the Cleveland Browns beat the Steelers in Three Rivers Stadium L (24-27). At Cincinnati's Riverfront Stadium on Oct 13, the Bengals beat the Steelers L (22-24) . At home in Three Rivers Stadium, the Patriots shellacked the Steelers L (0-34).

At home on Oct. 26, the Steelers beat the Cincinnati Bengals in Three Rivers Stadium W (30–9). Then, on Nov. 2 at home, the Steelers beat the Green Bay Packers in Three Rivers Stadium W (27–3). On Nov 9 at Buffalo's Rich Stadium, , the Bills beat the Steelers L)12–16. At home on Nov 16, the Steelers beat the Houston Oilers in Three Rivers Stadium W (21–10). Then, at Cleveland Municipal Stadium, the Browns beat the Steelers in OT L (31-37)

At Chicago's Soldier Field in OT, the Bears beat the Steelers L (10–13). At home on Dec. 7, the Steelers beat the Detroit Lions in Three Rivers Stadium W (27–17). At New York's Giants Stadium on Dec 13, the Steelers pounded the Jets W (45-24). In the final season home game on Dec. 21, the Kansas City Chiefs beat the Steelers in Three Rivers Stadium L (19–24).

1987 Chuck Noll #14

The 1987 Pittsburgh Steelers football team competed in their fifty-fifth season of Professional National Football League (NFL) football. The team was led by Chuck Noll in his nineteenth of twenty-three seasons as head coach of the Steelers. .The record improved from 6-10 in 1986 to 8-7 in 1986 using replacement players. The Steelers came in 3rd in the AFC Central this year and did not make the playoffs for the third straight season.

Chuck Noll was looked upon by most as a stoical character, but in complete contrast was his reaction to Jerry Glanville, the head coach of the Oilers. After the Steelers second meeting, Noll in the postgame handshake grabbed Glanville and told him he'd better watch out or he'd get jumped on. This was in reaction to Glanville's earlier comments on how the Oilers field was the 'house of pain' and his prediction that his players would intentionally hurt the Steelers. Noll cared about all his Steelers.

Top Steelers Players Rod Woodson

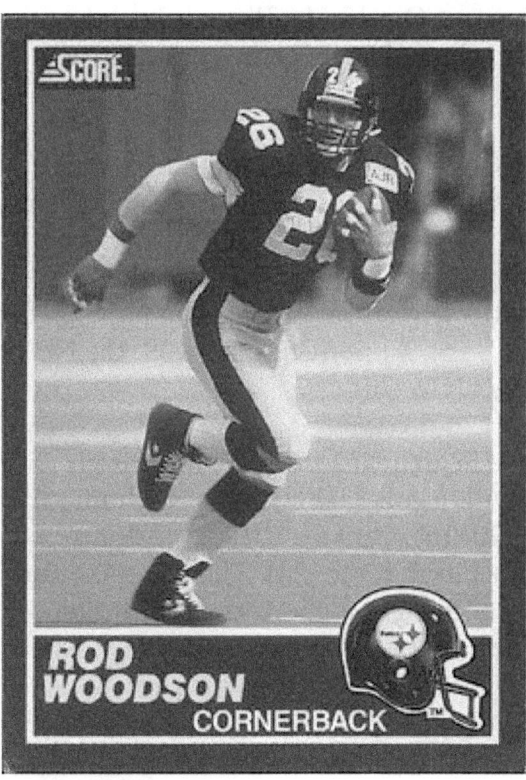

Cornerback (1987-'96) Elected: 2009 Roderick Kevin Woodson was the Steelers' first-round draft pick in 1987. He was the 1993 NFL Defensive Player of the Year and a member of the NFL's 75th anniversary team. A three-time team MVP, Woodson ranks fourth in team history with 38 interceptions. Woodson was selected to seven Pro Bowls, six AP All-Pro teams and was named to the 1990s All-Decade team. He returned five interceptions, two punts and two kickoffs for scores

Games of the 1987 season

In the season and home opener at Three Rivers Stadium on Sep 13, the Steelers beat the San Francisco 49ers W (30-10. At Cleveland on

Sept 20, in Municipal Stadium, the Browns beat the Steelers L (10-34). At home on Sep 27, the game between the Jets and Steelers was canceled due to the strike. At Atlanta, in Fulton County Stadium, the Steelers beat the Falcons W (28-12). At Los Angeles in Anaheim Stadium on Oct 11, the Rams beat the Steelers L (21-31). Then, on Oct 18, at home, the Indianapolis Colts lost to the Steelers W (21-7) . Then at home again, on Oct 25, the Steelers beat the Cincinnati Bengals in Three Rivers Stadium W (23-20).

At home in a Monday Night Football encounter on Sep 16, the Broncos beat the Steelers in Three Rivers Stadium L (10-21). At Minnesota in the HHH Metrodome, the Vikings beat the Steelers L (7-31). Then at Houston's Astrodome, on Sep 28, the Steelers defeated the Oilers W (22-16). At home on Oct 5, the Cleveland Browns beat the Steelers in Three Rivers Stadium L (24-27). At Cincinnati's Riverfront Stadium on Oct 13, the Bengals beat the Steelers L (22-24) . At home in Three Rivers Stadium, the Patriots shellacked the Steelers L (0-34).

At Miami on Nov 1, in Joe Robbie Stadium the Dolphins beat the Steelers L (24–35). Then at Kansas City's Arrowhead Stadium. The Steelers defeated the Chiefs by one-point W (17–16). At home on Nov. 15, the Houston Oilers defeated Pittsburgh in Three Rivers Stadium L 3–23). At Cincinnati's Riverfront Stadium on Nov 22, the Steelers beat the Bengals W (30–16). At home, on Nov 29, the New Orleans Saints beat the Steelers L (16–20).

At home on Dec. 6, the Seattle Seahawks lost to the Pittsburgh Steelers W (13–9). Then, at San Diego's Jack Murphy Stadium , the Steelers beat the Chargers W (20–16). On Dec. 20 at Houston's Astrodome, the Oilers beat Pittsburgh L (16–24). Then to close out the season, at home, on Dec. 26, the Cleveland Browns beat the Steelers in Three Rivers Stadium L (13–19.)

The Replacement Players

On the Steelers: Tales of 1987 strike

Post-Gazette archives

ED BOUCHETTE PITTSBURGH POST-GAZETTE

Mar 13, 2011 9:00 AM

Two games into the 1987 season, the NFL Players Association called a strike and Art Rooney Sr. called me into his office.

A press conference was being held down the hall, but the Chief waylaid me as I rushed toward the press room to grab a pen, paper and tape recorder.

"I want to talk to you," he said.

I tried to tell him I had to go to the press conference to learn what the Steelers' plans were during the strike.

"This is more important," he said sternly.

So I entered his office with none of my reporting tools. He gave me a pen and some pages from his personal stationary -- gold paper -- and told me to take notes.

Art Rooney went on to tell me that the strike would ruin football and explained why. I still have the notes on his stationary, but of course it did not ruin football. The strike eventually prompted a collective bargaining agreement that helped foster labor peace until, maybe, now.

Still, it was one big story the next day in the Post-Gazette, the first of many during the last NFL labor strife, which really did not last long. One game was canceled and then three more were played with "replacement" players. It remains perhaps the most unique season in NFL history because of it. Guys off the street playing next to Hall of Famers like Mike Webster.

The strike of 1987 even produced a bad movie -- "The Replacements," which could not hold a candle to what actually went on around the NFL during that one month.

The collective bargaining agreement had run out and there was little progress made toward a new one. The players' main goal during that time was to get some sort of free agency, and ownership stiffened on that topic. So, the players walked out. It ultimately led to a new CBA, free agency and the salary cap with a not-so-gentle push from a federal judge overseeing the case. Tunch Ilkin was the Steelers' union rep at the time, and it was my third season covering the team for the Post-Gazette.

Unlike some teams that had their heads stuck in the sand, the Steelers had prepared for the possibility of a strike and the NFL's determination to continue playing games with what NFLPA called scabs.

The Steelers held a replacement training camp in Johnstown, far enough from Pittsburgh that their striking players never came around to cause trouble -- except for one Saturday in which they drove up in a convoy and almost laughingly walked a picket line. Dan Rooney helped diffuse the situation by secretly giving Ilkin a key to the grass practice field outside Three Rivers Stadium and telling him to "keep the team together." The real Steelers practiced there throughout the five-week strike.

The Steelers stayed at the Holiday Inn in Johnstown for their two-week strike camp. The writers stayed there, too. The team's personnel people did a good job of lining up available players to play, and while many were not of NFL caliber, some were and remained on the team after the strike ended.

They did not allow the media into practices for the first three days nor let us know which players they had signed. So, the writers decided to use our collective resources to come up with as many names as possible and put together our own roster. We fanned out and compiled a Steelers replacement roster.

Every time we bumped into what looked like a football player at the Holiday Inn, we'd ask where he was from, what position he played and how big he was. I once slipped into an elevator with a guy who looked to me like he was the quarterback and on the ride up got all the info on Steve Bono I needed.

We wound up publishing a pretty complete roster, to the Steelers' surprise.

With word that practices would be closed for the first three days to us, the ingenuity flowed again. They held practices at the old baseball/football field in Johnstown's Point Stadium. Johnstown's Incline ran up the hill near the stadium, and a few writers took that to the top with binoculars to try to watch practice, including one from the old Pittsburgh Press. That newspaper also hired a helicopter to fly overhead to take photos.

A few of us took a different approach. Bob Labriola, then of the Greensburg Tribune-Review and now with the Steelers, and I scouted spots outside the stadium on the first day of closed practice. We noticed a handful of people on a third-floor porch across the street from the stadium watching practice. They invited us up.

There, we had a clear view of everything the Steelers were doing because the only barrier was a wall about 12 to 15 feet high. We were 30 feet above and right across the street with our binoculars. A Post-Gazette photographer joined us and the next day the newspaper had great photos and a good report of what was going on behind the almost-closed doors at the Steelers' replacement practices.

We watched practices from that vantage point until the Steelers finally opened them up to us. At one point as we watched practice through binoculars, Chuck Noll looked up and saw us and gave us a little wave of the hand.

As you might imagine, that band of replacement players was a pretty diverse bunch. The first day of open practice, we followed the players as they walked several blocks from the Holiday Inn to Point Stadium. One of them be-bopped along the way to the music on his Walkman. Problem is, he never took the thing off once they got onto the field.

This was a walk-through practice and the players were mostly in street clothes. As Noll spoke to his team on the field, the player still listened to his Walkman and not to Noll. I was chatting with the replacement kicker, David Trout, and mentioned it to him. Trout excused himself, walked over to the player and said a few words. The player sheepishly put the Walkman away.

One player the Steelers signed had been the fullback in high school in Passaic, N.J., for Craig "Ironhead" Heyward, the former Pitt player and 11-year NFL back who died of a brain tumor in 2006. His son, Cameron, will follow him into the league in next month's draft as the fine defensive end at Ohio State.

Heyward's fullback -- can't recall his name -- regaled us with stories about Ironhead and how they could not find a helmet big enough for him back in midget football. He said at one point they put a helmet on top of his head.

This was the kind of eclectic collection of players the Steelers strung together and somehow came up with a team to compete in three NFL replacement games. Several of their real players crossed the picket line to play -- led by Webster, who reported to Johnstown along with halfback Earnest Jackson before the first strike game. Later, John Stallworth and Donnie Shell joined them. So, two Hall of Famers, Webster and Stallworth, played in those games. Stallworth even caught his 500th NFL pass in a replacement game. He finished with 41 catches that season, his last, and finished his career with 537 -- the Steelers record until Hines Ward came along and obliterated it.

No one knows where the current labor strife will take everyone, but it won't take the Steelers to Johnstown and it won't produce any fun stories the way it did 24 years ago.
--- End of article --- First Published March 13, 2011, 5:00am

1988 Chuck Noll #14

The 1988 Pittsburgh Steelers football team competed in their fifty-sixth season of Professional National Football League (NFL) football. The team was led by Chuck Noll in his twentieth of twenty-three seasons as head coach of the Steelers. .The record declined from 8-7 in 1987 to 5-11in 1988. The Steelers came in 4th in the

AFC Central this year, and did not make the playoffs for the fourth straight season.

After fifty-six seasons of management by the CHIEF, Art Rooney, St. the Steelers community suffered a major setback this year with the death of Hall of Fame team founder & owner Art Rooney on August 25, at age 87 less than two weeks before the start of the season. The team honored the man who put the Steelers on the map by wearing AJR patches on the left shoulder the entire season in memory of "The Chief".

This year's record was the worst at 5–11, since finishing an NFL-worst 1–13 in 1969. As of 2018, the 5–11 mark remains the team's worst record since 1969, and have only finished with ten losses twice since, in 1999and 2003.

The 1988 squad never got off the dime. After winning their home opener against the Dallas Cowboys, the team lost 6 straight, their first 6 game losing streak since 1969. They never recovered after the skid, and at one point fell to a 2-10 record after a 27-7 loss to the Cleveland Browns.

Pittsburgh had several horrible and forgettable games during the season. One of those games was their week 10 game against the Cincinnati Bengals, a game in which they lost 42-7, the most points they had allowed in a game since 1985, when they allowed 54 points against the Chargers. The Steelers would, however, finish the season on a positive note, winning 3 of its last 4 games to finish the season 5-11.

Two of the last three remaining players who won all four Super Bowls retired in 1988 -- wide receiver John Stallworth and strong safety Donnie Shell. Both were both from the team's famous Class of 1974 that saw four players go on to the Pro Football Hall of Fame (although Shell was undrafted, he was still from the same rookie class), and in the case of Stallworth, retired as the team's all-time leading receiver. Stallworth's record was surpassed by Hines Ward in 2005. Mike Webster, who was also from the Class of 1974, stayed with the team through 1988. Webster would be released by the Steelers in the following offseason, officially ending the team's link to all four of its spectacular 1970's era Super Bowl clubs.

Top Steeler Players Greg Lloyd

Linebacker--Before Joey Porter and James Harrison, it was Greg Lloyd mean-mugging his way into the hearts of Steelers Nation. Like those men, Lloyd was known for providing big hits and shocking quotes in equal measure.

Between the 1991 and '95 seasons, Lloyd tallied 37 sacks and garnered five Pro Bowl bids. A 10-sack season in 1994 earned him the honor of the UPI's AFC Defensive Player of the Year award.

Lloyd, the unquestioned leader of the great "Blitzburgh" defenses in the 1990s, was known for wearing a shirt that read, "I wasn't hired for my disposition."

Truer words were never written.

Games of the season

In the season and home opener at Three Rivers Stadium on Sep 4, the Steelers beat the Dallas Cowboys W (24-21). At Washington on Sept 11, in RFK Stadium, Redskins edged out the Steelers L (29-30). At home on Sep 18, the Cincinnati Bengals defeated the Steelers in Three Rivers Stadium L (12-17). At Buffalo, in Rich Stadium, the Bills beat the Steelers L (28-36). At home in Three Rivers Stadium, on Oct 2, the Cleveland Browns beat the Steelers L (9-23). Then, on Oct 9, at Phoenix's Sun Devil Stadium, home, the Steelers lost to the Cardinals L (14-31) . Then at home again, on Oct 16, the Houston Oilers beat the Steelers in Three Rivers Stadium L (14-34).

At home on Oct. 23, the Steelers defeated the Denver Broncos in Three Rivers Stadium W (39–21). Then on Oct. 30 at Giants Stadium, the NY Jets beat the Steelers L (20–24). At Cincinnati's Riverfront Stadium, the Bengals pounded the Steelers L (7-42). At home on Nov. 13, the Philadelphia Eagles nosed out the Steelers in Three Rivers Stadium L (26–27) At Cleveland on Nov 20, in Municipal Stadium, the Browns beat the Steelers L (7–27).

At home on Nov. 27, the Steelers beat the Kansas City Chiefs in Three Rivers Stadium W (16–10). At the Houston Astrodome on Dec 4, the Steelers edged out the Oilers W (37–34). At San Diego's Jack Murphy Stadium on Dec. 11, the Chargers beat the Steelers L (14-20). Ending this terrible season, the Steelers put it away on the bright side with a win at home on Dec. 18 against the Miami Dolphins in Three Rivers Stadium W (40–24). It would be a much better year in 1989.

Top Steelers Players Dermontti Dawson

Guard. Dawson was selected by the Pittsburgh Steelers in the second round of the 1988 NFL Draft. In his rookie season he played guard alongside Hall of Fame center Mike Webster. When Webster left the team following that season, Dawson succeeded him as the starting center. He soon became one of the most respected players among the Steelers, and one of the best in the league at his position. He earned the name "Dirt" for the way he would try to grind defenders into the ground. In contrast, his friendly off-field demeanor led to a second nickname, Ned Flanders, after the annoyingly cheerful character from The Simpsons.

1989 Chuck Noll #14

The 1989 Pittsburgh Steelers football team competed in their fifty-seventh season of Professional National Football League (NFL) football. The team was led by Chuck Noll in his twenty-first of twenty-three seasons as head coach of the Steelers. .The record improved from 5-11 in 1988 to 9-7 in 1988. The Steelers came in 3rd in the AFC Central this year and did not make the playoffs for the fifth straight season.

The "being rebuilt" 1989 Pittsburgh Steelers were filled with many young players, especially after the release of longtime center Mike Webster in the offseason. The young team exuded inexperience in many positions. in the first game of the season, when the squad lost at home to archrival Cleveland Browns L (51–0). This loss marked the Steelers worst defeat in franchise history. The following week wasn't much better, with a 41–10 thumping from another division rival, the defending AFC Champion Cincinnati Bengals.

Nonetheless, the Steelers came back and snagged the final playoff spot in the last week in the season with a 9–7 record. Chuck Noll, operating in his 21st year as head coach, was named the NFL's Coach of the Year for the only time in his coaching career. Ironically the four Super Bowls had not swayed the judges.

The Steelers were in the playoffs again. That was big news after the five lean years. In the first round, they enjoyed a memorable come-from-behind overtime victory over the division-rival Houston Oilers 26–23. Kicker Gary Anderson was a big hero with his game-winning, 50-yard field goal in the extra period.

The following week, the Steelers were on their way to the Super Bowl as they nearly pulled off a major upset against the Denver Broncos at Mile High Stadium, losing by one point on Melvin Bratton's one-yard touchdown run with 2:22 remaining in the game. Though the Steelers would not make the playoffs again under Chuck Noll (missing in 1990 with an identical 9–7 record and again in 1991 at 7–9, despite a second-place finish that year), the season did set the tone for the team's return to prominence in the 1990s under his Chuck Noll's successor, Bill Cowher.

Until 2015, it was the last season the Steelers made the playoffs in a season the Super Bowl aired on CBS. Each of the next six such seasons (1991, 2000, 2003, 2006, 2009, 2012) would see the team missing the playoffs.

Top Steelers Players Carnell Lake

Defensive Back... As a defensive back, Lake played 12 seasons in the NFL from 1989 to 2001 for the Pittsburgh Steelers, Jacksonville Jaguars, and Baltimore Ravens.

As a rookie, Lake started 15 of 16 games and led the Steelers with 5 fumble recoveries.

He was a 5-time Pro Bowl selection. Over the course of his career he recorded 25 quarterback sacks, intercepted 16 passes, recovered 17 fumbles, and scored 5 defensive touchdowns. In 1997, Lake received a vote for MVP from Sports Illustrated writer Peter King, which created a situation where Barry Sanders and Brett Favre tied for the award that season.

Games of the season

In the season and home opener at Three Rivers Stadium on Sep 10, the Steelers were shellacked by the Cleveland Browns L (0-51). At Cincinnati on Sept 17, in Riverfront Stadium, the Bengals pounded the Steelers L (10-41). At home on Sep 24, the Steelers defeated the Minnesota Vikings in Three Rivers Stadium W (27-14). At Detroit in the Pontiac Silverdome, the Steelers beat the Lions W (3-3). At home in Three Rivers Stadium, on Oct 8, the Cincinnati Bengals beat the Steelers L (16-26). Then, on Oct 15, at Cleveland Municipal Stadium, the Steelers beat the Browns W (17-7). Then at Houston's Astrodome, on Oct 22, the Oilers shut-out the Steelers L (0-27).

At home on Oct. 29, the Kansas City Chiefs were beaten in Three Rivers Stadium by the Steelers W (23–17). On Nov. 5 at Denver's Mile High Stadium, the Broncos beat the Steelers L (7-34). At home on Nov. 12, the Chicago bears shut out the Steelers in Three Rivers Stadium L (0–20). On Nov. 19 at home, the San Diego Chargers were beaten by the Steelers in Three Rivers Stadium W (20–17). At Miami's Joe Robbie Stadium on Nov 26, the Steelers beat the Dolphins W (34–14).

At home on Dec. 3, the Houston Oilers beat the Steelers in Three Rivers Stadium L (16–23). At New York's Giants Stadium, the Steelers shut-out the Jets W (13–0). At home on Dec. 17, the Steelers beat the New England Patriots in Three Rivers Stadium W (28–10). Then, in the season finale on Dec 24, at Tampa Bay Stadium, the Steelers overpowered the Buccaneers W (31–22)

AFC Wild Card Playoffs Dec 31, 1989
Pittsburgh Steelers 26, Houston Oilers 23 (OT)

In their first playoff game in some time, the Steelers had their two comebacks in one event. They were back at the playoffs and they came back to win. In OT, Steelers defensive back Rod Woodson recovered a fumble to set up Gary Anderson's winning 50-yard field goal in overtime to give Pittsburgh the win. Go Steelers!

Houston started things their way with the opening kickoff and they drove to the Steelers 40-yard line but were stopped there. Their first attempted score failed with a Tony Zendejas 55-yard missed field goal. Later in 1Q, Steelers rookie Jerry Olsavsky blocked a punt from Greg Montgomery and Pittsburgh recovered on the Oilers 23. Eventually facing fourth and 1 on the Houston 9-yard line, Steelers coach Chuck Noll decided to go for the first down. This paid off as running back Tim Worley took a pitch and ran all the way to the end zone. He plowed right through safety Bubba McDowell on the way to a 7–0 Steelers lead with 2:36 left in the first quarter.

Houston picked up 3 on a stalled drive. They responded on their next drive, moving the ball 96 yards to the Steelers 3-yard line, but could go no further and settled for a 26-yard Zendejas field goal. After a fumble recovery, the Oilers had to settle for another Zendejas field goal, cutting the score to 7–6. Pittsburgh struck back and settled for an Anderson field goal to put them up 10–6 going into halftime.

The field goal battle continued . Zendejas got one and Anderson got two. Going in to the fourth quarter. QB Warren Moon finally got the oilers rolling with a 10-play, 80-yard drive and a score from his s 18-yard TD pass to Ernest Givins to tie the game. After a 3 and out, the Pittsburgh Punt went just 25 yds. to the Steelers 38-yard line. Five plays later Houston took their first lead of the game, on Moon's 9-yard pass touchdown pass to Givins. They were up 23–16 with 5:16 left in regulation.

The Steelers began on their own 18 after the kickoff, and they drove 82 yards, with a 22-yard run by receiver Dwight Stone (the only time he touched the ball all game) on a reverse play, to score on Hoge's 2-yard touchdown run with 46 seconds left. This tied the game and sent it to OT.

Pittsburgh won the coin toss and received the ball but could not move it. After that punt, and another short kick from Newsome gave Houston the ball, the Oilers had great position on the Steelers 45-yard line. On the Oilers first play, RB Lorenzo White fumbled after a big hit by Woodson and defensive end Tim Johnson. Woodson recovered the ball and brought it to the Oilers 46. The Steelers gained just 13 yards and it was punt or kick a FG.

Anderson had enough leg to kick a 50-yard field goal, his longest attempt of the season, which he sent perfectly through the uprights to give the Steelers the win.

Pittsburgh had been shut out three times, outgained by their opponents in ten consecutive games, and had to recover from a 4-6 record to get into the playoffs by winning five of their last six games.

AFC Division Championship January 7, 1990: Denver Broncos 24, Pittsburgh Steelers 23

The Broncos were down for the count a number of times in the game, but they recovered from two early 10-point deficits to eventually win on a 71-yard drive. The drive was capped by Mel Bratton's 1-yard touchdown run with 2:27 left in the game. For the second game in a row, Steelers running back Merril Hoge had a superb performance, rushing for 120 yards on 16 carries and catching eight passes for 60 yards. But this time it wasn't enough to lift his team to victory. Broncos receiver Mark Jackson caught five passes for 111 yards.

The Steelers were in charge early with a 3–0 lead from a 32-yard field goal by Gary Anderson. On the first play of the second quarter, Hoge pulled off a 45-yard run, the longest of his career. He ended up rushing for 60 yards on the Steelers drive, including a 7-yard touchdown carry to increase the Steelers lead to 10-0.

Denver came right back with a 12-play, 75-yard drive to score on Bratton's 1-yard touchdown run, cutting the lead to 10-7. But the Steelers fired right back, with Bubby Brister completing a 25-yard pass to tight end Mike Mularkey and rookie running back Tim Worley contributing a 19-yard carry on the way to a 9-yard scoring reception by Louis Lipps.

Before the half, however, Broncos kicker David Treadwell made a 43-yard field goal, putting the score at 17-10 going into intermission.

After the 3Q kickoff, Broncos defenders Karl Mecklenburg and Greg Kragen forced a fumble from Worley that defensive back Tyrone Braxton recovered on the Steelers 37-yard line. This set up John Elway's 37-yard touchdown pass to wide receiver Vance Johnson which tied the game at 17. Brister came right back with a 19-yard screen to Hoge and a 30-yard pass to rookie receiver Mark Stock on the way to a 35-yard Anderson field goal.

In the fourth quarter, Pittsburgh defensive back Thomas Everett picked off an Elway pass and returned it 26 yards to midfield, setting up Anderson's 32-yard field goal to make the score 23-17. The Steelers seemed like they were about to put the game away but their next time with the ball they missed a 1st down by 1-yard. It was fourth and Pittsburgh had to punt.

With 7 minutes left in the game, Elway found his range and led the Broncos 71 yards in nine plays. This drive included Elway completions of 36-yards to Jackson and 15-yards to Ricky Nattiel. Bratton finished the drive with his second 1-yard touchdown of the game. Pittsburgh had one chance left with 2:27 left.

Bad luck got the best of the Steelers, on first down of their possession, Brister fired a pass to a wide-open Stock, but he tried to turn upfield before securing the catch and it fell to the turf incomplete. After another incompletion, Brister fumbled a low snap from backup center Chuck Lanza (filling in for injured All-Pro center Dermontti Dawson) in shotgun formation, and Broncos safety Randy Robbins recovered the ball and it was all-over.

Brister had completed 19/29 passes for 224 yards and a touchdown. Elway threw for 239 yards and a touchdown, with one interception, and rushed for 44 yards. The Steelers would have to wait to get a restart on the dynasty.

1990 Chuck Noll #14

The 1990 Pittsburgh Steelers football team competed in their fifty-eighth season of Professional National Football League (NFL) football. The team was led by Chuck Noll in his twenty-second of twenty-three seasons as head coach of the Steelers. .The record stayed the same 9-7 in 1989 to 9-7 in 1990. The Steelers came in 3rd in the AFC Central this year and did not make the playoffs.

This was not Pittsburgh's best year; but it was far better than the years before Chuck Noll. The Steelers did not score an offensive touchdown until the 5th game of the season, but they did rebound to a 9–7 record (the same they had posted the previous season).

Unlike the previous season, all the other records competing for playoff berths were better this year. 9–7 was not enough to gain a playoff berth. The Steelers continued to show improvement overcoming a 1-3 start to find themselves in a showdown with the Oilers in Houston for the AFC's final playoff spot in the final game of the season. However, the Steelers were never in the game as the Oilers beat the Steelers 34-14 ending their season without entering the playoffs.

In the season opener at Cleveland Municipal Stadium, on Sep 9, the Steelers were beaten by the Cleveland Browns L (3-13). At home on Sept 16, in Three Rivers Stadium, the Houston Oilers were beaten by the Steelers L (9-20). At LA Memorial Coliseum, on Sep 23, the Raiders defeated the Steelers W (3-20). At home on Sep 30, the Miami Dolphins whipped the Steelers in Three Rivers Stadium L (6-28). At home in Three Rivers Stadium, on Oct 7, the San Diego Chargers were whipped by the Steelers W (36-14). At Denver's Mile High Stadium, on Oct 14, the Steelers beat the Broncos W (34—17). Then at San Francisco's Candlestick Park, on Oct 21, the Steelers were beaten by the 49ers L (7-27).

At home on Monday Night, Oct. 29 the Steelers pounded the Los Angeles Rams in Three Rivers Stadium at 9:00 p.m. on ABC W (41–10). Then on Nov. 4 at home, the Atlanta Falcons were beaten by the Steelers in Three Rivers Stadium W (21–9). The next week (Nov 11) was a league mandated bye. On Nov. 18 at Cincinnati's Riverfront Stadium, the Bengals blasted the Steelers L (3–27). At NY on Nov. 25, the Steelers pummeled the Jets in Giants Stadium W (24–7). At home on Dec. 2, the Cincinnati Bengals edged out the Steelers at Three Rivers Stadium L (12–16).

At home on Dec. 9, the New England Patriots were outmanned at Three Rivers Stadium by the Steelers W (24–3). At New Orleans in the Superdome, on Dec 16, the Steelers squeaked out a win from the Saints W (9–6). At home, playing against the Cleveland Browns in Three Rivers Stadium on Dec 23, the Steelers pounded forth a shutout W (35–0). Wrapping up an OK season, the Stealers showed up on Dec 30 at the Houston Oilers Astrodome and were beaten by the Oilers L (14–34).

1991 Chuck Noll #14

The 1991 Pittsburgh Steelers football team competed in their fifty-ninth season of Professional National Football League (NFL) football. The team was led by Chuck Noll in his twenty-third and last of twenty-three seasons as head coach of the Steelers. .The record reversed itself from 1990's 9-7 to 1991's 7-9. The Steelers came in 2nd in the AFC Central this year, and they did not make the playoffs this year.

There had not been an easy Pittsburgh season since the last Super Bowl from the 1970's as the team was looking to get its roster right and its plays more perfect during that time, while players were aging.

The Steelers struggled early in Chuck Noll's last season as Neil O'Donnell took over from Bubby Brister at quarterback. The Steelers ended the season winning their last two games, 17–10, over the Cincinnati Bengals and Cleveland Browns at Three Rivers Stadium to finish with a 7-9 record.

Following the season Chuck Noll had figured out the country was a better option and he announced his retirement. As much as he loved the Steelers, he knew he had not delivered like he accustomed the management and the fans to expect. This ended his 23-year career in which he won four Super Bowls while posting an overall record of 209–156–1.

Games of the season

In the season and home opener at Three Rivers Stadium, on Sep 1, the Steelers beat the San Diego Chargers W (26-20). At Buffalo's Rich Stadium, on Sept 8, Buffalo Bills beat the Steelers L (34-52).

At home on Sep 15, the New England Patriots were beaten by the Steelers W (20-6). At Philadelphia's Veterans Stadium on Sep 22, the Eagles beat the Steelers L (14-23). On Sep 29, the team drew a bye. At the Indianapolis Hoosier Dome, the Steelers beat the Colts W (21-3). At home on Oct 14, the Steelers were beaten by the Giants L (20—23). Then at home on Oct20, the Steelers were beaten by the Seahawks L (7-27).

On Oct 27, at Cleveland Municipal Stadium, the Browns beat the Steelers L (14–17). At Denver's Mile High Stadium, the Broncos beat the Steelers L (13–20). At Cincinnati on Nov 10, the Steelers beat the Bengals in Riverfront Stadium W (33–27). At home again on Nov. 17, the Washington Redskins pounded the Steelers in Three Rivers Stadium L (14–41). Then at home on Nov. 24, Pittsburgh beat the Houston Oilers in Three Rivers Stadium W (14–26).

At Dallas on Nov 28, in Texas Stadium, , the cowboys beat the Steelers L (10–20). At Houston on Dec 8, the Oilers beat Pittsburgh in the Astrodome L (6–31). At home on Dec. 15, the Steelers beat the Cincinnati Bengals in Three Rivers Stadium W (17–10). In the season ending game at home, the Steelers beat the Cleveland Browns in Three Rivers Stadium W (17–10).

From the PG Archives: The Curtain Falls

Morris Berman/Post-Gazette

Steelers' Noll decides it's time to get on with life's work

ED BOUCHETTEPITTSBURGH POST-GAZETTE

OCT 21, 2007

5:15 AM
This story from the Post-Gazette archives was first published on December 27, 1991.

Chuck Noll retired yesterday after 23 years as the Steelers' coach, holding an emotional news conference that left one question unanswered:

Why?

Ten days before his 60th birthday, Noll said he decided only yesterday morning to retire because "39 years in professional football is a goodly time."

He said he did not come to his decision easily and that he recently had gone through an up-and-down process about it.
But when he was asked if he would rule out coaching again, he paused, then said, "probably. One day at a time."

Noll, the only man to coach four Super Bowl champions, strode into the Steelers' offices at Three Rivers Stadium a few minutes after 10 a.m. for his scheduled meeting with Steeler President Dan Rooney.

They talked for about 45 minutes and Rooney told Noll that he wanted him back. Before Rooney could tell him about changes he wanted to make in the coaching staff and, perhaps, the front office, Noll told Rooney he had decided to retire.

Rooney had planned to tell Noll that he must fire offensive coordinator Joe Walton and maybe make a few more changes on his coaching staff. A source close to Noll said Rooney also wanted to take away some of the control Noll had over the football operation.

Noll had been dropping hints for the past three weeks that he had a decision to make at the end of the season but would never say why. At one point, he said he had not lost his desire to coach.

He said yesterday that a successful season in 1991 probably would not have changed his mind about retiring.

"It would have been great to have had 10 victories and been in the playoffs and have gone all the way and then said, 'Goodbye,' but it didn't work out that way."

He said he was not angry and "for you investigative reporters, there's no challenge to find a reason.

Whatever the reasons, an era ended yesterday. Noll's final record was 209-156-1, a .568 winning percentage in all games. His most important winning percentage came in Super Bowls, where he batted .1000 as the Steelers won them in the seasons of 1974, 1975, 1978 and 1979.

But Noll was never one for looking back, and he did not do much of that yesterday.

"Reminisce?" he said to a question. "When we get in rocking chairs, we'll probably do that. There are things to be done, and I'm sure I'll be busy from that standpoint. And I'll miss all the guys, I'll miss the training camps. I'll miss the season. That's going to be tough, but I'm sure you'll help me."

Rooney announced that Noll would stay with the organization, but Noll made it clear it would not be an active role.

"I don't want to get in the way."

Tom Donahoe, the Steelers director of football development, will lead the search for a new head coach, beginning immediately. Noll and Rooney conducted their joint news conference at 1:05 p.m., and it was televised live in Pittsburgh. Noll ended it 20 minutes later when he seemed near tears.

"You've got enough now," he told reporters, "before it gets tougher."

While Rooney read from a statement to open the press conference, Noll sat beside him with his hand on his forehead shielding his face and looking down.

Moments earlier, Noll had been chatting amiably with several reporters in the Steelers' lunchroom. He poured coffee for them and discussed various topics, football not among them.

He laughed and seemed to be in a good mood. But the mood turned somber as it came time for the press conference.

Rooney opened by reading a handwritten statement, saying Noll would remain a part of the team.

"It has been a wonderful 23 years. Chuck is a great man, and he hasn't changed from day one. He brought dignity and integrity to the coaching profession and that, even more than four Super Bowls, is what it means to be a Steeler. . .

"He ranks with the great coaches of the game, I always liked to compare him with Amos Alonzo Stagg. He ranks up there with George Halas, Vince Lombardi and Curly Lambeau. . .

"The greatest compliment that I know is what my wife said a long time ago, "If anything happens to us, I would like Chuck Noll to raise my kids."

Noll then thanked everyone.

"You know, it's much easier coming in than going out," said the man the Steelers hired on Jan. 27, 1969 when he was 37. "The emotions that build up and then attachments that build up over 23 years are tough to, I guess, sever. . .

"Thank you. I mean this is to everybody. The city of Pittsburgh, to the coaches that I've been associated with through the years, to the players. Especially to the players, because those are the guys that make it happen on the field, those are the guys that meant our success, and it's been great memories and a real upbeat experience for me and my family."

Noll laughed when he was asked what he would do now.

"That's the $64,000 question. . .I put in for a government program, so I could re-educate myself, so I could do something, but I don't think it's going to come through.

"I think after 39 years in it I have to step back and see what the flowers smell like for a little bit."

Asked if coaching burnout caused him to retire, Noll quipped: "Natural death."

"I can remember," he added, "running laps when I was in college, saying, 'What am I doing out here? This is terrible.' And then the next minute, 'This is the greatest thing that ever happened.'

"That's life. Right now, I'm not planning on coaching any more, although I've been accused of coaching all my life."

He was once asked how he would like to be remembered: "Don't leave anything on the beach but your footprints. I'm not big on history. Who is that masked man?"

Two minutes after the news conference ended, Noll pulled on his black overcoat and walked briskly out the front door, jumped in his car and was gone.

He never once glanced at the four Super Bowl trophies in the lobby as he passed within feet of them. They are his footprints.

Chapter 22 Coach Bill Cowher 1992 to 2006

Coach #15 Bill Cowher

Year	Coach	League/Conf/Div	Pl	Record	Pct.
1992	#15 Bill Cowher	NFLAFCCentral	1st	11 5 0	.688

- Lost Divisional Playoffs(Bills) 24–3
- Bill Cowher – NFL Coach of the Year
- Barry Foster – AFC Offensive Player of the Year

| 1993 | #15 Bill Cowher | NFLAFCCentral | 2nd | 9 7 0 | .563 |

- Lost Wild Card Playoffs(Chiefs) 27–24 (OT)
- Rod Woodson– Defensive Player of the Year

Yearly Summaries continued below picture >>>

| 1994 | #15 Bill Cowher | NFLAFCCentral | 1st 1 | 2 4 0 | .750 |

- Won Divisional Playoffs(Browns) 29–9
- Lost Conference Championship(Chargers) 17–13
- Greg Lloyd – AFC Defensive Player of the Year

| 1995 | #15 Bill Cowher | NFLAFCCentral | 1st | 11 5 0 | .688 |

- Won Divisional Playoffs(Bills) 40–21
- Won Conference Championship (Colts) 20–16
- Lost Super Bowl XXX(Cowboys) 27–17

| 1996 | #15 Bill Cowher | NFLAFCCentral | 1st | 10 6 0 | .625 |

- Won Wild Card Playoffs(Colts) 42–14

Lost Divisional Playoffs(Patriots) 28–3

- Jerome Bettis– Comeback Player of the Year

Year	Coach	League/Conf/Div	Pl	Record			Pct.
1997	#15 Bill Cowher	NFLAFCCentral	1st	11	5	0	.688

- Won Divisional Playoffs(Patriots) 7–6
- Lost Conference Championship(Broncos) 24–21

Year	Coach	League/Conf/Div	Pl	Record			Pct.
1998	#15 Bill Cowher	NFLAFCCentral	3rd	7	9	0	.438
1999	#15 Bill Cowher	NFLAFCCentral	4th	6	10	0	.375
2000	#15 Bill Cowher	NFLAFCCentral	3rd	9	7	0	.563
2001	#15 Bill Cowher	NFLAFCCentral	1st	13	3	0	.813

- Won Divisional Playoffs(Ravens) 27–10
- Lost Conference Championship (Patriots) 24–17
- Kendrell Bell – Defensive Rookie of the Year

Year	Coach	League/Conf/Div	Pl	Record			Pct.
2002	#15 Bill Cowher	NFLAFCNorth	1st	10	5	1	.656

- Won Wild Card Playoffs(Browns) 36–33
- Lost Divisional Playoffs(Titans) 34–31
- Tommy Maddox – Comeback Player of the Year

Year	Coach	League/Conf/Div	Pl	Record			Pct.
2003	#15 Bill Cowher	NFLAFCNorth	3rd	6	10	0	.375
2004	#15 Bill Cowher	NFLAFCNorth	1st	15	1	0	.938

- Won Divisional Playoffs(Jets) 20–17
- Lost Conference Championship (Patriots) 41–27
- Bill Cowher – Sporting News Coach of the Year
- Ben Roethlisberger– Offensive Rookie of the Year

Year	Coach	League/Conf/Div	Pl	Record			Pct.
2005	#15 Bill Cowher	NFLAFCNorth	2nd	11	5	0	.688

- Won Wild Card Playoffs(Bengals) 31–17
- Won Divisional Playoffs(Colts) 21–18
- Won Conference Championship(Broncos) 34–17
- Won Super Bowl XL(5) (Seahawks) 21–10
- Hines Ward – Super Bowl MVP

Year	Coach	League/Conf/Div	Pl	Record			Pct.
2006	#15 Bill Cowher	NFLAFCNorth	3rd	8	8	0	.500

1992 Bill Cowher #15

The 1992 Pittsburgh Steelers football team competed in their sixtieth season of Professional National Football League (NFL) football. The team was led by Bill Cowher in his first of fifteen seasons as head coach of the Steelers. .The record improved substantially from 1991's 7-9 to 1992's 11-5-0. The Steelers came in 1st in the AFC Central this year, and they lost in the divisional playoffs.

The Pittsburgh Steelers celebrated their 60th Anniversary season in 1992. Cowher led the Steelers to an 11–5 record in his first season and the top seed in the AFC playoffs. However, in what later became somewhat commonplace according to history and the pundits, in Cowher's reign as coach of the Steelers, the team failed to capitalize on the seeding and lost to the eventual AFC Champion Buffalo Bills in the divisional playoffs. Cowher did end the regular season record slide that had occurred during the second half of the Chuck Noll era.

In the season opener at Houston's Astrodome, on Sep 6, the Steelers won their opener by beating the Oilers W (29-24). At home on Sep 13, the Steelers beat the New York Jets W (27-10). At San Diego on Sep 20, the Steelers defeated the Chargers W (23-6). 20). At Green Bay's Lambeau Field, the Packers defeated the Steelers L (3-17). On Sun, Oct 4, Bye. On Oct 11 at Cleveland's Municipal Stadium, the Browns beat the Steelers L (9-17). At home on Monday Night, Oct 19, the Steelers shut out the Cincinnati Bengals W (20-0). On Oct 25, at Kanas City's Arrowhead Stadium, the Steelers pounded the Chiefs W (27-3).

Sep 29, the team drew a bye. At the Indianapolis Hoosier Dome, the Steelers beat the Colts W (21-3). At home on Oct 14, the Steelers were beaten by the Giants L (20—23). Then at home on Oct20, the Steelers were beaten by the Seahawks L (7-27).

At home on Nov. 1, the Steelers beat the Houston Oilers in a close match in Three Rivers Stadium W (21–20). Then, at Buffalo's Rich Stadium, on Nov 8, the Bills beat the Steelers L (20–28). At home on Nov. 15, the Steelers defeated the Detroit Lions W (17-14). On Nov. 22, at home, the Steelers beat the Indianapolis Colts in Three Rivers Stadium W (30–14). Then, at Cincinnati on Nov 29, the Steelers beat the Bengals in Riverfront Stadium W (21–9).

On Dec. 6, at home Pittsburgh defeated the Seattle Seahawks in Three Rivers W (20–14). At Chicago on Dec. 13, the Bears whipped the Steelers in Soldier Field L (6-30). At home on Dec. 20, the Minnesota Vikings beat the Steelers in Three Rivers Stadium in a low scoring game L (3–6). In the season finale, on Dec. 27, the Steelers defeated the Cleveland Browns in Three Rivers Stadium W (23–13).

Divisional Playoffs January 9, 1993
AFC Central: Buffalo Bills 24, Pittsburgh Steelers 3

The Divisional Playoff game for the AFC Central was not the Steelers finest hour. The Bills had numbers like we had once been accustomed to see in the Pittsburgh ledger. They forced four fumbles, three turnovers, and seven sacks as they held the Steelers to just one field goal.

Buffalo quarterback Frank Reich threw for 160 yards, two touchdowns, and no interceptions; while Buffalo running back, Kenneth Davis got 104 yards on the ground. Steelers back Barry Foster also rushed for 104 yards and he caught a pass for seven yards. Pittsburgh was up to their great "D" antics during the regular season having led the NFL with 43 takeaways, but they were not able to force any in this game. A different team seemed to show up for the playoffs.

Opening the game, the Bills were quickly on the Pittsburgh 46-yard line. But on fourth and 1, fullback Carwell Gardner was stuffed for no gain. The turnover on downs eventually led to Gary Anderson's 38-yard field goal to give Pittsburgh a 3-0 lead. However, that was it for scoring for the Steelers in this game.

Neil O'Donnell, Steelers QB, who had missed the last three games of the season with a leg injury, turning the ball over three times on the team's next four drives. First, he threw a pass that was deflected by Phil Hansen into the arms of Nate Odomes for an interception. Following a punt from each team, Bruce Smith forced a fumble from O'Donnell, which Hansen recovered on the Bills 41-yard line. Buffalo then advanced 59 yards, including a 19-yard catch by receiver Don Beebe on the Steelers 1-yard line. On the next play, the team scored on Reich's 1-yard touchdown pass to Mitch Frerotte, an eligible offensive lineman playing out of the fullback position.

Although there would be no more scoring in the first half, Pittsburgh's struggles would continue. On their next drive, O'Donnell was intercepted by defensive back James Williams. On the opening drive of the second half, the Bills moved the ball 80 yards and scored with Reich's 17-yard touchdown pass to James Lofton, increasing their lead to 14-3.

On the play before the touchdown, Reich threw the ball right into the hands of defensive back Richard Shelton while trying to connect with Beebe, but Shelton dropped it, costing Pittsburgh what would have been an easy touchdown return. "I was just running before I caught the ball, and that really hurt", Shelton said after the game. "I could have had six."

In the final quarter, the Steelers botched a field goal attempt, and this set up a 44-yard Bills drive that ended with kicker Steve Christie's 43-yard field goal. The next time Buffalo got the ball, they drove 86 yards and scored on a 1-yard run from Gardner.

1993 Bill Cowher #15

The 1993 Pittsburgh Steelers football team competed in their sixty-first season of Professional National Football League (NFL) football. The team was led by Bill Cowher in his second of fifteen seasons as head coach of the Steelers. .The record declined from 1992's 11-5 to 1993's 9-7-0. The Steelers came in 2nd in the AFC Central this year, and they lost in the Wild Card game.

The Steelers planned to continue the progress made under second year head coach Bill Cowher. However, the team would take a slight step backwards, finishing 9–7 (three games behind the eventual AFC Central champion Houston Oilers). Despite that, the Steelers did clinch the final wild card spot, making the playoffs for the second consecutive year.

The team had some tough close games, such as losing to the Kansas City Chiefs 27–24 in overtime in the AFC Wild Card Round of the playoffs, in what is considered one of the best playoff games in NFL history even though the Steelers were on the losing end.

In the second week, when the Steelers suffered a rare shutout loss to the Los Angeles Rams 27–0, it was one of the team's last visits to the Los Angeles area in the foreseeable future. The day highlighted rookie Jerome Bettis who spent the day running over the Steelers defense. Though no one knew it at the time, it would foreshadow what was to come with Bettis' career—as a member of the Steelers, who would acquire Bettis in a draft day trade with the Rams three years later.

1993 was also the season in which the Steelers began their policy of "blacking out" regular season contract negotiations. Early in the season the Steelers had reached contract extensions with Rod Woodson and Barry Foster and continued negotiations with other players. However, this led to discord in the locker room, and management felt that contract talk was taking the team's focus from winning. At mid-season the Steelers broke off all contract negotiations and have refused to negotiate contracts during the regular season ever since.

In the home and season opener on Sep 5, San Francisco defeated Pittsburgh L (13-24) in Three Rivers stadium. At Los Angeles on Sep 12, the Rams shut-out the Steelers in Anaheim Stadium L (0-27). Then, at home on Sep 19, the Steelers defeated the Cincinnati Bengals in Three Rivers Stadium W (34-7). At Atlanta in the Georgia Dome, the Steelers thumped the Falcons W (45-17). Oct 3 – bye. On Oct 10, at home Pittsburgh defeated San Diego W (16-3). Then, on Oct 17, the Steelers pounded the New Orleans Saints, in Three Rivers Stadium, W (37-14). At Cleveland on Oct 24, the Browns beat the Steelers in Municipal Stadium L (23-28).

On Sun. Oct. 31 Bye, Then, on Nov 7, at Cincinnati's Riverfront Stadium, the Steelers beat the Bengals W (24–16). On Monday Night, Nov 15, at home the Steelers shut-out the Buffalo Bills W (23–0). At Denver on Nov 21, in Mile High Stadium, the Broncos beat the Steelers L (13–37). At Houston on Nov. 28 in the Astrodome, the Oilers beat the Steelers L (3–26). Then at home on Dec 5, the Steelers beat the New England Patriots in Three Rivers Stadium in a close match W (17–14).

At Miami on Dec 13, in a Monday Night Football Game in Joe Robbie Stadium, in a one-point match, the Steelers defeated the Dolphins W (21–20). At home on Dec. 19, the Houston Oilers beat the Steelers in Three Rivers Stadium L (17–26). At Seattle's Kingdome, on Dec 26, the Seahawks beat the Steelers L (6–16). Then in the last day of the regular season on Jan. 2, 1994, at home, the Steelers beat the Cleveland Browns in Three Rivers Stadium W (16–9).

Wild Card Playoffs January 8, 1994
AFC Central: KC Chiefs 27, Pittsburgh Steelers 24 (OT)

It is tough to lose by any amount, especially a field goal. The Steelers had this game, but they let it get away. Chiefs kicker Nick Lowery was the game difference as he made the winning 32-yard field goal after 11:03 of overtime was played. Overall it was a great game in which both teams combined for 770 yards, no fumbles lost, and no interceptions. But the Steelers went home empty.

Pittsburgh scored first with a 66-yard drive, featuring a 32-yard reception by running back Merril Hoge. They scored on Neil O'Donnell's 10-yard touchdown pass to tight end Adrian Cooper. Later in the first quarter, Kansas City drove 75 yards in seven plays and tied the game after backup quarterback Dave Krieg, who temporarily replaced injured starter Joe Montana, threw a 23-yard touchdown to wide receiver J. J. Birden.

The Steelers came back with a clock-killing 15-play drive to retake the lead on Gary Anderson's 30-yard field goal. Now the score was 10–7. After a punt, Pittsburgh drove back to the Chiefs 35-yard line, only to lose the ball over on downs. KC then took over and made it to the Steelers 42. But, on 4th and 1, defensive end Gerald Williams sacked Montana for a 7-yard loss, giving Pittsburgh the ball on their own 49 with under a minute left.

The did well, scoring on O'Donnell's 26-yard touchdown completion to Ernie Mills that increased their lead to 17–7 at the end of the half. Most of the third quarter was a defensive struggle until the Chiefs put together a 49-yard drive to score on Lowery's 23-yard field goal.

Then in the fourth quarter, Montana connected with Willie Davis for 22 yards and Birden for 19 on the way to Marcus Allen's 2-yard touchdown run that tied the game at 17. O'Donnell led the Steelers right back though, completing a 26-yard pass to Dwight Stone before hooking up with Eric Green for a 22-yard touchdown throw to retake the lead, 24–17.

In the final minutes of regulation, tight end Keith Cash blocked a Pittsburgh punt and Fred Jones returned it 31 yards to the Steelers 9-yard line. On fourth down, Montana threw a game-killing 7-yard touchdown pass to wide receiver Tim Barnett, tying the game at 24 with 1:43 left in the game. Then after forcing Pittsburgh to punt, Kansas City drove 47 yards to set up Lowery's 43-yard field-goal attempt in the closing seconds, but the kick fortunately was wide right and thus the game went into overtime. Pittsburgh got its second chance in OT

Kansas City won the coin toss to receive the overtime kickoff but went three and out. Pittsburgh then drove to midfield before they had to punt. Then, Montana completed several passes, including an 18-yarder to Cash to move the Chiefs into position for Lowery's game winning score. Lowery cashed in with the three-pointer.

Montana finished the game 23/42 for 276 passing yards and a touchdown, with no interceptions. O'Donnell completed 23/42 passes for 286 yards and three scores. Pittsburgh went back for 1994 with some lessons learned.

1994 Bill Cowher #15

The 1994 Pittsburgh Steelers football team competed in their sixty-second season of Professional National Football League (NFL) football. The team was led by Bill Cowher in his third of fifteen seasons as head coach of the Steelers. .The record improved from 1993's 9-7 to 1994's 12-4. The Steelers came in 1st in the AFC Central this year. The advanced from their win in the Divisional playoff and lost in the Conference Playoff game. , and they lost in the Wild Card game.

This was Bill Cowher's third consecutive trip with the Steelers to the playoffs. For the second time in Cowher's three seasons as head coach of the Steelers the team was the top seed in the AFC playoffs. Pittsburgh won its first playoff game since 1989 with a win in the divisional playoffs over their division rival Cleveland Browns, but failed to advance to the Super Bowl after losing to the San Diego Chargers in the AFC Championship Game. Pittsburgh had again become an NFL force with which to reckon.

In the home and season opener on Sep 4, Dallas defeated Pittsburgh L (9–26) in Three Rivers stadium. At Cleveland on Sep 11, the Steelers beat the Browns in Municipal Stadium W (17-10). Then, at home on Sep 18, the Steelers defeated the Indianapolis Colts in Three Rivers Stadium W (34-7). At Seattle, in Husky Stadium, the Steelers thumped the Seahawks W (30-13). On Oct 3, at home Pittsburgh defeated Houston Oilers W (30-14). Oct 17 –bye. The Steelers edged out the Cincinnati Bengals on Oct 16, in Three Rivers Stadium, W (14-10). At New York in Giants Stadium, the Steelers squeaked by the Giants W (10-6)

At Arizona on Oct. 30, the Steelers lost in OT to the Cardinals L (17–20). At Houston on Nov 6 in the Astrodome, the Steelers edged out the Oilers in OT W (12–9). Monday Night Football game on Nov 14, saw the Steelers beat the Buffalo Bills in Three Rivers Stadium W (23–10). Then at home, on Nov 20, the Steelers played another OT game and this time beat the Miami Dolphins in Three Rivers Stadium W (16–13). At Los Angeles, on Nov 27, the Steelers whipped the Raiders in the Memorial Coliseum W (21–3)

At Cincinnati on Dec 4, in Riverfront Stadium, the Steelers pounded the Bengals W (38–15). At home on Dec 11, the Steelers beat the Philadelphia Eagles in Three Rivers Stadium W (14–3). At home in Three Rivers Stadium on Dec. 18, the Steelers beat the Cleveland Browns W (17–7). Finishing a great season with a loss was not part of the plan but it was a close game on Sat. Dec. 24 at San Diego's Jack Murphy Stadium when the Chargers beat the Steelers L (34–37).

Divisional Playoffs January 7, 1995[edit]
AFC Central: Pittsburgh Steelers 29, Cleveland Browns 9

Pittsburgh's 12-4 season was tops in the Central Division and so the Divisional playoffs was the first game for the Steelers. No Wild Card Game was needed. In this season, the Steelers had defeated the Browns twice and they were able to beat the Browns in this playoff game.

Barry Foster ran for 133-yards and this was more than enough for the Steelers to control the game. They scored on their first three possessions and held the ball for 42:27. Their offense was great with 424 yards, including 238 yards on the ground, while the D held the Browns to a mere 186 total yards.

When the game started, Pittsburgh's drove the ball 65 yards in 13 plays to score on Gary Anderson's 39-yard field goal. Cleveland then punted, Tom Tupa's kick traveled just 26 yards to the Steelers 47-yard line. Pittsburgh then greased through 53 yards in eight plays, including a 21-yard pass completion from Neil O'Donnell to Ernie Mills. Pittsburgh was quickly up 10–0 on O'Donnell's 2-yard touchdown pass to tight end Eric Green.

Next time with the ball, the Steelers' Foster rushed three times for 40 yards as the team went 74 yards to score on John L. Williams' 26-yard touchdown burst with 9:03 left in the second quarter. Cleveland was completely dominated at this point. They eventually caught a break when Mark Carrier returned Mark Royals' 43-yard punt 20 yards to the Steelers 30-yard line. They got on the board when Matt Stover's 22-yard field goal to cut the lead to 17–3.

However, in the closing seconds of the quarter, Steelers defensive back Tim McKyer intercepted a pass from Cleveland quarterback Vinny Testaverde and returned it 21 yards to the Browns 6-yard line. O'Donnell then completed a 9-yard touchdown to wide receiver Yancey Thigpen with 16 seconds left in the first half.

In the third quarter, the Steelers eased through 72 yards to go up 27–3 on a 40-yard Anderson field goal. In the final quarter, the Browns got a 35-yard pass interference penalty on Steelers defensive back Deon Figures, and they converted it into a score. Testaverde threw a 20-yard touchdown strike to wide receiver Keenan McCardell. But on their next drive, the Cleveland quarterback was sacked in the end zone by Pittsburgh defensive back Carnell Lake for a safety with 2:45 left in the game. It was all over but the final counting.

O'Donnell finished the game 18/23 for 186 yards and two touchdowns. His top receiver was Mills, who caught five passes for 117 yards. This was the first playoff win for Steelers coach Bill

Cowher, who had watched his team get eliminated from the playoffs in the first round in each of the past three seasons.

Conference championship January 15, 1995
AFC Championship: Chargers 17, Steelers 13

The Steelers were showing signs of the Chuck Noll dynasty, but Bill Cowher squad had developed a problem with finishing strong. The Steelers were set back by the Chargers scoring 14-unanswered points in the second half. In one of the greatest games in his career, Junior Seau recorded 16 tackles while playing hurt with a pinched nerve in his neck.

Although the Steelers led in stats such as total plays (80–47), total offensive yards (415–226), and time of possession (37:13–22:47), it was San Diego that made the big plays when it counted.

It looked like it would be a different game when the Steelers took the opening kickoff and drove 67 yards to a score on Neil O'Donnell's 16-yard touchdown pass to fullback John L. Williams. O'Donnell also made two big completions to Andre Hastings on the drive, the first for 18 yards, and the second for 11 yards on fourth down and 2.

Later in the quarter, the Chargers got a big opportunity when safety Darren Carrington recovered a fumble from Steelers running back Barry Foster on the San Diego 41, but Pittsburgh's defense stepped up and forced a punt. Pittsburgh then advanced the ball to the Chargers 27-yard line, but a holding penalty pushed them out of field goal range and they ended up punting it back.

San Diego's offense finally managed to get a drive going in the second quarter, with running back Natrone Means rushing for 17 yards and catching a pass for 15. On the next play, a long pass interference penalty gave them a first down on the Steelers 3-yard line, but they could not get into the end zone and settled for John Carney's field goal, cutting the score to 7–3.

Coming right back like they meant it, Pittsburgh struck with a 12-play, 51-yard drive, including three first down completions from

O'Donnell to receiver Ernie Mills, and the Steelers grabbed three points on Gary Anderson's 39-yard field goal with 13 seconds left in the half. Although their halftime lead was just 10–3, Pittsburgh seemed in control of the game. They had outgained San Diego in total yards 229–46, and first downs 13–4. San Diego had yet to do anything of consequence.

Pittsburgh kept looking better and better in the second half. Humphries was intercepted by cornerback Rod Woodson on the third play of the quarter, and O'Donnell's 33-yard aerial strike to tight end Eric Green set up Anderson's 23-yard field goal, increasing their lead to 13–3. But on the fifth play of the Chargers ensuing drive, quarterback Stan Humphries faked a handoff, fooling the Steelers defensive backs long enough to see tight end Alfred Pupunu wide open to complete a 43-yard touchdown.

The lead was cut to 13–10 and would remain so going into the fourth quarter. Early in the final quarter, Humphries completed consecutive passes to Pupunu for 31 yards, moving the ball across midfield. Then with 5:13 left in the game, Humphries threw a 43-yard touchdown strike to wide receiver Tony Martin, who out-jumped defensive back Tim McKyer to make the catch and give the Chargers a 17–13 lead.

O'Donnell then completed seven consecutive passes, the longest a 21-yard gain to Green that gave them a first and goal at the Chargers 9-yard line and put them in position for a potential winning touchdown. However, it did not happen as it should have and would have in the past.

Foster was dropped for a one-yard loss on the next play, followed by an incompletion and a 7-yard catch by Williams. On fourth down, Chargers linebacker Dennis Gibson sealed the victory by tipping away O'Donnell's pass intended for Foster. The Steelers lost for the first time during the season in which they held a lead at halftime. (In 1994, they were 9–0 when leading at halftime prior to this game.)

O'Donnell completed 32 of 54 passes for 349 yards and a touchdown. His top receiver was Mills, who caught eight passes for 106 yards. Humphries completed 11 of 22 passes for 165 yards, two touchdowns, and an interception. This would be the Chargers' last playoff win until 2007.

1995 Bill Cowher #15

The 1995 Pittsburgh Steelers football team competed in their sixty-third season of Professional National Football League (NFL) football. The team was led by Bill Cowher in his fourth of fifteen seasons as head coach of the Steelers. .The record declined slightly from 1994's 12-4 to 1995's 11-5. The Steelers came in 1st again in the AFC Central this year. They advanced from their win in the Divisional playoff and won the Conference Playoff game. They made it to the Super Bowl but were beaten by the Cowboys in a well-played tough game.

Yes, this season, the Steelers returned to the Super Bowl for the first time in sixteen years (Super Bowl XIV). The team's 11–5 finish was good enough for the AFC Central championship and the second seed in the conference.

For the second consecutive season Pittsburgh hosted the AFC Championship Game at home by virtue of the Indianapolis Colts' that upset the top-seeded Kansas City Chiefs at Arrowhead Stadium. The Steelers won the game, but then two-weeks later, lost to the 1995 Dallas Cowboys in the Super Bowl in a matchup of teams that were looking to join the San Francisco 49ers as the only other team (at the time) to win five Super Bowls.

It was the first time in three Super Bowl meetings that the Steelers had lost to the Cowboys. Pittsburgh coach Bill Cowher became (at the time) the youngest head coach to lead his team to the Super Bowl.
After the Super Bowl loss, quarterback Neil O'Donnell signed as a free agent with the New York Jets. The Steelers unfortunately would not return to the Super Bowl for the next 10 seasons.

In the home and season opener on Sep 3 Pittsburgh defeated Detroit W (23–20) in Three Rivers stadium. At Houston's Astrodome, the Steelers beat the Oilers on Sep 10, W (34–17). Then, at Miami on Sep 18, the Dolphins defeated the Steelers in Joe Robbie Stadium L

(10-23). At home on Sept 24, the Minnesota Vikings beat the Steelers in Three Rivers Stadium, L 24-44). On Oct 1, at home Pittsburgh defeated San Diego W (31-16). The Steelers were edged out by the Jacksonville Jaguars in Jacksonville Municipal Stadium, on Oct 8, W (16-20). Oct 15—Bye. At home on Oct 19, the Cincinnati Bengals beat the Steelers L (9-27).

At home on Oct. 29 the Steelers beat the Jacksonville Jaguars in Three Rivers Stadium W (24–7). At Chicago, on Nov 5, in Soldier Field, the Steelers beat the Bears W (37–34) in OT. Then at home again on Monday Night Nov. 13, Pittsburgh defeated Cleveland in Three Rivers Stadium W (20–3). On Nov 19, at Cincinnati's Riverfront Stadium, the Steelers beat the Bengals in a shootout W (49–31). At Cleveland on Nov 26, in Cleveland Municipal Stadium, the Steelers beat the Browns W (20–17)

On Dec. 3 at home, the Steelers defeated the Houston Oilers in Three Rivers Stadium W (21–7). At Oakland on Dec. 10 in the Oakland–Alameda County Coliseum, the Steelers beat the Raiders W (29–10). Then, at home on Dec 16, the Steelers defeated the England Patriots in Three Rivers Stadium W (41–27). In the season ender on Dec. 24 at Green Bay's Lambeau Field, the Packers took the joy of winning the last game of the season from the Steelers in a close match L (19–24).

Divisional Playoffs January 6, 1996
AFC Central: Pittsburgh Steelers 40, Buffalo Bills 21

The Steelers almost got themselves another Super Bowl and this game is where it began in the post season. It was running back Bam Morris, who scored two touchdowns in the fourth quarter as the Steelers stopped the Bills, from coming back from a 20-0 deficit. By the end of the game, the Steelers outgained them in total yards 409-250 and forced four turnovers. The Steelers were aided by the absence of Bruce Smith, who fell ill the day before the game,

The Steelers got it going with a 76-yard drive in which receiver Yancy Thigpen caught a 43-yard pass and fullback John L. Williams finished it off with a 1-yard touchdown run. The Bills came back with a drive to the Steelers 21-yard line, but then Darick Holmes was tackled for a 13-yard loss by defensive back Carnell Lake and Steve Christie missed a 52-yard field goal attempt. Morris then rushed for 44 yards on a 58-yard possession that ended on Neil O'Donnell's 13-yard touchdown completion to Ernie Mills.

Early in the second quarter, Steelers receiver Andre Hastings took a punt 12 yards to the Bills 43-yard line. This set up Norm Johnson's 45-yard field goal. Facing a 17-0 deficit, the Bills offense self-destructed on their next drive. With a 3rd and 8, Jim Kelly was sacked by linebacker Kevin Green and he fumbled the ball. Center Kent Hull recovered the fumble for Buffalo, but it didn't help much. On the next play, Lee Flowers stormed into the backfield and tackled punter Chris Mohr on the Bills 12-yard line, leading to another Johnson field goal giving the Steelers a 20-0 lead.

Buffalo came back with a drive to the Steelers 30-yard line, only to lose the ball when Lake forced a fumble from Thurman Thomas that was recovered by defensive back Chris Oldham. However, the Bills soon got the ball back with excellent field position after Rohn Stark punted the ball 33 yards to the Steelers 49. Kelley then got the team to the 1-yard line with three completions, hitting Tony Cline for 17 yards, Andre Reed for 5, and Steve Tasker for 26.

Thomas then ran the ball into the end zone, cutting the score to 20-7. Only 45 seconds remained in the half, but O'Donnell proved up to the challenge. He completed 4 consecutive passes for 53 yards to get the team to the Bills 16-yard line. Johnson finished the drive with his third field goal, giving the Steelers a 23-7 halftime lead. It looked like it was all over.

When the third quarter began, Lake intercepted a pass from Kelly and returned it 3 yards to the Buffalo 25-yard line, leading to Johnson's fourth field goal that Pittsburgh up 26-7. Both teams had to punt on their following drives, and Tasker returned Stark's 30-yard punt 4 yards to the Steelers 42-yard line. A few plays later, he took a handoff on a reverse and ran 40 yards to the 3. Alex Van Pelt (who replaced an injured Jim Kelly) finished the drive with 2-yard touchdown pass to Cline, making the score 26-14.

In the fourth quarter, Pitt had another bad punt from Stark. Buffalo capitalized on it. The 31-yard kick gave them the ball on the

Pittsburgh 36. Van Pelt then guided the team to the 11-yard line, where Kelly returned to the field and eventually hit Thomas for a 9-yard scoring completion, cutting the score to 26-21 with plenty of time (11:23) left in the game.

Needing to pull ahead, Pittsburgh rolled 76 yards down the field, with two O'Donnell 3rd down conversion passes to Thigpen and Andre Hastings for gains of 21 and 17 yards. The team scored a TD on Morris' 13-yard touchdown run, increasing their lead to 33-21.

The next three drives would result in interceptions, with Kelly throwing a pick to Jerry Olsavsky and Matt Darby nabbing a pass from O'Donnell. On the next play, Linebacker Levon Kirkland intercepted a pass from Kelly and returned it 4 yards to the Bills 23-yard line to set up Morris' 2-yard score with 1:58 remaining in the contest to clinch the victory.

This Steelers win snapped the Bills' 10 game postseason winning streak against the AFC dating back to 1990. Morris rushed for 106 yards and caught 2 passes for 7. Lake had an interception and a fumble recovery.

Conference Championship January 14, 1996
AFC Championship: Steelers 20, Colts 16

Bill Cowher deservedly or undeservedly got a reputation for not finishing seasons well by blowing the playoffs. Yet, here he was in his fourth season and he was four for four bringing the Steelers to the playoffs. In Chuck Noll's last nine seasons, he was three playoffs for nine seasons, and he missed his last three. Nonetheless after a losing season, Cowher came in and immediately got Pittsburgh moving. In his fourth year, he had them in the Super Bowl. That's not too shabby.

He had to get through this game to get in the big game and he did. From the first play of the Conference championship, Cowher had the big game plan in his mind. On the Steelers opening drive, O'Donnell's first pass of the game was tipped by defensive tackle Tony Siragusa and as luck would have it, intercepted by Jeff Herrod. Herrod brought it back it to the Pittsburgh 24-yard line.

This initial Colts drive was halted when Ray Seals tackled running back Lamont Warren for a loss on third down and one. On the next play, Cary Blanchard hit the right upright on his 34-yard field goal, but it still bounced in and the Colts took a 3–0 lead. After a punt exchange, Pittsburgh's Norm Johnson kicked a field goal to even the game with under two minutes left in the first quarter. The field goal occurred after Kordell Stewart dropped a pass in the end zone. Replays show Colts safety Jason Belser making contact with Stewart just before the ball arrived, but no penalty flag was thrown.

A 30-yard reception by Colts receiver Sean Dawkins set up Blanchard's second field goal in the second quarter. Later on, Pittsburgh drove 80 yards in 17 plays, featuring three third down conversion runs by Kordell Stewart, and they scored on O'Donnell's 5-yard third and goal touchdown pass to Stewart with 13 seconds left in the half to make it 10–6. Replays showed Stewart had put half a foot out of bounds before making the catch, which would have made him an ineligible receiver, but the penalty was not called. So, you lose one and then win one in the game of football.

On the Colt's first drive of the second half—61 yards in none plays--, there was a 29-yard completion from Jim Harbaugh to tight end Ken Dilger. Blanchard finished the drive with his third field goal to cut their deficit to 10–9. Then after forcing a three and out, the Colts drove 35 yards in nine plays to set up another field goal try, which would have put the Colts up 12–10. But this time Blanchard's 47-yard attempt sailed wide right.

Taking over on their own 37, Pittsburgh mounted a drive in Colts territory. Johnson's 37-yard field goal put them back up by four points, at 13–9.

Early in the fourth quarter, Andre Hastings returned a long punt to midfield. But all they got out of their great field position was a missed field goal. After that, Harbaugh threw a 47-yard touchdown pass to wide receiver Floyd Turner to grab the lead, 16–13. Then the Steelers were forced to punt, and the defense forced a Warren fumble deep in Colts territory. Guard Joe Staysniak recovered the ball in mid-air to keep the drive going. Later on, defensive back Willie Williams tackled Warren behind the line on third down and one to force a punt. Pittsburgh had a shot at the win with 3:03 left in the game.

The Steelers moved 67 yards to score the winning touchdown. Running back Byron Bam Morris scored the game-winning 1-yard touchdown run with 1:34 remaining in the game to pull Pittsburgh ahead for good. The drive was aided by O'Donnell's 9-yard completion to Hastings on fourth down and 3 from the 47-yard line, as well as an earlier dropped potential interception that went in and out of the arms of linebacker Quentin Coryatt.

On the next play after Hastings' fourth down conversion catch, O'Donnell completed a 37-yard pass to Ernie Mills on the Indianapolis 1-yard line, setting up Morris' 1-yard scoring run. The Colts got the ball back and took it to the Steelers' 29 with 5 seconds left. On the final play, Harbaugh attempted a hail mary pass which he lofted high and which came down into a crowd of players in the end zone; the ball momentarily was against the Colts' WR Aaron Bailey's chest, but it hit the turf before he could haul it in. Whew! The Steelers were off to the Super Bowl.

Super Bowl XXX Jan 28, 1996
Dallas Cowboys 27, Pittsburgh Steelers 17
Sun Devil Stadium, Tempe, Arizona Attendance 76,347

For the first time since the Chuck Noll dynasty in the 1970's, the Pittsburgh Steelers were in the Super Bowl. This would be their fifth shot and it was their first loss. The Cowboys defeated the Steelers by the score of 27–17. In a game played on January 28, 1996, at Sun Devil Stadium in Tempe, Arizona, both teams were trying for five wins, which at the time was the current record held by the San Francisco 49ers.

The Cowboys had a 12–4 regular season record, and the Steelers came in with an 11-5 regular season record. Both had won their two playoff games to get into the big contest. Another point of note on this game is this would be the fifth rematch between Super Bowl teams and it was the third meeting between the two longtime rivals—Cowboys & Steelers in a Super Bowl. This is the most Super Bowl rematches between any two NFL teams.

Dallas became the first team to win three Super Bowls in four years, while Pittsburgh's defeat was their first Super Bowl loss in team history.

Unlike many games, the QB was not the MVP this year. Instead it was Dallas' Larry Brown, a 12th-round draft pick. He became the first cornerback to gain the honor by recording two interceptions in the second half, (game difference), which the Cowboys converted into two touchdowns to prevent a Steelers comeback.

Dallas had a 13–0 lead in the second quarter before Pittsburgh scored with 13 seconds left in the half to cut the Cowboys' lead six points (13-7). Midway through the 3rd quarter, Brown made his first interception and brought it back 44 yards to the Pittsburgh 18-yard line. This set up Emmitt Smith's 1-yard touchdown run. The Steelers then rallied to cut their deficit to 20–17 in the 4th quarter. However, Brown got his second pick on the Steelers' next drive, and he brought it back 33 yards to the Steelers 6-yard line, setting up Emmett Smith's 4-yard rushing touchdown.

The NBC television broadcast averaged 95.13 million people in the United States, breaking the then-record for most watched sporting event ever on American television, and the second-most watched program of all, trailing only the final episode of M*A*S*H.[6]

Sometimes it is good to get another perspective on a game. The following recap is from NFL.COM:

> Cornerback Larry Brown's 2 interceptions led to 14 second-half points and helped lift the Cowboys to their third Super Bowl victory in the last four seasons and their record-tying fifth title overall. Brown's interceptions foiled the comeback efforts of the Steelers and earned him the Pete Rozelle Trophy as the game's most valuable player.
>
> Dallas scored on each of its first three possessions, taking a 13-0 lead on Troy Aikman's 3-yard touchdown pass to Jay Novacek and a pair of field goals by Chris Boniol. Neil O'Donnell's 6-yard

touchdown pass to Yancey Thigpen 13 seconds before halftime pulled Pittsburgh within 6 points, and the Steelers had the ball near midfield midway through the third quarter. But O'Donnell's third-down pass was intercepted by Brown at the Cowboys' 38-yard line, and his 44-yard return was carried to Pittsburgh's 18.

After Aikman's 17-yard completion to Michael Irvin, Emmitt Smith ran 1 yard for the touchdown that put Dallas ahead again by 13 points. The Steelers rallied, though, behind Norm Johnson's 46- yard field goal, a successful surprise onside kick, and Byron (Bam) Morris' 1-yard touchdown run with 6:36 to play in the game.

And when they forced a punt and took possession at their own 32-yard line trailing only 20-17 with 4:15 remaining, it appeared they might have a chance to break the NFC's recent domination in the Super Bowl. But on second down, Brown struck again, intercepting O'Donnell's pass at the 39 and returning it 33 yards to the 6. Two plays later, Smith barreled over from 4 yards out for the clinching touchdown with 3:43 to go.

Pittsburgh limited the Cowboys' powerful running game to only 56 yards and enjoyed a whopping 201-61 advantage in total yards in the second half but could not overcome the 3 interceptions (another came on the game's final play) thrown by O'Donnell, the NFL's career leader for fewest interceptions per pass attempt. In all, O'Donnell completed 28 of 49 passes for 239 yards. Morris rushed for a game-high 73 yards on 19 carries. For Dallas, Aikman completed 15 of 23 pass attempts for 209 yards. The Cowboys' victory was the twelfth in a row for NFC teams over AFC teams in the Super Bowl.

1996 Bill Cowher #15

The 1996 Pittsburgh Steelers football team competed in their sixty-fourth season of Professional National Football League (NFL) football. The team was led by Bill Cowher in his fifth of fifteen seasons as head coach of the Steelers. .The record declined slightly from 1995's 11-5 to 1996's 10-6. The Steelers came in 1st again in the AFC Central this year for the fourth time but did not win enough to get a first seed. / first round bye. They had to play a Wild-Card game, which they won; but then they lost in the Divisional playoff game.

In their first playoff game, a rematch of the previous year's AFC Championship Game, the Steelers defeated the Colts, However, their season would come to a halt a week later as the Steelers lost to the New England Patriots, 28–3.

In the season opener on Sep 1, at Jacksonville, the Jaguars defeated the Steelers L (9–24). At Baltimore on Sep 8, the Steelers beat the Ravens W (31–17). Then, at home on Sep 16, 8,the Steelers beat the Buffalo Bills in Three Rivers Stadium, W (24–6). Sep 22—Bye. On Sep 29, at home, the Steelers beat the Houston Oilers W (30-16). At Kansas City on Oct 7, in Arrowhead Stadium, the Steelers beat the Chiefs W (17-7). On Oct 13, at home Pittsburgh defeated Cincinnati W (20-15). 8 Sun. On Oct. 20 at Houston's Astrodome, the Oilers beat the Steelers L (13–23).

At Atlanta on Oct 27, in the Georgia Dome, , the Steelers beat the Falcons W (20-17). At home on Nov 3, the Steelers blasted the St. Louis Rams in Three Rivers Stadium W (42–6). At Cincinnati on Nov. 10 in Cinergy Field, the Bengals defeated the Steelers L (24–34). At home on Nov. 17, the Steelers beat the Jacksonville Jaguars in Three Rivers Stadium W (28–3). At Miami on Nov 25, the Steelers beat the Dolphins in Pro Player Stadium W (24–17).

Then on Dec 1, in Baltimore Memorial Stadium, the Ravens beat the Steelers L (17–31). At home on Dec, the Steelers beat the San Diego Chargers in Three Rivers Stadium W (16–3). The next two games were losses beginning at home on Dec 15 when the San Francisco 49ers beat the Steelers in Three Rivers Stadium L (15–25). Then, in the season finale on Dec. 22, the Carolina Panthers defeated the Steelers L (14–18).

Wild Card Playoffs December 29, 1996
AFC Central: Pittsburgh 42, Indianapolis 14

58,078 fans saw the Steelers blow a 13-point lead in the first half but then score 29 unanswered points in the second half. Meanwhile, Pittsburgh held the Colts to 146 total yards of offense, while gaining 407 yards for themselves (with 236 on the ground).

Starting the game, the Steelers put on a drive of 51 yards in eight plays, which included a 30-yard reception by receiver Charles Johnson, to score on Norm Johnson's 29-yard field goal on their first drive. After the Colts got the ball, and had to give it up, Steelers receiver Jahine Arnold returned their punt 36 yards to the Colts 31-yard line. One play later, Mike Tomczak completed a 20-yard pass to Charles Johnson at the 8.

Backup quarterback Kordell Stewart, who, because of his running ability, was routinely used by the team in short-yardage situations, eventually finished the drive with a 1-yard touchdown run, giving the Steelers a 10-0 lead with 4:55 left in the first quarter. Following another Colts punt, Pittsburgh added three points to their lead on Norm Johnson's 50-yard field goal 10 seconds into the second quarter.

The Steelers seemed to be taking control of the game, but with 4:35 left in the half, Tomczak threw a short pass intended for Ernie Mills that was too far behind the receiver. Defensive back Eugene Daniel intercepted the ball and returned it 59 yards for a touchdown. On the Steelers next possession, Tomczak threw another interception to safety Ray McElroy on the Colts 40-yard line. On the next play, Jim Harbaugh completed a 48-yard pass to Marvin Harrison at the Steelers 12, and he eventually converted a third and 7 with a 9-yard TD pass to receiver Aaron Bailey, giving the team a 14-13 lead with 31 seconds left in the first half.

It was actually too late for the Colts as the Steelers dominated the rest of the game. They started out the second half with a 16-play, 91-yard possession that stole 9:30 off the clock. Tomczak completed 5/5 passes for 37 yards on the drive, while Jerome Bettis caught one of them and rushed for 42 yards on eight carries, the last a 1-yard touchdown run.

Then Stewart got behind center and completed a 2-point conversion pass to tight end John Farquhar, giving the team a 21-14 lead. Harbaugh was intercepted by Levon Kirkland on the next drive, and after a Steelers punt, running back Marshall Faulk fumbled a pitch from him with safety Carnell Lake recovering on the Indy 18-yard line. Five plays later, was in again on one of his patented 1-yard touchdown runs to give the Steelers a 28-14 lead less than a minute into the fourth quarter.

Stewart ended up as the go-to guy for the Steelers for the rest of the game. He finished with just one pass attempt, but his 24-yard run on a quarterback draw set up running back Jon Witman's 31-yard touchdown play. Stewart added a 3-yard touchdown run with 3:10 left in the game, making the final score 42-14. It was the second straight year the Steelers eliminated the Colts from the playoffs.

Jerome Bettis rushed for 102 yards and two touchdowns (his 11th 100-yard game of the year), while he also caught a pass for four yards. Johnson caught five passes for 109 yards. Neither starting QB had a great day. Tomczak completed 13 of 21 passes for 176 yards, with two interceptions and no touchdowns. Harbaugh completed 12 of 32 passes for 134 yards and a touchdown with one pick. He was also sacked four times, three by lineman Chad Brown.

January 5, 1997 AFC Conference Championship
New England Patriots 28, Pittsburgh Steelers 3

The Patriots were about to enter their dynasty years as they hired a great coach with Super Bowl inning experience. Bill Parcells did not bring all the cigars and rings, but he helped move the program forward. In their first home playoff game in 18 years, New England blew away the Steelers 28–3 with a big show of 346 yards of total offense, while limiting the Steelers to 213.

The Steelers felt the pain from the beginning as on the very first play from scrimmage, the Steelers got to see Pats QB Drew Bledsoe complete a 53-yard pass to Terry Glenn that set up Curtis Martin's 2-yard touchdown run. Pittsburgh could not move the ball and were quickly forced to punt. New England took just four plays to score a second time. It was a 34-yard touchdown on a screen pass from Bledsoe to fullback Keith Byars, giving the team a 14-0 lead just over seven minutes into the first quarter. The onslaught was about to continue.

On the first play of the second quarter, Martin burst through a hole in the right line, dodged a tackle attempt by Carnell Lake, and scooted 78 yards for a touchdown. This was the second longest scrimmage run in NFL postseason history. Near the end of the half, Steelers defensive back Willie Williams gave the Steelers hope with an intercepted a pass from Bledsoe. But Pittsburgh did not use the opportunity. They turned the ball over on downs on the Pats 24-yard line and the teams remained at 21-0 going into halftime.

The Steelers finally got their lone score of the game with 3:50 left in the third quarter. Linebacker Chad Brown's intercepted a Bledsoe pass and it led to a 29-yard field goal by Norm Johnson. Pittsburgh then got the ball back on their own 36 following a Patriots punt, but any hope of a comeback was dashed when safety Lawyer Milloy intercepted a pass from Mike Tomczak on the New England 39-yard line.

Six plays later, Martin's 23-yard touchdown run increased New England's lead to 28-3. In the fourth quarter, the Steelers managed a drive to the Patriots 15, only to lose the ball again on an interception by linebacker Willie Clay. Sometimes you eat the bear and sometimes the bear eats you. This was a bad day.

Martin finished his day with 166 rushing yards and three touchdowns. Slick running back Dave Meggett returned seven punts for 72 yards and rushed for 18. Tomczak had a tough time getting things going as he was held to 110 passing yards and he threw two interceptions in the final postseason game of his NFL career.

He was periodically replaced by versatile quarterback Kordell Stewart, but Kordell fared no better, finishing the game 0/10 on pass attempts. Steelers running back Jerome Bettis, who rushed for 1,431 yards during the season and 102 yards in the previous playoff game, was held to just 43 yards on the ground and was limited by groin and ankle injuries. This was New England's first playoff win since their 1985 Super Bowl season. You would not have known it from a bleacher seat.

"That might be my longest run ever", Martin (a Pittsburgh native) said after the game about his 78-yard score. "College, Pop Warner, everything. To me, the Steelers are my second-favorite team. I kind of worry about when I go home, how infamous I'll be." Steeler fans like that thinking and there is great hope for continued good performance, knowing that Pittsburgh has the most Super Bowl victories among the best in the NFL.

Top Steelers Players Jerome Bettis

Running Back
Several players on this list finished their careers in different uniforms, but Bettis is the only one to start his in one.

The Steelers sent second- and fourth-round draft picks to the St. Louis Rams in 1996 in order to obtain Bettis, and the move proved fruitful to say the least.

Listed at 250 pounds (in some years that seemed generous), the aptly nicknamed "Bus" steamrolled defenders on his way to sixth on the NFL's all-time rushing list.

Bettis' first six seasons in Pittsburgh saw him top 1,000 rushing yards, but it may be his last season that proves most memorable.

Bettis considered retirement before the 2005 season but decided to stick around for one more shot at an elusive Super Bowl ring.

Of course, Steelers fans all know how this story ends. "The Bus" rode into his hometown of Detroit for Super Bowl XL and was able to close his career in a fashion befitting such a valued contributor.

1997 Bill Cowher #15

The 1997 Pittsburgh Steelers football team competed in their sixty-fifth season of Professional National Football League (NFL) football. The team was led by Bill Cowher in his sixth of fifteen seasons as head coach of the Steelers. .The record improved from 1996's 10-6 to 1997's 11-5. The Steelers came in 1st again in the AFC Central this year for the fifth time under Cowher . They won the Divisional Championship but lost again going for all the Conference marbles.

The 1997 season was considered a transitional year due to many key free agent losses in the offseason, as well as it being the first season of Kordell Stewart scheduled to start at QB.

Bill Cowher had not missed a playoff, and this would be his sixth in a row after Chuck Noll's 3 of 9 performance as Noll was approaching his Swan Song. In this effort, Steelers head coach Bill Cowher tied Hall of Fame coach Paul Brown with most consecutive playoff appearances to start a head coaching career in the NFL—a record Cowher still co-owns with Brown, as the Steelers missed the playoffs the very next year after the six in a row.

The Steelers had 572 rushing attempts in 1997, the most in the 1990s.Their 2,479 total rushing yards were third-most of the decade by any team.

The Steelers would host the AFC Championship Game for the third time in four years; however, they would ultimately lose to the eventual Super Bowl champion Denver Broncos. That game was the last playoff appearance for the Steelers during the 1990s and they did not return to the postseason until 2001. It helps to remember as you read that there is a Super Bowl coming up during the Cowher years. We'll keep it a secret as we approach it, so we can all enjoy it.

As of 2017, this remains the only time in their history the Steelers defeated the Patriots in the playoffs. In their first playoff game, a rematch of the previous year's AFC Championship Game, the Steelers defeated the Colts, However, their season would come to a halt a week later as the Steelers lost to the New England Patriots, 28–3.

In the season and home opener on Aug 31, the Dallas Cowboys belted the Steelers L (7–37) in Three Rivers Stadium. Then, at home on Sep 7, the Steelers nosed out the Washington Redskins at Three Rivers Stadium W (14–13). Sun Sep 14—Bye. On Sep 22, at Jacksonville, the Jaguars beat the Steelers L (21–30). At home on Sep 28, the Tennessee Oilers were beaten by the Steelers in Three Rivers Stadium W 37–24). On Oct 15 at Memorial Stadium, Pittsburgh beat Baltimore W (42-34). On Oct. 12 at home, the Steelers beat the Indianapolis Colts W(24-22). Then, at Cincinnati's Cinergy Field, the Steelers beat the Bengals W (26-10).

At home on Oct. 26, the Steelers beat the Jacksonville Jaguars in Three Rivers Stadium in OT W (23–17). Then, on Mon Night Football, on Nov. 3 at Kansas City in Arrowhead Stadium, the Chiefs beat the Steelers L (10–13). At home on Nov. 9, the Steelers pounded in a shutout to beat the Baltimore Ravens in Three Rivers Stadium W (37–0). Then, at home on Nov. 16 the Steelers beat the Cincinnati Bengals in Three Rivers Stadium W (20–3). At Philadelphia in Veterans Stadium. The Eagles beat the Steelers L (20–23).

At Arizona on Nov. 30, in Sun Devil Stadium, the Steelers beat the Cardinals W (26–20) in OT. At home on Dec. 7, the Steelers beat the Denver Broncos in Three Rivers Stadium W (35–24). On Sat Dec 13, playing at New England's Foxboro Stadium, the Steelers beat the Patriots W (24–21) in OT. At Tennessee om Dec 21, in Liberty Bowl Memorial Stadium , the Oilers won the final game v the Steelers L (6–16). And, so, other than the playoffs, that was another season.

AFC Divisional Playoffs January 3, 1998
Pittsburgh Steelers 7, New England Patriots 6

Working in front of an attendance: 61,228 at Three Rivers Stadium in Pittsburgh, it was Quarterback Kordell Stewart's 40-yard touchdown run in the first quarter that was the difference in a defense-dominated game.

Often at the end of the season, teams are at their injury peak. The Patriots were severely depleted by injuries, playing without star running back Curtis Martin. Pro Bowl tight end Ben Coates was limited to just a few plays, while receiver Terry Glenn was out of this game a few minutes into the fourth quarter.

On the third play of the game, rookie defensive back Chad Scott got the ball rolling as he intercepted a pass from New England quarterback Drew Bledsoe and he returned it 27 yards to the Steelers 38. Stewart then got the team to the Patriots 40-yard line, converting two third downs with 10-yard completions to Charles Johnson before taking the ball the rest of the way to the end zone all by himself on a 40-yard score. This was the longest touchdown run in Steelers playoff history at the time.

In the second quarter, Bledsoe tried to get the Pats in gear as he completed two passes to Shawn Jefferson for 29 yards and he threw a 36-yarder to Glenn on a 65-yard drive that ended with Adam Vinatieri's 31-yard field goal, making the score 7-3. Later on, Pittsburgh drove to the New England 33, but defensive back Steve Israel intercepted a pass from Stewart. It was a game without many highlights. The only remaining highlight of the quarter would be Steelers receiver Will Blackwell's 58-yard punt return on the last play of the half.

The whole third quarter was non-descript until the last play. Then, Bledsoe's 39-yard completion to Glenn led to a 46-yard field goal from Vinatieri, cutting the Steelers lead to one point at 7-6. After a punt from each team, the Steelers tried to put the game away with a drive to the Patriots 1-yard line. However, on fourth down, coach

Bill Cowher tried to ice the game with a TD attempt rather than a Field Goal. Stewart was stuffed for no gain with 3:24 left in regulation.

This gave New England their one last chance to go for a winning field goal and the best they could do was get to their own 42. The next play rookie linebacker Mike Vrabel stripped the ball from Bledsoe, and fellow linebacker Jason Gildon recovered it. That was basically it though the Patriots managed to get the ball back with 34 seconds left. Then, linebacker Levon Kirkland intercepted Bledsoe's Hail Mary pass on the game's final play.

This was the third time in four years that the Steelers would play and host the AFC Championship Game. Jefferson was the sole offensive star of the game with nine receptions for 106 yards. Jerome Bettis led the Steelers with 74 yards from scrimmage but was held in check by New England's defense. Blackwell had four punt returns for 78 yards and three kickoff returns for 36. Gildon had a sack and two fumble recoveries. It was like a high-scoring baseball game.

AFC Conference Championships Jan. 11, 1998 Denver Broncos 24, Pittsburgh Steelers 21

At Pittsburgh's Three River stadium before 61,382, Pittsburgh took its chance at another AFC Championship but failed. Denver had other plans. For Denver, it was the second week in a row, that the team eliminated a strong team on the road. Pittsburgh had beaten them in the regular season. In Week 15, Pittsburgh got the best of Denver 35–24.

At that time, Kordell Stewart threw for 303 yards and three touchdowns, while running for two more. This time, he did not have it. Denver intercepted three of Stewart's passes and recovered a fumble, while also sacking him three times. It was a miserable game for Kordell Stewart and yet the Steelers were very close.

Most of the scoring came right after the game began. Pittsburgh's Levon Kirkland intercepted a pass from Denver quarterback John

Elway on the Broncos 43-yard line to get things going. The Steelers took the ball to the 20, and normally accurate Norm Johnson missed a 38-yard field goal attempt.

Then Denver running back Terrell Davis took off for a 43-yard run to the Steelers 29-yard line, and the team went on to score on Davis' 8-yard touchdown run. Pittsburgh's Will Blackwell returned the ensuing kickoff 18 yards to the 35-yard line, where Pittsburgh went on to move the ball 65 yards for the score to tie the game.

On the final two plays of this scoring opportunity, Stewart completed a 20-yard pass to Yancey Thigpen and then ran the ball the final 33 yards to the end zone. Steelers defensive back Darren Perry ended Denver's next drive by forcing and recovering a fumble from Davis on the Pittsburgh 32-yard line. Pittsburgh then drove 68 yards in 11 plays to go up 14-7 on Jerome Bettis' 1-yard touchdown run a few minutes into the second quarter.

Denver got the ball back and went on a 10-play, 45-yard drive to score on kicker Jason Elam's 43-yard field goal. The teams then exchanged punts, and Blackwell's 19-yard return gave the Steelers a first down on the Broncos 43-yard line. Just two plays later, Stewart forced a throw into double coverage and safety Ray Crockett intercepted his pass in the end zone. After the turnover, Elway led the Broncos 80 yards to score on his 15-yard touchdown pass to fullback Howard Griffith, giving the Broncos the lead, 17-14.

The Steelers could not move on the next drive and punted. Darrien Gordon returned the ball 19 yards to the Broncos 46, setting up a 54-yard drive that ended on Elway's 1-yard touchdown pass to Ed McCaffrey. That gave Denver a 24-14 lead with 13 seconds left in the half. 34 of their 54 yards came from a pass interference penalty on Steelers defensive back Carnell Lake on the first play of the drive. Bad playing and bad luck.

Both defenses controlled the second half. The Steelers took the opening drive of the second half and moved the ball methodically down the field. They blew a great scoring chance at the Broncos 5-yard line. Allen Aldridge ended the possession with an interception in the end zone. The next time the Steelers got the ball, they moved it to the Broncos 32, only to lose it again when Neil Smith forced a fumble while sacking Stewart and Denver's Mike Lodish made the recovery. Bad playing and bad luck.

Looking for anything to get the team going to avoid the loss, late in the fourth quarter, Stewart completed seven of eight passes for 68 yards and rushed twice for 11 yards on a 79-yard drive that ended with his 14-yard touchdown pass to Charles Johnson. This made the score 24-21 with 2:46 left in regulation. The Steelers had a chance.

At the two-minute warning, facing third down and 5 on their own 15-yard line on their ensuing drive, Elway came through for Denver and hit on an 18-yard completion to Shannon Sharpe for a first down. Then, on the next play, he completed a 10-yard pass to McCaffrey for another first down, enabling his team to run out the rest of the clock.

Sharpe later said that Elway made up the converting play in the huddle, seconds before the snap. Davis rushed for 139 yards and a touchdown. Bettis rushed for 105 yards and a touchdown. This would turn out to be the final playoff game at Three Rivers Stadium as the Steelers would eventually move to Heinz Stadium but not for a while.

1998 Bill Cowher #15

The 1998 Pittsburgh Steelers football team competed in their sixty-sixth season of Professional National Football League (NFL) football. The team was led by Bill Cowher in his seventh of fifteen seasons as head coach of the Steelers. .The record improved from 1997's 11-5 to 1998's 7-9. The Steelers came in 3rd in the AFC Central this year. They did not qualify for the playoffs for the first time since 1991.

The Team was doing well but then finished 7–9 after starting the season 5–2. They lost their last five games which caused them to lose a spot in the playoffs. It was Bill Cowher's first losing record as coach of the Steelers.

Top Steelers Players Hines Ward

"The black and gold runs deep in me and I will remain a Steeler for life."
- Hines Ward

Wide Receiver ...Throughout his career, Hines Ward was an exemplary wide receiver. Wards ranks in the top 20 in NFL history in both receptions and receiving touchdowns. With 12,083 receiving yards, he ranks just outside the 20-mark. But it isn't solely Ward's receiving abilities that earned him a spot in this list's top 10. In fact, it's another aspect of his game that many fans will remember fondly. Ward played fearlessly. Never the biggest on the field, he had no problem laying a vicious block on any opponent. And he did it with a smile.

The season was marked by a controversial ending to the team's Thanksgiving Day game against the Detroit Lions, where Jerome Bettis claimed he called the coin toss in overtime as "tails" although referee Phil Luckett heard "heads." One of the first times if not the only time that hearing affected a football game. The Lions won the game 19–16 and this began the Steelers' losing streak to finish the season.

Kordell Stewart did not look good this year. It can be said that the inept plays of Kordell Stewart were cited as another conflict, as the fans slowly began to turn on him. After their 11–5 1997 season, Pittsburgh lost two key offensive components: Chan Gailey, the offensive coordinator who went on to become head coach of the

Dallas Cowboys, and their leading receiver, Yancey Thigpen, a Pro Bowler for Pittsburgh in 1997, who joined the Tennessee Oilers. The 1998 Steelers did not adapt.

Top Steeler Players Alan Faneca

Tackle. Faneca was picked by the Pittsburgh Steelers in the first round (26th overall) in the 1998 NFL Draft. He saw limited playing time at first, but other players misfortune became his early fortune as he got his chance to play because of injuries to fellow Steelers. For example, with Will Wolford and Jim Sweeney out of the lineup, it allowed him to get his first start against the Cincinnati Bengals. He earned the Joe Greene Award as the team's top rookie.

In 1999 against the Cleveland Browns he was having a bad season debut before leaving the game at halftime, after suffering a left ankle injury late in the second quarter of the game and played the rest of the first half after sustaining the injury but did not play during the second half.

Against Baltimore Ravens he returned from his ankle injury but was replaced in the second half by Roger Duffy. One of his best games on the Season was against the Cincinnati Bengals helping to pave the way for Jerome Bettis first 100-yard game of that season. Against the Carolina Panthers helped pave the way for Bettis season-high 137 yards rushing and the Steelers second highest rushing performance of the season.

In 2000, Faneca helped the Steelers rank fourth in the league in rushing, one of only 10 teams to compile more than 2,000 yards rushing in 2000.

In the season opener at Baltimore on Sep 6, the Steelers beat the Ravens in Ravens Stadium W (20–13). Then, at home on Sep 13, the Steelers beat the Chicago Bears in Three River Stadium W (17–12). At Miami's Pro Player Stadium, the Dolphins beat the Steelers L (0-21). On Sep 27, at home in Three Rivers Stadium, the Steelers beat the Seahawks W (13-10). Oct 4, Bye. At Cincinnati's Cinergy Field, the Bengals beat the Steelers L (20–25). At home on Oct 18, the Baltimore Ravens were beaten by the Steelers in Three Rivers Stadium W 16-6). On Oct 26, at Kansas City's Arrowhead Stadium, Pittsburgh beat the Chiefs W (20-13). On Nov 1 at home, the Steelers were beaten by the Tennessee Oilers in Three Rivers Stadium L (31-41).

At home on Monday Night Nov. 9, the Steelers beat the Green Bay Packers in Three Rivers Stadium W (27–20). At Tennessee, in Vanderbilt Stadium on Nov 15, the Steelers lost to the Oilers L (14–23). At home on Nov. 22 the Steelers beat the Jacksonville Jaguars in Three Rivers Stadium W (30–15).

At Detroit's Pontiac Silverdome 1on Nov 26, the Lions beat the Steelers L (16–19) in OT. Then on Dec. 6 at home, the New England Patriots beat the Steelers in Three Rivers Stadium L (9–23). At Tampa Bay on Dec 13, the Buccaneers beat the Steelers in Raymond James Stadium L (3–16). At home on Dec. 20, the Cincinnati Bengals beat the Steelers in Three Rivers Stadium L (24–25). At Jacksonville on Mon. Dec. 28 in the season finale, at Alltel Stadium, the Jaguars beat the Steelers L (3–21).

1999 Bill Cowher #15

The 1999 Pittsburgh Steelers football team competed in their sixty-seventh season of Professional National Football League (NFL) football. The team was led by Bill Cowher in his eighth of fifteen seasons as head coach of the Steelers. .The record declined from 1998's 7-9 to 1999's 6-10. The Steelers came in 4th in the AFC Central. They did not qualify for the playoffs for the first time since 1991.

For the second consecutive season the Steelers did not make the playoffs after starting off the season by winning 5 of their first 8 games. Losing seven of the remaining eight dropped Pittsburgh to 6–10 for the year, their worst record under Bill Cowher.

In the season opener at Cleveland on Sep 12, the Steelers shut out the Browns in a shellacking at Browns Stadium W (43-0). Then, at Baltimore at PSI Net Stadium Sep 19, the Steelers beat the Ravens W (23-20). At home on Sep 26, the Seattle Seahawks beat the Steelers in Three Rivers Stadium, L (10–29).At home, on Oct3, the Jacksonville Jaguars beat the Steelers in Three Rivers Stadium L (30–17). At Buffalo on Oct 10, in Wilson Stadium, the Bills beat the Steelers L (21-24). On Oct 17, at Cincinnati in Cinergy Field, , the Steelers beat the Bengals W (17-3). On Oct 25, at home, the Steelers beat the Falcons W (13-9). Oct 31, Bye

At San Francisco, on Nov. 7, the Steelers beat the 49ers in 3Com Park W (27–6). Then, at home on Nov. 14, the Cleveland Browns beat the Steelers in Three Rivers Stadium L (15–16). On Nov 21 at Tennessee's Adelphia Coliseum, the Titans beat the Steelers L (10–16). At home on Nov. 28, the Cincinnati Bengals beat the Steelers in Three Rivers Stadium L (20–27). On Thursday Night Dec. 2 at Jacksonville's Alltel Stadium, the Jaguars beat the Steelers L 6–20).

At home on Dec. 12, the Baltimore Ravens beat the Steelers in Three Rivers Stadium L (24–31). At Kansas City, on Sat. Dec. 18, the Chiefs beat the Steelers in Arrowhead Stadium L (19–35). At home on Dec. 26, the Steelers beat the Carolina Panthers in Three Rivers Stadium W (30–20). On Jan. 2, at home, in the season finale, the Tennessee Titans beat the Steelers in Three Rivers Stadium L (26–47)

2000 Bill Cowher #15

The 2000 Pittsburgh Steelers football team competed in their sixty-eighth season of Professional National Football League (NFL) football. The team was led by Bill Cowher in his ninth of fifteen seasons as head coach of the Steelers. .The record declined from 1999s 6-10 to 2000's 9-7. The Steelers came in 3rd in the AFC Central. They did not qualify for the playoffs for the first time since 1991.

This year, the Steelers were trying to get on with better seasons after hitting just 6–10 in 1999, a season in which they failed to qualify for the playoffs. While Pittsburgh did improve to 9–7 and had their first winning season since 1997, it was not enough for the team to qualify for the playoffs. This season also marked the Steelers' last year at Three Rivers Stadium.

Coach Bill Cowher named Kent Graham as the team's starting quarterback for the season, but after an auspicious 1–3 start, Graham got hurt, and Kordell Stewart, who was a backup, took over the starting job again. Graham was released at the end of the season.

In the season opener at home on Sep 3, the Baltimore Ravens shut out Steelers L (0-16). Sept 10 Bye. At Cleveland on Sep 17, in Browns Stadium, the Browns beat the Steelers L (20-23). At home on Sep 24, at home, the Tennessee Titans defeated the Steelers L (20–23). At Jacksonville in Alltel Stadium on Oct1, the Steelers beat the Jaguars W (24-13). At New York, on Oct 8, in Giants Stadium, the Steelers beat the Giants W(20-3). On Oct 15, at home in Three Rivers Stadium, the Steelers shut out the Cincinnati Bengals W (15–0). On Oct 22, at home, the Steelers shut out the Cleveland Browns W (22-0).

At Baltimore on Oct. 29 in PSInet Stadium, the Steelers beat the Ravens W (9–6). At Tennessee on Nov 5, in the Adelphia Coliseum, the Titans defeated the Steelers L (7–9). Then, at home on Nov. 12, the Philadelphia Eagles beat the Steelers in Three Rivers Stadium L (23–26) in OT. At home on Nov. 19, the Jacksonville Jaguars defeated the Steelers in Three Rivers Stadium L (24–34). On Nov. 26 at Cincinnati, in Paul Brown Stadium, the Steelers walloped the Bengals W (48–28).

On Dec. 3, at home the Steelers beat the Oakland Raiders in Three Rivers Stadium W (21–20). At New York Giants Stadium, on Dec. 10, the Giants beat the Steelers L (10–30). At home on Dec. 16, the Steelers beat the Washington Redskins in Three Rivers Stadium W (24–3). Then in the season closing game, on Dec 24 at San Diego in Qualcomm Stadium, the Steelers beat the Chargers W (34–21).

2001 Bill Cowher #15

The 2001 Pittsburgh Steelers football team competed in their sixty-ninth season of Professional National Football League (NFL) football. The team was led by Bill Cowher in his tenth of fifteen seasons as head coach of the Steelers. .The record declined from 2000's 9-7 to 2001's 13-3. The Steelers came in 1st in the AFC Central. They won the Divisional Playoffs and lost the Conference Championship.

After finishing the previous three seasons a combined 22–26, the Steelers were back and there was reason to think about a Super Bowl. They were back as the top seed in the AFC, rolling to a 13–3 record in their first season since 1997 and playing for the first time in the spectacular Heinz Field. The Steelers went 7–1 this year in their new home stadium, with the only loss coming to the defending Super Bowl champion Baltimore Ravens (a loss, which the Steelers avenged in the divisional playoffs).

However, for the third time in Bill Cowher's coaching tenure, the Steelers were beaten in the AFC Championship Game at home. This time, the eventual Super Bowl Champion New England Patriots defeated the top-seeded Steelers.

In the season opener at home on Sep 9, at Jacksonville in Alltel Stadium, the Jaguars beat the Steelers L (3–21). Sept 23 Bye. At Buffalo on Sep 30, in Ralph Wilson Stadium, the Steelers prevailed v the Bills W (20-3). At home on Oct 7, the Steelers beat the Cincinnati Bengals in Heinz Field W (16-7). At Kansas City on oct 14, in Arrowhead Stadium, the Steelers won W (20–17). At Tampa Bay, the Steelers beat the Buccaneers W (17-10). At home on Oct 29, the Steelers beat the Tennessee Titans in Heinz Field W (34-7).

At home on Nov 4, the Baltimore Ravens beat the Steelers L (10–13) in Heinz Field.

At Cleveland on Browns Stadium on Nov. 11, the Steelers beat the Browns W (5–12) in OT. At home on Nov. 18, the Steelers beat the Jacksonville Jaguars W (20–7) in Heinz Field. At Tennessee on Nov. 25, the Steelers beat the Titans W (34–24) at Adelphia Coliseum. At home on Dec. 2, the Steelers beat the Minnesota Vikings W (21–16) in Heinz Field. Then, on Dec 16 at home, the Steelers defeated the New York Jets W (18–7).

At Baltimore on Dec. 16 the Steelers beat the Ravens W (26–21) in PSINet Stadium . At home on Dec. 23, the Steelers thumped the Detroit Lions W (47–14) on Heinz Field. On Dec 30 at Cincinnati , the Bengals squeaked out a wain against the Steelers L (23–26) in OT in Paul Brown Stadium. The Steelers won their last game of the season on Sunday Jan 6, 1972, W(28–7) in Heinz Field

Top Steelers Players Casey Hampton

Defensive Tackle… The Steelers selected Hampton in the first round (19th overall) of the 2001 NFL Draft. He was the fifth defensive tackle drafted in 2001. He signed a five-year, $6.80 million contract on July 22, 2001 with a nice signing bonus of $3.10 million.

He did not have a free ride. Throughout training camp, he competed for the job as the starting nose tackle against Kendrick Clancy. Head

coach Bill Cowher named Hampton the backup nose tackle behind Kendrick Clancy to start the regular season.

His first game was in the Pittsburgh Steelers' season-opening 21–3 loss at the Jacksonville Jaguars. On October 26, 2001, Pittsburgh Steelers' head coach Bill Cowher named Hampton the starting nose tackle for the remainder of the season but stated he would still be rotated by Kendrick Clancy.

On October 29, 2001, Hampton got his first career start and recorded two combined tackles during a 34–7 victory against the Tennessee Titans in Week 7. In Week 9, he collected a season-high four combined tackles and made his first career sack on quarterback Tim Couch in the Steelers' 15–12 win at the Cleveland Browns.

In his rookie season in 2002, he had 22 combined tackles (nine solo) and a sack in 16 games and 11 starts.[13] The Steelers' defense was ranked as the No. 1 overall and also finished first against the run.

The Steelers finished first in the AFC Central with a 13–3 record and clinched a playoff berth. On January 20, 2002, Hampton started in his first career playoff game and recorded three combined tackles in a 27–10 victory against the Baltimore Ravens in the AFC Divisional Round. The following week, he made two combined tackles in the Steelers' 34–17 loss to the New England Patriots in the AFC Championship Game.

Sunday January 20, 2002 Divisional Playoffs
AFC: Pittsburgh Steelers 27, Baltimore Ravens 10

Every team has a star and often more than one. This year, the Steelers hoped to have Jerome Bettis lugging the ball for TD's all year long, but he was sidelined for much of the regular season. He was recuperated and was scheduled to make his return in this first playoff ever at the Steelers new home, Heinz Field. Unfortunately, Bettis came up with an undisclosed ailment at the last minute. The good news for this game was that it did not matter.

The Pittsburgh offense ran for 150 yards and held the ball for over 40 minutes. Their defense limited the defending champion Ravens to 150 yards and seven first downs, forced four turnovers, and recorded three sacks. Bettis' replacement, Amos Zereoué, rushed for two touchdowns.

The first half was all bad news for Baltimore. Their first six drives resulted in two interceptions, three punts without gaining a first down, and a fumble. Think about that. Steelers defensive back Chad Scott started out the Pittsburgh dominance by intercepting Baltimore quarterback Elvis Grbac's first pass of the game and returning it 19 yards to the Ravens 43-yard line.

The Pittsburgh offense subsequently gained 37 yards on their first three plays. Linebacker Jamie Sharper managed to halt the drive by tackling Chris Fuamatu-Ma‘afala for a 1-yard loss on third down and goal, but Kris Brown kicked a field goal to give Pittsburgh first score and a 3–0 lead.

Baltimore was forced to punt the next time they had the ball, right after linebacker Mike Jones sacked Grbac for a 10-yard loss on third down and 10. Pittsburgh's offense then drove 51 yards in seven plays, featuring two completions from Kordell Stewart to receivers Plaxico Burress and Hines Ward for gains of 17 and 20 yards. Zereoue finished the drive with a 2-yard touchdown run to make it 10–0.

In the second quarter, Baltimore defensive back Chris McAlister intercepted a Stewart Pass and took it 18 yards to the Steelers 7-yard line. But on the next play, safety Brent Alexander intercepted Grbac's pass in the end zone for a touchback. The Steelers took over and drove to the Ravens 9-yard line, but on third down, bad things began to happen.

Stewart was sacked for an 8-yard loss by Larry Webster and Brown's ensuing field goal attempt was wide left. Following another three and out for Baltimore, receiver Troy Edwards returned their punt 27-yards to the Ravens 43-yard line, setting up Zereoue's second touchdown run. Then linebacker Jason Gildon recovered a fumble from Terry Allen on Baltimore's next drive and the Steelers capitalized with a 46-yard field goal from Brown, increasing their lead to 20–0 with 4:23 left in the half.

After going all this time without a single first down, Baltimore responded on their next drive. Tight end Shannon Sharpe caught four passes for 48 yards on an 11-play, 57-yard drive. Matt Stover capped it off with a 26-yard field goal, cutting their deficit to 20–3 at halftime.

Late in the third quarter, Baltimore receiver Jermaine Lewis returned a punt 88 yards for a touchdown. But the Steelers responded by driving 83 yards in 12 plays and scoring with Stewart's 32-yard touchdown pass to Burress. The final score was 27 to 10 and the Steelers were off to the Conference Championship game. .

Conference Championship Sun Jan 27, 2002
AFC: New England Patriots 24, Pittsburgh Steelers 17

This was the first Conference Championship game played in the brand-new Heinz Field. The Steelers were hoping to apply some magical dust to their own season as in this game, they bumped into the Patriots' storybook season. The Steelers did their best but did not stop the Pats story as Drew Bledsoe came into the game in the second quarter in place of an injured Tom Brady. Brady had replaced Bledsoe himself early in the season when he suffered a sheared blood vessel. Despite the kinks, the Patriots were able to fire it up for the victory.

Defense was the name of the game for both teams early in the game. With just over four minutes left in the first quarter, the Steelers were forced to punt the ball from their own 13-yard line. Josh Miller hit a big 64-yarder which was well needed at the time. However, Steelers receiver Troy Edwards was penalized for going out of bounds before tackling Troy Brown on the return. This turned out to make a big difference, as the punt was redone and on the second attempt, Brown returned it 55 yards for a touchdown. In retrospect, it was the game.

Pittsburgh responded to the TD by driving 65 yards in 10 plays, one of them a 34-yard run by quarterback Kordell Stewart, and scoring with a 30-yard field goal from Kris Brown, cutting the score to 7–3. Later on, with under two minutes left in the half, Brady completed a 28-yard pass to Brown at the Steelers 40-yard line, but he was knocked out of the game by a hit from safety Lethon Flowers. Bledsoe took over like he had been playing the whole game.

He rushed for four yards and completed three passes to David Patten for 36 yards, the last one was an 11-yard touchdown strike which gave the Patriots a 14–3 lead.

On the first drive of the second half, New England linebacker Tedy Bruschi grabbed a fumbled snap on the Steelers 35-yard line. But the Patriots gained only two yards on their next four plays and ended up turning the ball over on downs. Pittsburgh then drove 52 yards to the 16-yard line to set up Brown's second field goal attempt, but this time his kick was blocked by defensive tackle Brandon Mitchell and Troy Brown recovered the ball. After returning it 11 yards, Brown threw a lateral pass to Antwan Harris, who took the ball the remaining 45 yards for a touchdown to increase New England's lead to 21–3. The Steelers had yet to step on the start pedal.

Pittsburgh struck back with Stewart completing a 24-yard pass to Hines Ward and a 19-yard screen pass to Amos Zereouéon an 8-play, 79-yard drive. Jerome Bettis finished it off with a 1-yard touchdown run, cutting the score to 21–10 with 5:11 left in the third quarter. New England had to punt when linebacker Jason Gildon sacked Bledsoe on third down, and Edwards returned the punt 28 yards to the Patriots 32-yard line. Five plays later, Zereoue scored with an 11-yard touchdown run, making the score 21–17.

Early in the fourth quarter, Adam Vinatieri nailed a 44-yard field goal at the end of a 45-yard drive. This added three points to New England's lead and brought the score to 24–17. Later in the quarter, the Patriots made two key stops to clinch the victory. First, safety Tebucky Jones intercepted a pass from Stewart and returned it 19 yards to the Steelers 34-yard line. The Pittsburgh's defense managed to prevent a first down and Vinatieri missed a 50-yard field goal attempt that would have sealed the game, giving the Steelers the ball back on their own 40-yard line.

A few plays later, however, Lawyer Milloy intercepted a pass from Stewart with 2:02 left to seal the game, and the Patriots were able to run out the clock. Close again but no cigar.

Brown was the top offensive performer of the day with eight receptions for 121 yards, along with three punt returns for 80 yards. Brady completed 12 of 18 passes for 115 yards, while Bledsoe completed 10 of 21 passes for 102 yards and a touchdown.

2002 Bill Cowher #15

The 2002 Pittsburgh Steelers football team competed in their seventieth season of Professional National Football League (NFL) football. The team was led by Bill Cowher in his eleventh of fifteen seasons as head coach of the Steelers. .The record declined from 2001's 13-3 to 2002's 10-5-1. The Steelers again came in 1st in the AFC North. Bill Cowher's team won the Wild Card Game, defeating the Cleveland Browns at home, but lost to AFC South champion Tennessee Titans in the divisional round.

As noted, the team was coming off a fine 13–3 record in 2001 and they had won an appearance in the AFC Championship Game. With their finish of 10-5-1 this year, the Steelers became the first champions of the newly created AFC North. Week 4 saw Kordell Stewart's final game as the Steelers' starting quarterback, as he was replaced by Tommy Maddox during the game and although he did relieve an injured Maddox, Stewart never regained his job as he was released following the season.

In the season opener at home on Sep 9, at New England, the Patriots whipped the Steelers L (14-30). On Sep 15, at home, the Oakland Raiders pounded the Steelers in Heinz Field L (17–30). Sept 23 Bye week. At home on Sep 29, the Steelers beat the Cleveland Browns in Heinz Field, W (16-13). At New Orleans on Oct 6, the Saints beat the Steelers in the Louisiana Superdome L (29-32) At Cincinnati on Oct 13, the Steelers squashed the Bengals in Paul Brown Stadium W (34-7). At home on Oct 21, in Heinz Field, the Steelers beat the Indianapolis Colts W (28-10). At

Baltimore on Oct 27, the Steelers beat the Ravens in PSINet Stadium W (31-18).

On Nov. 3 at Cleveland in Cleveland Browns Stadium, the Steelers beat the Browns W (23–20). Then on Nov. 10, the Atlanta Falcons tied the Pittsburgh Steelers T 34–34 in O. At Tennessee on Nov 17, the Titans beat the Steelers in Adelphia Coliseum L (23–35). At home on Nov. 24, the Steelers beat the Cincinnati Bengals W (29–21). On Dec. 1 at Jacksonville, the Steelers beat the Jaguars in Alltel Stadium W (25–23).

At home, on Dec. 8 the Houston Texans beat the Steelers L (6–24). On 15 Sun. Dec. 15 the Steelers beat the Carolina Panthers in Heinz Field W (30–14). Then at Tampa Bay, on Monday Night Dec. 23, the Steelers defeated the Buccaneers in Raymond James Stadium W (17–7). Wrapping up the 20012 season, at home, on Dec 29, the Steelers beat the Baltimore Ravens W (34–31).

2003 Bill Cowher #15

The 2003 Pittsburgh Steelers football team competed in their seventy-first season of Professional National Football League (NFL) football. The team was led by Bill Cowher in his twelfth of fifteen seasons as head coach of the Steelers. .The record declined from 2002's 10-5-1to 2003's 6-10. The Steelers came in 3rd and did not qualify for the playoffs.

The Steelers had an OK record in 2002 but they began 2003 looking to improve on their 10–5–1 record. They had lost to the Tennessee Titans in the Divisional round of the playoffs.

This was a big injury year. With the team suffering through injuries as well as less reliance on the running game than normal, the Steelers stumbled to a 6–10 record. They went through the entire season without winning consecutive games. Since moving to Heinz Field, this marked their first losing season as well as missing the playoff along with the 2006, 2009, 2012 and 2013. The team's 6–10 finish matched their worst record under Bill Cowher (1999).
This was linebacker Jason Gildon's last season. He had become the franchise's career sack leader during a game against the Arizona

Cardinals on November 9. As of the 2017 season, this was the most recent losing season for the Steeler. It never feels good.

Top Steelers Players Troy Aumua Polamalu

(/ˌpoʊləˈmɑːluː/; born Troy Aumua; April 19, 1981) is a former American football strong safety of Samoan descent, who played his entire twelve-year career for the Pittsburgh Steelers of the National Football League (NFL). He played college football for the University of Southern California (USC), and earned consensus All-American honors. He was chosen by the Steelers in the first round of the 2003 NFL Draft. He was a member of two of the Steelers' Super Bowl championship teams and was the NFL Defensive Player of the Year in 2010.

In the home and season opener on Sep 7, the Steelers beat the Baltimore Ravens W (34-15). On Sep 14, at Kansas City, in Arrowhead Stadium, the Chiefs beat the Steelers L (20-41). On Sep 21, at Cincinnati, in Paul Brown Stadium, , the Steelers beat the Bengals W (17-10). At home on Sep 28, the Tennessee Titans beat the Steelers in Heinz Field, L (13-30). At home against Cleveland, on Oct 5, the Browns beat the Steelers in Heinz Field L (13-33). At Denver on Oct 12, in Invesco Field, the Broncos beat the Steelers L (14-17). Oct 19 Bye week. Home on Oct 26, against St. Louis, the Rams beat the Steelers L (21-33).

At Seattle on Nov. 2, the Seahawks beat the Steelers in Seahawk Stadium L (16–23). On Nov. 9 at home the Steelers beat the Arizona

Cardinals in Heinz Field W (28–15). In a Monday Night Football game on Nov. 17 at San Francisco, the 49ers beat the Steelers in San Francisco Stadium L (14–30). At Cleveland Browns Stadium on Nov. 23, the Steelers beat the Browns W (13–6). Then at home on Nov. 30, the Cincinnati Bengals beat the Steelers in Heinz Field L (20–24).

On Dec. 7 at home, the Steelers defeated the Oakland Raiders in Heinz Field W (27–7). At New York, on Dec. 14 the Jets beat the Steelers in Giants Stadium L (0–6). Then on Dec. 21 at home, the Steelers beat the San Diego Chargers in Heinz Field W (40–24). In the season finale at Baltimore on Dec 28, the Ravens beat the Steelers in OT in M&T Bank Stadium L (10–13).

2004 Bill Cowher #15

The 2004 Pittsburgh Steelers football team competed in their seventy-second season of Professional National Football League (NFL) football. The team was led by Bill Cowher in his thirteenth of fifteen seasons as head coach of the Steelers. .The record improved from 2003's 6-10-1to 2004's 15-1. The Steelers came in 1st place in the AFC North, won the Divisional Championship and lost the Conference.

The team roared back after a disappointing 6–10 season the year before. This year's 15–1 record topped the 14–2 team record from 1978 and joined the 1984 San Francisco 49ers, the 1985 Chicago Bears, and the 1998 Minnesota Vikings as the only teams in NFL history to that point since the league adopted a 16-game schedule in 1978 to finish with such a record. Their 15-1 record also made the Steelers the first AFC team to achieve a 15–1 record.

Along the way, the Steelers ended the New England Patriots NFL-record 21-game winning streak in Week 8, then defeated their crosstown rival the Philadelphia Eagles the following week to hand the NFL's last two undefeated teams their first losses in back-to-back weeks, both at home. It was a good year.

After so many years from Bradshaw, finally, a consistently great quarterback began to play for Pittsburgh. The season was highlighted by the surprising emergence of rookie quarterback Ben Roethlisberger. He was the team's top pick in that year's draft. Originally the Steelers planned to sit "Big Ben" behind veteran Tommy Maddox the entire season. However, the plans abruptly changed when Maddox was hurt in the team's Week 2 loss to Baltimore.

Surrounded by talent in all positions, "Big Ben" went an NFL-record 13–0 as a rookie starting quarterback, shattering the old NFL record (and coincidentally, also the team record) of 6–0 to start an NFL career set by Mike Kruczek filling in for an injured Terry Bradshaw in 1976.

The Steelers were back hosting the AFC Championship. It was the fifth time in eleven years. However, for the fourth time under Bill Cowhers in that same span, the Steelers lost at home one game away from the Super Bowl. Just like in 2001, they lost to the Patriots in a rematch from Week 8.

It really was a heartbreak season and it was written up that way. The 2006 edition of Pro Football Prospectus listed the 2004 Steelers as one of their "Heartbreak Seasons." These were the seasons in which teams "dominated the entire regular season only to falter in the playoffs, unable to close the deal." Said Pro Football Prospectus, "

In the playoffs, Roethlisberger hit an inconvenient slump, just like the Pittsburgh quarterbacks who came before him. Roethlisberger threw two killer interceptions against the Jets, but the Steelers were bailed out when Jets kicker Doug Brien missed a game-winning field goal. The next week against New England, head coach Bill Cowher was clearly worried about Roethlisberger, letting him throw only once on first or second down in the first quarter. By the time the offense opened up, the Patriots were beating the Steelers by two touchdowns. A Roethlisberger interception was returned 87 yards for a touchdown by Rodney Harrison, and the game was effectively over. For the second time in seven years, a 15–1 team had failed to make it to the Super Bowl."

Games of the Season

In the home and season opener on Sep 12, the Steelers beat the Oakland Raiders in Heinz Stadium W (24-21). On Sep 19, at Baltimore the Ravens beat the Steelers in M&T Bank Stadium L (13-30). On Sep 26, at Miami's Joe Robbie Stadium, the Steelers beat the Dolphins W (17-10). At home on Oct 3, the Steelers beat the Cincinnati Bengals in Heinz Field, W (28-17). At home on Oct 10, against Cleveland, the Steelers beat the Browns in Heinz Field W (34-23). At Dallas on Oct 17, in Texas Stadium, the Steelers beat the Cowboys W (24-20) Oct 24 Bye week. At home on Oct 31, the Steelers beat the New England Patriots in Heinz Field W (34-20).

At home on Nov. 7, the Steelers pounded the Philadelphia Eagles W (27–3) in Heinz Field. At Cleveland on Nov. 14, the Steelers beat the Browns W (24–10) in Cleveland Browns Stadium. At Cincinnati, on Nov 21, the Steelers defeated the Cincinnati Bengals W (19–14) in Paul Brown Stadium . On Nov. 28 at home, the Steelers defeated the Washington Redskins W (16–7) in Heinz Field. At Jacksonville, on Dec. 5, the Steelers beat the Jaguars W (17–16) in Alltel Stadium.

On Dec. 12 at home, the Steelers beat the New York Jets W (17–6) in Heinz Field. Then on Sat. Dec. 18, at New York, the Steelers beat the Giants W (33–30) in Giants Stadium. On Dec. 26, at home, the Steelers defeated the Baltimore Ravens W (20–7) in Heinz Field. Then in the last game of the season, at Buffalo on Jan. 2, the Steelers beat the Bills W (29–24) in Ralph Wilson Stadium.

Divisional playoffs Saturday January 15, 2005
AFC: Pittsburgh Steelers 20, New York Jets 17 (OT)

The two-week breather did not help the Steelers before the Divisional Playoffs began. After 1 15-1 season, resting did not help the Steelers. They squeaked out a victory in this game but then lost the Conference championship again.

They won the Division game, however. The Jets came out on the losing end of this overtime game when placekicker Doug Brien missed two consecutive field goals at the end of regulation, setting an NFL record of 3 missed game winning field goals in a single post-season.

It was a subpar performance by Steelers' rookie quarterback Ben Roethlisberger. Nonetheless, the Steelers managed to win after Jeff Reed made a game-winning 33-yard field goal 11:04 into the OT period. Steelers running back Jerome Bettis finished the game with 101 rushing yards and a touchdown, along with a 21-yard reception.

The Steelers opened up the scoring with a 43-yard field goal by Reed. Then after the ensuing kickoff, Steelers safety Troy Polamalu intercepted a pass from Chad Pennington and returned it 15 yards to the Jets 25-yard line, setting up a 3-yard touchdown run by Bettis. New York Responded with a 42-yard field goal from Brien on their next drive to cut their deficit to 10–3. Later in the second quarter, Jets receiver Santana Moss returned a punt 75 yards for a touchdown to tie the game.

Jets defensive back Reggie Tongue intercepted a Roethlisberger pass midway through third quarter, and he took it back for a pick-6 -- 86 yards for a touchdown. Pittsburgh then drove all the way to New York's 23-yard line. But then Bettis fumbled and New York's Erik Coleman recovered it. The Steelers got into scoring range for the third consecutive drive, after having forced a punt. They got the TD with Roethlisberger's 4-yard pass to Hines Ward to tie it at 17.

The Jets came back bringing the ball inside the Steelers 30-yard line, but Brien missed a 47-yard field goal attempt with 2 minutes left in regulation. Two plays later, New York defensive back David Barrett gave his team another chance to score the winning points by intercepting a pass from Roethlisberger and returning it 25 yards to Pittsburgh's 36-yard line. But Brien missed another field goal, this one from 43 yards, as time expired in the fourth quarter, and the game went into overtime.

The Jets won the coin toss but were forced to punt. Pittsburgh then drove 72 yards in 14 plays and won the game with a 33-yard field goal from Reed. And then they moved to the Conference Championship game a week later.

AFC Championship: January 23 Heinz Field
New England Patriots 41, Pittsburgh Steelers 27
Attendance: 65, 242

A nice crowd of Pittsburgh fans assembled in Heinz Field hoping this would be the year when the Conference game jinx would end, and their beloved Steelers would be off to the Super Bowl.

It was a Pittsburgh cold game in mid-January with the game-time temperature of 11 °F (−12 °C). This marked the second-coldest game ever in Pittsburgh and the coldest ever in Steel City playoff annals. This should have given the Steelers the advantage, but New England was accustomed to the cold. The Patriots handed Ben Roethlisberger his first loss as a starter after a 14-game winning streak, the longest by a rookie quarterback in NFL history. The Steelers became the second NFL team ever to record a 15–1 record and fail to reach the Super Bowl.

The Patriots caused fumble-itis on the part of the Steelers and then they converted four Pittsburgh turnovers into 24 points, while committing no turnovers themselves. The Patriots' win also prevented an all-Pennsylvania Super Bowl from being played as Philadelphia was doing well on the other side of Pennsylvania.

The Steelers never recovered from their poor performance in the first quarter of this game. Patriots defensive back Eugene Wilson intercepted Roethlisberger's first pass of the game on his own 48-yard line. Vinatieri then knocked through a 48-yard field goal to take a 3–0 lead. Pittsburgh then drove to the Patriots 39-yard line. But then running back Jerome Bettis lost a fumble while being tackled by Roosevelt Colvin. Pats linebacker Mike Vrabel recovered it. On the next play, Tom Brady threw a 60-yard touchdown pass to receiver Deion Branch.

With 1:28 left in the opening quarter, the Steelers cut their deficit to 10–3 with Jeff Reed's 23-yard field goal. But after an exchange of punts, Branch caught a 45-yard reception on Pittsburgh's 14-yard line. Two plays later, Brady threw a 9-yard touchdown pass to David Givens. Then on the Steelers ensuing drive, safety Rodney Harrison intercepted a pass from Roethlisberger and returned it 87 yards for a touchdown, giving the Patriots a 24–3 halftime lead.

The teams scored three consecutive touchdowns when the second half began. New England was then forced to punt on the opening drive of the third quarter, and Antwaan Randle El returned the ball 9 yards to the Steelers 44-yard line. Then on the Steelers next possession, he caught two passes for 46 yards as they drove 56 yards in five plays. Bettis finished the drive with a 5-yard touchdown run, cutting their deficit to 24–10.

New England was ready to score again. They moved the ball 69 yards in seven plays and Corey Dillon's pulled off a 25-yard touchdown run. Pittsburgh stormed right back, driving 60 yards in ten plays and scoring with Roethlisberger's 30-yard touchdown pass to Hines Ward.

After Pittsburgh forced a Pats punt, Randle El returned the ball 22 yards to the Steelers 49-yard line. On the drive, Ward's 26-yard reception on the last play of the third quarter set up Reed's second field goal, making the score 31–20 with 13:32 left in the game. However, the Patriots took over the rest of the quarter. Their 49-yard drive took 5:26 off the clock and Vinatieri's nailed a 31-yard field goal. Then two plays after the kickoff, Wilson intercepted another pass from Roethlisberger at New England's 45-yard line.

The Patriots took off down the field on another long scoring drive, taking another 5:06 off the clock. Branch capped it off with a 23-yard touchdown run on a reverse play, giving the Patriots a 41–20 lead. The Steelers responded with Roethlisberger's 7-yard touchdown pass to Plaxico Burress on their next drive, but by then there was only 1:31 left in the game. It was over. One more year to wait for Cowher's Super Bowl.

Brady completed 14 of 21 passes for 207 yards and 2 touchdowns. Dillon rushed for 73 yards and a touchdown. Branch caught 4 passes for 116 yards, rushed for 37 yards, and scored two touchdowns. Roethlisberger threw for 226 yards and 2 touchdowns, and rushed for 45 yards, but was intercepted 3 times. Ward caught 5 passes for 109 yards and a touchdown.

Top Pittsburgh Players James Harrison

Outside Linebacker
Perhaps no permanently scowling face is more beloved in Pittsburgh than that of James Harrison.

I remember attending the Steelers/Ravens game in the 2010 AFC Divisional Round and being awestruck when Harrison exited the tunnel. The look on his face just told me Joe Flacco was in for a long day.

Of course, Harrison notched three sacks in that contest.
The undrafted product out of Kent State entered the NFL with low expectations and matched them by toiling on practice squads and in the NFL Europe through the early portion of his career.
Eventually, Silverback earned a spot in the starting lineup and made 31 teams regret overlooking him. Harrison tallied 60 sacks in six years as a starter and took home Defensive Player of the Year honors in 2008.

What he'll most be remembered for, though, is an astounding pick-six against the Cardinals in Super Bowl XLIII.

Top Steelers Players Ben Roethlisberger

Quarterback: Some may contend that a close to the top spot on a ranking site is a little high for Ben Roethlisberger, but they need only look at the years between his arrival and Terry Bradshaw's departure.

The Steelers fielded several competitive squads and All-Pro-caliber players, but quarterback play always seemed to be their downfall. Enter Roethlisberger.

Yes, he inherited a talented squad. But he also led it to heights not seen in decades.

With three Super Bowl appearances and two victories, Roethlisberger has already given younger Steelers fans a golden age of their own. His 32-career game-winning drives are good enough for 11th in NFL history.

And of course, one of those 32 drives stands well above the rest. Roethlisberger is the author of the game-winning drive against the Cardinals in Super Bowl XLIII. It firmly cemented his status as one of the all-time Steelers greats.

2005 Bill Cowher #15

The 2005 Pittsburgh Steelers football team competed in their seventy-third season of Professional National Football League (NFL) football. The team was led by Bill Cowher in his fourteenth of fifteen seasons as head coach of the Steelers. .The record declined from 2004's 15-1 to 2004's 11-5. The Steelers came in 2nd place in the AFC North, won the Divisional Championship, the Conference Title & the Super Bowl.

The Steelers failed to duplicate or improve on their 15-1 record from the year prior, but this time, even with an 11-5 2nd place finish, they did not lose the AFC Conference Championship game. tin which they lost to the New England Patriots in the AFC Championship Game at Heinz Field and finishing at 11-5.

The Steelers were lucky to get the sixth and final seed for the playoffs. They became just the second team ever (and the first in 20 years) to win three road games on their way to the Super Bowl. They got to the big game and they defeated the NFC Champion Seattle Seahawks in Super Bowl XL to secure their league-tying fifth Super Bowl title. In doing so, they also became the first team since the 1970 AFL-NFL merger to win a Super Bowl without playing a single home playoff game until the 2007 Giants. They are also the first 6th seeded team to beat the top 3 seeds on the road. Go Steelers!

In the home and season opener on Sep 11, the Steelers beat the Tennessee Titans in Heinz Field W (34-7). On Sep 18, at Houston, the Steelers beat the Texans in Reliant Stadium W (27-7). Then on Sep 25, at home, the New England Patriots beat the Pittsburgh Steelers at Heinz Field L (20-23). Oct 3 Bye Week. On Oct 10, at San Diego , the Steelers beat the Chargers W (24-22). At home on Oct 16, the Jacksonville Jaguars beat the Steelers in OT in Heinz Field L (17-23). At home on Oct 23, against Cincinnati, in Paul Brown Stadium, the Steelers beat the Bengals in Heinz Field W (27-13). At home on Nov 6, at Green Bay, the Steelers beat the Packers in Lambeau Field W (20-10).

At home on Nov. 13, the Steelers defeated the Cleveland Browns W 34–21 in Heinz Field. Then on Nov. 20 at Baltimore, the Ravens beat the Steelers L (13–16) in M&T Bank Stadium during an

Overtime Contest. On Monday Night, on Nov. 28 at Indianapolis, the Colts beat the Steelers L (7–26) in the RCA Dome. Then, on Dec. 4, the Cincinnati Bengals beat the Steelers L 31–38 in Heinz Field.

On Dec. 11, the Steelers beat the Chicago Bears W (21–9) in Heinz Field. Then at the Hubert H. Humphrey Metrodome in Minnesota, the Steelers defeated the Vikings W 18–3. As playoff time approached, on Sat. Dec. 24 at Cleveland Browns Stadium, the Steelers shellacked the Browns in a major shutout W 41–0. Then in the last regular season game on Jan. 1, 2006, the Steelers pounded the Detroit Lions W (35–21) in Heinz Field. The Steelers finished the season 11–5 and won all the way out of the playoffs. Great year!

Wild Card Playoffs January 8, 2006
AFC: Pittsburgh Steelers 31, Cincinnati Bengals 17

After a 15-1 season in which fans were looking for and somewhat expected a Super Bowl appearance, the Steelers got there this year, one year later with an 11-5 record. They got there on the skin of their teeth, having finished in 2nd place the AFC North and having to scratch their way through all away games beginning with having to compete in the Wild-Card games. Their win is a testament to continued play as opposed to getting a break in the action and losing the edge.

For the Bengals, this game was an unusual happening for them as it was their first playoff appearance in 15 years. It began with a rocky start for the Bengals when Pro Bowl quarterback Carson Palmer was knocked out of the game on the first drive of the game. Despite having Palmer on the sidelines, however, the Bengals still managed to build an early 10-point lead. But it was not too long before they had given up 24 unanswered points later in the game while turning the ball over three times.

On the Bengals second offensive play of the game, Palmer suffered a season-ending knee injury after being hit by Pittsburgh's Kimo von Oelhoffen. Nonetheless the play was successful. His 66-yard pass to wide receiver Chris Henry (who was also injured on the play) set up kicker Shayne Graham's 23-yard field goal. Then, after forcing a punt, backup quarterback Jon Kitna completed three consecutive passes for 40 yards and rushed for 11, while running back Rudi Johnson finished the drive with a 20-yard touchdown run, increasing their lead to 10–0.

Steelers defensive back Ike Taylor took the next kickoff 36 yards to the 40-yard line. Aided by a 15-yard penalty on cornerback Tory James, the Steelers then drove 60 yards in eight plays and scored with Ben Roethlisberger's 19-yard touchdown pass to Willie Parker. The subsequent kickoff was returned by Tab Perry for 32 yards to his own 43-yard line, and then the Bengals drove 57 yards in 14 plays. Kitna completed the drive with a 7-yard touchdown pass to T. J. Houshmandzadeh, retaking their 10-point lead, 17–7.

But on the Steelers consequent drive, Roethlisberger's 54-yard completion to Cedrick Wilson set up his 5-yard touchdown pass to Hines Ward, cutting the score to 17–14 at halftime.

The Bengals took the second half kickoff 62 yards to the Steelers 15-yard line. Graham then attempted a 34-yard field goal. However, center Brad St. Louis' lofted a high snap over holder Kyle Larson's head. Graham recovered the fumble, but the Steelers took over on the 34-yard line. On the seventh play of the drive, defensive back Kevin Kaesviharn was called for a 40-yard pass interference penalty on the Bengals 5-yard line. It was the perfect setup for Jerome Bettis to run the ball into the end zone on the next play.

Cincinnati was forced to punt, and then Pittsburgh receiver Antwaan Randle El took a direct snap, ran to his right, and threw the ball back to Roethlisberger. Big Ben then his Wilson for a 43-yard touchdown reception that increased the Pittsburgh lead to 28–17.

On the Bengals next drive, linebacker James Farrior intercepted a pass from Kitna and returned it 22 yards to the Bengals 40-yard line. This set up a 23-yard field goal by Jeff Reed. As the quarter progressed, the Bengals got another shot and managed to drive to the Steelers 43-yard line. However, safety Troy Polamalu ended the drive with an interception and the Steelers offense ran out the rest of the clock. It was off to the Divisional playoffs the next week for Pittsburgh.

AFC Divisional Championship January 15, 2006
Pittsburgh Steelers 21, Indianapolis Colts 18

Before 57,449 at the RCA Dome in Indianapolis, The Steelers became the first #6 playoff seed (since the league expanded to a 12-team playoff format in 1990) to defeat a #1 seed. They were also the first #6 seed to reach a conference championship game. Colts quarterback Peyton Manning, who struggled for years trying to win his first Super Bowl, would have to wait seven more years to get his trophy. But, he gave it a great go. Manning threw for 290 passing yards and a touchdown, but it wasn't enough to beat the Steelers.

The Steelers were the underdog and they literally stunned the Colts home crowd at the RCA Dome by driving 84 yards and scoring on their opening possession. Pittsburgh quarterback Ben Roethlisberger completed six consecutive passes for 76 yards, including a 36-yard completion to tight end Heath Miller and a 6-yard touchdown pass to Antwaan Randle El.

Before the quarter was finished, Roethlisberger had fired a 45-yard completion to Hines Ward moving the ball to the Colts 8-yard line. Big Ben scored another touchdown with his 7-yard pass to Miller, increasing the Steelers' lead to 14-0.

Just five minutes into the second quarter, Indianapolis managed to get its team moving. They drove 96 yards to the Steelers 2-yard line, taking 9:39 off the clock. Despite being on the doorstep, the colts could not open the door and they were forced to settle for a field goal from Mike Vanderjagt, cutting their deficit to 14-3.

In the waning moments of the third quarter, on third down, Steelers linebacker James Farrior (who finished the game with eight tackles and 2.5 sacks) got to Manning for a sack at the Colts 1-yard line.

Randle El returned Hunter Smith's ensuing punt 20 yards to the Indianapolis 30. Five plays later, Jerome Bettis scored a 1-yard touchdown run, making the score 21–3. This time, the colts did not just take it. They came back, driving 72 yards in six plays and scoring with Manning's 50-yard touchdown pass to tight end Dallas Clark.

The punted on their next drive, but only after taking over seven minutes off the clock, leaving just 6:03 left in the game by the time Indianapolis got the ball back.

Right after the punt, an interception by Pittsburgh safety Troy Polamalu was overturned by instant replay (a reversal that the league would later admit was a mistake). Manning took advantage of his second chance and he completed a 9-yard pass to Clark, a 20-yard pass to Marvin Harrison, and a 24-yard pass to Reggie Wayne, moving the ball to the Steelers 3-yard line. Running back Edgerrin James finished the drive with a 3-yard touchdown run, and then Manning threw a pass to Wayne for a successful 2-point conversion, cutting the Colts deficit to 21–18.

The Steelers were forced to punt on their next drive. However, with 1:20 left in the game, Pittsburgh sacked Manning on fourth and 16 at the Colts' 2-yard line, and the ball was turned over to the Steelers on downs.

At this point, the game appeared to be over, but the Steelers were forced to play ball instead of taking a quarterback kneel because the Colts still had three timeouts remaining. On Pittsburgh's first play, in which Bettis tried to punch it in for an insurance touchdown, he fumbled for the first time all season. Actually, he had some help. Linebacker Gary Brackett popped it from Bettis' hands with his helmet. Indianapolis defensive back Nick Harper recovered the ball and appeared to be on his way for an Indy touchdown that would have given the Colts the lead when Ben Roethlisberger showed what he was made of as he made a season saving tackle at the Colts' 42-yard line, spinning around and grabbing his ankle. The game was on the line.

Eventually, the Colts advanced to the Pittsburgh 28-yard line, but Vanderjagt, who had been perfect at home in the playoffs, missed a

46-yard game-tying field goal attempt wide right with 17 seconds left, and the clock ticked down.

This game was the beginning of the end for Vanderjagt, who entered the game as the NFL's all-time leader in field goal percentage. The following year, the Colts decided to let his contract expire. He spent the next season with the Dallas Cowboys, where he made just 72% of his field goals before leaving the NFL for good. To stay in pro football, you must play like a professional.

AFC Conference Championship: Jan 22, 2006
Pittsburgh Steelers 34, Denver Broncos 17

In perfect football weather at 34 degrees in Denver's Mile High Stadium, the Steelers played their third playoff game on the road. This was the first time since 1984, that the Steelers played on the road in the AFC Championship Game. Pittsburgh was on their game and the home field did not matter as the Steelers forced four turnovers and went into halftime with a 24–3 lead on the way to advancing to their sixth Super Bowl appearance in team history.

Pittsburgh thus became the first #6 playoff seed (since the league expanded to a 12-team playoff format in 1990) to advance to the Super Bowl. Second-year quarterback Ben Roethlisberger, with a 15-1 season and an 11-5 season behind him was already in his fifth career playoff game. Like a seasoned pro, Big Ben completed 21 of 29 passes for 275 yards and two touchdowns (one each to Cedrick Wilson and Hines Ward) and ran for a third. Steelers running back Jerome Bettis rushed for the other touchdown.

Pittsburgh's good omens began when the Steelers scored on their opening drive. They moved the ball 62 yards in 12 plays and ended it with a Jeff Reed field goal. Three plays after their kickoff, Broncos quarterback Jake Plummer lost a fumble as he was being sacked by Joey Porter. Steelers lineman Casey Hampton recovered the ball at the Denver 39-yard line. Four plays later, Roethlisberger's 12-yard touchdown pass to Wilson increased the Steelers lead to 10–0 on the first play of the second quarter.

The Broncos did not just sit by. Plummer responded by driving 55 yards and positioning the team for a field goal courtesy of Jason Elam. The Steelers ripped right back, marching 80 yards in 14 plays and scoring with Bettis' 3-yard touchdown run. This gave Pittsburgh a nice 17–3 lead.

Then on the first play after the next kickoff, defensive back Ike Taylor intercepted a pass from Plummer on the Broncos 39-yard line. Four plays later, a Bettis touchdown run was called back because of a penalty on Ward. But Ward made up for his mistake by catching a touchdown pass on the next play, giving the Steelers a 24–3 lead with seven seconds left in the half.

Plummer finally got the Broncos moving in the third quarter by completing four consecutive passes for 80 yards. The last pass was for a 30-yard touchdown to Ashley Lelie. However, Wilson caught two passes for 45 yards on Pittsburgh's next possession, setting up Reed's second field goal to make the score 27–10.

As the game was wrapping up in the fourth quarter, Lelie nailed a 38-yard reception. This plus a 22-yard pass interference penalty on Taylor set up a 3-yard touchdown run by Mike Anderson, cutting the Steeler's lead to 27–17. The game was not over.

After a Steelers punt, defensive end Brett Keisel forced a fumble on fourth down from Plummer and Travis Kirschke recovered the ball on the Broncos 17-yard line. Four plays later, Roethlisberger ended any chance of a Denver comeback with a 4-yard touchdown run. This game was the Broncos' last playoff game with Mike Shanahan as their head coach, and last with any coach until 2011. It would also be Shanahan's last playoff game until 2012, when he was with Washington.

Super Bowl XL February 5, 2006:
Pittsburgh Steelers 21, Seattle Seahawks 10

This game was played indoors at Ford Field in Detroit Michigan before 68,206 fans. This was Super Bowl XL (40). The National

Football Conference (NFC) champion Seattle Seahawks played the American Football Conference (AFC) champion Pittsburgh Steelers. The outcome of this game would decide the National Football League (NFL) champion for the 2005 season. The Steelers defeated the Seahawks by the score of 21–10.

With this win, the Steelers tied the San Francisco 49ers and the Dallas Cowboys with the then-record five Super Bowls. Right now, Pittsburgh leads the pack with six wins but in 2006 for this game, that was just a nice thought.

The Steelers' victory was their first Super Bowl victory since Super Bowl XIV in 1980. Pittsburgh had finished the regular season with an 11–5 record, and this got them into the action. They had to play in the wild card playoffs to get their chance. And, so, they became the fourth wild card team, the third in nine years, and the first ever number 6 seed in the NFL playoffs, to win a Super Bowl. The Seahawks, on the other hand, in their 30th season, were making their first ever Super Bowl appearance after posting an NFC-best 13–3 regular season record.

Pittsburgh was on its game and they capitalized on two big plays that were converted into touchdowns. They jumped to a 14–3 lead early in the third quarter with running back Willie Parker's Super Bowl record 75-yard touchdown run. Seahawks defensive back Kelly Herndon's Super Bowl record 76-yard interception return then set up a Seattle touchdown to cut the lead 14–10. However, Pittsburgh responded with Antwaan Randle El's 43-yard touchdown pass to Hines Ward. This was the first time a wide receiver threw a touchdown pass in a Super Bowl. This action clinched the game in the fourth quarter.

Hines Ward, who caught 5 passes for 123 yards and a touchdown, while also rushing for 18 yards. He was then named Super Bowl MVP. There was criticism of the officiating in Super Bowl XL. Members of the media piped in soon after the game, leading NFL Films to rank it as one of the top ten controversial calls of all time.

It was the last Super Bowl game broadcast on ABC. Although the Super Bowl had largely been presented in high definition since Super

Bowl XXXIV, Super Bowl XL was the first Super Bowl where all aspects of the game itself were aired in HD.

The Steelers' catchphrase for the playoffs was "One for the Thumb", a phrase originally made popular by Joe Greene as an allusion to a fifth Super Bowl ring. The Steelers got their thumb ring.

The first four tries with the ball in Super Bowl XL resulted in punts. There are always big game jitters in these big games. Seahawks punt returner Peter Warrick eventually gave the team good field position when he returned Chris Gardocki's 37-yard punt 12 yards to Seattle's 49-yard line. QB Matt Hasselbeck then started off the drive with a pair of completions to receivers Darrell Jackson and Joe Jurevicius for gains of 20 and 11 yards, respectively. The Seahawks were forced to settle for a 47-yard field goal by kicker Josh Brown.

By the end of the first quarter, the Steelers had failed to gain a first down, and quarterback Ben Roethlisberger had completed one of five pass attempts for one yard. On their first second-quarter possession, Pittsburgh had to punt again in a three-and-out. However, they benefited from another Seahawks holding call that nullified Warrick's 34-yard punt return. The Steelers forced a Seattle punt, but Seattle safety Michael Boulware intercepted a Roethlisberger pass at the Seattle 17-yard line, but the Seahawks ultimately punted.

As the quarter moved on, Roethlisberger hit receiver Hines Ward out of a scramble with an against the grain pass for a 37-yard gain to keep the drive going. Jerome Bettis carried the ball on the next two plays, taking his team to the one-yard line but not into the end-zone. On the third-down play, after the two-minute warning, Roethlisberger faked a handoff and dove into the end-zone himself.

Confusion reigned after Big Ben's score. The referee hesitated for a bit after the play ended, but he eventually signaled a touchdown, and it was upheld after a replay challenge.

After a 19-yard Jurevicius reception, Seattle took the ball to the Pittsburgh 36-yard line, but, after the drive stalled, Brown's field goal attempt from 54-yards failed and the Steelers ran out the clock to end the first half.

Pittsburgh got the ball to begin the second half, and on the second play, running back Willie Parker broke through for a 75-yard touchdown run, giving his team a 14–3 lead and setting a record for the longest run in Super Bowl history. It beat Marcus Allen's Super Bowl XVIII mark by one yard.

The Seahawks were into Pittsburgh territory on the next drive, sparked by a 21-yard run by Alexander. However, Brown again missed a field-goal attempt, this one from 50 yards, as Seattle could not close the 11-point deficit.

Pittsburgh then took the ball 54 yards to the Seattle six-yard line to put themselves in position to take a large lead, but Seahawks defensive back Kelly Herndon picked off a Roethlisberger pass and brought it 76-yards for a Super Bowl record. The next play began on the Steelers 20-yard line. From there, the Seahawks took just two plays to score on Hasselbeck's 16-yard touchdown pass to tight end Jerramy Stevens, cutting the Pittsburgh lead to four points (14–10).

After an exchange of punts (two from Pittsburgh, one from Seattle), which occupied most of the third quarter, the Seahawks had taken the ball from their own two-yard line to near midfield as the fourth quarter began. .

The drive continued, and the Seahawks reached the Pittsburgh 19-yard line. Stevens then caught an 18-yard pass, but it was negated on a penalty call against Seattle tackle Sean Locklear for holding. This kept the Seahawks from getting a first-down-and-goal from the 1-yard-line.

Just three plays later, Pittsburgh defensive back Ike Taylor intercepted a Hasselbeck pass at the 5-yard line and took it back 24 yards. While tackling Taylor, Hasselbeck was flagged for blocking below the waist. The penalty added 15 yards to the return and gave the Steelers the ball on their own 44-yard line.

Pittsburgh ran a wide receiver reverse after having run four prior plays. This play turned out to be a pass play by wide receiver Antwaan Randle El, who played quarterback while in college. Parker took a pitch from Roethlisberger and handed off to Randle

El, who was running in the opposite direction. Randle El then pulled up and threw a 43-yard touchdown pass to a wide-open Hines Ward, giving the Steelers a 21–10 lead. This was the first time a wide receiver threw a touchdown pass in a Super Bowl.

On the next possession, Hasselbeck ran for eighteen yards and was briefly touched by Steelers linebacker Larry Foote as the QB fell to the ground. Though the play was initially ruled a fumble, with the ball recovered by the Steelers, a Seahawks challenge proved successful, as officials ruled Hasselbeck was down prior to his having lost the ball. Hasselback hit Jurevicius for a thirteen-yard reception, and he drove the team to the Pittsburgh 48-yard line but could go no further. Tom Rouen punted, and the ball was in the end-zone for a touchback. The Steelers got possession on their own 20-yard line.

Pittsburgh held the ball for about nearly four-and-one-half minutes on their next drive, as Bettis carried seven times. Seattle had to use all three timeouts to stop the clock. There was 1:51 left when they took the ball from their own 20-yard line following a Gardocki punt.

Jurevicius then snagged a 35-yard reception taking the Seahawks into Pittsburgh territory. This was followed by a 13-yard Bobby Engram reception which took the team to within field-goal range. Poor clock-management and play-calling left the team with just 35 seconds remaining> Then an incompletion and a three-yard pass to Stevens over the middle of the field took another 26 seconds, and Hasselbeck threw incomplete near Stevens on fourth down, giving the Steelers the ball on downs with just three seconds remaining. Roethlisberger was pleased to kneel-down to end the game. Pittsburgh were Super Bowl Champions for the fifth time.

2006 Bill Cowher #15

The 2006 Pittsburgh Steelers football team competed in their seventy-fourth season of Professional National Football League (NFL) football. The team was led by Bill Cowher in his fifteenth and last season as head coach of the Steelers. .The record declined from 2005's 11-5 to 2006's 8-8. The Steelers did not make the Playoffs

Ben Roethlisberger suffered a near death accident in the offseason while riding his motorcycle in downtown Pittsburgh. An out of state vehicle failed to yield and hit him. Roethlisberger was not at fault but was moments away from dying due to a cut artery> However medics stopped the bleeding in time. This set him back for training camp and the Preseason. However, he did manage to play in part of the Preseason games.

Shortly after the Preseason however, Roethlisberger needed an emergency appendectomy which caused him to miss the first game of the season. Between both of these events, Ben reportedly lost 15 pounds and was not up to regular form with the team due to lack of practice time and time spent in camp. His health early in the year is pointed to as the cause for this rough season.

He experienced continued problems in the Atlanta Falcons game in Atlanta during the year. He was hit after throwing the ball by multiple defenders, one of which caused a helmet to helmet collision. Roethlisberger was diagnosed with a concussion and had to sit out the rest of the game and appeared to have difficulties in the next couple of games. Obviously, the health Of Ben Roethlisberger was a paramount reason for the poor season.

In the home and season opener on Sep 7, the Steelers beat the Miami Dolphins in Heinz Field W (28-7). On Monday Night Sep 18, at Jacksonville, the Jaguars beat the Steelers in Alltel Stadium L (0-9). Then on Sep 24, at home, the Cincinnati Bengals defeated the Pittsburgh Steelers at Heinz Field L (20-28) Oct 1 Bye Week. On Oct 8 at San Diego , the Chargers beat the Steelers in Qualcomm Stadium L (13-23). W (24-22). At home on Oct 15, the Steelers pounded the Kansas City Chiefs in Heinz Field W (45-7). At Atlanta on Oct 22, the Falcons beat the Steelers beat the Bengals in the Georgia Dome, L (38-41). At Oakland on Oct 29, in the McAfee Coliseum, the Raiders beat the Steelers L (13-20).

At home on Nov. 5, the Denver Broncos beat the Steelers L (20–31) in Heinz Field. On Nov 12, at home, the Steelers beat the New Orleans Saints in Heinz Field W (38–31). Then, on Nov. 19 at Cleveland, the Steelers beat the Browns W (24–20) in Cleveland Browns Stadium. At Baltimore, on Nov. 26 the Ravens shut-out the

Steelers L (0–27) in M&T Bank Stadium. On Dec 3 at home, the Steelers beat the Tampa Bay Buccaneers W (20–3) in Heinz Field.

At home on Dec. 7, the Steelers beat the Cleveland Browns W (27–7) in Heinz Field. Then at Carolina's Bank of America Stadium, the Steelers beat the Panthers W 37–3. On Dec 24, at home, the Baltimore Ravens beat the Steelers L (7–31) in Heinz Field. Then, on New Year's Eve, Dec 31, in the season finale, in OT, the Steelers beat the Cincinnati Bengals W (23–17) in Paul Brown Stadium. This was Bill Cowhers last game as the Steeler's head coach.

Chapter 23 Coach Mike Tomlin 2007 to 2017+

Coach #16 Mike Tomlin

Year	Coach	League/Conf/Div	Pl	Record	Pct.
2007	#16 Mike Tomlin	NFLAFCNorth	1st	10 6 0	.625

- Lost Wild Card Playoffs(Jaguars) 31–29

2008	#16 Mike Tomlin	NFLAFCNorth	1st	12 4 0	.750

- Won Divisional Playoffs(Chargers) 35–24
- Won Conference Championship (Ravens) 23–14
- Won Super Bowl XLIII(6) (Cardinals) 27–23
- James Harrison – Defensive Player of the Year
- Santonio Holmes – Super Bowl MVP
- Mike Tomlin – Motorola NFL Coach of the Year

Continued below picture

Year	Coach	League/Conf/Div	Pl	Record	Pct.
2009	#16 Mike Tomlin	NFLAFCNorth	3rd	9 7 0	.563
2010	#16 Mike Tomlin	NFLAFCNorth	1st	12 4 0	.750

- Won Divisional Playoffs(Ravens) 31–24
- Won Conference Championship (Jets) 24–19
- Lost Super Bowl XLV(Packers) 31–25
- Troy Polamalu– Defensive Player of the Year

2011	#16 Mike Tomlin	NFLAFCNorth	2nd	12 4 0	.750

- Lost Wild Card Playoffs(Broncos) 29–23 (OT)

Year	Coach	League/Conf/Div	Pl	Record	Pct.
2012	#16 Mike Tomlin	NFLAFCNorth	3rd	8 8 0	.500
2013	#16 Mike Tomlin	NFLAFCNorth	2nd	8 8 0	.500
2014	#16 Mike Tomlin	NFLAFCNorth	1st	11 5 0	.688

- Lost Wild Card Playoffs(Ravens) 30–17

2015	#16 Mike Tomlin	NFLAFCNorth	2nd	10 6 0	.625

- Won Wild Card Playoffs(Bengals) 18–16
- Lost Divisional Playoffs(Broncos) 23–16

2016	#16 Mike Tomlin	NFLAFCNorth	1st	11 5 0	.688

- Won Wild Card Playoffs(Dolphins) 30–12
- Won Divisional Playoffs(Chiefs) 18–16
- Lost Conference Championship (Patriots) 36–17

2017	#16 Mike Tomlin	NFLAFCNorth	1st	13 3 0	.813

Lost Divisional Playoffs(Jaguars) 42–45

2007 Mike Tomlin #16

The 2007 Pittsburgh Steelers football team competed in their seventy-fifth season of Professional National Football League (NFL) football. The team was led by Mike Tomlin in his first season as head coach of the Steelers. .The record improved from 2006's 8-8 to 2006's 10-6. The Steelers came in first in the AFC North and made the playoffs in their first year under Mike Tomlin. They lost their first wild card game against Jacksonville L (29-31).

This Steelers' season contained two notable playoff rematches. The Steelers again played the New England Patriots on December 9. This was the first time in the regular season since 2005, when the Steelers lost at home on a last-second Adam Vinatieri field goal 23–20. The 34–13 loss was also the Steelers' first visit to Foxboro, Massachusetts since 2002.

The Steelers shut-out the Seattle Seahawks 21–0 in week 5 on October 7. This was the teams' first meeting since the Steelers' 21–10 victory in Super Bowl XL20 just months earlier. The week 5 match was the Steelers' and Seahawks' first meeting in Pittsburgh since 1999 as well as the Seahawks' first-ever visit to Heinz Field.

Another notable game occurred December 20 when the Steelers defeated the St. Louis Rams, 41–24, for their first-ever road win over the "new" Cleveland/Los Angeles/St. Louis Rams (1–9–1). It was the two teams' first-ever meeting in St. Louis, a city the Steelers last visited in 1979 (a 24–21 win over the then-St. Louis Cardinals at Busch Memorial Stadium).

In the season opener on Sep 9, the Steelers beat the Cleveland Browns in Cleveland Browns Stadium W (34-7). On Sep 16, at home, the Steelers beat the Buffalo Bills in Heinz Field W (26-3). Then on Sep 23, at home, the Steelers beat the San Francisco 49ers in Heinz Field W (37-16). On Sep 30, at Arizona, in University of Phoenix Stadium, the Cardinals beat the Steelers L (14-21). At home on Oct 7, the Steelers shut-out the Seattle Seahawks in Heinz Field W (21-0). Oct 14 Bye Week. At Denver on Oct 21, the Broncos beat the Steelers in Invesco Field L (28-31). At Cincinnati the Steelers beat the Bengals in Paul Brown Stadium W (24-13).

At Atlanta on Oct 22, the Falcons beat the Steelers beat the Bengals in the Georgia Dome, L (38-41). At Oakland on Oct 29, in the McAfee Coliseum, the Raiders beat the Steelers L (13-20).

On Monday Night at home on Nov. 5, the Steelers stuffed the Baltimore Ravens W (38–7) in Heinz Field. At home on Nov 11, the Steelers defeated the Cleveland Browns, W 31–28 in Heinz Field. At New York on Nov 18 in OT, the Jets defeated the Steelers

L (16–19) in Giants Stadium. On Monday Night, at home, Nov 26, the Steelers defeated the Miami Dolphins W (3–0) in Heinz Field . On Dec. 2, at home, the Steelers beat the Cincinnati Bengals W (24–10) in Heinz Field.

On Dec 9, at New England , the Patriots beat the Steelers L (13–34) in Gillette Stadium in Foxboro, Mass. On Dec. 16, the Jacksonville Jaguars beat the Steelers L (22–29) in Heinz Field. Then on Thu. Night, Dec. 20, at St. Louis, the Steelers beat the Rams W (41–24) at the Edward Jones Dome. In the season closing game at Baltimore, the Ravens beat the Steelers on Dec. 30 L (21–27) in M&T Bank Stadium 10–6 Summary

2008 Mike Tomlin #16

The 2008 Pittsburgh Steelers football team competed in their seventy-sixth season of Professional National Football League (NFL) football. The team was led by Mike Tomlin in his second season as head coach of the Steelers. .The record improved from 2007's 10-6 to 2008's 12-4. The Steelers came in first in the AFC North and made the playoffs in their second year under Mike Tomlin. They won it all including the Super Bowl Pittsburgh become the first franchise in the NFL with six Super Bowl titles.

The Steelers entered the season as defending champions of the AFC North Division, coming off a 10–6 record in 2007. Based on the previous season's results, the team faced the most difficult schedule in over 30 years; however, they were identified as Super Bowl contenders by ESPN.

The team opened their regular season in Mike Tomlin's second season on September 7, with a win over the Houston Texans while headed to a fine 12-4 record, and a second straight AFC North Division title. Mike Tomlin was selected in fan balloting as the Motorola Coach of the Year.

Linebacker James Harrison was named the NFL's Defensive Player of the Year after leading a defense which set the standard for the league in nearly every defensive category, including total yardage allowed, points allowed, passing yardage allowed, first downs allowed, yards per play, and yards per pass, among others. The playoffs began on January 11, 2009, with a win over the San Diego Chargers. The following week saw the third victory of the season over the Baltimore Ravens in the AFC Championship game and the advancement to Super Bowl XLIII, where the Steelers defeated the Arizona Cardinals on February 1, 2009. Go Steelers!

In the home and season opener on Sep 7, the Steelers beat the Houston Texans in Heinz Field W (38-17). On Sep 14, at Cleveland Browns Stadium, the Steelers beat the Browns W (10-6). Then on Sep 21, at Philadelphia, the Eagles beat the Steelers in Lincoln Financial Field L (6-15). On Sep 29, at home in Heinz Field, the Steelers beat the Baltimore Ravens W (23-20). At Jacksonville Municipal Stadium on Oct 5, the Steelers beat the Jaguars, W (26-21). Oct 12 Bye Week. At Cincinnati on Oct 19 in Paul Brown Stadium, the Steelers beat the Bengals W (38-10). At New York on Oct 26, the Giants beat the Steelers at Giants Stadium L (14-21).

On Monday Night, Nov. 3, at Washington the Steelers beat the Redskins W (23–6) in FedEx Field. On Nov. 9, at home, the Indianapolis Colts beat the Steelers L (20–24) in Heinz Field. At home again, on Nov. 16, the Steelers edged out the San Diego Chargers W (11–10) at Heinz Field. On Thursday Night, Nov 20, the Steelers beat the Cincinnati Bengals W (27–10) in Heinz Field. Then on Nov. 30 at New England, the Steelers beat the Patriots W (33–10) in Gillette Stadium.

On Dec. 7, at home, the Steelers beat the Dallas Cowboys W (20–13) in Heinz Field. At Baltimore on Dec 14, the Steelers beat the Ravens W (13–9) in M&T Bank Stadium. On Dec. 21 at Tennessee, the Titans beat the Steelers L (14–31) in LP Field. In the last game of the season, on Dec. 28, Pittsburgh shut out Cleveland Browns W (31–0) in Heinz Field

Notes on the wild card round: Pittsburgh bye week

After the Dec 28 game, the team took a well-deserved rest on December 29—the day following their final regular-season game.

They began to prepare for their first post-season game on Tuesday, December 30 through Thursday, January 1, before three days of a nice weekend rest. Bog Ben Roethlisberger did not practice until Monday, January 5. Tomin was quoted as follows: "We will proceed slowly with him because we have that luxury. But we feel comfortable with where he is relative to Sunday and where he's capable of being next week."

The Steelers January 1 practice was expected to be normal, but Tomlin allowed players to leave after team meetings and a walk-through. Multiple Steelers stated that they would watch the Wild Card games. Some including James Farrior and Ryan Clark watched as fans; however, Chris Hoke said, "I will be watching the guys I am going against... That is how I watch it." The Steelers wanted this ring to start their second hand.

AFC Divisional Round: January 11, 2009
Pittsburgh Steelers 35 San Diego Chargers 24

Heinz Field was alive on Jan 11 as the Pittsburgh Steelers hosted the San Diego Chargers. The Chargers' were fresh from an overtime victory over the Indianapolis Colts during the Wild Card round.

As the game began to move, the Chargers scored on the game's first drive with a 41-yard pass from Philip Rivers to Vincent Jackson for a touchdown. After the Steelers defense stopped the Chargers on their next drive, Pittsburgh's Santonio Holmes returned a punt 67 yards to tie the game at seven. With just two minutes remaining in the first half Nate Kaeding was perfect with a 42-yard field goal to re-grab the lead for the Chargers.

Pittsburgh's offense did not stand still after the Chargers score. They came back with a 7 play, 66-yard drive in just one minute and 33 seconds to take their first lead of the game. The score came on a 3-yard touchdown run from Willie Parker.

The Steelers took off right after the second-half kickoff. They opened up with a 7:56, 13 play drive which concluded with a Ben Roethlisberger's touchdown pass to Heath Miller. San Diego had one offensive play in the third quarter, which resulted in an interception. The Steelers entered the fourth quarter with a 21–10 lead that they needed to protect and/or expand.

Gary Russell scored on a 1-yard touchdown rush to extend the Steelers lead. The Chargers scored again on their next possession, when Legedu Naanee received Rivers' second touchdown pass of the game to conclude a 73-yard drive. With 4:17 remaining Willie Parker scored his second touchdown of the game—with a 16-yard run.

The scoring was not complete until Darren Sproles finished off the game's scoring for the Chargers with a 62-yard touchdown reception. This brought the final score to 35–24. Pittsburgh was heading to the AFC Conference Championship.

AFC Championship: January 16, 2009
Pittsburgh Steelers 23 Baltimore Ravens 14

The Pittsburgh Steelers rallied at the Allegheny County Courthouse before the game. It was a big deal.

The Ravens were "guests" of the Steelers for the AFC Conference game. The Baltimore Ravens had defeated the Miami Dolphins and Tennessee Titans in the Wild Card and Divisional rounds respectively to get into the AFC Championship Game.

During the week before the game, the City of Pittsburgh was celebrating. Mayor Luke Ravenstahl temporarily changed his name to Luke Steelerstahl in order to remove the "Raven" from his name—all in good fun. The change was not official, but the mayor was compelled to comment that "As soon as he heard the idea, [he] thought it was a great idea." Pittsburgh is a great, fun city.

Eventually, the teams had to play the game. The Steelers scored the game's first points, with Jeff Reed converting on field goals from 34 and 42 yards in the first quarter. Santonio Holmes received a pass from Ben Roethlisberger in the second quarter and ran for a touchdown to give the Steelers a 13-0 lead.

Baltimore's Willis McGahee got himself a touchdown with 2:44 remaining in the second quarter—bringing the halftime score to 13-7. Reed converted his third field goal of the game from 46 yards in the third quarter.

McGahee scored his second touchdown of the game with 9:32 remaining in the final quarter bringing the Ravens within two points of a bad day for the Steelers. Thankfully, Troy Polamalu intercepted a pass from Joe Flacco and returned it 40 yards to score the final touchdown of the game. Pittsburgh got itself a fine 23-14 victory with a Super Bowl just two weeks away.

Super Bowl: XLIII (48) February 1, 2009
Pittsburgh Steelers 27   Arizona Cardinals 23

Super Bowls are often fraught with a bunch of nervous players, especially the quarterbacks who have to rely on their accuracy to lead their teams to victory. The games are often dull in the beginning as the teams get the feel of the game. In this game it took some time, but Jeff Reed concluded the first drive of Super Bowl XLIII with a field goal—giving the Steelers a 3-0 lead over the Arizona Cardinals.

The next go was also successful as Gary Russell scored on a 1-yard touchdown rush on the Steelers' second drive. The Cardinals stopped watching the Steelers score and so they responded by going for a touchdown on their next opportunity with the ball.

On the final play of the first half Kurt Warner threw a pick-6 that was snagged by James Harrison and returned 100 yards for a touchdown. As he did in the first quarter, Reed scored the sole points of the third quarter giving the Steelers a 20–7 lead entering the final quarter.

Nothing is ever sure but the score on the final game whistle. The Cardinals scored three consecutive times in the fourth quarter—with two Larry Fitzgerald touchdown receptions and a Steelers' holding call in the end zone that resulted in a safety. It could have been a Steelers loss as there was a 23–20 Cardinal lead with just 2:37 remaining in regulation.

Pittsburgh needed to score and so Big Ben drove 78 yards in 2:02 and scored on a touchdown pass from Ben Roethlisberger to Santonio Holmes. The Steelers four-point lead held until the end as time expired and the Pittsburgh Steelers became the first team to win six Super Bowl titles. Go Steelers.

Lots of people were celebrating and no practice was scheduled for Monday. Santonio Holmes was voted the game's Most Valuable Player. Mike Tomlin became the youngest coach to win a Super Bowl. Harrison's interception return was logged as the longest play in Super Bowl history.

On February 3 a parade was held in the city of Pittsburgh to celebrate the victory. The town was excited. According to the Pittsburgh Post-Gazette an estimated 400,000 people attended. The City's name was ceremonially changed to "the City of Sixburgh" for the duration of 2009. Go Steelers. Amen to the 2008 season.

2009 Mike Tomlin #16

The 2009 Pittsburgh Steelers football team competed in their seventy-seventh season of Professional National Football League (NFL) football. The team was led by Mike Tomlin in his third season as head coach of the Steelers. .The record declined from 2008's 12-4 to 2009's 9-7. The defending Super Bowl Champions Steelers came in third in the AFC North and did not qualify for the playoffs.

The team thinkers in the front office had a lot of off-season work to do to keep the Steelers a vibrant team. The major goals were to retain most of the team's own free agents and to look to add talent primarily through the draft rather than free agent acquisitions. This had been the primary philosophy of the Steelers since Chuck Noll took over as head coach in 1969.

There were a number of other major items that needed to be accomplished such as extending the contracts of certain players who were coming into the final year of their contracts–such as linebacker and 2008 NFL Defensive Player of the Year, James Harrison, tight end Heath Miller, and tackle Max Starks. The overall objective was to keep the winning Super Bowl team intact as much as possible

The front office managed to accomplish their highest-priority task by signing Harrison on a six-year, $51.175 million contract. They were also successful in extending the contracts of Starks (four years, $26.3 million)[8] and Miller (six years, $35.3 million), both of whom were potential free agents after the season. Additionally, important contract extensions were accomplished with receiver Hines Ward (five years, $22.1 million), guard Chris Kemoeatu (five years, $20 million), center Justin Hartwig (4 years, $10 million) and defensive end Brett Kiesel (5 years, $18.885 million). Can you imagine Art Rooney having bought the whole team in 1933 for $2500.00?

The team's recognized needs coming into 2009 were seen as bolstering the offensive line and perfecting the performance of special teams, primarily at kick returner. Moreover, they had to replace free agent losses such as starting cornerback Bryant McFadden and number three wide receiver Nate Washington.

The team management were also looking at those elements of the team that were still vital but beginning to age -- Aaron Smith[13] and cornerback Deshea Townsend, 33 and 34 respectively at the start of the season. ESPN got their two cents in on the Steelers needs suggesting that their pre-draft needs (in order), were defensive end, offensive tackle, wide receiver and cornerback. With a 9-7 season in 2009, it was clear not all aspects of the needs were fulfilled.

The season after a Super Bowl is not always the best. Such was the case for the 2009 after winning all the marbles in 2008. They were coming off a season in which they compiled a 12–4 regular season record and capped the season by winning the franchise's record sixth Super Bowl. The team's coaching staff remained the same for the third consecutive year.

As the defending champions, the Steelers opened the season by hosting the NFL Kickoff Game on Thursday, September 10, 2009. They scored an overtime victory against the Tennessee Titans. The team compiled a 6–2 record over the season's first half, but then began a five-game losing streak which included losses to all three division opponents. Three late wins led to a 9–7 record, but the team failed to qualify for the playoffs. This was the third straight time the team has missed the playoffs following a Super Bowl victory; 1980and 2006 being the previous two. Mike Tomlin would have the team ready for 2010.

Games of the season

In the home and season opener on Thursday Sep 10, the Steelers beat the Tennessee Titans in OT in Heinz Field W (13-10). On Sunday Sep 20, at Chicago, the Bears beat the Steelers in Soldier Field, W (10-6). Then on Sep 27, at Cincinnati, the Bengals beat the Steelers in Paul Brown Stadium L (20-23). On Oct 4, my wedding anniversary, at home, the Steelers beat the San Diego Chargers in Heinz Field, W (38-28). At Detroit on Oct 11, the Steelers defeated the Lions at Ford Field W (28-20). On Oct 18, at home, the Steelers beat the Cleveland Browns, in Heinz Field W (27-14). At home against Minnesota on Oct 25, the Steelers beat the Vikings W (27-17) in Heinz Field. Nov 2 Bye Week.

On Monday Night on Nov. 9 at Denver, the Steelers beat the Broncos W (28–10) in Invesco Field at Mile High. After this Monday Night win, the Steelers lost five in a row. On Nov 15, at home, the Cincinnati Bengals beat the Steelers L (12–18) in Heinz Field CBS . At Kansas City on Nov 22, the Chiefs beat the Steelers in Arrowhead Stadium L (24–27). At Baltimore on Nov. 29, the Ravens beat the Steelers L (17–20) in M&T Bank Stadium. At home on Dec. 6, the Oakland Raiders edged out the Steelers L (24–27) in Heinz Field.

At Cleveland on Dec 10, the Browns beat the Steelers L (6–13) in Cleveland Browns Stadium. At home on Dec. 20, the Steelers nosed out the Green Bay Packers W (37–36) in Heinz Field. Fox on Dec. 27, the Steelers beat the Baltimore Ravens W (23–20) in Heinz Field. Then, in the regular season finale at Miami on Jan. 3, the Steelers beat the Dolphins W 30–24 in Land Shark Stadium.

2010 Mike Tomlin #16

The 2010 Pittsburgh Steelers football team competed in their seventy-eighth season of Professional National Football League (NFL) football. The team was led by Mike Tomlin in his fourth season as head coach of the Steelers. This was also the eleventh season under the leadership of general manager Kevin Colber. The record improved from 2009's 9-7 to 2010's 12-4. The defending Super Bowl Champions Steelers came in first in the AFC North and they made it to the playoffs but were beaten L (25-31) by Green Bay in Super Bowl XLV in their eighth Super Bowl appearance in a try for a seventh Super Bowl victory. The Steelers allowed the fewest points in the NFL in 2010, with 232 (14.5 points per game). It was a fine season with a disappointing ending.

After a 9-7 season, the Steelers looked to make some changes before the 2010 season began. They traded Santonio Holmes, and they endured the six-game suspension (then reduced to four games) of quarterback Ben Roethlisberger for off-the-field issues. The team did not re-sign free agent running back Willie Parker, who had been with the team since 2004. They added receiver Antwaan Randle El and linebacker Larry Foote, who were both with the team for their Super Bowl XL victory.

In the home and season opener on Sep 12, the Steelers beat the Atlanta Falcons in OT in Heinz Field W (15-9). On Sunday Sep 20, at Tennessee, the Steelers beat the Titans in LP Field W (19-12). Then on Sep 26, at Tampa Bay, the Steelers thumped the Buccaneers in Raymond James Stadium W (38-13). On Oct 3, at home, the Baltimore Ravens beat the Steelers in Heinz Field, L (14-17). Oct 10, Bye Week. On Oct 17, at home, the Steelers beat the Cleveland Browns, in Heinz Field W (28-10). At Miami in Sun Life Stadium, on Oct 24, the Steelers nosed out the Dolphins W (23-22) On Oct 31, at New Orleans the Saints beat the Steelers L (10-20) in at the Louisiana Superdome.

At Cincinnati on Mon day Night Nov. the Steelers beat the Bengals W 27–21 in Paul Brown Stadium. On Nov. 14, at home the New England Patriots beat the Steelers L (26–39) in Heinz Field. On Nov 21, at home, the Steelers pounded the Oakland Raiders W (35–3) in

Heinz Field. At Buffalo on Nov. 28, the Steelers beat the Bills in OT W (19–16) in Ralph Wilson Stadium. At Baltimore on Dec. 5, the Steelers beat the Ravens W (13–10) in M&T Bank Stadium.

On Dec. 12 at home, the Steelers beat the Cincinnati Bengals W (23–7) in Heinz Field. At home on Dec 19, the NY Jets beat the New Steelers L (17–22) in Heinz Field. On Thursday Night, Dec. 23, the Steelers beat the Carolina Panthers in Heinz Field W (27–3). In the final game of the regular season, on Jan 2, in Cleveland Browns Stadium, the Steelers lambasted the Cleveland Browns W (41–9).

AFC Divisional Playoffs January 15
Pittsburgh Steelers 31 Baltimore Ravens 24

Beginning their postseason at Heinz Field before 64,879, after a fine 12-4 season, the Steelers enjoyed reasonably good weather for football, 32 degrees and cloudy

This year, the Steelers entered the postseason as the AFC's No. 2 seed. They did not compete in the wild card playoffs but began their playoff run at home in the AFC Divisional Round against their AFC North rival, the #5 Baltimore Ravens, for the third time in the season. Pittsburgh got on the board first with an opening strike in the first quarter. It was a quick 1-yard touchdown run from running back Rashard Mendenhall.

The Ravens took the lead back with running back Ray Rice getting a 14-yard touchdown run, followed by defensive end Cory Redding returning a fumble 13 yards for a touchdown. Baltimore got even more in the second quarter as quarterback Joe Flacco completed a 4-yard touchdown pass to tight end Todd Heap.

The Steelers needed some fire and got it when they struck back to tie in the third quarter as quarterback Ben Roethlisberger found tight end Heath Miller on a 9-yard touchdown pass. Then, he found wide receiver Hines Ward on an 8-yard touchdown pass. Pittsburgh regained the lead in the fourth quarter with a 35-yard field goal from kicker Shaun Suisham, yet the Ravens tied the game with kicker Billy Cundiff getting a 24-yard field goal.

The Steelers soon afterwards got another score with a 1-yard touchdown run from Mendenhall. With this win, Pittsburgh improved its overall season record to 13–4.

Also, since the New York Jets defeated the top-seeded New England Patriots in the divisional round the next day, Pittsburgh would get to host the AFC Championship Game at Heinz Field the following week.

AFC Championship Game January 23, 2011
Pittsburgh Steelers 24 New York Jets 19

With the Patriots out of the picture, the Steelers hosted the Conference Championship game at Heinz Field before 66,662 after their fine 12-4 season, It was a cold, crisp day, 12 degrees and clear.

It was a nice advantage staying at home after the win against the Ravens. This game for the AFC Championship Game pitted the Steelers against the No. 6 New York Jets. The Steelers were prepared to avenge their Week 15 loss.

Pittsburgh started like the team meant business by scoring the first TD on a 1-yard run from running back Rashard Mendenhall. Pittsburgh added onto their lead in the second quarter with a 20-yard field goal from kicker Shaun Suisham, followed by a 2-yard touchdown run from quarterback Ben Roethlisberger, along with cornerback William Gay returning a fumble 19 yards for a touchdown. The Jets closed out the half with kicker Nick Folk getting a 42-yard field goal. The game would get closer, but this was a good start.

Mark Sanchez got New York going in the third quarter with a 45-yard touchdown pass to former Pittsburgh wide receiver Santonio Holmes. The Jets tried to keep it going in in the fourth quarter as Roethlisberger fumbled the snap and then got tackled by Mike DeVito for a safety. Sanchez then completed a 4-yard touchdown pass to wide receiver Jerricho Cotchery, yet Pittsburgh held the Jets to preserve the victory for the Steelers.

With the win, the Steelers improved their overall season record to 14-4 while also advancing to Super Bowl XLV, which would be played two weeks later. In the Super Bowl, unfortunately, Pittsburgh would be defeated by the NFC Champion, Green Bay Packers.

Super Bowl XLV February 6, 2011
Green Bay Packers 31 vs. Pittsburgh Steelers 25

This was the Steelers' eighth time in a Super Bowl, tying the record at the time with the Dallas Cowboys for the most appearances in Super Bowl history. They were denied their seventh ring, however, by the Green Bay Packers, who defeated them 31-25.

Super Bowl XLV was a great football game between the American Football Conference (AFC) champion Pittsburgh Steelers and the National Football Conference (NFC) champion Green Bay Packers to decide the National Football League (NFL) champion for the 2010 season. The Packers edged out the Steelers by the score of 31–25. The game was played on February 6, 2011, at Cowboys Stadium in Arlington, Texas, the first time the Super Bowl was played in the Dallas–Fort Worth area.

Not all Super Bowls have such title-abundant franchises competing. Coming into the game, the Packers held the most NFL championships with 12 (9 league championships prior to the Super Bowl era and 3 Super Bowl championships), while the Steelers held the most Super Bowl championships with 6. The Packers entered their fifth Super Bowl in team history and became the first number 6-seeded team in the NFC to compete in the Super Bowl, after posting a 10–6 regular season record. The Steelers finished the regular season with a 12–4 record, and advanced to a league-tying 8th Super Bowl appearance.

The Packers dominated most of the first half of Super Bowl XLV, jumping to a 21-3 lead before the Steelers brought it down to 21–10 just before halftime. After the teams exchanged touchdowns, the Steelers pulled within 28–25 midway through the fourth quarter with wide receiver Mike Wallace's 25-yard touchdown reception from quarterback Ben Roethlisberger and a two-point conversion. But the Packers came back and answered with Mason Crosby's 23-yard field goal with 2:07 remaining. They then prevented the Steelers from scoring on their final drive of the game. Packers quarterback Aaron Rodgers was named Super Bowl MVP, completing 24 of 39 passes for 304 yards and three touchdowns.

The game was decided in the fourth quarter, but Green Bay was winning most of the game. The Steelers were having bad luck. For example, on the first play of the fourth quarter, the Steelers lost their third turnover of the game when Mendenhall fumbled the ball while being tackled behind the line by Matthews and Ryan Pickett. Bishop recovered the ball and returned it 7 yards to the Packers 45.

Just five plays later on third down and 10, Rodgers completed a 38-yard pass to Nelson at the Steelers 2-yard line. Pittsburgh linebacker LaMar Woodley fortuitously sacked Rodgers for a 6-yard loss on the next play, but Rodgers picked himself up, dusted himself off, and on the next play threw an 8-yard touchdown pass to Jennings thereby increasing the Packers lead to 11 points -- 28–17.

Roethlisberger led the Steelers right back with 6 of 7 completions. After a 9-yard pass to tight end Matt Spaeth, he threw three completions to receiver Mike Wallace for 27 yards to the Green Bay 40-yard line. Then after a 15-yard completion to Ward, he finished the drive with a 25-yard touchdown pass to Wallace.

Pittsburgh went for two. On the two-point conversion play, Roethlisberger faked a handoff to Mendenhall and ran up to the line before pitching the ball to Randle El, who scored on an outside sweep, cutting the Steelers deficit to 3 points at 28–25.

There was just over 7 minutes left when Green Bay got the ball back. They soon found themselves facing third down and 10 after two plays, but Rodgers kept the drive going with a 31-yard completion to Jennings over the middle. Starks then ran 14 yards to the Steelers 30. Two plays later, James Jones caught a 21-yard pass at the 8. The Steelers defense kept Green Bay out of the end zone, forcing the Packers to settle for a 23-yard field goal by Mason Crosby that gave

Green Bay a 31–25 lead with 2:07 left in regulation. There was still an opportunity for Pittsburgh.

The Steelers did not get a good kickoff return and took over on their own 13-yard line following a penalty on the kickoff. On their first play, Roethlisberger completed a 15-yard pass to Miller. But after a 5-yard reception by Ward, his next three passes were incomplete, turning the ball over and allowing the Packers to run out the rest of the clock. Nice try but no cigar.

There were a ton of people across the world who saw this game including 111 million FOX viewers, breaking the record for the most-watched program in American television history. The game's attendance was 103,219, just short of the Super Bowl record 103,985 set in Super Bowl XIV at the Rose Bowl in Pasadena, California. The halftime show featured the American hip hop group The *Black Eyed Peas*, with additional performances by *Usher and Slash*.

2011 Mike Tomlin #16

The 2011 Pittsburgh Steelers football team competed in their seventy-ninth season of Professional National Football League (NFL) football. The team was led by Mike Tomlin in his fifth season as head coach of the Steelers. This was also the twelfth season under the leadership of general manager Kevin Colber. The record stayed the same from 2010-'s 12-4 to 2011's 12-4. The defending Super Bowl Champions Steelers came in second the AFC North and they made it to the playoffs for the wild card game but lost 29-23 in OT to the Denver Broncos. .

The Steelers played all of their home games at Heinz Field in Pittsburgh, Pennsylvania. The Steelers' defense allowed the fewest points, passing yards, and total yards in the 2011 NFL season. So close, yet…

In the season opener on Sep 11, the Baltimore Ravens pounded the Steelers in M& T Bank Stadium L (7-35). On Sep 18, at home, the Steelers shut out the Seattle Seahawks, W (24-0) in Heinz Field. On Sep 25, at Indianapolis, the Steelers beat the colts in Lucas Oil Stadium. At Houston on Oct 2, the Houston Texans beat the

Steelers L (10-17) in Reliant Stadium. On Oct 9 at home, the Steelers beat the Tennessee Titans W (38-17) in Heinz Field. At home again on Oct 16, the Steelers beat the Jacksonville Jaguars W (17-13) at Heinz Field. On Oct 23, at Arizona, the Steelers beat the Cardinals W (32-20) at University of Phoenix Stadium. Then, on Oct 30, at home, the Steelers beat the New England patriots W (25-17) in Heinz Field

At home on Nov 6, the Baltimore Ravens beat the Steelers L (20–23) in Heinz Field. At Cincinnati on Nov. 13 the Steelers beat the Cincinnati Bengals W (24–17) in Paul Brown Stadium. At Kansas City, on Nov 27, the Steelers beat the Kansas City Chiefs W (13–9) in Arrowhead Stadium. Then, on Dec 4, at home, the Steelers whipped the Cincinnati Bengals W (35–7) in Heinz Field.

On Dec. 8, the Steelers beat the Cleveland Browns W (14–3) in Heinz Field. At San Francisco on Dec. 19, the 49ers beat the Steelers L (3–20) in Candlestick Park. Then, on Sat. Dec. 24, the Steelers shutout the St. Louis Rams W (27–0) in Heinz Field. Then in the Season Finale, on Jan. 1, at Cleveland the Steelers beat the Browns W (13–9) in Cleveland Browns Stadium.

Postseason Wild Card Playoffs January 8, 2013
Pittsburgh Steelers 23 v Denver Broncos 29 in OT

This game was played in Sports Authority field in Mile High Stadium in Denver. It was great weather at 40 degrees and sunny—perfect day for a nice football game. For the Steelers, that's about all that was perfect.

Pittsburgh had a second of back-to-back 12-4 seasons and they were riding high. They were the AFC's number 5 seed, playing the number 4 seed, the 8–8 Denver Broncos in the wild card contest. Pittsburgh got off to a good start and they had a 6–0 lead after the first quarter. Then, things changed.

The Broncos got 20 unanswered points, and as a result they led 20–6 lead at halftime. The Steelers did regroup after the second quarter debacle and after that allowed just one Matt Prater field goal. They recovered a key fumble in the fourth quarter that set up the tying touchdown.

Pittsburgh had one last possession at the end of regulation, but Ben Roethlisberger was sacked while he prepared for a hail mary attempt. This forced overtime with the game tied at 23.

This game then became notable for being the first non-sudden death overtime game in NFL history, with the new playoff overtime rules. However, the new rules only applied if the team that got the ball first did not score a touchdown, because if a touchdown or safety was scored at any time, the game would end. This meant that only field goals could be kicked, and the game would not end without the other team gaining possession.

The Steelers OT bad luck began when they lost the overtime coin toss, and the Broncos elected to receive. Shaun Suisham delivered a kick out of the back of the end zone for a touchback, but on the first play, the Steeler defense allowed Demaryius Thomas to go from the Denver 20 all the way to the end zone for a touchdown, ending the Steelers' season. Amazing. I bet Mike Tomlin and the team would like to have that play back.

2012 Mike Tomlin #16

The 2012 Pittsburgh Steelers football team competed in their eightieth season of Professional National Football League (NFL) football. The team was led by Mike Tomlin in his sixth season as head coach of the Steelers. This was also the thirteenth season under the leadership of general manager Kevin Colber.The record declined substantially from 2011-'s 12-4 to 2012's 8-8. The Steelers came in third in AFC North and they did not make it to the playoffs.

In the season opener on Sep 11, at Denver, the Broncos beat the Steelers in Sports Authority Field in Mile High L (19-31). Then, at Heinz Field, the Steelers beat the New York Jets W (27-10). On Sep 23, at Oakland, the Raiders beat the Steelers L (31-34). Sept 30 Bye Week. Then at home, the Steelers beat the Philadelphia Eagles W (16-14) in Heinz Field. At Tennessee, the Titans beat the Steelers

L (23-26) in LP Field. Then, at Cincinnati on Oct 21, the Steelers beat the Bengals W (24-17) in Paul Brown Stadium. At home on Oct 28, the Steelers beat the Washington Redskins W (27-12) in Heinz. On Nov 4, at New York, the Steelers beat the Giants W (24-20, in Met Life Stadium.

On Nov 12, the Steelers beat the Kansas City Chiefs in OT W (16–13) in Heinz Field. On Nov 18, the Baltimore Ravens beat the Steelers L (10–13) in Heinz Field. On Nov 25 at Cleveland , the Browns beat the Steelers L (14–20) in Cleveland Browns Stadium. Then on December 2 at Baltimore, the Steelers beat the Ravens W (23–20) in M&T Bank Stadium.

On Dec 9 at home, the San Diego Chargers beat the Steelers L (24–34) in Heinz Field. At Dallas on Dec 16, the Cowboys beat the Steelers in OT L (24–27) in Cowboys Stadium. Then, on Dec 23, the Cincinnati Bengals beat the Steelers L (10–13) in Heinz Field. In the sixteenth and last game of the season on Dec 30, the Steelers beat the Cleveland Browns W (24–10) in Heinz Field.

2013 Mike Tomlin #16

The 2013 Pittsburgh Steelers football team competed in their eighty-first season of Professional National Football League (NFL) football. The team was led by Mike Tomlin in his seventh season as head coach of the Steelers. This was also the fourteenth season under the leadership of general manager Kevin Colber.The record stayed the same year to year from 2012-'s 8-8 to 2013's 8-8. The Steelers came in second in AFC North and they did not make it to the playoffs.

The Steelers had a chance at the playoffs 'til the end. The Ravens, Dolphins, and Chargers were 8–7 going into Week 17, while the Steelers were 7–8. This meant that the Steelers had to win and the Ravens, Dolphins, and Chargers all had to lose. Despite a win from the Steelers and losses from the Ravens and Dolphins, the Chargers went on to beat the Kansas City Chiefs 27–24 in overtime, taking the playoff spot. It was the first season since 1999 the Steelers would miss back-to-back postseason playoffs.

In the season and home opener on Sep 8, at Tennessee, the Titans defeated the Steelers in Heinz Field L (9-16) Then, at Paul Brown Stadium, the Cincinnati Bengals beat the Steelers L (10-20). On Sep 22, at home, the Chicago Bears beat the Steelers L (23-40) in Heinz Field. At Minnesota on Sep 29, the Vikings beat the Steelers L (27-34) in Wembley Stadium. In England. Oct 6 Bye Week. On Oct 13, at New York, the Steelers beat the Jets in Met Life Stadium W (19-6). At home on Oct 20, the Steelers beat the Baltimore Ravens W (19-16) in Heinz Field. At Oakland on Oct 27, the Raiders beat the Steelers in the Coliseum L (18-21). At New England in Gillette Stadium, on Nov 3, the Patriots smothered the Steelers L (33-55).

At home on Nov 10, the Steelers beat the Buffalo Bills W (23–10) in Heinz Field At home again on Nov 17 the Steelers beat the Detroit Lions W (37–27) in Heinz Field. At Cleveland, on Nov 24, the Steelers beat the Browns W (27–11) in FirstEnergy Stadium. At Baltimore, on Nov 28 the Ravens beat the Steelers L (20–22) in M&T Bank Stadium

On Dec 8 at home, the Miami Dolphins beat the Steelers L (28–34) in Heinz Field. At home on Dec 15, the Steelers beat the Cincinnati Bengals W (30–20) in Heinz Field. At Green Bay on Dec 22 in Lambeau Field, the Steelers beat the Packers W (38–31). Then the Steelers ended the season at home on Dec 29 hammering the Cleveland Browns W (20–7) in Heinz Field.

Top Steelers Players Le'Veon Bell

When we were finishing up this book in 2018, Le'Veon Bell's future with Pittsburgh was in doubt and he was not working out with the team.

Nonetheless, few will argue that this Pittsburgh Steelers running back, Le'Veon Bell, has been arguably the best running back in the NFL for the last two years. NFL Spin Zone recently said they "could not agree more."

"Le'Veon Bell has been a force in this league for years, now. Even if his offseason is being spent searching for a long-term deal instead of improving, he's still considered one of the most exciting players to look forward to in 2018.

"For the second-straight season, Bell has surpassed 1,200 yards on the ground and 600 yards receiving, with 11 total touchdowns in 2017. Averaging 128.9 yards per game last season, Bell proved to be Pittsburgh's greatest force all over the field.

"NFL Spin Zone took on the challenge of ranking all 32 starting running backs. Not all Steelers fans are going to be happy with the rankings. Despite missing all of last offseason and still performing well, Randy Gurzi acknowledges that not showing up over the summer is hurting his stock.

"Gurzi ranks Bell as the second best starting running back in 2018. Bell could've topped the list with his talent and versatility. He's a game changer at running back and receiver. But the more time he misses during the summer, the less of certain anyone is of his success in the future.

"If Bell was attending offseason workouts, he would probably rank first. Gurley proved he's right on Bell's level. With him participating in Rams' OTAs and summer camps, he gets an early leg up on Bell before the season starts.

At this point, the future is pretty shady for Bell. No one knows if he'll be in Pittsburgh after 2018. For now, though, the hope is that he continues the same success he's had the last two years.
NEXT: 4 players who must improve in 2018

?No. 2 isn't bad in a league full of talented runners. Even without showing up during the summer, Bell is expected to be a top three running back in every aspect. Something that'll keep the Steelers as a Super Bowl favorite in 2018.

2014 Mike Tomlin #16

The 2014 Pittsburgh Steelers football team competed in their eighty-second season of Professional National Football League (NFL) football. The team was led by Mike Tomlin in his eighth season as head coach of the Steelers. This was also the fifteenth season under the leadership of general manager Kevin Colber. The record improved from year to year from 2013-'s 8-8 to 2014's 11-5. The Steelers came in first in the AFC North and they made the playoffs in the wild card round.

It's tough to believe that we have chronicled 40 years of games since the Steelers won their first Super Bowl. Terry Bradshaw still looks to me like he can suit up on Sundays and help the team. Don't you think?

The Steelers made a big celebration of the honor of the 40th anniversary of their first Super Bowl winning team, Super Bowl IX. They put this on during their Week 13 game against the New Orleans Saints at Heinz Field on November 30. (The Steelers played the Super Bowl at Tulane Stadium that year.)

The team wore a special patch and honored the players at halftime. Though it also serves as the team's annual alumni weekend, the team did not wear their alternate 1934 "Bumblebee" throwbacks for this game. Instead, the Steelers wore the "Bumblebee" jerseys vs. the Indianapolis Colts on October 26.

The Steelers managed to improve from their 8-8 record from each of their previous two seasons with their week 15 victory against the Atlanta Falcons, and ensured their first winning season since 2011. They also clinched a playoff berth for the first time since that same year with their week 16 victory over the Kansas City Chiefs. The Steelers won the AFC North division title, but the success was overwhelming, and they lost to the Baltimore Ravens in the Wild Card round of the playoffs by a score of 30–17.

The Steelers were so good, yet they did not close the deal. They became the first team in NFL history to have a 4,500-yard passer, 1,500-yard receiver and 1,300-yard rusher in the same season.

In the season and home opener on Sep 7, Steelers defeated the Cleveland Browns in Heinz Field W (20-27) Then, at M & T Bank Stadium, on Sep 11, the Baltimore Ravens beat the Steelers L (6-26). At Carolina, on Sep 21, in Bank of America Stadium, the Steeles beat the Panthers W (37-19). On Sep 28, at home, the Tampa Bay Buccaneers beat the Steelers L (24-27) in Heinz Field. At Jacksonville on Oct 5, the Steelers beat the Jaguars W (17-9). in EverBank Field. At Cleveland, in First Energy Stadium, the Browns beat the Steelers L (10-31) . At home on Oct 20, the Steelers beat the Houston Texans W (30-23) in Heinz Field. At Indianapolis on Oct 20, , the Steelers beat the Colts in a Shootout W (51-34) in Heinz Field.

On Nov 2, the Steelers beat the Baltimore Ravens W (43–23) in Heinz Field. At New York, on Nov 9 the Jets beat the Steelers L (13–20) in MetLife Stadium. At Tennessee on Nov 23, the Steelers beat the Titans W (27–24). Then, on November 30, the New Orleans Saints beat the Steelers L (32–35) in Heinz Field.

At Cincinnati on December 7 the Steelers beat the Bengals W 42–21 in Paul Brown Stadium. At Atlanta, on Dec 14the Steelers beat the Falcons W (27–20) in the Georgia Dome. Then, on December 21, the Steelers beat the Kansas City Chiefs W (20–12) in Heinz Field. At home for the season finale, on Dec 28 the Steelers bat the Cincinnati Bengals W (27–17) in Heinz Field.

2015 Mike Tomlin #16

The 2015 Pittsburgh Steelers football team competed in their eighty-third season of Professional National Football League (NFL) football. The team was led by Mike Tomlin in his ninth season as head coach of the Steelers. This was also the sixteenth season under the leadership of general manager Kevin Colber.The record declined from year to year from 2014-'s 11-5 to 2015's 10-6. The Steelers came in 2nd in the AFC North and they made the playoffs.

For the first time since 2003, safety Troy Polamalu was not on the opening day roster, as he announced his retirement on April 9. The Steelers clinched the last AFC playoff spot, finishing tied with the New York Jets with a 10–6 record but winning the tiebreaker over the Jets based on a better record vs. common opponents. The Steelers defeated the Cincinnati Bengals in the Wild Card round but lost to the eventual Super Bowl champion Denver Broncos in the Divisional round.

In the season opener on Sep 10, the New England Patriots defeated the Steelers in Gillette Stadium L (21-28). Then, at Heinz Field, on Sep 20, the Steelers shellacked the San Francisco 49ers W (43-18). At St. Louis, on Sep 27, the Steelers defeated the Rams in the Edward Jones Dome W (12-6). On Oct 1, at home, the Baltimore Ravens beat the Steelers in OT L (20-23) in Heinz Field. At San Diego, on Oct 12, the Steelers defeated the Chargers W (24-20) in Qualcomm Stadium. At home on Oct 18, the Steelers beat the Arizona Cardinals W (25-13) in Heinz Field. At Kansas City on oct 25, the Chiefs beat the Steelers L (13-23) in Arrowhead Stadium. On Nov 1, in Heinz Field, the Cincinnati Bengals beat the Steelers L (13-23).

At home on Nov 8, the Steelers beat the Oakland Raiders W (38–35) in Heinz Field. On November 15 at home, the Steelers beat the Cleveland Browns W (30–9) in Heinz Field. On November 29 at Seattle, the Seahawks beat the Steelers L (30–39) on CenturyLink Field. On Dec 6 at home, the Steelers smothered the Indianapolis Colts W (45–10) in Heinz Field
1
At Cincinnati on Dec 13, the Steelers beat the Bengals W (33–20) in Paul Brown Stadium. At home on Dec 20, the Steelers beat the Denver Broncos W (34–27) in Heinz Field. At Baltimore, on Dec 27, the Ravens beat the Steelers L (17–20) in M&T Bank Stadium. In the season finale, on Jan 3, at Cleveland, the Steelers defeated the Browns W (28–12) in FirstEnergy Stadium

AFC Wild Card Game January 8, 2016
Pittsburgh Steelers 18, Cincinnati Bengals 16

Before 63,257 at Paul Brown Stadium in Cincinnati Ohio, with 51-degree weather, what was supposed to be a light rain turned out to be a rain-soaked vicious battle between two AFC North rivals, filled with injuries and personal fouls on both sides.

The Bengals seemed to start out behind 15–0, but they had had the ball enough to punt four times before they got behind. Then, out of nowhere, they got the spark and scored three times in the fourth quarter to take a 16–15 lead over Pittsburgh. Until the final whistle, nothing in pro-football is permanent.

With less than a minute left in the game, two consecutive personal fouls were called against the Cincinnati defense. The term shooting yourself in the foot comes to mind as this helped the Steelers get close enough for Chris Boswell to make a 35-yard field goal with 18 seconds left on the clock. The Steelers moved on to the Divisional Playoffs.

The game began as a defensive struggle with both teams punting at the end of its first eight drives. With less than six minutes left in the second quarter, Bengals linebacker Vontaze Burfict forced a fumble from Markus Wheaton that safety George Iloka recovered on the Cincinnati 47-yard line. But a few plays later, Bengals quarterback AJ McCarron fired an interception right to Antwon Blake, who returned it 35 yards to the Bengals' 41-yard line.

This was quickly followed by A Ben Roethlisberger 23-yard completion to Antonio Brown on the next drive, setting up Boswell's 39-yard field goal. Following a punt, Roethlisberger completed a 16-yard pass to running back Fitzgerald Toussaint and a 24-yard pass to Wheaton – with a personal foul penalty on safety Shawn Williams adding another 15 yards – to set up Boswell's 30-yard field goal just before halftime. Despite the Steelers' slim 6–0 lead, they had dominated the stat sheet, holding Cincinnati to just 56 yards and two first downs.

The second half started with the Bengals going for a score when Jeremy Hill broke free for a 38-yard run to the Steelers' 29-yard line. But on the next play, McCarron lost a fumble due to a hit by linebacker Jarvis Jones. Defensive end Cam Thomas recovered the ball and ended up losing it while being tackled, then defensive back William Gay picked it up and returned it for a touchdown.

Replays showed that Thomas was down by contact before he lost the fumble, and a 15-yard penalty against Gay for excessive celebration moved the ball all the way back to Pittsburgh's 36-yard line. Receiver Martavis Bryant's 44-yard run on an end-around play then set up Boswell's 34-yard field goal that gave the Steelers a 9–0 lead.

Following another punt, Roethlisberger completed a 60-yard pass to Brown on the Bengals' 10-yard line. Then he threw a pass in the back of the end zone to Bryant, who made a diving somersault catch and maintained possession for a touchdown by pinning the ball against one leg while falling to the ground. The two-point attempt failed, so the score remained 15–0.

Cincinnati came back to the Steelers' 23-yard line but committed another turnover when running back Giovani Bernard lost a fumble that was forced and recovered by linebacker Ryan Shazier. He had leveled Bernard with a devastating helmet leading hit that knocked the running back out of the game.

Moving to the last play of the third quarter, Burfict sacked Roethlisberger for a 12-yard loss. Pittsburgh had to punt from their own -yard line. This play temporarily knocked Roethlisberger out of the game with a shoulder injury.

After Jordan Berry's 41-yard punt gave the Bengals a first down on the Pittsburgh 46-yard line, Steelers defensive back Will Allen was called on a 42-yard pass interference penalty trying to cover A. J. Green. Hill then got the ball into the end zone with consecutive carries. He got in on his second try, a 1-yard touchdown run that made the score 15–7.

With Big Ben on the bench, Landry Jones led the Steelers on their next drive. Jordan Todman rushed for a 25-yard gain on the second play. But Jones was nailed with for an 11-yard sack by Carlos Dunlap and this forced the Steelers to punt.

McCarron started the Bengals' drive off with two completions to Hill for 24 total yards. McCarron soon faced a 4th-and-2 situation but converted with a 9-yard completion to Marvin Jones. Then with a 3rd-and-7, he launched a 25-yard touchdown pass to Green. After their two-point conversion failed, the Bengals were ready for a victory celebration with a 16–15 lead and just 1:45 left.

On the first play after the kickoff, Landry Jones threw an interception to Burfict on the Steelers' 26-yard line. He celebrated by running all the way through the tunnel. Shazier forced a fumble from Hill that was recovered by defensive back Ross Cockrell. Would the Steelers get the job done?

They were their own 11-yard line with 1:23 left, when Big ben Roethlisberger returned to the game to lead the Steelers 74 yards in nine plays to get the winning score. It started with several short completions which got the ball to the 37-yard line, Pittsburgh did not make their first down on three attempts and were facing a 4th-and-3. Big Ben his Brown's for a 12-yard reception.

On the next play, with just 22 seconds left, Roethlisberger threw a pass intended for Brown. The pass was incomplete, but Burfict was flagged for a personal foul for contact with Brown's helmet. Brown was injured on the play, and as he was being attended and officials were dealing with both teams, Adam Jones was flagged for a personal foul after an altercation with Steelers linebackers coach Joey Porter, giving the Steelers another 15 yards and moving the ball to the Bengals' 17-yard line.

On the next play, Boswell kicked a 35-yard field goal with 18 seconds left to win the game for Pittsburgh.

Ben Roethlisberger completed 18 of 31 passes for 221 yards and a touchdown, while Brown caught seven passes for 119 yards and Todman was the game's leading rusher with 65 yards. Shazier had 13 tackles – nine of which were solo tackles – a pair of forced fumbles, and a fumble recovery.

AJ McCarron completed 23 of 41 passes for 213 yards, with a touchdown and an interception. Hill rushed for 50 yards and a touchdown, while also catching three passes for 27 yards. Green caught five passes for 71 yards and a touchdown, while Burfict had six tackles, a sack, an interception, and a forced fumble. The Steelers began preparation for the Divisional Championship game the following week.

AFC Divisional Championship January 17, 2016
Denver Broncos 23, Pittsburgh Steelers 16

At the Sports Authority Field at Mile High in Denver Colorado the Steelers and Broncos basked in sunny 43-degree weather before 76,956 in their encounter for the AFC Divisional Championship.

It was one of those tough defensive struggles in which both teams could work the ball into the end zone once, Denver looked like the game was theirs when they pulled ahead by scoring 11 points in the final three minutes of the game.

The Broncos started the scoring when after the opening possession, Broncos safety Omar Bolden returned a punt 42 yards to the Pittsburgh 30-yard line. This set up a 28-yard field goal by Brandon McManus. Later in the same quarter, Britton Colquit sailed a 57-yard punt pinning the Steelers back at their own 3-yard line.

Pittsburgh could not squeeze out a first down with this drive and they did not punt well. Jordan Berry's 27-yard punt gave Denver a first down on the Steelers 31. Despite a great starting position, the Broncos did not get into the end zone and they settled for another McManus 3-pointer to grab a 6–0 lead.

Pittsburgh found some fire in their step and they stormed 80 yards in just five plays. First, Roethlisberger completed a 23-yard pass to receiver Martavis Bryant. Then Bryant grabbed his part of a reverse and raced 40 yards to the Broncos 16-yard line. Fitzgerald Toussaint got the score after two carries; the first for 15 yards and the second a 1-yard score that gave Pittsburgh a 7–6 lead with less than two minutes left in the first quarter.

Next time with the ball, Roethlisberger's 58-yard completion to Darrius Heyward-Bey set up a 43-yard Chris Boswell field goal. Pittsburgh was then up 0–6. Denver then turned the ball over with an incomplete pass on 4th-and-3.

Late in the second quarter, Berry booted a 50-yard punt that gave the Broncos the ball at their own 5-yard line. But a 34-yard burst by running back C. J. Anderson sparked a 62-yard drive then ended with McManus' 51-yard field goal, cutting the score to 10–9 on the last play of the first half.

Denver was forced to punt of the first drive of the second half, and then the Steelers put together a nice 69-yard scoring drive featuring a 58-yard reception by Bryant. Boswell finished it with a 28-yard field goal, increasing the Steelers lead to 13–9. Touchdowns were tough to come by.

Denver had to punt again on their next drive, and Colquitt once again whacked a big one 51-yards down the field to the Steelers 6-yard line. Pittsburgh could not get a first down, and Berry got them out of the jam with a 43-yard punt. Denver took over on their own 47-yard line. They moved the ball 30 yards. It was enough for McManus to make a 41-yard field goal, trimming their deficit to one point at 13–12.

Pittsburgh got the ball back and took off to the Broncos 34-yard line, where they were stopped cold. They chose to punt instead of going for the long field goal. The Broncos then also punted, and the Steelers came right back to the Denver 34-yard line after three consecutive Roethlisberger completions totaling 39 total yards.

On the very next play, safety Bradley Roby forced a fumble from Toussaint that was recovered by linebacker DeMarcus Ware. This was the first turnover of the game.

With 9:52 left in the game, 39-year old Broncos quarterback Peyton Manning took to the field to spark his team and he came through by leading the team 65 yards in 13 plays for the go-ahead score. The key play of the drive was a 31-yard completion from Manning to rookie receiver Bennie Fowler on 3rd-and-12 from the Broncos 33-yard line.

Running back Ronnie Hillman also made a big impact in this series, with five carries for 18 yards. After Fowler's catch, the Broncos would not face another third down on this drive until the last play, when Anderson converted a 3rd-and-goal with a 1-yard touchdown run. Then Manning completed a pass to Demaryius Thomas for a 2-point conversion, giving the Broncos a 20–13 lead with three minutes left on the clock. Would the Steelers be able to come back?

Pittsburgh started off their next drive with an 18-yard catch by Bryant, but soon faced 4th-and-5 on their own 43-yard line with less than two minutes left. They tried to pick up a first down, but Ware sacked Roethlisberger for a 13-yard loss. Taking over at the Steelers 30-yard line, Denver forced Pittsburgh to use up all their timeouts with three consecutive running plays. Then McManus kicked a 45-yard field goal that gave the Broncos a 23–13 lead with 53 seconds to go.

There was a 20-yard pass interference penalty on safety T. J. Ward and a 22-yard reception by Bryant enabled Boswell to bring the deficit back to one score with a 47-yard field goal. But Anderson eliminated any chance of a comeback by recovering Boswell's ensuing onside kick. The Steelers were out of the playoffs.

2016 Mike Tomlin #16

The 2016 Pittsburgh Steelers football team competed in their eighty-fourth season of Professional National Football League (NFL) football. The team was led by Mike Tomlin in his tenth season as head coach of the Steelers. This was also the seventeenth season under the leadership of general manager Kevin Colber. The record improved from year to year from 2015-'s 10-6 to 2016's 11-5. The Steelers came in 1st^d in the AFC North and they made the playoffs, winning the wild card and divisional championships and losing the conference championship.

For the first time since 2004, tight end Heath Miller was not on the opening day roster, as he announced his retirement on February 19,

2016. The Steelers were the first team since the 2011 Green Bay Packers to play on both Thanksgiving and Christmas Day. The Steelers won the AFC North for the second time in three years and made the playoffs for the third straight year.

The team also improved upon their 10–6 record from 2015. Le'Veon Bell made his career first playoff appearance with the Steelers in the 2016–17 playoffs. The Steelers went on to defeat the Miami Dolphins in the Wild Card round and the Kansas City Chiefs in the Divisional round before losing to the eventual Super Bowl champion New England Patriots 36–17 in the AFC Championship Game. This was the Steelers' first appearance in the AFC Championship Game since the 2010–11 NFL Season. This was also the final season under the ownership of Dan Rooney, as he died on April 13, 2017.[1]

In the season opener on Sep 12, the Steelers defeated the Washington Redskins in FedEx Field W (38-16). Then, at Heinz Field, on Sep 18, the Steelers beat the Cincinnati Bengals W (24-16). At Philadelphia on Sep 27, the Steelers were defeated by the Eagles L (3-34) in Lincoln Financial Field. On Oct 2, at home, the Steelers pummeled the Kansas City Chiefs W 43-14) in Heinz Field. At San Diego, on Oct 9, the Steelers defeated the New York Jets (31-13) in Heinz Field. At Miami on Oct 16, the Dolphins beat the Steelers L (15-30) in the Hard Rock Stadium. At home, on Oct 23, the New England Patriots beat the Steelers in Heinz Field L (16-27). Oct 30, Bye Week. On Nov 6, at Baltimore, the Ravens beat the Steelers L (14-21) in M&T Stadium.

At home on Nov 13, the Dallas Cowboys beat the Steelers L (30–35) in Heinz Field. At Cleveland on Nov 20, the Steelers beat the Browns in at FirstEnergy Stadium W (24–9). At Indianapolis on Nov 24 , the Steelers beat the Colts W (28–7) in Lucas Oil Stadium. At home in Heinz Field on December 4, the Steelers beat the New York Giants W (24–14).

At Buffalo on Dec 11, Pittsburgh defeated the Bills W (27–20) in New Era Field. At Cincinnati on Dec 18, the Steelers beat the Bengals in Paul Brown Stadium W (24–20). Then, at home on Dec 25, the Steelers beat the Baltimore Ravens in Heinz Field W (31–27)

. On January 1, at home in OT, the Steelers beat the Cleveland Browns in the season finale in Heinz Field W (27–24).

Wild Card Playoffs Sunday, January 8, 2017
AFC: Pittsburgh Steelers 30, Miami Dolphins 12

When Miami and Pittsburgh played on Oct 16, Miami racked up 474 yards and they whopped the Steelers 30–15. This game played before 62,726 in 17-degree weather at Heinz Field would have a very different outcome. Pittsburgh pounded Miami for 387 yards, forced three turnovers, recorded five sacks and scored three touchdowns in the first half on the way to a great 18-point win. There was little doubt.

The Steelers drove 85 yards after the opening kickoff in 5 plays, scoring on Ben Roethlisberger's pass to Antonio Brown, who hauled in the short screen and took it 50 yards to the end zone. Then after a punt, the Steelers moved the ball 90 yards in 6 plays on the way to a 62-yard touchdown completion from Roethlisberger to Brown.

Miami responded this time, helped by Kenyan Drake's 33-yard kickoff return to the 41-yard line. When faced with 3rd-and-13 after two plays, Matt Moore completed a 36-yard pass to receiver Kenny Stills, setting up Andrew Franks' 38-yard field goal cutting Pittsburgh's lead to 11 points at 14–3.

However, after getting the ball back, Steelers running back Le'Veon Bell carried the ball 9 times for 79 yards on a 10–play, 83-yard drive that ended with his 1-yard touchdown run, giving the team a 20–3 lead after Chris Boswell missed the extra point. The Steelers were on a roll.

The Dolphins then took off for 39 yards in 12 plays, and they scored when Franks nailed a 47-yard field goal with less than 5 minutes left in the second quarter. The Steelers came back with a drive to the Dolphins' 34-yard line. There was 1:12 left on the clock. Roethlisberger threw an interception on a pass destined for the outstretched hands of Brown, but the ball bounced off him and it was intercepted by safety Michael Thomas.

He took the ball 16 yards to the Dolphins' 27-yard line. Miami then moved the ball to the Steelers' 8-yard line. This drive included a 37-yard completion from Moore to DeVante Parker. But on the next play, Moore lost a fumble while being sacked by James Harrison and Steelers defensive end Stephon Tuitt recovered the ball, allowing Pittsburgh to go into the half maintaining their 20–6 lead.

Soon after the third quarter action began, safety Mike Mitchell forced a fumble while sacking Moore. Leterrius Walton recovered for the Steelers at their 41-yard line. Bell then rushed 3 times for 49 yards on the way to a 34-yard Boswell field goal that increased their lead to 23–6.

Then after the kickoff, linebacker Ryan Shazier intercepted a pass from Moore and returned it 10 yards to the Dolphins' 25-yard line. Miami's defense forced a 4th down, but a neutral zone infraction penalty against Dolphins defensive back Tony Lippett on the field goal attempt gave Pittsburgh a new set of downs.

The Steelers took full advantage of the opportunity, scoring on Bell's 8-yard touchdown run that made the score 30–6 with 2 minutes left in Q3. Miami came back with a drive to the Steelers' 42-yard line but lost the ball when Tuitt tackled Moore for a 2-yard gain on 4th-and-4.

Miami finally got its first TD in the fourth quarter – with 5:57 left. They moved the ball 70 yards in 9 plays and scored on Moore's 4-yard pass to running back Damien Williams. After a failed onside kick attempt, the Dolphins got one last chance to score when Xavier Howard intercepted Roethlisberger's pass and returned it 11 yards to the Miami 43-yard line. But the Steelers created a turnover on downs at the Steelers' 33-yard line and ran out the clock to win the game.

Roethlisberger was on the mark with 13 of 18 passes for 197 yards and two touchdowns, with 2 interceptions. Brown caught 5 passes for 124 yards and two scores, while Bell rushed 29 times for 167 yards – surpassing the previous franchise playoff record of 158 yards set by Franco Harris in Super Bowl IX – and a touchdown.

Linebacker Lawrence Timmons had 14 tackles (8 solo) and 2 sacks. James Harrison had 10 tackles (6 solo), 1.5 sacks and a forced fumble. Moore finished with 29 completions on 36 passing attempts for 298 yards and a touchdown, with one interception. His top receiver was Jarvis Landry, who caught 11 passes for 102 yards. Pittsburgh was off to the Divisional Playoffs looking for the Super Bowl.

AFC Divisional Championship January 15, 2017 Pittsburgh Steelers 18, Kansas City Chiefs 16[edit]

Oh, the weather outside was frightful so the 75,678 fans lined up to see the game in Arrowhead Stadium in Kansas City had to sit around from the proposed 1:05 PM start for about seven hours until 8:00 PM Ironically, because of the time pushback, this was the first ever divisional round playoff game in NFL history to premiere on Sunday Night Football.

Although Pittsburgh was unable to get into the end zone all night, Chris Boswell's nailed a postseason record of six field goals, which was just enough for the Steelers to become the first team to win a playoff game without scoring a touchdown since the 2006. Indianapolis Colts on their run to a victory in Super Bowl XLI.

Pittsburgh scored on the game's opening drive, taking the ball 65 yards in 11 plays on the way to Boswell's 22-yard field goal. Kansas City quickly struck back after Demetrius Harris returned Boswell's short kickoff 25 yards to their 45-yard line. The Chiefs then drove 55 yards in six plays, including a 21-yard catch by Travis Kelce, to score on Alex Smith's 5-yard touchdown pass to Albert Wilson, giving them a 7–3 lead.

Pittsburgh came right back, with Big Ben's 52-yard completion to Antonio Brown leading to another Boswell field goal. This made the score 7–6. On their next drive, they went 53 yards in 14 plays, scoring on Boswell's third field goal, to put them up 9–7 lead. At this point, there was just over 9 minutes left in the half.

Pittsburgh got another chance to score when linebacker Ryan Shazier intercepted a pass from Smith on the Chiefs' 44-yard line.

Three plays later, Roethlisberger threw an interception to Eric Berry in the end zone. Kansas City ended up punting after three plays and Brown returned it 6 yards to the Chiefs' 45-yard line.

Le'Veon Bell took over and carried the ball 5 times for 32 yards on a drive that ended with Boswell's 4th field goal, this one from 45 yards, increasing the Steelers lead to 12–7. Shortly before halftime, the Steelers had another scoring chance when defensive back Artie Burns recovered a fumble from Charcandrick West on the Chiefs' 40-yard line. Roethlisberger then completed a 29-yard pass to Brown, but he was tackled on the 11-yard line as time expired.

With its first possession of the second half, Pittsburgh's Bell carried the ball five times for 49 yards, including a 38-yard rush on the first play, as the team drove to a 43-yard Boswell field goal that put them up 15–7. Both teams had to punt on their next possessions and Jordan Berry's 35-yard kick gave Kansas City the ball with good field position on the Steelers' 46-yard line.

QB Smith then completed a 20-yard pass to Jeremy Maclin that set up Cairo Santos' 48-yard field goal, cutting their deficit to 15–10 with 10 seconds left in the third quarter. Roethlisberger then nailed completions to Eli Rogers and Jesse James for gains for 14 and 23 yards respectively on their next drive moved the team into position for Boswell to kick a record-setting sixth field goal of the game, which he made from 43 yards to give the team an 18–10 lead.

For the Chiefs, Smith then hit Kelce for a 24-yard gain on their first play and then Spencer Ware gained 11 yards on the ground. After a penalty pushed them into a 2nd-and-25, Smith completed a 17-yard pass to Kelce and a 12-yard completion to Chris Conley on 4th-and-8 allowed them to keep the ball. Several plays later, they faced 4th-and-2 on the Steelers' 4-yard line; but they converted again with Smith's 3-yard pass to fullback Anthony Sherman. Ware scored on a 1-yard touchdown run on the next play that cut their deficit to 18–16. It was getting tense at Arrowhead Stadium

Smith got the two-point conversion with a pass to Harris, but it was negated by a holding penalty on Eric Fisher as he tried to block an outside blitz from linebacker James Harrison. Their second attempt was incomplete.

With 2:43 left and one timeout remaining, Kansas City was still fighting to win. They still had a chance to get the ball back, especially after Justin Gilbert was tackled on the 5-yard line during the kick return. However, Roethlisberger was on the mark and not about to give up the ball. He completed passes to Rogers and Brown for gains of 5 and 7 yards respectively. This gave the Steelers a first down, which allowed the team to run out the clock, and get the team ready for the Conference Championship the following week.

AFC Championship Game January 22, 2017
New England Patriots 36, Pittsburgh Steelers 17

New England had recently become a Pittsburgh nemesis. The Patriots had not begun their resurgence to prominence in football when the Steelers along with Bradshaw and Noll were tearing up the gridiron with four Super Bowl Championships.

The Patriots advanced to their seventh Super Bowl in the last 16 seasons under quarterback Tom Brady and coach Bill Belichick. The weather was balmy for the New England area and the 66,829 fans enjoyed 41 degrees weather and the clouds kept the earth's heat from escaping. The Patriots wacked the Steelers with 431 yards and 26 first downs.

Pittsburgh's Roethlisberger and Pittsburgh's offense did not lay down on the job with 368 yards, but could only score 17 points, eight of them on a touchdown late in the game with the outcome already decided. Meanwhile, the Steelers' rushing attack, that had been so critical to their earlier playoff wins, was crippled by an early injury to running back Le'Veon Bell, finishing the game with just 54 total yards on the ground.

On the opening drive, Brad hit a 41-yard completion to Julian Edelman, which set up Stephen Gostkowski's 31-yard field goal. This gave the Pats a 3–0 lead less than two minutes into the game. Following several punts, New England went off on an 80-yard, 11-play drive, the longest gain being a 26-yard catch by receiver Chris

Hogan. Brady finished it off with a 16-yard touchdown pass to Hogan, for a 10–0 lead.

It was on the second play of Pittsburgh's next drive that Bell suffered a game-ending groin injury. However, his replacement DeAngelo Williams caught two passes for nine yards and rushed four times for 25 yards, the last carry a five-yard touchdown run to complete the 13-play, 84-yard drive early in the second quarter. Chris Boswell missed the extra point, with the score remaining 10–6.

New England answered right away, moving 82 yards in nine plays and scoring on Brady's 34-yard touchdown pass to Hogan on a flea flicker play. Pittsburgh then moved the ball to the Patriots' 19-yard line, where Ben Roethlisberger threw a pass to tight end Jesse James that was ruled a touchdown, but a replay review determined James was down on the 1-yard line. On the next play, Williams was dropped for a one-yard loss by Dont'a Hightower and Patrick Chung. On second down, Williams was tackled for a three-yard loss by nose tackle Vincent Valentine. On third down, Roethlisberger's pass was incomplete, so the team was forced to settle for Boswell's field goal to make the score 17–9. Lady Luck was not shining.

The Patriots dominated the second half, overpowering the Steelers with four unanswered scores. After forcing them to punt, New England drove 55 yards in nine plays, 24 of them coming on a catch by Hogan. Gostkowski finished the drive with a 47-yard field goal that put the team up 20–9. Following another punt, Brady's 39-yard completion to Hogan led to a one-yard touchdown by LeGarrette Blount, giving the team a 27–9 lead with 2:44 left in the third quarter.

On the first play after the kickoff, Kyle Van Noy forced a fumble from Eli Rogers that was recovered by linebacker Rob Ninkovich on the Steelers' 28-yard line. Brady completed an 18-yard pass to Edelman on the next play, and eventually found him in the end zone for a 10-yard touchdown pass. Gostkowski missed the extra point, but the Patriots had effectively put the game away with a 33–9 lead going into the fourth quarter.

In the fourth quarter, it was all but over. The Steelers drove to New England's 2-yard line but turned the ball over on downs. Then after a punt, Eric Rowe intercepted a pass from Roethlisberger and returned it 37 yards to the Steelers' 32-yard line, leading to a Gostkowski field goal that increased New England's lead to 36–9.

Roethlisberger's eventually hist a 30-yard touchdown pass to Cobi Hamilton and a subsequent 2-point conversion pass to Williams that made the final score 36–17. Brady completed 32 of his 42 passing attempts for 384 yards and three touchdowns. Hogan caught nine passes for 180 yards and two touchdowns, while Edelman had eight receptions for 118 yards and a touchdown. Roethlisberger threw for 314 yards, with a touchdown and an interception. This game got away from the Steelers.

2017 Mike Tomlin #16

The 2017 Pittsburgh Steelers football team competed in their eighty-third season of Professional National Football League (NFL) football. The team was led by Mike Tomlin in his eleventh season as head coach of the Steelers. This was also the eighteenth season under the leadership of general manager Kevin Colber. The record improved from year to year from 2016-'s 11-5 to 2017's 13-3. The Steelers came in 1st^d in the AFC North and they made the playoffs.

The Steelers won the AFC North division title for the second consecutive season with a 39–38 win over the Baltimore Ravens in Week 14, and they got a first-round playoff bye for the first time since 2010 following a 34–6 win over the Houston Texans in Week 16. In the Divisional Round however, the Steelers lost to the Jacksonville Jaguars by a score of 45–42 after falling behind 28–14 at halftime. After their loss, the Steelers were criticized for looking past the Jaguars and anticipating a rematch with the New England Patriots. With a fine record of 13-3, the Steelers posted their best mark since 2004.

In the season opener on Sep 10, the Steelers beat the Cleveland Browns in First energy Stadium W (21-18). Then, at Heinz Field, on Sep 17, the Steelers defeated the Minnesota Vikings W (26-9). At Chicago on Sep 24, the Bears beat the Steelers L (17-23) at Soldier

Field. On Oct 1, at M&T Bank Stadium, the Steelers defeated the Baltimore Ravens W (26-9.) At home on Oct 8.m in Heinz Field, the Jacksonville Jaguars defeated the Steelers L (9-30). At Kansas City on Oct 15 in Arrowhead Stadium, the Steelers beat the Chiefs W (19-13). On Oct 22, at home, the Steelers beat the Cincinnati Bengals W (29-14) in Heinz Field. At Detroit, on Oct 29, the Steelers defeated the Lions at Ford Field W (20-15). Nov 5, Bye Week.

At Indianapolis on Nov 12, the Steelers beat the Colts W (20–17) in Lucas Oil Stadium. At home, on Nov 16, the Steelers pounded the Tennessee Titans W (40–17) in Heinz Field. At home again on Nov 26, the Steelers beat the Green Bay Packers W (31–28) in Heinz Field. At Cincinnati, on Dec 4, Pittsburgh beat the Bengals W (23–20) in Paul Brown Stadium

At home on December 10, the Steelers beat the Baltimore Ravens W (39–38) in Heinz Field. On Dec 17, at home in Heinz Field, the New England Patriots barely beat the Steelers L (24–27) in Heinz Field. At Houston, on Christmas Day, Dec 25, the Steelers trounced the Texans W (34–6) in NRG Stadium. To finish off a fine season, the Steelers beat the Cleveland Browns on Dec 31 in Heinz Field W (28–24).

AFC Divisional Playoffs January 14, 2018
Jacksonville Jaguars 45, Pittsburgh Steelers 42

With sunny, 18-degree weather in Heinz Field, before 64,524 fans, Jacksonville took the opportunity to build up a 28–7 first-half lead. Then, they held off a second-half Steelers comeback to win the fourth highest scoring NFL playoff game of all time. For both teams, it was week 5 game rematch between the 2 teams, which the Jags had won 30-9 thanks to a defense that intercepted Steelers quarterback Ben Roethlisberger 5 times. It was not as easy for the Jaguars in this game but nonetheless, they prevailed.

Jacksonville started the game by driving 66 yards in eight plays on their opening drive. Blake Bortles completing passes to tight ends

Ben Koyack and James O'Shaughnessy for gains of 21 and 19 yards on the way to a one-yard fourth-down touchdown run by Leonard Fournette. Later in the first quarter, linebacker Myles Jack intercepted a pass from Steelers quarterback Ben Roethlisberger on the Steelers 18-yard line, and Fournette increased Jacksonville's lead to 14–0 with a touchdown run on the next play.

Pittsburgh came back with a drive to the Jacksonville 21-yard line, but on fourth-and-1, running back Le'Veon Bell was tackled by Jalen Ramsey and Malik Jackson for a four-yard loss. The Jaguars then drove 75 yards in 11 plays and scored on T. J. Yeldon's 4-yard touchdown run, increasing their lead to 21–0 with just over 11 minutes left in the half.

The Steelers roared back with a 64-yard scoring drive. Highlights included a 21-yard run by Bell and Roethlisberger's 23-yard touchdown pass to Antonio Brown. Nobody is perfect but perfect play does win games. The next Pittsburgh possession saw Roethlisberger losing the ball on a fumble while being sacked by Yannick Ngakoue. Linebacker Telvin Smith recovered the ball and returned it 50 yards for a touchdown, making the score 28–7 with less than two minutes left until halftime.

On the play, Jaguars were penalized 15 yards for excessive celebration, and then Cameron Sutton returned the ensuing kickoff 22 yards to the Jacksonville 49-yard line. Pittsburgh went on to drive 51 yards and cut their deficit to 28–14 on Roethlisberger's 36-yard touchdown completion to Martavis Bryant with 25 seconds remaining.

The Steelers drove 77 yards in 10 plays at the opening of the second half. The deficit then stood at 7, 21-28–21 with Roethlisberger's 19-yard touchdown pass to Bell. Early in the final period, the Steelers got the ball on the Jags' 48-yard line due to a deflected punt but ended up turning the ball over with an incomplete pass on fourth-and-1.

On the next Jacksonville drive, Bortles' 45-yard completion to Keelan Cole put them on the Steelers' 3-yard line, and Fournette ran the ball in for a touchdown on the next play, giving the Jaguars a

35–21 lead. This was the start of a scoring run from both teams. Together both teams accumulated 38 points in the fourth quarter.

After Fournette's score, Roethlisberger started the next drive with a 21-yard completion to Brown. He finished with a 43-yard touchdown pass to Brown that cut the score to 35–28. Jacksonville did not sit still. They came right back, 75 yards in eight plays. One of the plays was a 40-yard completion from Bortles to Yeldon on third-and-5. Fullback Tommy Bohanon caught a 14-yard touchdown pass from Bortles with 4:19 left, giving the Jaguars a 42–28 lead. The Steelers responded by taking the ball 75 yards in 12 plays, the longest a 22-yard reception from Bell. Bell finished the drive with an eight-yard touchdown run, reducing the jags lead to 7 at 35–42 with 2:19 to play.

Pittsburgh tried an onside kick which resulted in Jacksonville getting the ball back on the Steelers' 36-yard line with Josh Lambo nailing a field goal that put the Jaguars up 45–35. Pittsburgh then drove 75 yards in 10 plays, including a 42-yard completion from Roethlisberger to Brown. He ended up throwing a four-yard touchdown pass to JuJu Smith-Schuster, but by then, just one second remained. It was over, and the Steelers were forced to wait for the 2018 season to try again for the Super Bowl.

Other books by Brian Kelly: (amazon.com, & Kindle)

Great Moments in Pittsburgh Steelers Football All the best from the Pittsburgh Steelers
Great Moments in New England Patriots Football Great football moments from Boston to New England
Great Moments in Philadelphia Eagles Football. The best from the Eagles from the beginning of football.
Great Moments in Syracuse Football The great moments, coaches & players in Syracuse Football
Boost Social Security Now! Hey Buddy Can You Spare a Dime?
The Birth of American Football. From the first college game in 1869 to the last Super Bowl
Obamacare: A One-Line Repeal Congress must get this done.
A Wilkes-Barre Christmas Story A wonderful town makes Christmas all the better
A Boy, A Bike, A Train, and a Christmas Miracle A Christmas story that will melt your heart
Pay-to-Go   America-First Immigration Fix
Legalizing Illegal Aliens Via Resident Visas   Americans-first plan saves $Trillions. Learn how!
60 Million Illegal Aliens in America!!! A simple, America-first solution.
The Bill of Rights By Founder James Madison Refresh *your knowledge of the specific rights for all*
Great Players in Army Football Great Army Football played by great players..
Great Coaches in Army Football Army's coaches are all great.
Great Moments in Army Football Army Football at its best.
Great Moments in Florida Gators Football Gators Football from the start. This is the book.
Great Moments in Clemson Football CU Football at its best. This is the book.
Great Moments in Florida Gators Football Gators Football from the start. This is the book.
The Constitution Companion. A Guide to Reading and Comprehending the Constitution
The Constitution by Hamilton, Jefferson, & Madison – Big type and in English
PATERNO: The Dark Days After Win # 409. Sky began to fall within days of win # 409.
JoePa 409 Victories: Say No More! Winningest Division I-A football coach ever
American College Football: The Beginning From before day one football was played.
Great Coaches in Alabama Football Challenging the coaches of every other program!
Great Coaches in Penn State Football the Best Coaches in PSU's football program
Great Players in Penn State Football The best players in PSU's football program
Great Players in Notre Dame Football The best players in ND's football program
Great Coaches in Notre Dame Football The best coaches in any football program
Great Players in Alabama Football from Quarterbacks to offensive Linemen Greats!
Great Moments in Alabama Football AU Football from the start. This is the book.
Great Moments in Penn State Football PSU Football, start--games, coaches, players,
Great Moments in Notre Dame Football ND Football, start, games, coaches, players
Cross Country with the Parents   A great trip from East Coast to West with the kids
Seniors, Social Security & the Minimum Wage. Things seniors need to know.
How to Write Your First Book and Publish It with CreateSpace
The US Immigration Fix--It's all in here. Finally, an answer.
I had a Dream IBM Could be #1 Again   The title is self-explanatory
WineDiets.Com Presents The Wine Diet Learn how to lose weight while having fun.
Wilkes-Barre, PA; Return to Glory Wilkes-Barre City's return to glory
Geoffrey Parsons' Epoch... The Land of Fair Play Better than the original.
The Bill of Rights 4 Dummmies! This is the best book to learn about your rights.
Sol Bloom's Epoch ...Story of the Constitution The best book to learn the Constitution
America 4 Dummmies! All Americans should read to learn about this great country.
The Electoral College 4 Dummmies! How does it really work?
The All-Everything Machine Story about IBM's finest computer server.
ThankYou IBM! This book explains how IBM was beaten in the computer marketplace by neophytes

Brian has written 155 books in total. Other books can be found at amazon.com/author/brianwkelly

www.ingramcontent.com/pod-product-compliance
Lightning Source LLC
Chambersburg PA
CBHW070732170426
43200CB00007B/505